THIN ICE

THIN ICE

Coming of Age in Grand Rapids

edited by

Reinder Van Til & Gordon Olson

William B. Eerdmans Publishing Company

Grand Rapids, Michigan / Cambridge, U.K.

Wm. B. Eerdmans Publishing Co.
2140 Oak Industrial Drive N.E., Grand Rapids, Michigan 49505 /
P.O. Box 163, Cambridge CB3 9PU U.K.

Printed in the United States of America

12 11 10 09 08 07   7 6 5 4 3 2 1

Library of Congress Cataloging-in-Publication Data

Thin ice: coming of age in Grand Rapids /
edited by Reinder Van Til & Gordon Olson.
p. cm.
ISBN 978-0-8028-2478-3 (pbk.: alk. paper)
1. Grand Rapids (Mich.) — Biography — Anecdotes. 2. Grand Rapids (Mich.) — Social life and customs — Anecdotes. 3. City and town life — Michigan — Grand Rapids — Anecdotes. 4. Children — Michigan — Grand Rapids — Social life and customs —Anecdotes. 5. Authors, American — Michigan — Grand Rapids — Biography — Anecdotes. 6. Authors, American — Homes and haunts — Michigan — Grand Rapids — Anecdotes. I. Van Til, Reinder. II. Olson, Gordon L.

F574.G7T48 2007

977.4′56 — dc22

2007004321

www.eerdmans.com

To our comrades on "the committee"

Hank Meijer

Larry ten Harmsel

Bob VanderMolen

. . . for their erudition and common sense, not to mention their reading of the contributions and their acquaintance with some of the writers we pursued — all of that invaluable advice rendered on long afternoons at the Cottage Bar, and all of it an immense support to our humble efforts.

The Reverend Jonathan Booth's drawing of Grand Rapids in 1831

Grand Rapids Public Library, Grand Rapids History and Special Collections Department, Art and Graphics Collection, hereafter cited as GRPL, with name of collection.

Contents

Contents

Preface

Van Til's Note on the Origins of This Book

The idea for this anthology of memoir pieces by writers who grew up in Grand Rapids goes back as far as 1969, when I read an article in *Harper's* magazine that was entitled "Yesterdays in Grand Rapids." *Harper's,* then as now, offered a sophisticated diet of literary, cultural, and political commentary, and the magazine had just installed Willie Morris as its editor-in-chief. Early in his tenure, Morris started up a series of articles, entitled "Going Home in America," in which writers reflected on growing up in their hometowns across America — and on returning to them as adults. Writers in that series included Walker Percy on New Orleans, John Hollander on New York City, Midge Decter on St. Paul, Marshall Frady on Gary, Indiana, and Morris himself on his hometown of Yazoo City, Mississippi.

The essays all tended to be period pieces about those towns and cities because the writers were looking back from a distance of thirty or forty years. As the editors put it: "Leaving home in America and returning to it in one's dreams and emotions are essential to what we are as a transient, displaced people; these have been the main themes in much of our literature, and the very words themselves, *going home,* have a special American resonance." The inaugural piece in that series particularly caught my eye because it was about my own hometown — Grand Rapids, Michigan. The author was John Thompson, a poet, novelist, essayist, and the book review editor for *Harper's* under Morris. Thompson had grown up on the east side of Grand Rapids and was in 1969 a professor of English at the State University of New York at Stony Brook.

That essay — and that whole concept in *Harper's* — stayed in the back of my mind for years. Then, in 1982, another essay about coming of age in Grand Rapids appeared, again in *Harper's,* this time by Pulitzer Prize–winning columnist and civil rights activist Roger Wilkins, entitled "Confessions of a Blue-Chip Black." This was a sizable teaser from Wilkins's autobiography, *A Man's Life,* which was to be published later that year. (*Harper's* was known for publishing large chunks of books — even whole books by Norman Mailer and William Styron, for example — between its magazine covers in those halcyon years.) That piece was not meant to be a simple memoir about growing up in Grand Rapids; but since Wilkins had spent his formative adolescent years through his graduation from Creston High School — and into his college years — in Grand Rapids, it portrayed a significant and profoundly moving segment of his life. Both of these remarkable essays — by Thompson and Wilkins — are reprinted in this anthology.

Then, in the mid-1990s, when Bill Brashler and I were invited to read from one of our murder mysteries at the Ford Presidential Museum — neither of us having lived in Grand Rapids for two or three decades — I wrote a sentimental little piece for that occasion about growing up in Grand Rapids. Some people indulged my whim and enjoyed the reminiscence at the time; some even wondered about the possibility of a book that would be a compendium of writers' musings about coming of age in Grand Rapids.

Gordon Olson, whom I have known and worked with since before he became the official city historian of Grand Rapids in 1978, was naturally aware of some historical reflections written by earlier Grand Rapids natives, in-migrants, and immigrants — work that I would have had no way of knowing about. So Gordon has been the perfect person to help me pursue that trail. Initially, neither of us knew what or how much we would find that had already been published in some form; so we did not begin with a set number of contributions for this anthology in mind.

As it happens, we have excerpted exactly half of the narratives in this collection from existing books (autobiographies and memoirs), journals, and magazines; the other half we have directly solicited from active writers as new pieces specifically written for this book. The earliest pieces go back to lives lived in Grand Rapids as long ago as the 1830s and 1850s, and the most recent are a cluster of contemporary pieces that describe coming of age in the Grand Rapids of the 1960s through the 1980s. They represent not only sharp personal writing by some of the best writers that Grand Rapids has produced but also a kind of impressionistic historical portrait of that community during a century and a half of its own coming of age.

REINDER VAN TIL

Olson's Note on the Origins of a Partnership

I was not born in Grand Rapids and did not grow up there. My own coming of age took place in a remote, sparsely settled northwest corner of Wisconsin. It was not until 1973 that my wife, Christine, and I came to Grand Rapids from Laramie, Wyoming, where we were both graduate students at the University of Wyoming. I had been appointed assistant director of the Grand Rapids Public Museum, and since my degrees were in American history, I was put in charge of history exhibits at the museum. That assignment included Grand Rapids history, and I embarked on a reading of the city's history. One of the first books I took up was Albert Baxter's *History of the City of Grand Rapids,* and within its pages I encountered Hattie Burton's poignant account of trekking westward across Michigan Territory in 1832, with several members of her party ill, running low on food and supplies. When one of the sick children died in the wilderness, the group could only pause a brief moment for a simple burial before pressing on.

There were other gripping narratives in Baxter's 900-page tome, and subsequently I found accounts of growing up in Grand Rapids in other books as well. But while politics and government, military campaigns, immigration groups, and other subjects have captured the attention of American historians, I had become aware of the paucity of interest in the history of children and childhood in the United States — the stories of young people who were seldom "seen or heard."

Preface

In the 1970s, I became friends with Reinder Van Til, whose editing work more than once saved me from my own grammatical shortcomings. Our work and discussions together covered Potawatomi beadwork, Civil War veterans in Michigan, and even vintage baseball in Michigan. But it was not until many years later that we discovered a mutual interest in first-person accounts of coming of age in Grand Rapids. As we began discussing stories that we had read over the years, it was clear that our combined experience covered a wide swath of the community. I knew of numerous historical accounts, and through his work at Eerdmans Publishing Company and his interest in literature generally, Reinder knew about some of the contemporary writers who grew up in Grand Rapids. We had both read Roger Wilkins's story in *Harper's* magazine, which helped push our thinking ahead until we had more than enough material for this book. Once we began comparing notes, it did not take long for the idea of a collaboration to germinate.

We wish to express appreciation to the writers who have told their stories of coming of age in Grand Rapids here for the first time, as well as to those writers who told their stories in earlier publications — going back to Albert Baxter's Grand Rapids history accounts, first published in the 1890s. And we know that there are many thousands more such stories out there. Whether you grew up in Grand Rapids or not, we hope that you will use these stories as a springboard to reflect on your own coming of age, and that you will share those reflections with your family and friends.

GORDON OLSON

Acknowledgments

We want to thank those writers (authors of half the pieces in this book) who responded positively to our invitation to write a new piece, something specifically for this anthology. Since there is no model or precedent for this volume — indeed, it started out as a kind of shot in the dark — these writers were responding in a spirit of friendship with us and perhaps a sense that this project could become a unique collection of memoirs. We think readers will agree that the resulting narratives are sharp and moving observations of life, full of human warmth and humor. We are grateful to the writers who came through for us.

A book like this also relies on the contributions of a number of people whose names do not appear on the cover or in the table of contents. In our efforts to run down early Grand Rapids narratives, pictures, and other graphic illustrations in the following pages, we benefited from the assistance of the staff of the Grand Rapids Public Library's Grand Rapids History & Special Collections Department: Richard Vettese, Chris Byron, Karolee Hazlewood, Marcie Beck, and Jennifer Morrison. They care for the area's finest collection of historical books, magazines, newspapers, and images, and they helped us locate several personal recollections of growing up in historic Grand Rapids — and the illustrations to go with them. The department's staff is an important and often underappreciated resource for Grand Rapids historians and writers. We are also grateful to David Horrocks, director of the Gerald R. Ford Library in Ann Arbor, for his assistance in cutting through layers of bureaucratic protection to get us permissions to reprint the excerpts by Gerald and Betty Ford.

We want to extend a special word of appreciation to Fred Meijer for his assistance in the publication of this book.

At the publishing house, Bill and Sam Eerdmans have been supportive of and enthusiastic about this project right from the beginning, as they have been about books on local Grand Rapids and west Michigan subjects in general — past and future. We also wish to thank Bobbi Humbracht at the press: she persistently pursued publishers for permission to reprint the memoirs that were published earlier in books and magazines. This is a job that can require nerves of steel and gloves of kid, and Bobbi developed both as she pressed forward. Klaas Wolterstorff not only created an aesthetically pleasing design for the book but also helped us with the illustrations, and Willem Mineur produced a cover that has historic and artistic resonance. Jennifer Hoffman, as always, moved the project smoothly through the production phase. We are grateful to all of them.

We also want to acknowledge the support and help of our spouses, Dorothea Schneider and Christine Olson, who not only tolerated but profitably joined in during many of our brainstorming sessions.

Most of all, we want to thank our "ad hoc committee" — Larry ten Harmsel, Bob VanderMolen, and Hank Meijer. During periodic meetings at a venerable Grand Rapids establishment, the Cottage Bar, they kept us focused, made sure we were aware of the writers we needed to pursue, and came up with the title. We dedicate this book to them.

Introduction

Early in this collection of memoirs, Charles Belknap, in his selection entitled "At the Shipyard Forge," tells the story of an ice-skating mishap on the Grand River in the 1850s: "One winter day when the ice was all islands with narrow glades of water dividing them, that in the crisp sunlight looked like liquid race courses, the weather was at its best and all the skaters in town were out. It was like a carnival, except that it lacked the music.

"The islands within safe reach were crowded, but there was one large glare place just beyond jumping distance that was tempting the daring. A party of Holland girls came down an open space like a whirlwind and going into the air one by one in their short skirts they cleared the glade and landed safely on this island of temptation.

"This challenge was too much for the American boys and several crossed successfully and were soon linked arm in arm with the rosy cheeked, sensibly dressed Netherlands girls. A dark haired American girl saw her beau cutting 'pigeon wings' and doing the 'long roll' with a pretty blonde and she tried to jump. When she left the ice her short skate caught in the long skirt and she plunged head first into the water with such force that she came up under the ice on the farther side.

"In about a minute the crowd was frantic; all except a twelve-year-old boy — a 'water rat' they called him — who pushed his way through the crowd and followed the girl under the ice, where she could be plainly seen floating and being carried along by the current. Men yelled and women fainted or fell upon their knees sobbing. Those who could see said the boy had caught her hand and with his feet braced on the bottom was struggling for a place in the open.

"It was a Holland girl lying on her face at the channel's edge who caught the boy's hand and pulled them out. Men brought planks and bridged the glade and the unconscious girl was wrapped in blankets and rushed to her home." Thanks to the boy's quick action, the girl survived, and her story became a much-repeated part of the lore of Grand Rapids, Michigan.

This story about the pure "carnival" joy but also the potential peril of skating on thin ice provides an illuminating metaphor for this book's twenty-eight personal reflections on coming of age in Grand Rapids. The writers tell stories of the carnival of growing up there, but also of the precarious thin ice of life-and-death situations (Jim Harrison, Sheri Venema, John Hockenberry), of growing up in poverty (David C. DeJong, Glen Peterson, Al Green), of family deaths and separations (Gerald and Betty Ford, Max Apple, Roger Wilkins, Laura Kasischke), of conflicts concerning religious beliefs and practices (DeJong, Apple, Peterson, Green, Venema, Kasischke, Paul Schrader), and of the perils of first loves (Albert Baxter's Potawatomi, Roger Wilkins, John Otterbacher, Kaye Longberg).

Those who immigrated to Grand Rapids from foreign countries (Muste, DeJong, Bich Minh Nguyen); those who were members of ethnic groups different from the predominant ones (Edward Gillis and Max Apple); those who experienced racism in direct and explicit ways (the early Potawatomi and Levi Rickert, Nguyen, Wilkins and Green) — all of them were skating on thin ice as they sought to form their identities while encountering the ethnic prejudices and racial stereotypes forced on them by the dominant white Grand Rapids society. Also pulsating in these stories is the very precariousness of the growing-up experience itself: of being an adolescent, poised between teenage vulnerability and hardened adulthood, of working to establish one's identity in the face of the ambivalence and complexity of the looming adult world.

Challenges and Conflicts

The most dramatic examples of precarious lives, of course, are of those who survived life-threatening accidents and whose stories are of coming of age in Grand Rapids hospitals. Jim Harrison recalls coming to Blodgett Hospital from Reed City in 1944 after being poked in the eye with a broken bottle, when "my sight and a great deal of my blood leaked out on my shirt." He describes a seven-year-old boy's fears about what he *heard* when both of his eyes were covered for the first ten days of his month-long stay. Thirty years later, John Hockenberry had escaped a fatal car crash with his life, only to realize that he had to live the rest of it as a paraplegic. His coming-of-age story is set in the Mary Free Bed Rehabilitation Hospital, where he learned — along with several loony fellow paralytics and the nurses who tried to keep the lid on their behavior — how to face the continuation of his life with a major spinal-cord injury. Sheri Venema's Aunt Mux hovers between life and death as an infant born very prematurely in 1911. But she spends those harrowing first months of her life not in a hospital but at Ramona Park, because amusement parks were the only places where the incubation "hatcheries" for preemies were to be found.

There was also the thin ice of growing up in poverty. In his novel *Belly Fulla Straw,* David Cornel DeJong gives a fictional account of the arrival of a new immigrant family, the Idemas, in Grand Rapids from the Netherlands, carrying a few trunks that contained all their worldly belongings, to be met at the train station by their sponsor, a fellow immigrant (from an earlier immigration) named Kuiper. Rolf, the narrator, recounts how Kuiper turns out to be unscrupulous, overbearing, and exploiting. In addition, their fellow Dutch-Americans on the block are cold and uncaring, and most of the local teenagers are hostile and mock the strange ways and appearance of the children newly arrived from Europe. Young Glen Peterson, sensing the difference in means between his family and fellow church-goers, used his little wagon to bring home coal that had fallen off trains. But his mother forbade him to do so, unwilling to have others see the family acknowledge that they were poor.

Al Green portrays the deprivation of a black family that came to Grand Rapids from Arkansas in the mid-1950s, when opportunities for his father to get work, which were "supposedly around every corner in Grand Rapids, seemed instead to always be just out of reach." Al was cooped up in a tiny two-room flat with seven or eight of his siblings, and his family found a whole lot of black people around them that were in the same boat — "all come to the promised land on a wing and a prayer and all wondering what happened to the pot of gold at the end of the rainbow."

The loss of a parent — through illness, death, or divorce — is another childhood trauma that is recounted in these memoirs. Betty Bloomer Ford's life was changed irrevocably the year she was sixteen, when her father died of accidental carbon monoxide poisoning one summer day while he was working on his car. It was the closing bracket on an early life that Betty describes as a "sunny childhood . . . and a wonderful girlhood." Roger Wilkins lost his father, Earl Wilkins — first to a tuberculosis sanatorium before Roger's second birthday and then to death before he was nine.

Max Apple's family lost three of its members in a winter auto accident near Lansing in 1936, including two cousins and the uncle who was to be his namesake. For his family, it became the "single defining event that changes everything." The two predominant characters in Apple's memoirs — his grandmother, Gootie, and his grandfather, Rocky — never got over that loss. And they invested more of the family's hopes in the young Max, born five years later, than he was willing to accept. Laura Kasischke's mother, whose tales of a world of ghosts Laura dismissed while her mother was living, died when Laura was twenty. Her memoir paints a picture of how that trauma was so difficult for her to accept that she continued to see her mother and hear of her appearances as a ghost in her own young life.

Religious faith and its potential for community cohesion — but also for family conflict and youthful rebellion — pops up as a recurring theme in these narratives. DeJong's portrait of the fictional Idema family and their struggle to fit in with the early twentieth-century Dutch Calvinist community of Grand Rapids is a bitter example. Mr. Idema finds out what ostracism means for those who are Dutch in Grand Rapids and do not go to church. People react in horror when they learn that his children have not been baptized; and he realizes that, if the family is to be accepted by their fellow immigrants — indeed, if Idema himself is even to get a job — they will have to attend church and lie about having a religious faith.

In describing the competing educations he was getting on the street and in school, Peterson says that, "while the church and Christian school were laying a foundation of guilt and shame, the Creston neighborhood was slowly eroding the protective layers of Dutch Calvinism and exposing me to alleged evils that sometimes turned out to be rather banal." Along with its anti-Catholicism and its emphasis on Old Testament stories of swift, violent, and excessive punishments for small sins, the church of Peterson's youth gave a mixed message about wealth and poverty. The minister "glorified" poverty, impressing on everyone the fact that Jesus was poor; yet the church seemed to hold in high regard all the trappings of wealth, and the well-to-do parishioners had the better positions in the church hierarchy. But the clincher for Peterson's early assessment of church rules was when he learned, in an argument with his mother, that the no-swimming-on-Sunday rule he was challenging was actually about *having fun* on Sundays — "that was the real sin."

While Apple was growing up as a young Jew in Grand Rapids, his grandfather would regularly introduce him to rabbis who were on a kind of circuit in west Michigan by saying, "Do something. Teach him. He's growing up like a goy." But as he sat with the Hebrew prayerbook in front of him, young Max realized that his heart was "too American": he was thinking of baseball. His conflicts with his grandfather became the mirror image of the Calvinist youths' arguments with parents and ministers who gave out anti-Catholic and anti-Jewish warnings. When he wanted to become a Cub Scout, and the den was scheduled to meet in the basement of the St. Peter and Paul church, his grandfather forbade him to go: "A Jew doesn't go to church." When Max assured him there would be no priests or nuns present, just the den mother, his grandfather replied: "First they tell you den mother, pretty soon they'll start talking about a Holy Mother." Ultimately, Rocky gives up on his dream that his grandson will become a rabbi. But Max, whose bar mitzvah is approaching, goes one step further: since his hero is now Albert Einstein, who has indicated that he does not go to synagogue, Max announces one Sabbath that he is through with synagogue. Luckily for their continuing relationship, his conflict with his grandfather is resolved just in time for the bar mitzvah.

The orthodoxy question in Al Green's family was about the kind of music one was allowed to pursue. Al's father was a gospel singer with "stern admonitions against worldly music"; he tried to restrict young Al's access to music that was not religious, and he would not hesitate to destroy the popular 45s Al brought home. "Daddy wasn't about to let me loose to scorch my ears with the sound of hell's own house band. . . . To his way of thinking, there was God's music and the devil's music . . . nothing in between and no two ways about it." Though Green later made a celebrated return to gospel music, indeed established his own church in Memphis, his rebellion against parental strictures was based on the music he chose to sing.

Paul Schrader's father was converted to the Christian Reformed Church (a condition of his marriage to Paul's mother), and though he was unable to fulfill his dream of studying at Calvin Seminary and becoming a minister, he was determined that his sons would do so. This became a source of profound father-son conflict, and the battles produced "scars that were never healed." Sheri Venema found that the faith she had thrilled to as a younger child had turned to ashes in her mouth when her confession of faith came due as a teenager. The process of faith profession turned out to require not a statement of her beliefs but a parroting of the Heidelberg Catechism. Severely disappointed and disillusioned, "cut off and abandoned," she left her questions — and their answers — in the consistory room, and she stood before the congregation feeling like "an empty vessel."

Reacting to the Sunday observance compulsions of what one wag has called a "severely overchurched community," Laura Kasischke thought when she was a child that it was actually *illegal* to mow one's lawn on a Sunday in Grand Rapids. She so dreaded and loathed Sundays that "it seems to me possible that it was the very force of my desire that altered that terrain, as if I were Carrie — hating Sundays with such passion that I could move lawn mowers out of their garages and push them around on the grass, break the locks on the convenience stores, throw open the gates to the zoo, the doors to the skating rinks, the libraries, the arcades, activate the electrical eyes on the doors to the supermarkets so that they slid open freely when a shopper passed by."

Religious faith is clearly a powerful force in all segments of Grand

Rapids life, as it is in American culture in general, which has now become obvious in every political election analysis. But it is also clear from these narratives that it evokes and provokes an equally powerful negative reaction in its youth, a rebellion that has lasted a lifetime for some of the community's writers and artists.

Sex and Race

Perhaps the only force more powerful than religion in those who are coming of age is that of sex and love, its denial and loss, a theme that emerges dramatically in some of these narratives. Adoniram Judson (not his native name but the one given to him by missionaries) was a Grand Rapids Potawatomi who, in the 1820s, was among those educated at the Carey Mission School to become fit for "superior usefulness among [his] own countrymen." These young men were of exceptional scholarship and character, and they came back to their Potawatomi "countrymen" wanting to establish schools, churches, and "all the blessings of civilization." But they were rejected by their peers, who did not want — indeed had contempt for — their white ways and what they took to be a renunciation of their Indian ways. Now they were in no man's land — neither Indians nor white men.

So Judson used his education credentials to get a job as principal of a white academy in Gull Prairie, where his prospects were good and "every house was open to my visits." But when he fell in love with and proposed to marry a young woman of the community, her parents (who had become his friends) said: "Our daughter marry an Indian! You are crazy! She might as well marry a Negro. You will never be anything but an Indian for all your education." Judson's humiliation forced him to acknowledge the reality of their devastating pronouncement: he returned to "live and die among [his] own people." Toward the end of this anthology, Levi Rickert, a Grand Rapids Potawatomi of the twentieth and twenty-first centuries, gives us an update on American Indian life in west Michigan today — and the racial realities that are still part of that life.

Judson's aching story of a love denied on racial grounds is echoed in Roger Wilkins's moving account of the humiliation of his thwarted romance. As the only black person at Creston High School in the late 1940s, Wilkins was a good athlete, a gifted student, and president of the student council. He had many friends among white males and especially among white females: "Because I was a boy, I had insight. But I was also Negro, and therefore neuter." As Wilkins notes, there are few more powerful obsessions than "a teenage boy's fixation on a love object." So it was only natural for him to ask for a date with one of those white girls who were fond of talking with him. When he did, however, the girl shrieked in horror and fled — leaving him to "writhe with mortification."

Kaye Longberg's fictional heroine is in love with Chris — though they are too young to do anything about it — and all the while she knows that she will inevitably lose him because his family is of a "higher" social stratum. It seems that in the 150 years between the opening vignette about the Potawatomi in the small white community of the 1820s on "the Rapids" and Longberg's East Grand Rapids setting along Fisk Lake in the mid-1970s, not much has changed in matters of the heart.

The most sustained story of ultimately unrequited young love is that of John Otterbacher, whose love object, Judy, "renders me almost entirely mute on those rare instances when we are alone together." And Judy grows tall while John remains short; her voice attains a new resonance and even sophistication, while John's voice "lingers an octave above those of [his] peers." He feels Judy "slipping away from me, lapping my elongated childhood."

The longing for members of the opposite sex is, of course, most pronounced among the adolescent male of the species, though that strong urge to come of age sexually was either ignored or openly discouraged by older members of the community. William Brashler says he learned early on that "lust of the flesh would result in eternal damnation . . . and everywhere I turned, from age ten on, there was flesh and lust." Like Glen Peterson, though, he waited in vain for his older brothers or father to give him any sex education or advice that would be of any use. His secret auto-eroticism and collecting of nudy magazines only brought forth his brother's "do pushups instead" mantra. Brashler concludes that the "Dutch Calvinist method of sex education was either through osmosis or via the bad kid on the playground."

In matters of race, Grand Rapids mirrored the life of many communities in the upper Midwest. Like Chicago or Minneapolis, it had multicultural beginnings: white settlers arriving from the state of New York and other points east came to a culture and economy started nearly a decade earlier by French and American Indian fur trade. Merely navigating a common language among those groups was a challenge (Louis Campau's French-speaking wife, Sophie, never did learn English). By the late 1840s, immigrants were coming from Germany and the Netherlands. However, the intermingling of these groups and the fact that they lived in or near the same town did not mean that the dark-skinned and uneducated "savages" were welcome in the churches, schools, or other white institutions (as is obvious from the Potawatomi narrative). Grand Rapids became more ethnically diverse (Poles, Lithuanians, Irish, and so forth) by the turn of the twentieth century, but those ethno-religious groups kept to themselves in their own enclaves.

African-Americans first came to Grand Rapids in the mid-nineteenth century and began settling in significant numbers during the first half of the twentieth century, especially after both of the two World Wars. As we read in Al Green's boyhood memory of moving there, their numbers had begun to make up a large migration from southern states by the 1950s — blacks who were seeking employment in the automotive and related industries in western Michigan. For Al's father, who was steadfastly and desperately looking for work, "the line formed at the rear, and there were a whole lot of other displaced dirt farmers with no prospects standing in front of Daddy." When Al wasn't singing, he was part of a neighborhood that was basically segregated, and he was one of many children who were "scared kids, staring down poverty and despair and a generally hopeless future, all trying to act like we had the world on a string."

Vietnamese immigrants began arriving in Grand Rapids after the fall of Saigon in 1975. Bich Minh Nguyen tells her story of trying to fit in with her white school environment as an immigrant kid by being as quiet as possible and being the best student in the class. She notes that a large billboard in downtown Grand Rapids declared it "an All-American City." But for her, "that all-American designation meant all-white." Like Wilkins, she was terrified as a student when she had to give a school report about her family's origins and history: "I loathed this task, for I was dreadfully aware that my history could not be faked; it already showed on my face. . . . Some kids, a few of them older, took to pressing back the corners of their eyes with the heels of their palms while they chanted, 'Ching-chong, ching-chong!' during recess."

All of the normal perils and pains of coming of age were exacerbated by the peculiar racial, ethno-religious, social, and family circumstances of each individual writer.

Comfort and Humor

And yet, coming of age in Grand Rapids was not all made up of perils and precariousness. The personal memoirs in this book also express the more benign, heart-warming, and joyous aspects of life growing up in Grand Rapids, which are juxtaposed to those of the hostility and rejection elaborated above. In point of fact, most of these narratives are ambivalent: they portray childhoods and adolescences that contained experiences of both fear and security, both pain and happiness, sorrow and joy, criticism and praise, discouragement and encouragement.

The first narratives portray a settlement at the rapids of the Grand River that in the 1830s was in its infancy. The white migrants who were moving into this settlement were mostly Americans coming from New York and other eastern states and territories to seek their future and fortunes in the "wild west" of the Michigan territory. They came of age quickly because of the sheer physical hardships they encountered hacking their way through the wilderness that stood between Detroit and the settlement on the Grand — an atmosphere that bred diseases and agues, not to mention wild beasts. And when "Aunt Hattie" Burton's family did arrive at the settlement, they found a compound of a few unadorned, drafty log cabins, with a couple of streets or paths that turned into mud holes when it rained. But they also found hospitable and colorful people, such as Louis Campau, who spoke his native French and passable Indian languages but little English, and his non-English-speaking but welcoming wife, who "did her utmost to make [the newly arrived] comfortable" — providing lodging and wholesome game and vegetables to those who had been reduced to eating their horses' meal on their journey from Detroit.

Grand Rapids' first frame house, built by Joel Guild in 1833
GRPL, Art and Graphics Collection

A. J. Muste, who was seven when he emigrated with his family from the Netherlands in 1892, gives an immigrant's view of coming to Grand Rapids at the turn of the twentieth century that is in stark contrast to David C. DeJong's. Even though the ocean voyage made his mother so sick that it took her a whole month to recover in the New York Harbor, once they got to Grand Rapids they were greeted at the train station by loving uncles and aunts and escorted by horse and carriage to his cousins' warm and commodious home. A. J. embraced his life in the "new world" as a "pleasant and stimulating sensation." He befriended the Quimbys, one of the prominent and privileged families of Grand Rapids, and he thrived in school — winning an essay contest and a cash award when he was only twelve.

Charles Belknap gives an even more positive — even boosterish — picture of the settlement on the Grand where he grew up from the age of eight. His optimistic disposition saw him embracing the town by becoming a volunteer fireman as a young boy and later its mayor, and then serving on all the important civic boards, serving as a U.S. congressman from west Michigan, and as the national commissioner of the Boy Scouts. His friendly, often lyrical, descriptions of the storage and consumption of food; spearfishing for giant sturgeon; ice-skating on the Grand; and even humorous stories of drunken firefighters — all show him to be an acute observer who could always find the humorous sides of humans and animals and the positive view of a developing town. John Thompson, who calls Belknap's book *The Yesterdays of Grand Rapids* "one of my favorite books for as long as I have been able to read," says that Belknap was a "wonderful writer gifted in natural comedy. . . ."

Betty Ford had an innate love of growing up in Grand Rapids even though she wanted to leave to become a professional dancer with Martha Graham's company in New York (which she did). But even in little Grand Rapids she had a venerable dance teacher, Calla Travis, who introduced her to a complete program of dance, and Betty loved it all. After her Martha Graham experience, she became a model and a dance instructor in New York City, and she taught many young dance enthusiasts before marrying into the world of politics in 1948. "When you say you've had a sunny childhood," she said of growing up in Grand Rapids, "the assumption is that you're smart enough to know you've been lucky. I did know it."

Edward Gillis, with his enthusiasm for everything about the West Side and Lithuanian Town, was clearly in love with growing up in Grand Rapids. His word pictures of fire stations, old locomotives in train yards, and hobos, as well as his portrayal of neighborhood gangs, are decidedly upbeat and affectionate. Gillis also thrilled to the arrival of the gypsy camps on Ann Street between Turner and the Grand River (in the 1920s and '30s), and to the vaudeville atmosphere of the medicine shows that had started coming to Lithuanian Town as early as 1915. Gillis regales his readers with the favorite sports of Lithuanian-Americans: hockey on the frozen parts of the Grand River; boxing in the Golden Gloves; bowling at Wenger's in Lithuanian Town.

Grand Rapids athletics in general — from ice-skating to boxing and Buster Mathis, to Little League baseball and Mickey Stanley, to high school football and Rocky Rozema, to the Tackers and Delton Heard —

come in for affectionate and humorous treatment in a number of these memoirs. Bill Brashler and Bob VanderMolen, coming up as youths through the Grand Rapids world of sports during exactly the same era, provide both fond and irreverent views of the value of athletics for "building character" and "developing manhood."

Some of these writers not only grew up in Grand Rapids but also continued living there or came back to live there in adulthood. Former newspaperman Hank Meijer and *Grand Rapids Press* columnists Tom Rademacher and Charles Honey, all now in their fifties, portray a metropolis that they have carefully observed for half a century, a city that has experienced great growth in population, cultural gifts, racial and ethnic diversity, and educational and medical facilities during that time. They know that, as much as their fair city has meant in the formation of its sons and daughters, the city has, in turn, been formed by those sons and daughters — even those who were skating on the thin ice of adolescence while here, and even those who left it a long time ago, never to return.

John Thompson observes: "How impossible to believe that these kids we see now, fifteen or sixteen years old, our own children perhaps, are living as we lived then in a turmoil of pain and discovery and elation, living in a world of heroes and heroines . . . learning the language and customs of that country, acquiring the ways of feeling and acting which will never be lost no matter what passports we acquire and what other lands we may come to inhabit. . . . [T]hose who found adolescence to be an entire world, well, many of us were lost there and it can take years and years to get out."

REINDER VAN TIL AND GORDON OLSON

Potawatomies on Waterloo Street

Albert Baxter

In 1855, Albert Baxter went to work for the *Grand Rapids Eagle* newspaper as a business and editorial assistant. After five years he left the *Eagle* and began work at the *Detroit Tribune*. After a period of bad health (a recurring problem), he returned to Grand Rapids and the *Eagle* in 1865, where he would stay until he began work on the first comprehensive history of Grand Rapids in January 1888. He spent the next three years of his life interviewing and digging, amassing a voluminous amount of original research.

Because he was close enough to the times of the first white pioneers to learn a good deal of Grand Rapids' history first hand, Baxter's work — drawn from over 150 interviews — can be characterized as a nineteenth-century form of oral history. Z. Z. Lydens put it this way in the *Grand Rapids Press* of May 26, 1963: "Historians would agree, because of the fact that Baxter lived with the things he wrote about, that his material is 'primary.'" Unfortunately, he was cheated out of all but a small remuneration for his labors by the firm that contracted him to write it, a publisher in Dodge City, Kansas.

Baxter claimed that he experienced only six years of happiness in his life, the time he lived with Elvira Guild, the sister of "Aunt Hattie" of the second of these vignettes. After losing a young daughter and experiencing repeated bouts of ill health, Baxter went off to live in a hut on a sand farm near Muskegon, where he died in 1905. In this first remarkable narrative from his history, the report by a New York paper shows all the prejudices toward American Indians that were prevalent in the white culture of the time. However, Baxter allows the principals of this story, the young Potawatomi men, to tell their own tragic and moving story. Both of these first two narratives are excerpted from Baxter's *A History of the City of Grand Rapids, Michigan.*

In the spring of 1838, during the days of an Indian payment at which, it was said, more than one thousand two hundred, of several different tribes, were present, a few young people were practicing for choir service, singing with flute accompaniment, in the counting-room of the store of A. H. Smith, on Waterloo street. A crowd of the natives gathered to enjoy the music and admire the instruments. One who was present related the incident several years ago in the columns of the New York *Christian Union,* and from his story the following is extracted:

Great was our surprise when from the assembled crowd of savages a young brave of about twenty-five years, as dirty and as unkempt as any of his associates, picked up the Boston Handel and Haydn note book, from which we had been playing, and turned over the leaves as any of his rude companions would have done, apparently wrapped in a sort of dazed admiration, as we supposed, of the fabric and the printing, always so mysterious to the superstitious savage. But suddenly, with kindling eye and flushing cheek, he beckoned from the crowd one of his companions — a young man about his own age, and, like himself, a thorough-bred savage in appearance — and turning pleasantly to us and pointing to the tune indicated, in unexceptionable English said: "Will you play 'St. Martin's,' if you please?" which I wonderingly did, carrying the air with the flute, when he taking the tenor and his companion the bass, they sang from the book the words of the hymn as sweetly and as correctly as the best of us of the Court House choir could have done; and not only that, but through tune after tune, and hymn after hymn, anthems and all, for an hour or more the young savage led the way with a fluency and correctness as to both music and words which demonstrated no superficial ear-work, but knowledge born of much study and intelligent practice; and his companion was not one whit behind him. Here now was a new thing, and of a most surprising nature. A full-blooded Potawatomie with moccasins and leggins, calico shirt, gay cotton head-dress, ringed ears, blankets, and above all that indescribable Indian odor of blended wood-smoke, fish and muskrat, and yet with the manners of a gentleman, and the accent of a scholar, singing readily by note our most elaborate hymn tunes and set pieces; and here too was an apparently equally accomplished companion, but equally dirty and unkempt, and of equally pure Indian blood, accompanying him. Of course there must be a history behind it, and as there were yet to be two or three days remaining before the camps would be broken up, we set ourselves to the work of winning the confidence of these wondrous savages and learning their history. This is in substance what they told us:

Their names (as known among the whites) were Adoniram Judson and George Dana Boardman. They were two of the Indian boys (Potawatomies) selected by the Rev. Isaac McCoy from among the pupils of the Carey Mission School, then located south of the St. Joseph River, in Michigan. It was part of Mr. McCoy's plan, as appears from his history of the Mission, to fit for enlarged usefulness among their countrymen some of the most hopeful Christian pupils. His own language is simply expressive. He says: "We were allowed the peculiar felicity of church fellowship with a considerable number of Indian pupils; and from among them we proposed to make a selection of some who appeared to possess the most promising talents, whom we should endeavor to qualify for superior usefulness." This was in 1826, and Judson and Boardman were two of the seven youths who that year entered the Literary and Theological Institute (now Madison University) at Hamilton, New York, to fit themselves for "superior usefulness among their own countrymen." These youths, it appears from their record while in college, were of unexceptionable character and deportment. As I afterward learned, they became to a degree the pets and protégés of the good citizens in and around Hamilton. All houses were open to their visits. They had full companionship with those of their own age, in all companies, and with both sexes. They became largely imbued with a devoted missionary spirit, and having completed their prescribed course of study, after several years' absence they returned to their destined field of labor, "fitted for superior usefulness among their own countrymen." And now we will let Judson, who was the chief speaker, give his own experience, and the substance of his explanation of his present condition. He said:

"I went home among my own people full of purpose and sanguine

An unknown artist's romanticized depiction of Adoniram Judson, from a book published in 1889

Darius Cook, *Six Months Among the Indians.* Niles, MI: Niles Mirror Office, 1889

expectation. They should have schools. They should have churches. They should learn mechanics and farming, and have crops and stock and books, and all the blessings of civilization. Our work was before us. We were young and strong and patient. What should hinder? So we thought. But everything did hinder. Our people did not want such things. They turned from us with contempt and derision. Our civilized clothing was an unceasing object of their ridicule. Our names, which they made ridiculous by their pronunciation, were a sign that we had renounced our parents and our people. We were neither Indians nor white men. We were not wanted by either. Having no Indian virtues or accomplishments, we were useless in the woods; and the whites did not need us, for they were our superiors. Even the young girls, when we approached them, showed their contempt. At last we could no longer stand the scorn and ridicule which overwhelmed us. We gave it up in despair. Our own people fairly drove us away from them as useless and disagreeable members of their society. We left them, completely cowed and disheartened, and returned to the settlements.

"Hearing that a teacher was wanted for an academy at Gull Prairie, I presented my credentials of character and scholarship to the trustees, and was appointed Principal. Life now opened very brightly for me. I had a good school, loved teaching, loved my pupils, was active in religious meetings, taught the choir and singing school, and every house was open to my visits. The whole community seemed to love me, and I was happy. Especially was I fond of a bright and beautiful young lady, one of my best pupils. We went together everywhere: to church, to singing school, evening parties and social visits. Everywhere she went with me, and seemed proud of my devotion. After a few months I proposed to marry her, and was referred to my warm friends, her parents. And this is what they said to me: 'What! You, an Indian, presume to address our daughter! Our daughter marry an Indian! You are crazy. She might as well marry a Negro. You will never be anything but an Indian for all your education. Remember this, and never presume again with your attentions. We are your friends, and if you will consider it, you will see that it must be as we state it.'

"All that night I did consider it. Crushed to the earth in my humiliation, bruised and half stunned by the cruel scorn which accompanied my rejection, I saw clearly that it could never be different. I was an Indian, and could never be anything but an Indian. God help me! So the next day I resigned my position, dismissed my students, gave away my broadcloth suit, boots, and beaver, put on moccasins, leggins and blanket, and took to the bush, where I shall thus live and die among my own people. This was three years ago, and for the future I can only be an Indian, as God has made me."

A year or two later [i.e., after the incident of joining the choir on Waterloo Street], these men, moccasined and blanketed, went west of the Mississippi with their people, carrying with them their gentle culture, fair scholarship, and humbled aspirations.

Aunt Hattie's Story

Albert Baxter

Harriet Guild Burton was the oldest daughter of Joel Guild and part of a Yankee pioneer family (six daughters and one son) that migrated from the state of New York and reached the "Rapids" in 1833. The members of the Guild family were considered the first permanent white settlers in Grand Rapids. At Ionia the Guilds had left a larger party of migrants who were making their way west from Detroit; they came down the Grand River on a float boat and landed on a bank where Huron Street came to be. Joel Guild bought a parcel of land from Louis Campau, and he immediately began building the first frame house in the valley. Hattie was twenty when they arrived at the site of Grand Rapids, on June 23, 1833. Less than a year later (April 13, 1834), she married Barney Burton, a young pioneer who had taken up a homestead in Paris Township. Theirs was the first wedding of white people in what is now Grand Rapids. It was held at the bride's parents' home, and the young couple immediately set up housekeeping in a log house Mr. Burton had built in the woods southeast of the "Rapids."

"Aunt Hattie" lived another sixty-two years in Grand Rapids, outliving her husband and all her siblings by some years. She had a life membership in the Union Benevolent Association (predecessor of Blodgett Hospital), and she had a home there during the last few years of her life. Her obituary in the *Grand Rapids Herald* of August 2, 1895, reads in part: "She was known by a larger number of people than any other woman who ever lived in Grand Rapids, and had

---

From Albert Baxter, *History of the City of Grand Rapids, Michigan*

seen more of the growth and development of the city than any person now living — over sixty-two years. For many years she was the central figure at nearly all gatherings of the old settlers, her name occupies a prominent place in all histories of the city, and the papers have published column after column on the incidents and events in her pioneer life and that of her father's family."

After the surveys of public lands had been extended as far north as Grand River, reports of an enticing nature as to the inducements for settlement in this region began to reach the eastern people, probably from some of the surveyors and their assistants, and from now and then an explorer who ventured into the wilderness; though of the latter there is very little record. Then followed the land-lookers who had already traversed the more southerly portions of the Territory, where many settlements were established between the years 1828 and 1832. And speculators as well as pioneer settlers were searching further north for "fresher fields and pastures new."

In the fall of 1832 Samuel Dexter, of Herkimer county, N.Y., came to Grand River and selected the spot where now is Ionia, and entered there a quarter section of land. He also entered four eighties — a tract two miles long and eighty rods wide — close by where now is the very heart of this city of Grand Rapids, along the east side of the Division street line, from Wealthy Ave. to Leonard street. He then went back to Herkimer county and set about organizing a colony of emigrants. In the spring of 1833 they started. The company numbered sixty-three persons. . . .

That was a long and tedious expedition; but those who were of it soon forgot its few hardships and through life remembered and loved to recount its many exciting incidents and pleasures. Cutting their way through the previously untrodden wilderness, and camping at night in the woods, wherever darkness stopped them, was no frolic in the ordinary sense; but they were vigorous and healthy and companionable, and the adventure was novel and exhilarating. There was brush to be cut through, swamps and jungles to pass around, streams to be crossed, and many a hard lift for the men of the party; while the women aided with as much good will in preparing their frugal lunches and their resting places, and the children were in the very spirit of play. Only one seriously sad incident occurred — the death of a child of Mr. Dexter, by scarlet fever. But the entire narrative may perhaps best be told by one of the pioneer party, Mrs. Harriet Burton, a daughter of Joel Guild, who was one of that colony. . . . "Aunt Hattie" relates the following story of that journey and its incidents:

We (Joel and Edward Guild, and their families) started from Paris, Oneida county, N.Y., taking goods and teams. At the Erie Canal we went aboard a boat purchased by Samuel Dexter for the party. In all there were sixty-three of the company. We had our horses to draw the boat, and the boys to drive. At Buffalo the boat was sold, and we shipped our goods and took passage on the steamer *Superior* for Detroit, where we selected only such goods as we could carry overland, and left the rest to be sent around to the mouth of Grand River. We stopped in Detroit two or three days, buying oxen and cows, and laying in supplies. Every family had a wagon. From there we went to Pontiac, where we staid two nights in a tavern. The third day we went about ten miles and camped near a tavern, where the women and children found shelter, and the rest slept in tents. The next day we left the roads and went into the wilderness, with no guide except a compass and a knowledge of the general direction to be taken. That night, I think, we reached the cabin of a Mr. Gage, twenty miles from any other white man's habitation. As many as the small house would accommodate slept in it; the others camped. All were quite weary. Mr. Winsor, who was lame, Mrs. Winsor, with her sick girl, Rosalind, and the small children, rode. The rest of us walked, and it was hard walking. After leaving there, all had to camp out. Each family had a tent; the six tents were pitched together as one long tent, and every night twenty-three beds were made upon the ground. At Pontiac Mrs. Dexter's youngest child, a boy, became sick with scarlet fever, and seemed to grow worse every day. But we could not stop, for our progress was slow and our supplies running short, so we traveled on to the Shiawassee, where we procured a guide. It was raining when we reached the Looking-glass River, and that night the little boy was so sick that his mother and Mrs. Yeomans, whose babe was but four weeks old when we started, and myself, sat up all night, holding umbrellas over the two little ones, and nursing them. It was late when we started the next day, and we went only about four miles before reaching heavy timbered land. Thus far we had been traveling through burr oak openings. That night the boy grew worse, and his mother and I sat up nearly all night with him.

Death in the Woods

Our provisions were nearly gone, and we could not stop, but about noon Mrs. Dexter called a halt, noticing a change in the boy. Dr. Lincoln gave him some medicine, but in a few minutes the little sufferer was dead. We could not tarry, but went sadly on carrying his body, and camped early; when my mother furnished a small trunk that had been used for carrying food and dishes, which served for a coffin, and by Muskrat Creek, as the sun was going down, the little one was buried. A large elm by the grave was marked, and logs were put over the mound and fastened there, to protect it from wolves that were then plenty in that vicinity. The only service over the little grave was a prayer by Mr. Dexter. The mother seemed broken-hearted, and we all were grieved, but could not tarry there.

At Grand River

We had reached the point where we had to use meal that father bought at Pontiac for the horses, letting the latter pick their living as best they could from grass and twigs by the way. Each family had cows — in all fifteen or twenty. We made log-heap fires, filled a large brass kettle with water, placed it over the fire, stirred in meal and made hasty-pudding, which, with milk from the cows, was our only food. After reaching the timber land, we girls had to rise very early and get breakfast for the young men, who would then start ahead to cut out the road, and only came in when it was time to camp at night. At the end of sixteen days we reached Grand River at Lyons, where father and his family made a brief stop, while the rest proceeded at once to Ionia.

On to the Rapids

In a few days father and Mr. Dexter started from Ionia, on horseback, by way of the Rapids of Grand River, for the land office at White Pigeon. On reaching the Rapids they met Uncle Louis Campau, who wanted them to settle here, the lands having come into market the year before. He had taken some land, and was platting it into lots; he did not "talk Yankee" very well, he said, and he wanted a settlement of Yankees here. So father went and took up the forty that is now the "Kendall addition," and also took up some pine land a little southeast of here. When he came back from the land office, he bought, for $25, a village lot of Mr. Campau. Uncle Louis, and some of his French help, went to Ionia for us with bateaux. All of our family came down. At the mouth of Flat River we went ashore. Dan Marsac was there, in a log shanty. There was no clearing. Many Indians were about. We next landed at Rix Robinson's. Found Indians there also. Soon after, some Indians met us, and Uncle Louis talked with them in their own language. He said they informed him that a Catholic Priest, Mr. Baraga, had just arrived. We reached the Rapids and landed that evening on the east side by the foot of Huron street, near where the Butterworth & Lowe iron works are. Two log houses and a shop were there. All about were woods, mostly. We were received with a warm welcome by that good woman, Mrs. Louis Campau, who did her utmost to make us comfortable. This was Saturday, June 23, 1833 — the day that I was twenty years old. We staid there a few days; then removed to Mr. Campau's fur-packing house and store, where we lived till about the first of September, when we removed into the new house that my father built.

[Albert Baxter's note: The story teller, Harriet Guild [Aunt Hattie], was the oldest of six daughters (the youngest was three) of Joel Guild and his wife; they also had one son, Consider Guild, then 18 years old. They came from West Winfield, Herkimer county, N.Y., to Paris, Oneida county, and then here [Grand Rapids]. The lot which Mr. Guild purchased was on the east side of Monroe at its junction with Pearl street, and at the base of "Prospect Hill." There he immediately set about building a house, which he so far completed as to be able to move into it in ten weeks. It was the first frame-house built at Grand Rapids, and the lumber for it was procured at the Indian saw mill which had been built for the Slater mission.]

Harriet Guild Burton ("Aunt Hattie"), pictured late in life

GRPL, Library Photo Collection

At the Shipyard Forge

Charles E. Belknap

Charles Belknap's family moved from the state of New York to Grand Rapids, arriving on the Grand River by boat from Grand Haven, in 1854, when Charles was eight years old. He often worked in his father's blacksmith and ship-repairing shop. During the Civil War, Belknap enlisted as a private; but while still seventeen, he was promoted to captain, and when the war ended, the U.S. Senate voted him to the rank of Brevet Lieutenant Colonel in recognition of his outstanding war service.

Long before the automobile appeared, Belknap built up his Belknap Wagon Company, which was located near the No. 3 Fire Engine House. He joined the fire department in 1870 as an active volunteer; in those days of frame store buildings and wood construction, fire service was strenuous. Captain Belknap rode a high-spirited Kentucky-bred mare who was eager to reach the scene of the fire as soon as the alarm sounded. She was stabled at the Belknap home barn at night, but during the day she had a stall at the wagon company — always ready for when the alarm would sound.

Captain Belknap served on the Grand Rapids Board of Education, the Board of Aldermen, and was mayor of Grand Rapids. He also served two terms in the United States Congress. He was active on numerous state boards and civic boards, and he arranged many parades — usually riding in the lead as the mounted marshal. A bronze statue of Captain Belknap, in his uniform as Boy Scout Commissioner, still stands at the little park at the intersection of Lake Drive and Fulton Street. The following segments of his memoir have been excerpted from his book *The Yesterdays of Grand Rapids* (Grand Rapids: The Dean-

Hicks Co., 1922; reprinted for the benefit of Mayflower Congregational Church, 1958).

In the early fifties [1850s], when as a boy I came to the "faraway waters," forests covered the hills and valleys. In the windings of the river the steamboat passed between banks bordered with wild fruit trees, fragrant grape vines and meadows of wild flowers. In places the banks were blue with violets. Indian pinks were everywhere. It was an enchanted land from which came wild brooks, often bearing canoes loaded with native Americans.

Indians were not strangers to me, my father having lived all his life among the St. Regis tribe in the St. Lawrence river country. I sometimes think that I breathed into my system a lot of Indian spirits that float about in the maze of the autumn days. I would have willingly quit the river steamer for a seat in one of those canoes with its Ottawa paddler.

We came to Michigan because the government had given my grandfather a quarter-section of timber land as a reward for his services in the war of 1812. Father came to do the iron work on the boats being built in the shipyard located where the Pantlind hotel now stands.

By stage, river, canal, lake and railroad we arrived in Chicago, then known to the Indians as Chi-cog — "skunk water." In the getaway from this rightly named place we secured passage on a lumber schooner for Grand Haven, sleeping on the deck without blankets; then by steamer to Grand Rapids.

Until the white man came with a Bible in one hand but a jug of whiskey in the other, the Indian was a pretty good fellow. When the smithshop was in order and the fires glowing with heavy forgings for the shipbuilder the Indian began to come in for gun repairs.

The first work my father did for one of them was a fish spear. With a grunt of approval he stepped into his canoe, went away upon the rapids and soon returned with a sturgeon long as a rail with which he paid his bill. North of the shipyard were sawmills, livery stables, and Butterworth's foundry, whose factory bell was official time.

Artist Sarah Nelson's 1856 painting of the Grand River at "the Rapids" captured Grand Rapids as it looked during Charles Belknap's youth.
GRPL, Art and Graphics Collection

Canal Street north was a streak of black mud. On foggy days the wornout corduroy looked like alligators. Boys on adventure bound rolled up their trousers when going over.

The first business place south was Bentham's restaurant, then Daniel Ball's bank and beyond the tangle of streets afterward known as Grab Corners, a very proper term.

The shipyard forge soon became the roosting place for the loafers, traders, politicians, scandal peddlers and would-be statesmen. All territory south of Monroe-av. was "Shantytown," north of Monroe "Kent," and west side men were "Three B's." All stores were on the cash and carry plan. There not being many stores on the west side of the river every man going to work in the morning carried a bag, basket and bottle, the bottle for New Orleans molasses. The boys of these three sections seldom went abroad except in gangs. Because I lived on Waterloo and dad's shop was on Canal, I was neutral and had a chance to save my alley. . . .

As I remember now Bentham's restaurant was to me the most important place in town. It stood where the Pantlind now stands and it may be the Pantlind's reputation for good things to eat is an inheritance rightly handed down. Bentham specialized in smoked venison. Sometimes he had boiled ham, venison stew with onions; in the winter oysters that came through in gallon wooden kegs; usually a kettle of pea soup to draw French trade, but dried venison always.

Nobody need go hungry, for if a fellow's credit was low he could set his traps for muskrat and trade the skins to Bentham for his daily bread. Ice Cream had not been invented, but the present-day girl and boy has nothing over the boy who had a chunk of dried venison to gnaw on. Molasses candy was the great confection in those days, paid for with our big copper cents.

The floors and table tops at Bentham's were not scrubbed to excess, but all the same he liked the boys and the boys liked him. We watched him grow gray and when the Indians with canoe loads of bucks no longer came, the taste of the town changed to beer and pretzels and Bentham's became a thing of the past. . . .

The Pioneers' Winter Food

One of the serious problems of the pioneer settler of any northern country is the storing of provisions for the winter months. Southern Michigan offered an abundance of game and wild fruit to the man who sought a home within its boundaries. Boys then, as now, had a great capacity for food and I remember my father's preparations for winter much better than I do my school lessons, and the cellar of our first home comes to mind more clearly than the parlor, for all its dulcimer, what-not, wax wreaths, and shell baskets.

This cellar had a dirt floor and riverstone walls. Along one side were the potato and apple bins; on the other the pork, beef, pickle and sauerkraut barrels and a bin for turnips, carrots and beets. Mother's spiced wild pigeons were a specialty and every fall father made an outing with others to Battle Point down the river and put up barrels of black bass in salt. It was possible to get a twenty-five-pound kit of salt whitefish at [Grand] Haven for two dollars. When it was time for Thanksgiving turkey we went over toward the John Ball Park country and shot one. And if we got two, mother made us give one to the minister.

This was long before the time of glass fruit jars or before one could buy canned stuff of any kind, but all during the summer we gathered the wild fruits, blackberries for jam, wild plums and verily the apple of temptation must have been the wild crabapple stewed down in maple syrup. During autumn days the kitchen was the drying place for pumpkins. A spokeshave was used to pare the rind, then they were sliced in rings and hung on a pole to dry. When well dried they were stored in the attic and rings were brought forth about once a week to be stewed for sauce or pies.

Apples, and peaches, when we could get them, were pared, quartered, strung on twine and hung to dry over the kitchen stove, where they made a fine place for flies to roost. Housewives who were finicky covered the stuff with netting.

Ham and shoulders — beef and venison — were dried in the old smokehouse. Then the cellar had its barrel of soft soap, kept well covered because for some reason or other it seemed always to be a trap for the family cat; and also its barrel of vinegar and cider. Beside them stood kegs of wild grapejuice and elderberry wine.

Some families that had a member afflicted with shaking ague had a keg of wild cherries covered over with whisky. The mayor of the village added some of the inner bark of the cherry tree to his keg and one needed the appetite of a Georgia goober-grabber to share in his hospitality.

In some homes these fancy medicinal barrels fairly crowded the pork kegs and potato bins out of the cellar.

Nearly every family had its own chickens and the price of eggs did not go up every time the sun went behind a cloud; it also had a cow and a pig. The pig ran at large and one year the village council found it necessary to pass an ordinance restraining people from emptying the dregs of their cherry whisky in the gutters. . . .

A Day on the *Olive Branch*

One spring morning in 1857, drifting away from the pier at the yellow warehouse, the steamer *Olive Branch* set forth for the Haven [Grand Haven] with a cargo of package freight, a top deck laden with passengers, and Capt. Robert Collins, Pilot Tom Robbins and Cook Jim Daily, with a full crew of husky Irishmen. We were soon winding between banks heavily wooded and bordered with wild fruit trees in full bloom — plum, cherry, crab and thornapple — all festooned with wild grape vines.

At the dock of Hovey's plaster mills a hundred barrels of land plaster were taken aboard. Then angling across the river we were against the bank at Grandville, the place nature intended should be a town site. The settlement got an early start with some of the best men who came out of the east in those pioneer days. Here we left package freight and took aboard a few passengers.

At Haire's landing we gathered up a lot of maple sugar in tubs and a pile of slabwood for the boilers.

At the mouth of Sand Creek, where there had once been an Indian village, we added a couple going to the Haven to be married. Coming down from the upper road they crossed the creek on a tree footbridge and the young lady had taken a tumble and had to swim out.

They built a fire to dry out as well as to signal the boat. Once aboard the women passengers fitted the young woman out in dry clothing and the couple were seated at the captain's table for the noon meal. The bride-to-be was game all right. She had come west to teach at the Sand Creek school, but the first month she found a better job and the log shack's pupils had a vacation.

At the Blendon hills two families of Hollanders, all wearing wooden shoes, were met by a man with a yoke of cattle. Their goods were piled high on his cart and the boat tooted a goodbye as they trailed away into the forest.

It was a short run to Lamont, a beautiful place so spread along the bluffs — for every man wanted a home on the river front — that it looked four miles long and four rods wide.

All the morning a couple had occupied a bench on the top deck in front of the pilot house. The man smoked a fancy shaped pipe and they talked only in German. Lamont evidently touched his heart and with arm outstretched he recited "Bingen on the Rhine." I did not understand then as I did in Civil war days, when I served with men who often in battle days sang of "Bingen on the Rhine."

There have been many changes since those days, but time cannot blot out pretty Lamont as it looked to me in my boyhood.

At Eastmanville Mr. Eastman came aboard with a party of ladies and gentlemen. The ladies were carrying many things made by the Indian women of the vicinity, beaded belts and beaded money bags; some had traveling bags of smoke-tanned buckskin ornamented with native dyes and woven designs of porcupine quills. The freight taken here consisted of many packs of ax helves shaved out of white hickory.

The long dining table was crowded at the evening meal. Capt. Collins toasted the bride-to-be who was garbed in the best that several "carpet sacks" afforded.

At the landing at Bass river Mr. Eastman took charge of the dining cabin and with song and story the *Olive Branch* rounded Battle point, paddling past great river bottom meadows of cattail and wild rice, from which flocks of wild duck came swirling overhead.

There were many inviting channels and waterways and the pilot needed to be well informed.

As we neared the Haven the sun in the golden west disclosed smoking mill stacks, forests of ship masts and drifting sand dunes. Beyond was a great sea of white caps. This was the end of a "perfect day." . . .

The Fisk Lake Log Tavern

From the days of the very first settlers of Grand Rapids there was a forest trail from the east which, as years have passed, has developed into Robinson road [named after Rix Robinson]. More people travel this road in one hour now than covered the trail in all the first year of its existence.

The Fisk family were among its very first followers and in 1837 John W. Fisk built a log tavern on the site now owned by Ben West.

The Fisk Lake House, as it was called, was made from the timber growing on the high bluffs which bordered the lake. Across the road, north from the tavern, was built a log stable to shelter the horses of the travelers.

How welcome the blaze of the great stone fireplace must have been to men and women after long miles of travel on a rough road, skirting swamps, fording streams or winding about the hills through an unbroken forest.

Can you not imagine this man Fisk as he came from the east and looked upon the gem of a lake that for all the years since has borne his name? Fisk kept this tavern for two years, then engaged in other building enterprises. The two years following James Fosget was the landlord. His ancestors were soldiers from France, under Lafayette, during the Revolutionary war. The girl who afterward became his bride was a niece of President Adams and came with her parents from the east; the last part of the journey down Grand river on a raft of logs and lumber. She was then thirteen years old. After her marriage to Mr. Fosget she became the landlady at the tavern and was as fine a type of American womanhood as the valley ever received, and at least one of her capable daughters is living near Grand Rapids at this time. The Fosgets afterward ran the Grandville hotel and their history will sometime make a story by itself.

The log tavern was in time replaced with a brick structure and for two years was operated by Jerome Trowbridge, afterward by Napoleon B. Carpenter. If ever a man was born to entertain people it was "Boney" and likewise there was no man, woman or child who knew her, that did not love and respect Auntie Carpenter.

Along in the seventies the Fisk Lake House was a great resort for saddle men and their ladies. Many of the cavalry and mounted soldiers of the Civil war had kept their horses. The ladies of that day rode side saddle and wore long, flowing skirts, tight-fitting waists, military collars and derby or stiff silk hats. They rivaled their escorts in horsemanship and the straight stretches of road witnessed many a merry race; ditches, stumps, loads of hay and stray cattle were no obstacle to cavalryman speed. Many a sentimental soul lost his heart along the winding Thornapple river road.

The popular stunt was to stop and leave orders for dinner, then gallop to Cascade, follow the river road to Ada and back to the tavern where Pat McCool looked after the horses and Boney Carpenter served chicken and the finest steaks that ever came from a charcoal broiler.

Frequently the evening ended with dancing in the upstairs ballroom, noted as having one of the finest floors in the city. Mr. Carpenter played the "bones" and set the pace. So here is just a word of appreciation for the good old landlords and their ladies — the Fisks, Fosgets and the Carpenters. . . .

The Head and the Tail of the Sturgeon

As the whale is the monarch of the ocean, so the sturgeon was monarch of the river years ago. In the spring of the year it was in the nature of many kinds of fish to come to the "Bow-e-ting" [the Ottawa term for "rapids"] to spawn. At this season it was not unusual to capture sturgeon weighing one hundred and fifty pounds and if Aaron Benneway was alive he could tell you of one that weighed two hundred and ten pounds.

All fishing with nets and spearing was done below the dam. The walks of Bridge street bridge were often lined with people looking at the fish and watching the canoe men spearing them in the water below. At night the scene was enlivened by the torches of the fishermen who with pitch-pine jacks, set on short staffs in the bow of their canoes, lighted up the shallow water for many feet about. With a man behind the light and another in the stern of the boat, both with heavy two-tined spears, they poled up near the dam and then floated back with the current.

There was one record night when Oscar Blumrich, still with us, and Aaron Benneway, long since fishing in the streams "beyond," went out under a jack light and brought in during the night seventy-two of the fish.

The sturgeon had a standard commercial value: they sold for twenty-five cents, large or small. Some smart Frenchmen in Shantytown gathered the spawn, pickled it in salt brine and sold it as Russian caviar in eastern cities.

When properly prepared the fish made tempting food. Farmers brought them in as a change from salt meats. Often a farmer would take several and pass them out to his neighbors. To dress them they were hung from a limb of a tree and skinned, the offal fed to the hogs and the spawn to the poultry. The meat wanted for immediate use was parboiled, to extract the oil, which was offensive, then fried with salt pork — a white, flaky fish, very good indeed. If not wanted at once the fish was hung in the smoke-house over a fire of chips that drew all the oil out and then put in salt for a day before the finish in the smoke-house.

Sturgeon like this one, caught in the Grand River at the turn of the twentieth century, were common in the river in the 1850s.

GRPL, Godfrey Anderson Collection

Today we pay large prices for smoked salt water fish not nearly so good as the sturgeon. Many people utilized the oil of the fish for making soft soap, for in those days it was a poor cellar or woodshed that had no barrel of soft soap. Somebody always had an iron cauldron and over a fire on the river bank the parts undesirable for food were boiled and the oil skimmed off the water.

This oil also made very good lamp oil and was often burned in the torches used in night parades and even in the lanterns that lighted the streets. In some cases it made the "witch lights" that our mothers used; a simple contrivance of a saucer half full of oil and a rag wound around a hickory nut with a loose end sticking above the oil. Light this end with a wisp of paper started in the stove, for matches were not plentiful, and you had a light as long as the oil lasted. I remember my mother sewing on trouser buttons and patches by just such a light after she had her five small boys tucked in bed.

Sometimes men who had no tallow to grease their boots used sturgeon oil and it was the cause of many family jars when the old man came home with cold feet and stuck them in the missus' oven to warm. I knew one man who used it for hair oil, but he was intoxicated at the time.

In one thing the sturgeon was a source of joy to the boy. In its head was a semi-bone growth that had all the pliable, bouncing properties of rubber. The boy chopped this out with an ax, whittled it round with his knife and had a ball. He wound it up to the desired size with yarn from an old sock. This winding required skill that was gained only by practice. Then as to the finishing touch — if he could lay hands on an old bootleg of split calf or sheepskin in those days, for the outside cover, mother sewed it on — or if he could spare a quarter of a dollar he went to Moses DeLong, the shoemaker on Bridge street, and came away with the finest kind of a ball, one that would bound clear over the house.

Men and boys played all the ball games from "two old cat" to hotly contested games that were the big event of the Fourth of July celebrations and a boy who could produce a fine ball was as happy as a bob-o-link swinging on a cattail in the swamp. . . .

Winter Sports and Perils

Before the river bed on the rapids was cleared of its great hard-head boulders and narrowed by the west side canal — for this canal was a part of the river and its present retaining wall is entirely in the river bed — all the water of the river, except the small flow that passed down the east side canal, came over the dam and spread out in swirls and channels between the rocks in a combat for the right of way to the foot of the rapids.

In the winter these great boulders made anchorage for ice formations and the entire river surface resembled islands of ice with narrow glades of clear water between.

In long spells of cold even the channels would close up and if snow covered the ice the canal gate would be closed and all the water coming over the dam [would] flood the ice below and make it fine for the skaters.

Of all the winter sports skating was the most popular and there developed many expert men and women skaters. Most of the skates were home made. Factory made skates were just finding their way into the hardware stores and distinctly American in style: short as the boot and blunt in taper, which was all right on clear, hard ice.

When the Hollanders began coming over they brought their skates, long in front and gradual taper. They were an innovation and looked odd, as did the people who wore them.

Our American girls wore long skirts and trim shoes while the Holland girls dressed in short corduroy skirts, heavy wool stockings and stout shoes that supported the ankle. When one of these girls went down, which was not often, she made a dent in the ice, but it was a modest tumble, while the home girl cut capers and blushed.

One winter day when the ice was all islands with narrow glades of water dividing them, that in the crisp sunlight looked like liquid race courses, the weather was at its best and all the skaters in town were out. It was like a carnival, except that it lacked the music.

The islands within safe reach were crowded, but there was one large glare place just beyond jumping distance that was tempting the daring. A party of Holland girls came down an open space like a whirlwind and going into the air one by one in their short skirts they cleared the glade and landed safely on this island of temptation.

This challenge was too much for the American boys and several crossed successfully and were soon linked arm in arm with the rosy cheeked, sensibly dressed Netherlands girls. A dark haired American girl saw her beau cutting "pigeon wings" and doing the "long roll" with a pretty blonde and she tried the jump. When she left the ice her short skate caught in the long skirt and she plunged head first into the water with such force that she came up under the ice on the farther side.

In about a minute the crowd was frantic; all except a twelve-year-old boy — a "water rat" they called him — who pushed his way through the crowd and followed the girl under the ice, where she could be plainly seen floating and being carried along by the current. Men yelled and women fainted or fell upon their knees sobbing.

Those who could see said the boy had caught her hand and with his feet braced on the bottom was struggling for a place in the open.

It was a Holland girl lying on her face at the channel's edge who caught the boy's hand and pulled them out. Men brought planks and bridged the glade and the unconscious girl was wrapped in blankets and rushed to her home.

The boy refused to be helped out but waded to the shore side of the glade and climbing up to the roadway he hiked for the blacksmith's shop. Here he was stripped and wrapped in a horse blanket while his clothes were drying. He was sitting on the forge by the fire surrounded by an admiring crowd when a big hearted Irish woman came in with a stew-pan of hot soup, saying, "There is nothing like hot soup to drive the cold out of his insides."

That boy had made his own skates. The blades were ground out of old mill files and he had worked many long evenings at the grindstone. The skates were fastened on his feet with buckskin laces. But Mr. Wilder D. Foster, who had a fine assortment of skates in his store, sent a pair of the best he had as a reward for his bravery.

In the late seventies there were several winters when the ice was unusually good above the dam, mainly because the drift ice was held back by the logging booms above the city. Hundreds of people gathered for the skating and in the evenings great driftwood fires were built along the shore. On holidays Squire's brass band played and added to the pleasure.

To skate on Reeds lake in those days simply never came to mind. It would have called for a walk of three miles before one could put on skates and was just altogether "out in the country." . . .

Along in the fifties it became necessary to enlarge the schoolhouse on the west side of the river, so the wise men of the school board decided to build it large enough for all time. River stone was plenty and cost only the digging and hauling; building lumber was a drug on the market and good mechanics one dollar per day of ten hours.

The school was built where the Union High now is. The top, or third floor, was used as the Armory; each lower floor had a large study room and two recitation rooms. In the large rooms were two box stoves — one on the girls' and one on the boys' side of the room — which burned two-foot wood usually carried upstairs by the boys. The tuition of the country boys was often paid with wood.

The stoves were in one corner of the room and the pipe ran to the other corner overhead, so no heat was lost. When the men drilled in the armory above, the vibrations parted the pipe joints and the soot sifted down upon the pupils of Prof. Boardman Taylor's night school; special classes for spelling and penmanship were very popular because it gave the boys a chance to beau the girls home.

There was no janitor at first and when one was supplied, he was known as the moderator and assisted the principal when he got hold of a boy he could not manage single handed.

Everything was lovely in the spring and fall, when the older boys worked outside, but in the winter when they came in from the country the principal went armed with a six-foot hickory pointer. The moderator earned his salary, for in the battles the stove and all its pipe frequently came down. The small boys crawled under the desks and the older ones tried to be neutral. They wanted to see the country chaps downed but could not forget that the same hickory pointer often beat the dust out of their own trousers. Some of the principals were short term men, the length of service depending upon their muscle. Prof. Ballard, Prof. Clark, and Prof. Kent stayed the longest, but they really applied tact along with zeal and stick.

The schoolyard, inclosed by a board fence with a post entrance at either corner — not so much to keep the pupils in as to keep the cows and pigs out — was one city block in size except for the home of Mrs. Stephen Cool, who owned two lots at the corner of Turner and Fourth. She had declined to give these up but the board was not much concerned since the nearest well and supply of water was on her ground. She had a fine vegetable garden and was a lover of flowers and chickens. As the school grew her corner became quite a problem. She was at war with the boys all the time. They batted their balls through her windows, trampled the garden down and that sweet two-hundred-pound woman was worried to a frazzle but could not be persuaded to sell out and go to a quieter locality.

All the school ground west of the building was piled high with cord wood for the winter fire. There on the top of the high piled wood the little girls made houses and played with their dolls. One of their innocent stories of a cave in the wood pile revealed a fraud perpetrated by a south end farmer, many cords short in his contract to the city. West of Broadway was a swamp, with a thick tangle of alders and other marsh growth, through which ran a tame sort of a creek where frogs held concerts. The boys who loved adventure cleaned out the snakes, but the crop of frogs seemingly grew no less though many found their way into the schoolrooms in coat pockets and were let loose to hop about on the girls' side. In this swamp the boys made robber dens in accordance with the fiction of the day.

There was a woman who had a home on the bank of the creek above Fifth street. In a willow thicket below her house some girls innocently built a dam which blocked the water and drowned all the chickens. Of course, the engineering feat was laid to the boys. I always liked that woman, but not well enough to give to her the names of the girls who played in that heaven of mud, water and pollywogs.

It seems to me there never was a schoolhouse with so many natural attractions for the boys and girls, but along with the years came the big ditch and swallowed the creek and the dump of the city buried the alders, willows and cattails. Mrs. Cool's garden, chickens and pump were outlawed. The old stone schoolhouse was condemned in 1872 as a worn-out building and unsafe for the increasing numbers. While replacing it school was held in a long wooden shed built the length of the Third street side. The rooms were so exactly alike that small children became confused and had to be escorted to their places. The third school now stands on this location and enrolls more children than lived in all the city at the time the old stone school was built. Above the swamp where Dick built a robber's roost with a dime novel for a guide, his great-grandson is taught "how to play" and teeters on a board with a caretaker to see he does not fall off. The stone school that seemed built for eternity has become but a legend. . . .

With the City Firemen

One afternoon in 1857, I occupied a reserved seat on the top of a house on Monroe street along with some forty odd boys and girls and saw twenty-five business places destroyed by fire. The fire started in a drug store on Monroe between Waterloo and Ottawa streets.

There were three fire companies at that time and Number One and Number Two were in the crater, while Number Three was working to save surrounding property. It looked from my position as if all the people of the town were helping; throwing glass and china from upper windows and lugging feather beds down stairways.

From one of the stores many large boxes of dry paints were carried into the street. Every store kept whisky in those days, none of them drinking water. As a result the male population, thirsty and hard pressed by the flames, got a little dizzy and began tumbling into the paint boxes. Yellows and greens and purple began to blend with the blue and gray of smoke and ashes. If any of you have a desire to know how funny a man really can look, fill his inside with fire water and his outside the colors of the rainbow.

Were it not that the wind-driven fire brands threatened the entire town it would have been the most successful carnival the people ever put on the street.

From the doctor's office some fellows salvaged a pickling cask. It tipped into the gutter and scattered the contents and an Indian with a scalping knife could not have stampeded the crowd more quickly.

Number One and Number Two fire companies became badly demoralized by evening. Overcome by spirits and crusted with color they disappeared from the scene of conflagration. Number Three saved the town by working until daylight next morning, the women keeping them going by carrying coffee and sandwiches. The following Sunday every church in town was given a sermon on temperance.

As a reward of merit to Number Three company for keeping sober, the women of the town expressed their appreciation by the gift of a beautiful satin banner, which now is among the treasures of the Kent Scientific Museum.

This fire had all the thrills of a great battle. It was the fireside story of the year and while it distressed many people for a long time, now that the paint is washed off they can smile, even at the foreman of the company, who, lying on his back in a box of red paint, waved his brass trumpet vaguely and shouted: "Play away, Number Two." . . .

My Fire Service before the Civil War

When about fourteen years old I became interested in Number Three fire company. My father was a member and it was every boy's ambition to run with the engine.

No salaries were paid; in fact, one had to pay fifty cents annual dues and fifty cents fine for missing a fire or monthly meeting. I was assigned the duty of bearing the torch, a brass globe that held about a quart of fish oil on the end of a four-foot staff. I must be the first man at the engine house and with the torch run ahead of the machine to light the road to the fire. Once there and the machine set, I must go with the pipemen and light the way into stairways and other dark places. It certainly was a life of adventure.

It was my start in public affairs and caused many sleepless hours, with no pay, in return. I rather think those men and boys would have felt insulted if pay had been offered them.

Mother made me a red shirt and embroidered in silk on the front a figure three. Every time I carried the torch mother had to wash the fish oil out of my clothes. That was one of the penalties she paid for the glory of having a fireman in the family.

I had the trade pretty well learned by the beginning of the Civil war and when the various war organizations absorbed nearly every able-bodied man in Number Three company it became necessary to make up a new hose company.

I was elected foreman with a silver plated trumpet as a badge of authority. I had reached the top round of the ladder. Boys had attained a commercial value then and the common council announced they would pay five dollars each at the end of a year's service.

When the year ended the city clerk, Mr. Doubleday, sent each one of the company an order for five dollars, but there was no money in the treasury. Then John W. Squires, the miller, said he would give us a two-hundred-pound barrel of flour for each order.

I went to his mill, built of river stone on the river's east bank, not far south of the bridge, and took my flour home in my canoe to save expense. It was the proudest moment of my fire fighting life when I rolled that barrel of flour into mother's kitchen. My father was in the army and a whole barrel of flour at one time was cause for a jubilee. I was one of twenty boys who made their mothers happy that day.

Sketches for an Autobiography

A. J. Muste

Abraham Johannes (A. J.) Muste, 1885-1967, was the foremost pacifist in the United States during the first half of the twentieth century. He was an influential figure in the major social movements of that era and served as a mentor to a diverse group of activists, including Martin Luther King, Jr., Bayard Rustin, the Reuther brothers, David Dellinger, and Barbara Deming. His career ranged from a beginning as an ordained minister in several Protestant denominations to a labor organizer and educator, socialist agitator, and peace activist. He played an important role in the founding or development of such organizations as the American Civil Liberties Union, Brookwood Labor College, the Committee for Progressive Labor Action, the Fellowship of Reconciliation, the Congress on Racial Equality, the World Peace Brigade, and the War Resisters League.

Muste was also a founder and editor of *Liberation* magazine and the author of numerous articles and several books, including *Nonviolence in an Aggressive World* (New York, 1940) and *Not by Might* (New York, 1947). There are two published biographies of A. J. Muste: *Peace Agitator: The Story of A. J. Muste* by Nat Hentoff (New York: Macmillan, 1967; reprinted by the A. J. Muste Memorial Institute, New York, 1982), and *Abraham Went Out* by Jo Ann Ooiman Robinson (Philadelphia: Temple University Press, 1981). The following autobiographical memoir is excerpted from *The Essays of A. J. Muste,* edited and with an introduction by Nat Hentoff, preface by Jo Ann O. Robinson (2nd ed., 2001), published by the A. J. Muste Memorial Institute, Murray Rosenblith, Executive Director.

Sketches for an Autobiography

Since I am trying to write an autobiography, the question that intrigues me at the moment is: what is the connection between me today and the baby who was born early in January of 1885 in a small town named Zierikzee, in the province of Zeeland in the Netherlands, to whom his parents, Martin Muste and Adriana Jonker, gave the sonorous name Abraham Johannes?

My mother more than once in later years remarked that during the first year of my existence I cried virtually without interruption all day but slept like a top all night. This was a pattern which I have in some sense followed most of my life, since I am usually sounding off about something a good part of every day and practically never have any trouble about sleeping at night.

As for Zierikzee, when in later years I went back to the Netherlands and told Dutch friends, in answer to their questions, that I was born in Zierikzee, they invariably exclaimed: "Not Zierikzee!" and then let go with a hearty laugh. It seems that Zierikzee is a sort of equivalent of our Podunk. There is in fact a popular song in the Dutch night clubs, the chorus of which starts with "I was born in Zierikzee." It sounds much more tuneful and jocular in Dutch than in English. . . .

It was about the time of the death of [my] pet bird that life in our family entered a period of continuous excitement. Four of my mother's brothers, in the period before or just after my birth, had moved their families to the United States. They had been poorly paid agricultural laborers in Zeeland. They had not taken up farming in America, but small businesses — groceries, drugs, scrap metal in Grand Rapids, Michigan, where, in the decades since 1847, thousands of Hollanders had settled. All four of them had done fairly well and were making a much better living than would have been possible in the Netherlands at that time.

Having achieved a measure of security for themselves, they considered the plight of their youngest and favorite sister, my mother, and one of them paid us a visit and proposed that our family emigrate. The brothers were ready to finance the trip. I know from conversations that took place after we had settled in this country that the two arguments against undertaking the venture that weighed most heavily with my parents were leaving the country of their birth and of their fathers, and a doubt as to whether they would ever be able to pay back the (to them) huge loan which my uncles were prepared to make. . . .

We embarked on an old Holland-America Line steamer named Obdam which took nearly two weeks in a stormy January [1891] to reach Hoboken. We traveled, of course, in the steerage. Families staked out preserves for themselves on the platforms, one above another, which served as beds. Those who were near the wall, as we were, climbed over the families between them and the aisle when the occasion arose. Occasionally soup was passed out, but the migrants had brought their own supplies of bread and cheese with them and, in some instances, cakes, which they occasionally shared with families like ours who had no cakes. Again, it was all new experience; it was adventure and it was to my liking.

There was only one qualification. Mother became ill. Early in the voyage she was removed to the ship's hospital. A vivid memory is of one of the last days of the journey. The storm had abated. My father took me on deck with him. The ship was still rolling. The sky was not yet clear. The ocean was a blur. We made our way to a window, where my mother's face appeared. We could converse a little. She was not too ill to smile. There was a feeling that everything was going to be all right. It must have dominated the hours that followed very powerfully, because I have not been able to bring to the surface any definite memories of the end of the voyage or the debarkation in Hoboken or the transfer to a hospital on an island in New York harbor, where we were kept for nearly a month because mother was still not well enough to undertake the journey to Grand Rapids.

Here the photograph on the plate of memory becomes clear again. Mother is in one wing of the building. Father and the children are in another, but we know she is near by. The harbor is beautiful. Here I consciously experience for the first time the sensation of the beauty of scenery composed of water, island, and shore. Little tugboats ceaselessly plied the blue waters and left a white wake. We called them "doctors' boats," because it was in a tug that a doctor came each day to see the patients on our island.

Inside the hospital there was delicious food, and more than enough of it. There were corridors in which to play and, as far as my recollection goes, our play was uninhibited. We had, however, been strictly brought up and I am quite confident we were not noisy.

In our section of the hospital there was an attendant whose name was John. We did not understand his English, nor he our Dutch, but we were friends. John learned that my first name was Abraham. So, when he appeared in the morning, he said, "Hello, Abraham Lincoln," and when he left in the evening it was, "Goodnight, Abraham Lincoln."

We did not know whether Abraham Lincoln was the name of a gadget, a town, or a person dead or alive. It was natural that one of the things we did when we got settled in Michigan was to find out. So it came about that early in life I began to read everything by and about Lincoln that I could lay my hands on. I learned about the boy studying by the light of the hearth in the log cabin. I followed him on the trip down the Mississippi River and I heard him say when he saw a slave sold on the block at New Orleans: "By God, if ever I get a chance to hit that thing, I'll hit it and hit it hard."

Early I learned to chant: "Four score and seven years ago our fathers brought forth upon this continent a new nation, conceived in liberty and dedicated to the proposition that all men are created equal."

In time I learned, of course, about certain distinctions between Lincoln the myth and Lincoln the human being, between the "American Dream" and the reality. Nevertheless, being called "Abraham Lincoln" by John on the island in New York harbor, and passing my youth in Michigan, next door to Illinois, not far from Springfield, in the 1890's when the economy of the Middle West, in its own imagination and feeling, still lived in the days of John Brown, the Emancipation Proclamation, the martyred President — all this is part of my inmost being.

There came a morning when mother was well and we all got into a "doctor's boat" and were taken to Castle Garden, which was then the immigrant station, at Battery Park, New York. A later generation knew the building as the Aquarium.

Father left for Hoboken to reclaim the baggage which had been left in storage there. We waited for his return anxiously as the day wore on. What might not have happened to him in this strange land? May it have been a mistake to undertake this journey into the unknown? But no; toward evening father returned, the business taken care of.

Then we were on a train all night and all the next day and, because of February fog and rain, not much lighter in the day than in the night. I was sick on the train as I had not been on the ocean.

Then, in late afternoon, we stood on the platform of the Grand Trunk Railway station in the east end of Grand Rapids, where I lived for a dozen years, my parents for over four decades, my sisters to this day. Uncles and cousins are there to greet us. In a pouring rain we drive in a carriage to the home of an uncle. The rain is not so important as the carriage — in America even ordinary people may have their own carriages and are not confined to being someone's coachman if they want to ride and not walk.

Now we are in a warm, brightly lighted room at the home of an uncle. We are eating supper. My mother laughs happily at her brother's jokes. This I recall, but also that there were cousins, girls a few years older than I, who make much of me. By that time the younger children were probably sound asleep. The cousins told me the English words for "table," "chair" and so on, and were delighted when I imitated them precisely. They made me feel that I was the Traveler they had been waiting for.

So the first journey into the unknown had a happy ending. The new country was livable, hospitable, even exciting.

You are a boy six years old and you are living on Quimby Street in Grand Rapids, Michigan. The drab frame house is set back in a yard, unlike the houses in Holland, which front directly on the street. In the back there is a considerable garden in which potatoes are planted. There is a street which seems very wide, in contrast to the narrow Dutch streets, and very dusty. There is a wooden sidewalk, but the housewives do not go out to scrub it on their hands and knees. A hundred yards or so to the west the Grand Trunk railroad trains clamor over the crossing, heading for the bridge over the Grand River. Beyond the railroad track is the factory, where your father luckily got a job, a day or two after arriving in the town, at six dollars a week for a sixty-hour week. These are the "hard times" of the early Eighteen Nineties. . . .

My own experience of absorption into the "new world" was certainly a pleasant and stimulating sensation. As I have looked back upon it and sought to understand its influence on my character and destiny, it has also seemed to me singularly fortunate. It came, of course, at an early age when one is impressionable and to some extent aware of what is taking place — for example, that one speaks a different language, is an object of curiosity, an outsider in some measure — and is also malleable. The ocean voyage had had its enigmas, its apprehensions, its quality of near terror and at times its feeling of bewilderment at being carried along one knew not whither. Yet it had ended well. A place to settle had been found which seemed advantageous compared with the place we had left behind. Might not this experience mark voyaging of another kind than geographical?

The Hollanders who settled in the Middle West in the decades before World War I formed a fairly numerous group in Grand Rapids (without, however, making it a predominantly Dutch center). With the rarest of exceptions, every Dutch family belonged to a church, the Reformed or Christian Reformed, to which it had belonged in the old country. The services and preaching were all in Dutch.

In the larger population in Grand Rapids the Dutch constituted a lower stratum. The owners of the furniture factories and saw mills were of English stock. Until after the first World War, Hollanders were the cheap labor in the factories, the small shopkeepers in the outlying parts of town, the poor farmers on the land. In my early youth it was still an event when a girl from one of the Dutch families, who well may have been born in the United States, became a clerk in one of the fashionable department stores downtown. The girl's family, for its part, still wondered whether it would not have been better if she had remained in domestic service instead of, for a little more money and a lot more prestige, being exposed to all the lures of life in the English-speaking stratum of the town. Had not the Calvinistic God assigned them their place as hewers of wood, though often highly skilled ones, and would it not be best for the children to remain close to the fold of their humble elect?

There was no semblance of a ghetto, of course. There was no barrier of culture as there was to be later with immigrants from Eastern Europe, and no barrier of color as with Negroes and Asians. The Dutch were considered especially desirable immigrants. Almost without exception they were sober and industrious. Many of them became skillful cabinet makers. They were allergic to unions or "agitators" of any kind.

They were not numerous enough, nor did they have the kind of his-

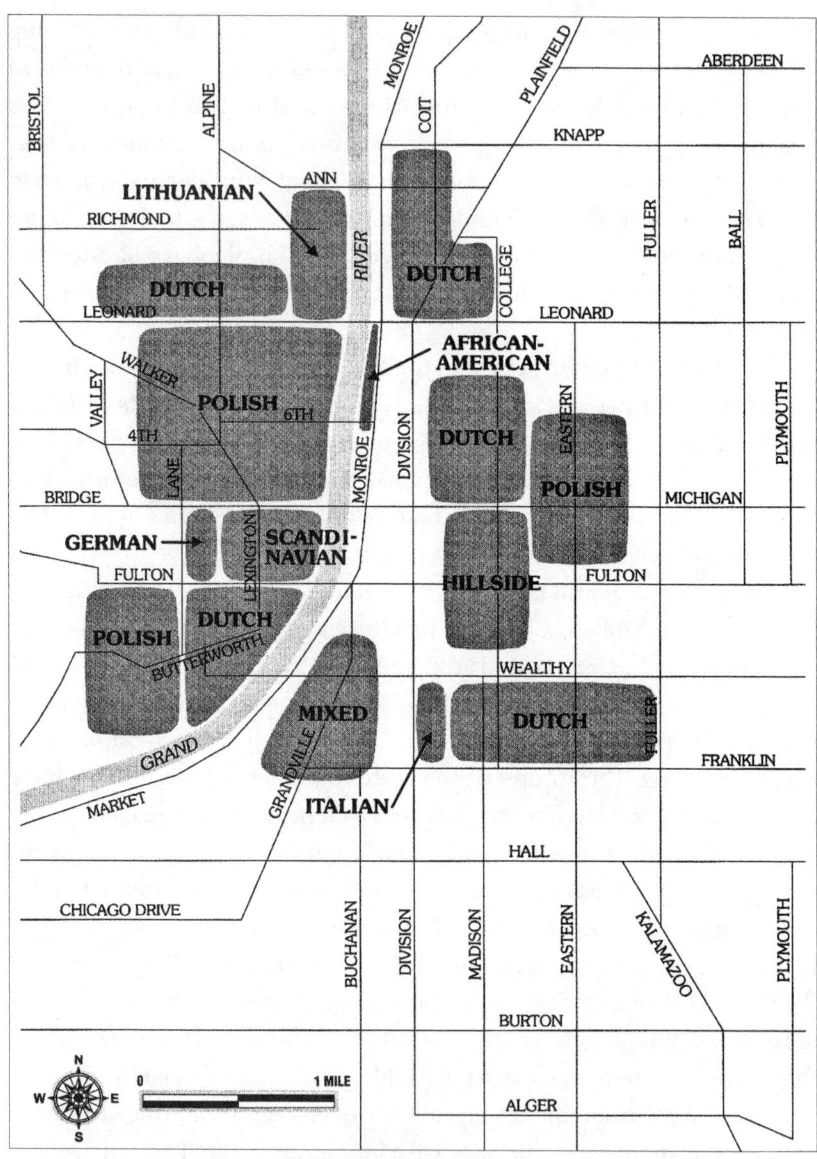

Grand Rapids' several ethnically distinct neighborhoods at the beginning of the twentieth century

Map by Chris Gray, courtesy of Grand Rapids Historical Commission

tory or cultural pattern which led them to want to perpetuate a separate Dutch minority over and against the American nation which to them was, in spite of such doubts as I have suggested, a land of opportunity and freedom, the land to which God had led the Pilgrim fathers, a land of peace where youth was not conscripted, and a Christian land, though unfortunately not entirely peopled by orthodox Calvinists.

It was in line with common practice among the Hollanders of Michigan that my father took out his first papers as soon as he was eligible and became a citizen at the earliest opportunity in time to cast his vote for William McKinley in the crucial election of 1896. Voting Republican is a habit which the descendants of that generation who have remained in Michigan still have. In my own youth, one no more thought that a church member could vote the Democratic ticket than that he could beat his wife, or steal, or have extramarital sexual relations. . . .

My formal schooling began, soon after our arrival in Grand Rapids, in a Reformed Church parochial school run by a somewhat rotund schoolmaster about whom I had the feeling that he was, as I would subsequently have put it, a stuffed shirt. There are two things I remember easily about that school. One is that we were put to memorizing all the verses of the metrical version of Psalm 119, which was chosen because it is the longest of all the Psalms. This suffices to indicate the pedagogical principles which prevailed in this institution of safe and sacred learning. The other memory has to do with one of the older boys in the school, a lad of nine or ten. He was at that tender age distinguished among us because he chewed tobacco. For some reason he had taken a liking to me and I felt that in him I had a sort of protector. One afternoon when we were going out of school he offered me a chew from his plug of tobacco. There may have been an admixture of devilishness with his generosity and a hope that he might witness my discomfiture. If so, he was disappointed. With my urge to be obliging to anyone who is nice to me, I took the chew, but at the same time took off briskly for home. It was not long before I had to seek relief for my stomach behind a lumber pile. When I reached home, Mother remarked on my paleness. I indicated ignorance of any reason for this condition. By supper time I had a near normal appetite, so the incident passed without further ado.

In a year or two, when my sister was old enough to go to school, we were sent to the nearby public school. The reason was undoubtedly that my parents preferred free public education, despite its non-religious character, to paying the fees at the parochial school for more than one child. Nor did we have to go to a school where Dutch was spoken in order to get along. The fact is that I do not have the slightest recollection of a time after arrival in Grand Rapids when I could not speak English, though there must have been an interval when this was the case. From the time I started in the public school I was the best speller and reader in the class, partly no doubt because in the beginning I had had to concentrate. The teachers made something of this, which served to increase my interest in school.

School was an utter fascination. That apparently there would never be an end of things to learn frequently produced a state of delightful intoxication. I learned with the rapture of the explorer, "silent upon a peak in Darien," that, when I had graduated from the eighth grade, there would be awesome subjects ahead, like algebra, physiology, geology, psychology, not to mention the ultimate wonderlands of theology, predestination, apologetics, eschatology. The words themselves were blessed.

School never started too early in the morning for my taste. The school days always seemed to rush by. The start of vacation was in its way an occasion, but the opening day of school after Labor Day was a much more joyful and momentous one. My impression of my public school teachers is that they knew their business; their classrooms were orderly; they knew how to handle children. They certainly inspired me.

After living for a year or two in the drab frame house we moved across the Grand Trunk railway tracks into a house which belonged to the owners of the furniture factory after whom Quimby Street was named and for whom father drove a team, hauling logs and delivering lumber. Directly across the street was one of the finer mansions in the city, the home of the Quimby family. To the west and on the same side of the street was the sprawling one-story mill from which the music and the lovely smell of lumber being sawed and planed came all day long. Quimby Street came to an end at Canal Street. The considerable strip of land between Canal Street and the Grand River was occupied by the company's lumberyard, stable and dry kiln.

The Quimby family, in those days, consisted of the elderly and stately widow of the founder of the business; a spinster daughter named Ethel; another daughter, Mrs. Morley, a widow; her son, Lawrence, a handsome youth older than I; and Irving Quimby, an orphan of about my age who was being brought up by his grandmother, the founder's widow. Mrs. Morley was the manager of the factory and, I have no doubt, of the family.

Irving Quimby did not go to public school, at least at that time. He was being tutored by Aunt Ethel. No other family of his social set lived in that part of town. The only available playmates for him were my brother and I. My recollection of the relationship is that Mrs. Morley gave my father to understand that he was under no obligation but that it would be appreciated if Irving were permitted sometimes to come across the street and play in our yard. I always had the feeling that we were doing Irving a favor, and he certainly never gave the impression that he felt that he was condescending in playing with us. He was shy and clumsy at games at which my brother and I were adept.

Irving tended to become tired or bored and took to inviting me over to the mansion in the late afternoon to keep him company. The first time the invitation was extended my mother told me that of course I could not go; the Quimbys would be angry at the intrusion of the teamster's son. I realized afterward that she was afraid that father would be fired for such presumption on our part. But somehow, presumably via Mrs. Morley, word came that if my parents would let me go, it would be not only quite proper but a real kindness.

So one day I ascended the long flight of steps leading up to the first floor of "the big house." Irving and I turned into a large room at the left, which was the library, and which had shelves upon shelves of books. Irving suggested a book of stories about life at Princeton. This was the first university I knew by name. I have very pleasant, if very vague, memories of the stories, and I still root for Princeton football teams against Yale or Harvard because of those tales.

Soon, however, I found for myself a greater treasure. There were bound volumes of *Harper's* and *Century,* which had been running series of articles on the battles of the Civil War.

For me, as a result of the experience described in the first installment, the Civil War was Lincoln's War. Breathlessly, day after day, I followed the accounts of the battles, marches, sieges. Though the figure of

Lincoln and the concept of freeing the slaves dominated the panorama as a whole, I do not remember that I thought of the Northern soldiers as heroes and of the Southern as villains. There were heroes and villains on both sides, but the distinction I made was mainly between the more romantic and the less romantic figures. But this distinction was not really important. The main impression was of a drama of epic proportions being enacted before my eyes.

As I think back, I can still hear the names of battles ringing in my ears: Antietam; the Wilderness; Bull Run; Fredericksburg; Gettysburg; Vicksburg; the battle between the *Monitor* and the *Merrimac;* Chickamauga. I can still recall Sheridan riding through the Shenandoah Valley, leaving behind not enough food to keep a crow alive, and Sherman's March to the Sea.

Daily the bugles sounded. Nightly the songs went through my youthful mind, sometimes mingled with the more martial psalms. I marched through Georgia. I witnessed "the trampling out the vintage where the grapes of wrath are stored." I heard the summons: "O be swift my soul to answer Him; be jubilant my feet!" I looked at the men that "are tenting tonight on the old campground" and into their "hearts that are weary tonight wishing for the war to cease."

Such scenes and sounds came back to me in later years when I read Whitman's Civil War poems or Stephen Vincent Benet's magnificent *John Brown's Body.*

In those days I began to take notice of the veterans from the Old Soldiers Home, which was located a mile or so to the north of where we lived. After the noon-day meal, many of them walked the three miles from the Home to what we called downtown. Their route lay partly along the same street that I used going from home to the afternoon session at the North Ionia Street School. I tried each day to summon my courage to speak to one of these awesome figures. When I did, I was usually grumpily rebuffed and this was hard to understand: why should they not be eager to speak of the glorious battles they had fought? Occasionally, one of them talked: "Yes, I lost a leg at Chickamauga," and proceeded to spin a tale. What a day that was!

It was to be quite a few years before I knew that what my heroes went downtown for was booze, and that veterans of wars are not always, not nearly always, heroic noblemen who volunteered to lay down their lives that some great cause might not perish from the earth.

The moral of all this may be that there is no telling what goes into the education of a pacifist.

I surmise that in the life of every child there are incidents which reveal a deep-seated behavior pattern; in a crucial and unanticipated moment the child does what he does without having had time or often even the inclination to reflect and plan, because this is the way he is made. With minor alterations, this is the way he will find he always has to behave.

Such an incident occurred when I was eleven and in the seventh grade in public school. One afternoon, the big boy in the class, who was also something of a bully, was called to the front by the teacher to be reprimanded for some shenanigan. His seat was in the back row. As he passed my seat, near the front, I surreptitiously stuck out my foot. He stumbled over it and barely avoided landing in a heap at the teacher's feet. She had not seen my foot sticking out and would not easily have suspected me of being a foot-sticker-outer. She assumed that what had occurred was some more "monkey business" on the part of the other boy — evidence of his lack of respect for the dignity and authority of teachers — and so he got a double reprimand.

The other children sensed what had really happened and were consequently aware that there would be excitement when school let out. My recollection is that we did not pay much attention to arithmetic or whatever it was we were supposed to be doing the rest of the time. When closing time came we marched out, probably with more than the usual angelic innocence written on our faces. One of the teachers stood on the front porch of the frame schoolhouse and watched us go down the sidewalk until we got beyond a high solid fence which hid us from her sight.

I stopped there and so did several other boys. In a moment the big boy arrived and, as he faced me, his pals gathered round. For some unfathomable reason I no longer felt afraid or nervous, as I had up to that moment. He said in a belligerent tone, "You tripped me." I looked him in the eye and quietly said, "Yes, I did." I suppose this development was unexpected to him. He probably had felt I would try to lie out of it, or possibly put up my fists and make the best fight of it that I could. The response I did make took him off his guard. He hesitated, shifted his weight to the other leg, hitched one of his shoulders, then turned and walked away without saying a word. His pals followed him. In a moment the other boys walked off, considerably disappointed.

I have no recollection of what my own thoughts were as I walked home. It was not until twenty years or so later that the incident came back to me for the first time. The fact that thereafter I did at intervals recall it indicates that it had made a considerable impression. It was not, however, until about 1940 — that is, about forty years after the occurrence — that it came home to me that it illustrated several aspects of pacifist philosophy which I had consciously adopted in 1915 but toward which I had, no doubt, an inclination many years earlier. . . .

One other incident in my grade school days points to a later interest, that in the labor movement. In the year that I was in the eighth grade, the Trades and Labor Council of Grand Rapids, Michigan, instituted an essay competition for children in the city's grade schools. The subject was Child Labor. The prize was $15 worth of books and publication of the prize essay in the souvenir book issued by the Council, on Labor Day. The principal of the North Ionia Street School, Miss Amanda Stout, whose name went well with her figure and who was a pleasant and noble lady, called me into her office one day, told me I should go into the contest, and expressed the opinion that I'd win if I did. The ideas of writing, of winning, and of books to own, were all delightful. In any case, a boy brought up as I had been had no alternative but to enter the contest, once the principal had proposed it.

I have no idea even now as to what children of twelve or thirteen are supposed to know about child labor — I mean as a subject to write about. Certainly I had practically no idea then. Miss Stout placed in my hands some information about the subject, provided by the Trades and Labor Council. Writing about a subject I could hardly be expected to know much about did not seem too formidable an undertaking to me. After all, by that time, instead of committing somebody's Christmas poem to memory and reciting it at the Sunday School Christmas Festival, I was writing and delivering my own sermonettes on such themes as "Christ as Prophet, Priest and King." So I wrote a moral essay on Child Labor and handed it to Miss Stout. Some weeks later, the matter had gone out of my mind, chiefly because I was full of excitement about going away from home soon, to the Hope College Preparatory School in the town of Holland, twenty-five miles away, to prepare for the ministry, a goal which was eleven years distant — four years of prep school, four of college and three of theological seminary intervening — but which was predestined and therefore in a sense already realized. However, one summer day, the announcement came through Mrs. Morley that I had won the prize.

Some days later, she and a representative of the Trades and Labor Council took me to the big bookstore downtown to help me select the books, that is, to pick them out for me. The packages which I carried home included *Self Help* by Samuel Smiles, the standard work of that time for teaching people how to succeed, i.e., make money, by frugality, sobriety and industry. I read it. I have never been drunk. I am, I suppose, industrious — but from preference, not from a sense of duty. My tastes are simple, but I have a considerable aversion to saving, and a strong aversion to money-making.

My prize collection also included Dickens' *Our Mutual Friend,* a novel I was never able to read, and Scott's *Ivanhoe,* which I did read a good many years later and liked. But there were also real prizes. One was an anthology of poems gathered by Agnes Repplier, which helped develop a love for poetry which has been one of life's greatest and most enduring joys. A second was J. B. Green's *Short History of England,* which opened up another field which I have cultivated vigorously through the years and which sometimes tempted me in my youth to desert the ministry and go in for teaching history. Finally, there was a volume of Emerson's *Essays,* which was, I am sure, the most seminal influence of all on my thinking. With Lincoln, Emerson was a creator of that "American Dream," which, along with the great passages of the Hebrew-Christian Scriptures, molded and nourished my mind and spirit.

In September of 1898 I entered the Preparatory School of Hope College, the institution which the pioneer Dutch Reformed settlers of Western Michigan had founded in 1847. Earlier in 1898, I had been solemnly accepted into membership in the Fourth Reformed Church in Grand Rapids. It was unusual to be received into membership at thirteen, as I was. I was accepted shortly thereafter as a student for the ministry by a higher ecclesiastical body, and granted the small stipend which made enrollment in the denominational prep school possible.

The curriculum, both in the prep school and the college, was heavily loaded on the side of Greek and Latin and Bible study. There were a couple of competent and inspiring teachers, another couple who were abysmally incompetent and uninspiring, and a larger number who fell between these two extremes. But, on the whole, solid foundations for further study were laid, and I am grateful for what the institution did for me. Moreover, I was not without extracurricular stimulation. Early in prep school, I was given a job in the college library to eke out my income. This gave me access to books on evolution, for example, which were kept locked away from younger students, and were issued only to college upperclassmen and then only under strict supervision. I remember being scolded by a seminarian from my home church in Grand Rapids for tasting, surreptitiously, of the forbidden fruit. He threatened to tell my parents, which caused me some apprehension, but did not stop me from slipping into the stacks. However, he did not carry out his threat. He also predicted that "all this will come to no good end" and here, of course, he was right.

Graduating from Hope, in 1905, at the age of twenty, I took a year off to teach Greek and English in what was then known as Northwestern Classical Academy, in Orange City, Iowa. There were two cogent reasons for this. One was that at the beginning of my senior year at Hope I had fallen in love, at first sight, with the girl who, later, for over forty-five years, was my wife. Her home was in a town called Rock Valley, in the extreme northwestern corner of Iowa. Though transportation was extremely primitive in that corner of Iowa, I managed to spend longish weekends with her. This involved dashing out of class at noon on Fridays, walking three miles to a railroad station to catch a freight for the heavenly regions, and getting up at four o'clock on Monday mornings to be driven by horse and buggy to a railroad connection for Orange City by one of Anne's obliging brothers. The other cogent reason for taking off a year to teach Greek and English to the sons and daughters of devout Iowa corn growers was that my closest college friend was to graduate a year after me, and I thought it would be nice if I waited a year to enter the theological seminary, so that we could be classmates as well as roommates. Since, also, I loved Greek and English, I think the youngsters did not lose on the deal.

The Cut of My Jib

ARNOLD GINGRICH

Arnold Gingrich was born in 1903 in Grand Rapids, where he attended elementary and secondary schools. In 1925, after graduating from the University of Michigan with a Phi Beta Kappa key and a B.A., he became an advertising copy writer. In 1931, while he was creating copy for Kuppenheimer Clothes and writing radio scripts in his spare time, William Weintraub and Robert Smart asked him to become the editor of *Apparel Arts* (now *Gentleman's Quarterly*) in Chicago. Then, in March 1933 — during the depths of the Depression — Weintraub, Smart, and Gingrich started up *Esquire* magazine, whose slick-paper pages featured intelligent articles, fiction by famous writers, and luxury ads. During the first three years of its publication, with Gingrich as its editor, *Esquire* sold more than 10 million copies. By 1937 he was supervising ten editors in the Chicago office.

Gingrich served as vice president of Esquire, Inc., from 1933 to 1945, and also editor-in-chief of its publication *Coronet*. From 1945 to 1949 he was the European editor of *Esquire* and *Coronet*. On his return to the United States, he became a vice president of Cowles Magazines, Inc., and the general manager of *Flair*. In 1952 he returned to *Esquire* as its senior vice president and publisher when the company's offices moved to New York. From that point on, he emphasized the literary quality of the magazine and played down its illustrations. With Gingrich at the helm as moderator, *Esquire* sponsored three literary symposia on college campuses in the late 1950s, at which *Esquire* writers such as Saul Bellow, Ralph Ellison, Norman Mailer, Truman Capote, Leslie Fiedler, Wright Morris, Dorothy Parker, John Cheever, James Baldwin, and Philip Roth gave their views on contemporaneous American writing.

The Cut of My Jib

In addition to editing several anthologies, or "treasuries," of *Esquire* writers, Gingrich edited *The Well-Tempered Angler* (1965) and *American Trout Fishing* (1966), reflecting his lifelong passion for trout fishing. He was an essayist and novelist as well as an editor and publisher. In 1935 he published the novel *Cast Down the Laurel* (New York: Knopf), set in — and on its publication quite controversial in — Grand Rapids; it is an experimental novel within a novel that is significant for its musical background and its criticism of the novelist's art. The following memoir is excerpted from his autobiography, *Toys of a Lifetime* (New York: Knopf, 1966).

I was walking along the curbstone, kicking the first fallen leaves ahead of me, one early autumn day before the re-opening of school in the year I was six, when I saw coming toward me one of the idols of my life, a "big boy" whose name was Roger Verseput. In my eyes he was a lordly creature, a sort of super-adult, and much more glamorous to me than any of the mere grown men I had watched coming and going on their way to and from work. He was beyond attending any longer my neighborhood elementary school, in which the year before I had barely escaped the ignominious fate of being stuck into kindergarten, having been allowed into first grade after considerable argument partly because, before that year was out, I would be turning six. That in itself was still not enough, because according to the rules your sixth birthday had to fall in the first half of the year to enter first grade, but what had finally tipped the scales in my favor was the happenstance that I could already read, having taught myself from constant poring over the Sears Roebuck catalogue. But he was now going to go to something far away and practically downtown, that I had never seen but knew was called a Junior High School. He must have been pushing thirteen, because his voice was changing, and he had in consequence acquired a new nickname, which was Squeech.

I wondered whether I dared address him individually, away from the multivoiced yelling of a group of boys playing in the streets together, where any remark addressed to him, as most of them were (hey, Squeech, lookit what I can do), would have seemed much less presumptuous.

I finally decided to risk it, when he had drawn even with me with no apparent sign of having remarked my minute presence, and looking up at him with overtones of *adoremus* in my voice, ventured a very diffident and tentative "Hello, Squeech."

He appeared to be passing on without deigning to answer but then, much worse, he turned back and down to regard me, with the air of a robin reconsidering a worm that he had at first thought too insignificant to be worth the bother of digging up, and said,

"Hullo, yuh darn ol' Arnie — with yer girl's coat on!"

I ran home howling, to tell my mother what he had said.

My coat, which she had made, was a double-breasted bright red jacket, of the type known to sailors as a pea-jacket, and she had deemed it not only very natty but manly too, an opinion in which, up to that awful moment, I had fully concurred. But of course she had made it to button, like anything of her own, from right over left, instead of left over right, as any male garment should.

This was a detail I couldn't have known, and I doubt she discovered for herself until it was later pointed out to her by somebody else, perhaps my father, because my distinct recollection is that she was as mystified as I, seeking to understand why a coat, made for a boy and worn by him, could possibly be considered a girl's coat.

But I would not wear it again, even after she had learned what its fault was and had remedied it by making new buttonholes on its inner left-hand flap, thus permitting it to be buttoned from left over right, in the correct masculine manner. Although she made the most of the fact that its color was that of the fireman's shirt and of guardsmen's tunics, still I couldn't help harboring the suspicion that it might have been the color, as well as the way it buttoned, that had provoked the mighty wrath of Squeech.

I had already labored for a full school year under the dreadful handicap of a given name that, I was still convinced, was a girl's name, and had been worried, all year long, lest some new pupil, a girl also named Arnold, might someday join our class and, because our names would be the same, be assigned a double desk that, worst of infamies, I would have to share with her.

Everybody had assured me that there weren't any girls named Arnold, but then as far as I could determine there weren't any other boys with the name either, and now this about the coat had served to redouble my inner doubts.

My reading, based as it was on merchandise descriptions in the Sears Roebuck catalogue, had not yet wandered far enough afield to have encountered either Arnold von Winkelried or even, though perhaps that was just as well, Benedict Arnold.

And now, as school was re-opening, and I was going into a new room, with a new teacher, and thus for all I could see to the contrary, a chance to start fresh, I resolved at last to do something about that girl's name.

So I just plain ditched it, in favor of the most masculine-sounding name I could think of.

For three days nothing happened. Nobody said anything, but I didn't get my papers back either, though I took pains to notice that all the other kids did.

So I stayed after class that day to ask the teacher about it.

"Miss Brodie," I began bravely, "I didn't get my papers back, but all the other children did."

"What's your name?"

"Everett," I said, proud of the choice all over again, now that I heard the manly way it resounded.

"Oh, I don't think it is," she said, eyeing me with an amusement that she seemed to be making no great effort to conceal and that, in any event, I thought most uncalled for.

"Why not?" I countered as impudently as I knew how, to hide my panic as I scanned my person to see if there was anything betraying the fact that I was not indeed so called.

"I think if your name were really Everett," and now she was looking at me levelly, her eyes seeming almost to probe my own, "I think you'd know how to spell it."

So that jig was up. But what a foul and dirty blow, to have a fine name like that taken away on a mere technicality.

She had my papers, all right, and she duly showed me that my chosen name was not spelled the way it sounded, and as I had it — "E-v-r-i-t" but with two "e's" and an added "t."

So I had to continue to live with my hated girl's name, but now the more resigned to it because, unlike before, I now could feel that at least it was my fault that I was stuck with it, since I had muffed my one chance of getting away from it. It never once entered my head that some nefarious grown-up intelligence network might be capable of forestalling such ingenuous efforts as mine by passing on, from one teacher and one room to the next, the names of the pupils who were being promoted to the next grade.

Before long my mother had replaced the hated red coat with a more acceptable one, both properly buttoned and of a more suitable shade, navy blue. I liked that. It was the color that virtually all grownups wore, in those days of the universal reign of the blue serge suit, to the near-exclusion of everything else.

Besides, I was no longer running such a frequent risk of an adverse comment from Squeech, who didn't seem to be around as much since starting to attend that other school downtown, and anyway I had a new hero now, from around the other side of the block. He was Sybrand Buys, called Syb for short. He was as tall as Squeech, and I suppose must have been very nearly as old — he had an older brother Adrian who was a *man* — but must have been much less adept academically, because he was now repeating the penultimate grade in that same Congress school where I was, whereas Squeech had completed its last grade before going to the old Central Grammar which was now and thenceforth to be known as Junior High.

Syb offered to be my manager, for such fights as I could pick with my peers, at recess and after school. Picking the fights was no problem at all, as there was always somebody ready to dispute whether it was your turn or his, on the slides or the swings or the teeter-totters or wherever, but winning them now also suddenly ceased to be a problem. There was no kid of anywhere near my size who, after having accepted with almost insulting alacrity my suggestion that "all right, I'll see ya after," didn't quail when, having reached the appointed scene of combat in the alley outside the schoolyard, he saw that he might be obliged to contend, if he persisted too long against me, with my much more awesome and presumable ultimate weapon, in the hulking person of my "manager," Syb. Alexander-like, I ran out of scope for further conquest, much too soon.

I was almost eight before my mother, unable to cope with my request that she make me something as complicated as the Norfolk suit that I had found in the pages of the newest Sears Roebuck catalogue, decided that she would have to give up trying to make my clothes. Previously, she had been able to "make me one like that" whenever I had showed her some admired costume in the catalogue. But this time she decided she'd have to send away for it. I remember very well when it was, because the suit seemed slower in arriving than anything else we had ever ordered. Although she had taken my measurements for the order and sent for it before my birthday, in early December, it still hadn't come when the time came to take down the 1911 calendar and put up the one for 1912, and I remember doing it, and that it was the first time I had been able to do it myself, without having to be hoisted for the ceremony by my father.

Possibly, with Christmas so near, and Sears offering no such installment-plan purchasing conveniences then as they do now, she may have had to wait a while before actually sending in the order. But there must also have been some other factor to account for the long delay in filling the order for that particular item. Probably they duly explained it, but I can't remember now what the story was. All I can remember is how I kept bellyaching from my bedroom, night after night, and it still seems to me now as if I must have kept it up all winter through, about how long it was going to be before, if ever, I got my Norfolk suit. The punch line of my evensong of complaint, that winter of my extreme discontent, comes back to me clearly even now, as I can remember bitterly ending up, every night, and merely remembering it makes me re-experience some of the same bitter sense of disappointment even now, with the sad refrain, "Well, I s'pose when it finally does come, you can always hang it on my grave."

At least it shows that my interest in clothes was early and intense, as I can't imagine that most kids would make such an unholy fuss over the mere matter of whether or not a suit was delivered on a given day.

The next great stimulus to my interest in attire came through uniforms, and in particular those of the Boy Scouts. In Canada in the summers, one of my aunts had made soldier suits for me and one of her sons who was close to my age, and as she was an accomplished seamstress, able to copy very skillfully all the details we showed her from the pictures in the pictorials, they were a great success. But it was the related appurtenances, things like canteens and mess-kits, hunting knives and hatchets, all those things that couldn't just be sewn out of cloth, that I wanted and could seem to find, at least back in Michigan, only among official Boy Scout items, the sale of which turned out to be restricted to bona fide members of the Boy Scouts of America. You couldn't buy them if you weren't a Boy Scout, and you couldn't be a Boy Scout until you were twelve, and one of the prime considerations of membership it seemed, as my first anguished enquiries elicited, was the discouraging one that "a Scout is truthful." There was no side door around this, in the form of Cub Scouts, then as there is now. The organization itself was still quite new, having been founded by Baden-Powell in England only a matter of a couple of years earlier, and quite possibly they were stickier about the rules then than they might have been at a later time. But I soon saw that there was no way to sneak any of that coveted equipment out if I couldn't first manage somehow to sneak myself in. The dilemma was complicated by the fact that I had formed a neighborhood army, for war games, and could be sure of my authority over it only as long as I possessed the ability to bestow, or to withdraw, desirable items of equipment, in accordance with the degree of obedience to my orders manifested by any one of my soldiers.

A way around this difficulty soon presented itself, when a new Boy Scout Troop was formed by the church where I sang in the choir, in conjunction with the camp that it maintained for the choirboys. The choirmaster, as ex officio director of the camp, became the Scoutmaster by the same token. And those of us who were attending the camp as choirboys were permitted to buy the same equipment as those who attended as Boy Scouts. I attended two summers, the first before I was eleven, when it was still known as Camp Anderson, and the second, before I was twelve, when the name had been changed to Camp Roger, the name change having been made presumably in connection with its altered status after it became a camp for Scouts as well as choirboys.

So, though I was both in and out before reaching the required age, my peculiar needs as a neighborhood quartermaster, junior grade, had long since been served.

But it was some time before my always lively interest in clothes became more than personal and began to be in any way professional. And my first attempt to turn pro, at the age of twelve, was a failure.

Because I liked clothes, the first place I went to try to get a summer job was the best haberdashers in town, a small exclusive shop called Mackenzie-Bostock-Monroe. I thought the tie silks and shirtings in their windows were among the most beautiful objects, of any kind, that I had ever seen, and it occurred to me that one way to overcome the obstacle presented by their prohibitively high prices would be to work there, where I might thus be enabled to buy them somewhat more cheaply. I was even willing, if it came to that, to take my pay in merchandise allowances. But that point didn't even come up. It seemed they didn't want a boy, whether for cash or credit. Before giving up the idea, I tried it on my second choice as a place to buy clothes, The Giant, a clothing store later known as A. May and Sons. It wasn't a small exclusive shop, and in fact its location, opposite the Pantlind Hotel, marked the last outpost of the elegance associated with Upper Monroe Street. On Lower Monroe, beginning with the next block, quality and prices went pretty abruptly down from there. But they didn't want a boy either.

In my dejection at this second rebuff I wandered on down their side street toward the river, not to throw myself in, but just to sit and think, and see if I could figure out some other job to apply for. But before I reached the river, I saw a sign, in a sort of warehouse, reading Boy Wanted. So I went in and got the job, just like that, at three dollars a week. The contents of the warehouse were reams and quires of paper, for folders, brochures, and letterheads, to be delivered by hand, as called for, to various job printers in the more-or-less immediate vicinity, and I was the hand to deliver them. Literally by hand, it turned out, in the case of ten quires of letterheads, or with a small pushcart for larger orders, such as body and cover stock for small quantities of booklets or folders. All I had to do was sit there, at the back of the warehouse, where there was a table and chair, and wait for orders to come in for me to deliver. There was a lamp on the table, and the boss had no objection to my reading, to pass the time between filling and delivering those small orders, as aside from that I had nothing else to do, once I had swept out the place in the morning. It was a wonderful job, and I read dozens of books, getting them and exchanging them for others at the Public Library during my

The Monroe Avenue and Campau Square area in downtown Grand Rapids was western Michigan's retail center in the early years of the twentieth century.

GRPL, Library Photo Collection

noon hours. I kept it, feeling guilty about taking three dollars each week because for the most part I was being paid only for reading things I would have wanted to read anyway, all that summer of '16 and the next one too. I read all of Mark Twain, most of Henry James, and as much of George Moore as I could get my hands on, and even started there again the summer of '18, still at three dollars a week, and feeling very lucky to get it, under the circumstances. I had a quiet cool place where I could sit and read with actually fewer interruptions than I would have had at home or in school or anywhere else, and I was getting paid for it. It was the best job I've ever had, and for quite a while I had sense enough to realize it. In fact, I wish I had it now.

But the second week of that third summer I first bit into the worm of discontent as I munched my large apple of happiness. On the way to work one morning, across the street from The Giant, where I had tried to get a job, I saw a Boy Wanted sign in one window of Collat Brothers, and I knew that, though I didn't want to, I ought to take that job. Collat's was a cheap cut-rate store where I wouldn't have bought anything for myself on a bet, unlike The Giant where I had really wanted to work and where, next to Mackenzie-Bostock-Monroe, they had the best stuff in town and I could conceive of wanting, personally, practically anything they had in the store. But still, Collat's was in the clothing business too, and that was the business, I reminded myself, that I had first thought I wanted to be in, and if I still did, then I had to start somewhere.

What did I want to be, I asked myself sternly, just the best-read boy of my age in town? Wasn't that perhaps just another way of saying the laziest? What had I allowed to happen to my once bright ambition to be the best-dressed?

I argued with myself, for the better part of the morning, and, finally falling victim to my own syllogistic reasoning, talked myself into walking back to Collat's, from my old and happy home with the E. R. Lee Paper Company, and taking their lousy job. It was only a couple of short blocks, and I kept hoping that by the time I got there the sign would no longer be in their window, but I could see from a block away that it still was. So, feeling by now that it was fate, I went in and got the job. The final determinant was that it paid three dollars and fifty cents a week — or almost twenty per cent more than I had been getting for the last two summers.

I was hired by Julius Collat, who seemed all right but had a brother, whom I didn't meet until after I was on the job, who was a stinker. I can't recall his name, undoubtedly because I don't want to, and didn't even then, always thinking of him simply as The Other One. There was no reading on this job, nor was there even any standing around, for as much as a minute, without being given something to do by The Other One. He might send me to the basement, to clean the furnace, and just as I had started that filthy chore, summon me back upstairs with,

"Arnold! Front! Show customer sport shirt!"

Back up I would come, sooty as a chimney sweep, to do as I was told, though the white sports shirts I would then display and handle would never be the same again. Or he would send me out to wash the windows, again, no matter how recently I had washed them. Or, again and again, he would make me sweep out the place, unlike the Lee Paper Company, where once a day was all that was ever expected. Not only was there no reading, nor even standing around idle, though that was all the grown-up clerks ever did, but there was not even any whistling or humming, let alone singing, at my work. Once he snatched me by the ear from out in front of the store where I was washing the windows and, squeegee and pail still in hand, dragged me inside to give me a terrible dressing down. For several seconds I didn't even know what my crime had been, until it developed that it had something to do with "the music of the enemy" and it dawned on me that, all unconsciously, I had been whistling as I washed the windows, and that what I had been whistling must have been Schubert's Serenade.

But most of all, what The Other One kept me doing, when he couldn't think of anything else to do and the sight of me standing idle would have driven him crazy, was Making Sizes. This he would shout, no matter what counter he caught me standing behind. Shirts, socks, underwear, bathing suits, no matter what, everything but ties had to have Sizes Made.

Making Sizes was simple work, though I never saw how it could possibly fool any but the simple-minded. What you did, to Make Sizes, was remove the size tickets from anything you had too many of and replace them with the size tickets of anything else, of the same kind, that you had too few of. If you had too many bathing suits, for instance, in size 44, and not enough in 40, you simply re-ticketed enough 44's to make enough 40's. But if you didn't have that many 44's, you could just as readily remedy the deficiency by taking as many as you needed the other way, from the 38's, the 36's, or the 34's, until you had Made the required number of 40's.

The only possible consequence of this policy of Making Sizes that I could foresee was that of getting long lines formed of angry customers demanding their money back, but that only showed how stupid I was. The policy of Making Sizes went beautifully with the policy of Money Back, because the full reading of the Money Back policy was "Money

Back on All Merchandise Unless Worn." Those last two words were the joker in the deck. If you told a man you didn't have his size, he would walk out. But if you gave him what he thought was his size, he would buy it. If he came back and said it wasn't his size, then you still had him hooked, because if he hadn't worn it, how had he known it wasn't his size? And of course once he had admitted that he had found it out by putting it on, he was admitting that the merchandise had been worn and was therefore no longer eligible for refund, but only for exchange. He could exchange it, again and again, until he stopped complaining. But as long as he could do no more than exchange it, once he had bought it, what did it matter if it had been, so to speak, pre-exchanged by my Making Sizes, before he ever got his hands on it in the first place? It was a beautiful policy, because it meant in effect that the customer was always wrong, and this made sure of it from the start.

I learned less than nothing about the art of wearing clothes from this first experience in selling them, but I did learn one thing about men's attitudes toward clothes, as opposed to women's. If I showed a woman a shirt for her husband and she complained about any detail of it as being something she didn't like, I could always shut her up by saying "Oh, that's what they're all wearing now." But if I tried that on a man who was looking at a shirt for himself, he'd be much more likely to say that he neither knew nor cared what "they" were wearing, but wanted to see something that "he" liked.

I hated every minute at Collat's, and though I stuck it out for the rest of that summer I never went back. But that one lesson learned there stood me in good stead when, later in my schooling, I got some merchandise I wanted from the campus men's shop in Ann Arbor by writing some ads for them. And after college, when my second job was writing ads for men's clothing, I found that the telling phrase was indeed never "this or that is what they're wearing" but rather "this or that is what you'll like" about whatever it was I was describing.

Men are, actually, every bit as prone as women to follow fashion, though at a much slower gait, but the big difference is that they will never admit it and will stoutly deny it, even when it's proved. This is a subject that I've never been very far away from, and then never for very long, in over forty years, and it's one that I therefore tend to back away from, as every man always hesitates to talk shop. But there are a few fundamental things about it that have not changed an iota in the past four decades, despite the fact that the period has in every other respect been one of kaleidoscopic change, and that I therefore doubt ever will. The whole subject can still be summed up in a sentence, really, and though it's a very simple one, there will still be a lot of people, even forty years hence, who will still not understand it. But in men's clothes the equation that answers everything is still this:

Style is what the maker wants to sell, and fashion is what the customer is ready to buy.

Books could be written, and doubtless will be, that could say no more about it than that, though they run to a thousand pages. The trade press, whether in the field of men's clothes or of automobiles, often confuses style and fashion, being so narrowly specialized in their outlook as all too often to be unable to see the forest for the trees, to become so close-focused on style, and styling, as to lose perspective on fashion.

In automobiles, because they are so much more costly, mistakes that have been made in this respect, from as long ago as the Chrysler Airflow to as recently as the Edsel, have been much more generally remarked upon than similar mistakes could ever be in the field of men's clothes. But all of us can readily recall occasions when cars have become so long on style, that thing the maker would like to sell, that some of the most stylish of them have been caught embarrassingly short of fashion, that sometimes quite different thing that customers are ready to accept.

Belly Fulla Straw

David Cornel DeJong

David Cornel DeJong was born in 1901 in the town of Blija, province of Friesland, the Netherlands, and immigrated with his parents to Grand Rapids in 1918. After completing grammar school at Baldwin Street Christian School, he took a short business course at McLaughlin's (now Davenport University) and worked at a variety of offices and banks for the next several years. He later said that, at age eighteen, he "did not even know who Shakespeare was except from fishing tackle by that name."

Once he returned to school, he read voraciously. He earned a high school diploma at Calvin Preparatory School and graduated from Calvin College in 1929. He made his way through school as a soda jerk, a butcher boy, a mason, and a grave digger — primarily in Fulton Street Cemetery. After a year of teaching high school in Edmore, Michigan, he went to Duke University on a fellowship and received an M.A. degree there in 1932. Under a second fellowship, he moved to Brown University and was in his second year of Ph.D. work when Alfred Knopf published his first novel, *Belly Fulla Straw,* which describes the experiences of a fictional Dutch immigrant family in Grand Rapids. DeJong dropped out of the program at Brown and devoted all his time to writing, though he continued to live in Providence and West Barrington, Rhode Island.

From the time he was a junior in college, DeJong's poetry and short fiction appeared in *Atlantic Monthly, Scribner's, Esquire, Poetry, The New Yorker, Redbook, Virginia Quarterly, Nation, American Mercury, Saturday Review of Literature,* and many other magazines. By the time of his death in 1967, he had published thirteen novels, five children's books, three volumes of poetry, numerous short stories, and hundreds of poems in magazines. He was the editor of *Smoke,* a poetry magazine published in Providence, and he taught creative writing at Brown, the University of North Carolina, and the University of Rhode Island. His later novels include *The Desperate Children, The Walls of Everything,* and *Around the Dom.* The following selection is an excerpt from his novel *Belly Fulla Straw,* which was published in 1934.

All of them were already lined up in the aisle when the train slowed to a stop. Idema was ahead, then the children, and Detjen came last; each with his share of bags and packages — the children eager and hard to control, Detjen pent and uneasy, Idema with all the semblance of courage and alertness. It was a large station anyway, Rolf decided; it was too large and busy, Detjen thought; it was very dark and squirmy, Gerda told Ka, while Ka was watching a tall man with a cane who might be Mr. Kuiper, who was going to meet them at the station. Dirky had no opinions whatsoever. He leaned drowsily back against his mother's dress, for the ride from New York in a dusty day-coach had been very tiresome. Detjen wanted to stroke his hair down, but with both her arms filled she could do little but worry over his disheveled hair. Therefore she also looked through the window and saw the man with the cane, though not even for one moment did she think that it was Mr. Kuiper. Then the train shook suddenly to a stop.

There seemed to be no one at the station to welcome them, so they all crowded a little desperately around Harmen, each depositing his bundle at Harmen's feet, where he had already put his own. After that the children looked at their mother, and then they stood politely waiting for father to speak, for they had been instructed by Detjen to show their best manners as soon as they arrived at their new destination. Idema looked around, but he hardly knew what to look for. He had never seen this Mr. Kuiper in whose hands their fate had suddenly been thrust through the ardent efforts of an enterprising uncle, who at the time had displayed a yellowed semblance of Mr. Kuiper, wooden and clumsy, photographed at the age of seventeen or thereabouts, before he had gone to America. It was rather hopeless, Harmen thought, considering that that was all of forty years ago. So he said to Detjen: "I think we had better sit down in the waiting-room and see what happens."

"But what are we going to do if he doesn't come?" she worried.

"Oh, he'll come. He said so definitely in his letter. We could even find our way to his address, but we might miss him." The possibility of offending a man who had done well in America and who was going to be very influential in giving them their start was a matter not to be taken too lightly. Idema picked up his bags and each one of the children followed his example. Then they proceeded down to the waiting-room, where several people sat and stared at them, and two girls in white dresses with purple clover leaves tittered, so that Ger wanted to stick out her tongue at them. But that might not be done in America.

They sat down on a bench and waited, Harmen and Detjen next to each other, both watching the people that entered, Rolf deciphering the "No Smoking" and other signs, Dirky now wide awake against his mother's arm, smiling at a red-faced woman who sat opposite him and who had smiled at him first. Gerda said to Ka: "Come on, let's walk around," and to her mother, "We may, mayn't we, mother?"

After Mrs. Idema had given a preoccupied nod of approval, Ger took Ka's hand and led her at once to those [girls] in the white dresses who had tittered at them when they had come in. If she couldn't do anything else, she could at least stare defiantly at them. Self-conscious in her revenge, she walked up to the girls, who started to giggle again when they saw Ger and Ka approach. The one with the pink ribbon around her hair stopped her giggling and said in unmistakable Dutch: "Wat denk je van America, he?" Then the other one was rocked with laughter, while the one who had spoken pressed her lips together and smirked. Ger and Ka had stopped in front of them. For one moment Ger was almost jubilant that someone had spoken in Dutch, until she recalled the tittering and saw the silly laughing faces. She looked hastily back, ready for revenge, but she saw that her mother was watching her. Suddenly she jerked Ka's hand and led her away — her back and neck held very straight — to a large poster with a huge locomotive. Ka, amazed at what had happened, looked back at those ladies who had spoken to them in Dutch and who now sat stooped over with laughter.

"Are they Hollanders?" she asked Ger.

"Yes," answered Ger grimly. "Oh, look at this big locomotive, Ka!"

While they were still looking at the poster, Ger too ardently and Ka already impatient, and while the two Holland girls were still shaking their pink and blue bows in unconcealed laughter over their green countrymen, a large red, and angle-faced man entered from the hot sun outside, took off a browned straw hat with a stained band, and wiped his face with a large blue handkerchief. Then he adjusted the hat firmly on his head again, spat a stream of tobacco juice at a cuspidor, and stopped to survey the whole waiting-room. Among the two score people who waited there, the couple with the two boys and all manner of baggage at their side were unmistakably the ones he was looking for. He stopped unceremoniously in front of the man. "I take it you are Harmen Idema," he announced.

Idema jumped up, and Rolf, aroused by the sound of Dutch, concluded at once that Mr. Kuiper must have sent his gardener to meet them. When the man had shifted his wad of tobacco to the other cheek and announced that he was Mr. Kuiper, Rolf, who had risen and stood next to his father, looked with misgiving at his mother, who was also rising, clutching Dirky with one hand. Finally, when his father presented her to the sun-reddened man, Rolf took Dirky's other hand and waited politely. It was all somehow wrong, he decided.

"And this is my oldest boy, Rolf," Idema explained to the man.

Mr. Kuiper ignored Rolf's extended hand and looked him over from top to toe. "Looks like a healthy kid. I can use him on the farm this summer."

"And this is the youngest boy."

But Dirky looked away. It hardly mattered, for Mr. Kuiper had not even looked at him. Instead he was saying: "Well, we better get going and catch the next streetcar. I bet you never rode on one of those in the old country, did you?"

When Idema protested that he certainly had, and many a time, and Rolf was ready and eager to help his father in protesting, Mr. Kuiper went on complacently: "I've got to get back to the store for a while this afternoon. You see, from your letter I couldn't tell whether you'd be here yesterday or today, so I've been coming down here about five times yesterday and already twice this morning. I tell you, Idema, this is America, and that means you've got to hustle. None of your old-country slowness. Did you have a good trip?" Before anyone could answer, he continued: "Didn't have a hard time picking you out, as it was. You can always tell Hollanders when they first come." He stopped to study both Harmen and Detjen once more, and then, pointing at Rolf's short straight pants, which did not reach even to his knees, he said: "Like those pants your kid has on there, we don't use them here. We give our kids plenty of room in the seat and around the legs. That's America for you. Lots of room and lots of space so that you can stick out your elbows and hustle. Did you say you had a good trip? Seasick or anything?"

While he had been speaking, Detjen had surveyed him carefully, in spite of all her fear and shyness. When he had spoken of their manner of dress, she looked even more than stealthily at his baggy trousers, the too large, shapeless coat, and the blue work-shirt, with its wrinkled ribbon of a soiled wash tie. Then she recalled that he had not even removed his hat for her. She bit her lips and tried hard not to listen to her husband's polite explanation about the trip and the seasickness. Instead she watched Gerda and Ka approach. They had also discovered the man, as she knew from their puzzled faces. Past Mr. Kuiper she shook her head at them and signaled them carefully with one finger. Ka came and took her hand timidly, but Ger placed herself boldly in front of the man to whom her father was explaining, in a tone which he always used when he was polite: "So we really did have a fine trip, even though the train was terribly tiring. We didn't have any idea that Grand Rapids was so far from New York. Well, of course I had read about it, but that somehow wasn't like actually experiencing it."

"Oh, this is a big country, I tell you," Mr. Kuiper interrupted as if he personally was responsible for all its bigness, though actually he had never been outside of the boundaries of Michigan since he had entered the state forty years ago. "Well, we'd better get a move on us." Then he became aware of the two girls. "Oh, is them the other kids? Boys would have been better. But there's plenty of work for girls too. Plenty of money here for them who goes after it, Idema."

They moved toward the door, each with his share of the baggage. Mr. Kuiper for some reason condescended to take one of Mrs. Idema's bags. Then they stood in the hot sunshine, such sunshine as they had not known in their cold district across the ocean, each clinging to his burden, waiting for a street-car. Mr. Kuiper went on exclaiming about the bigness and cost of everything they saw, and all the modern improvements, in which America beat every other country of the globe by at least two hundred years. During this time — according to Rolf's count — Mr. Kuiper spat five times at the sewer-hole and missed twice, picked his nose three times, and scratched his hair once, all things which his mother had told him never to do in America. Somewhat glumly in the intense heat of the sun he told himself that he was not going to work on a farm with this man before he knew what the rest of the family had to say about it. But he feared that very likely they would have to give in to this man, who in the conversations of the last few days had loomed so important and formidable. However, in spite of himself, he started to watch the passing automobiles with interest, while his father had found a short interlude during which he explained to Mr. Kuiper that he knew some English, though it needed brushing up.

A little later they jangled along a busy street in a rocking street-car. Mr. Idema and Mr. Kuiper were sitting together, the latter talking about wages and rents. Mrs. Idema held Dirky's hand, while the other children sat scattered through the car, each on a separate seat, and exclaimed enthusiastically to each other about all they saw.

The street-car clanged away, and they soon stood in front of Mr. Kuiper's house, a wooden structure in bright yellow with white borders, between a grocery store on one side and a hardware store on the other. The whole side of the grocery store toward Mr. Kuiper's house was painted over with a sign in huge letters announcing: "LILY WHITE FLOUR, THE FLOUR THE BEST COOKS USE," with a ruddy-cheeked boy stepping over a large loaf of gold-colored bread. The side of the hardware store toward Mr. Kuiper's house announced: "FISK TIRES. TIME TO RE-TIRE," with a sleepy boy holding a tipsy candle as he stepped through a tire. Ger liked the picture of the sleepy boy.

While they followed Mr. Kuiper to the back door along the high, awkward house, with its odd curvings and lattice-work along the porch, Mrs. Idema took the opportunity to remind all the children quietly that they should be very polite and quiet. Mr. Kuiper stopped on the back porch to finish what he had been saying to Idema. "So I said, well, with the boy being able to run the store, I may as well have a few acres of farm land to work in my spare time. That's America for you, Idema. Never shirk at anything. If one job don't keep you busy, take two or three." Even the children had gathered by this time that Mr. Kuiper, besides having a feed store, also had a farm, also eight other pieces of property, a half-interest in the grocery store next door, fifty chickens, a cow, and a horse. . . .

Mr. Kuiper, who seemed to be precise and emphatic enough on all other points, had vaguely hinted something about a job for [Idema], something so indefinite that he had not dared to ask, for evidently American ways were strange and broad and immense, and one performed widely and sweepingly without any concern whatsoever for details. And after he had cut the pork once more, he assured himself that it was his duty to dedicate these first days to the comfort of Detjen and the children — to build fences around his roof so that no one would fall off and no blood come on his head. High and firm fences, right from the very start; later also for neighbors. As he watched Detjen's too calm and drawn face and her uncertain way of pecking at the food on her plate, he realized that she felt miserable. The sooner they were beneath their own roof, the better. He watched one of the boarders peel an orange for Dirky. He beamed an appreciative smile at the young fellow, who colored a little, thus accentuating the white splashes of paint on his face. Then when Mrs. Kuiper had seated herself as if she actually expected to remain sitting for several minutes, he heard Mr. Kuiper demand abruptly at his side: "What church to you belong to, Idema?"

He hesitated momentarily; then, cutting his pork with some precision, he said as negligently as possible: "I'm afraid we don't belong to any particular church, Mr. Kuiper. The truth is, neither Juffrouw Idema nor I ever go."

Mr. Kuiper laid his knife firmly aside and, poising his fork near his chin, turned in his chair and looked unbelievingly at Idema. All the boarders were silencing their eating also and were all looking at him. "Do you mean to say, Idema, that none of those children have been baptized?" Mr. Kuiper asked.

Idema shook his head. "No, they haven't."

Ka stopped eating and looked frightened at Mr. Kuiper. Gerda looked unashamed into the faces of the staring boarders, as if to show that this matter of not having been baptized did not concern her in the least. But Detjen lowered her eyes to her plate.

Mr. Kuiper still held the fork aloft. "I tell you this, Idema, you won't get far here in Grand Rapids among us Hollanders unless you belong to church. You'd better go with me to church next Sunday. You can come and some of the kids. My wife is too busy getting dinner ready, but if your wife wants to come, it's all right, too. I tell you, you can't get along in America without going to church."

Idema nodded vaguely, and everybody started to eat once more. Detjen looked up and saw that Mrs. Kuiper was regarding the children almost piteously. Through the renewed clanging of forks and knives Mr. Kuiper demanded suddenly: "You're not one of them there Socialists, are you, Idema?"

Idema wanted to smile. Then, seeing everything clearly, he looked up and shook his head, for, after all, the matter didn't seem important enough at that moment to cause additional turmoil. "Don't worry about that," he said calmly, and looked steadily at Detjen, who colored and looked aside to wipe Dirky's mouth.

"Well, that's a good thing. We don't want any of that ilk here." Mr. Kuiper attacked his food viciously, and after that there seemed to be little left to talk about until the prayer which officially ended the dinner was finished. . . .

Three o'clock that afternoon, when the heat was still greater . . . they were all on their way to see their first house in America, which Mr. Kuiper had rented for them. . . . Kloosterman Place ran treeless and as narrowly as possible between a row of meager houses — all alike, with slanting porches — and a row of more formidable buildings, first a printing shop, then a livery stable, and last a carpenter shop, from which came loud pounding. There was no room for sidewalks, but since the whole street had been cemented, that seemed hardly to matter. A narrow, straight runnel in the center took care of excess water. The whole looked decidedly unprepossessing, Harmen Idema thought; it looked awful and cheap, Mrs. Idema thought, for she was becoming self-conscious when curtains were parted and women's faces peered out at them. An old fat man with tobacco dribbling from his beard raised the handle of an ax in salute from his little back-yard vegetable garden and yelled, "Welcome in America," in Dutch. Only Ka smiled at him.

Mr. Kuiper announced loud enough for all of them to hear that the people on the street were excellent people, all Hollanders and all clean and religious, and that the Idemas were certainly going to enjoy living among them. When they passed the livery stable, with huge piles of steaming manure, which two men were shoveling into a wagon, he explained: "There's dollars in everything in America, Idema. That man who has those stables makes money hand over fist just from selling the manure," as if back in Holland there were no animals and no manure, or if there should happen to be, people were simply too stupid to know what to do with it. The children sniffed at the manure odors, Mrs. Idema looked away from a hawk-nosed woman who was watching them from behind a screen door and who nodded curtly to Mrs. Kuiper. Harmen Idema looked again at the flimsy wooden houses — something which he himself would be expected to build in the future, something new, for he had never seen wooden houses before. Mr. Kuiper had been right. Over the whole street dominated a sort of desperate Dutch cleanliness which accentuated the cheapness all the more. It was all utterly respectable, with a scoured air of almost fanatic respectability, which banned everything that was fickle and gentle. "A very respectable neighborhood," Mr. Kuiper mumbled. . . .

"Welcome to your house," Mr. Kuiper shouted heavily jovial, and they all put their baggage down and stood looking at the house mutely, without enthusiasm and without disappointment, with no feeling whatsoever evident, until Ger shouted: "Oh, mother, look, it has a little veranda in the back, too, and a lilac bush and two trees. Isn't that great?"

Mr. Idema looked at the bare and sandy back-yard with its two reeking heaven-trees and a clump of lilacs. "Yes, that's nice," he said with a little show of enthusiasm.

"It's not so nice for the wash, though," said Mrs. Kuiper. "There ain't much sun there any time, I'm afraid."

"You don't want sun here in the summer," Mr. Kuiper outshouted her, while he proceeded to the door and unlocked it. They filed in behind him.

They examined the furniture, which had already been bought for them by Mr. Kuiper. In the largest room stood a square kitchen table and six straight, cheap chairs along the wall. In the kitchen was an old and battered round table which wobbled on the floor at a touch, and one old chair with a broken seat, and a pile of browned and cracked dishes. In the little parlor hung one picture, which contained a waterfall, a mill, a sunrise, and a woman in green with a red parasol. There was nothing else in the room. Ger thought the picture was beautiful, especially the very intricate, gilded frame.

Then they filed into the narrow alcoves which were going to serve as bedrooms and which contained one bed each. Mr. Kuiper turned around and looked at Rolf. "That big boy can't sleep with the girls any more. We'd better sell them that old cot we have, hadn't we, mamma?" When Mrs. Kuiper nodded in vague, unwilling approval, he added hurriedly: "We can let you have that cheap, Idema." Then no one spoke for a while as they stood lined along the pinkish wall-paper with purple asters and blue moonflowers, until Mr. Kuiper said with sonorous finality: "Well, now that you are all settled in a house and everything, I guess I'd better run up to the store for a while."

Politely Mr. Idema thanked him for all he had done, hiding from Detjen all the misgiving and chagrin which made his voice sound unreal even to himself. But the sooner the man was gone, the better.

Loftily and unconcerned with Idema's thanks, Mr. Kuiper continued: "Tomorrow morning I'm going out to the farm. That means getting up at five. I should have been there today and yesterday, but I didn't know just when you were gonna come. I've got a farmer's kid doing some weeding now, but you can't trust those louts when they're alone." He regarded Rolf critically once more, and continued: "I won't be a bit surprised I can use that young fellow this summer. It'll come you all in good stead, because he can work for vegetables and winter potatoes. And I always say, you can never learn too much. That's America; be master of all trades and you can get anywhere you want."

Suddenly Rolf ran outside through the back door, and Gerda followed him. A few minutes later he and Ger stood beneath the lilac, watching Mr. and Mrs. Kuiper depart. "I'm not going to work for that old codfish," he said grimly.

"Let's play something," said Ger.

In the house Mr. and Mrs. Idema sat next to each other on the bare mattress, which had large brown stains and rings on it. They had not yet spoken since the Kuipers had left. In the other room Ka and Dirky were romping and rolling on the other mattress. Suddenly Detjen jumped up and rushed toward them. "Get off those filthy beds at once," she shrieked. She grabbed Dirky so that he started to whimper. Ka stood straight and scared against the wall, staring at her. "Don't you touch those filthy things again. I won't let you sleep on them. I'm going to burn them, even though the smoke chokes those Kuipers and this whole damned street. I'd rather sleep on the floor on old newspapers."

Then she broke down, sobbing. Ka ran outside and Dirky wailed louder. Harmen stood in the doorway, helpless, looking away from her and also from the old stained mattress. "God damn them," he said.

She stopped her crying and looked at him. Then she smiled at him, suddenly desperate in her rage. He walked up to her and took her hand. "Come, let's sit down and talk it over as quietly as we can."

She cried a little more, but together they went to the six straight chairs lined along the wall and sat down, almost prim and straight, next to each other without speaking, until Dirky crawled up on Detjen's lap and fell asleep at once. The other children were shouting outside. Then Idema said slowly: "We'll beat ourselves out of this. We have to and we can."

Then they talked in slow, precise, determined voices, never even mentioning the horror that was Mr. Kuiper.

So Ger found them when she came bursting in through the back door and shouted: "Oh, mother, the toilet is outside in a special little house. Isn't that funny? And right next to ours is the neighbor's, and we just watched the neighbor lady go in hers. She's awful fat."

Somehow by four that afternoon they had achieved a grim determination, which was hardly yet courage. Idema could smile at the new discoveries of the children, and he and Detjen together set what little they had in order. After that there seemed little else to do, for their trunks had not yet arrived. They decided to have some tea. That at least could be had, even though there was hardly room for anything else on the little gas-plate when the large tin tea-kettle occupied it. But when they went to the pump in the corner of the kitchen and pumped water from the cistern, they found that the water was brown and filled with squirming things and that it stank. Detjen poured it away at once and sat down in a corner, for a few minutes losing hope again. Harmen somewhat hopefully opened the trapdoor which opened to the cellar, for that part of the house had not yet been explored. But the exploration proved nearly fatal to his new-born courage, for the cellar was little but a mudhole with stagnant pools, while it reeked of cats, which could enter freely through the paneless windows. He let the door fall shut and did not look at Detjen.

Thus it happened that they decided to appeal to the fat neighbor woman, who, as Ka had reported some minutes after Ger's initial announcement, had emerged again from her little backhouse and waddled back to her kitchen. The house next door had many beer-bottle tops strewn around it, which Rolf and Ger were already collecting for a game they were going to play with them.

With a new empty pail Idema stood in front of the woman's screen door. After he had introduced himself, the woman, who quite unwillingly told him that she was Mrs. Jansen, stood implacably on the other side of the screen door. She explained plaintively, yet unflinchingly: "So I says to your landlord I can't bother with his renters using my water. After all, I've got to pay for it. So I says to him why doesn't he put it in? And the other neighbors says likewise. No, I tell you, you'd better go to the livery stable there; it's all right to them. That's what the people who lived here last year did, too." Then she was through and looked at him complacently.

Mindful of the inexorableness of her voice, he asked politely: "But Juffrouw Jansen, can't you let us have one pailful now?"

She shook her head. "No, there's no use making a start. I can't have just anybody running through the yard for water." While Idema looked at her bare yard, which was littered with egg-shells, coffee-grounds, and fruit-peelings, she continued: "Especially not with a pile of kids."

Then because he was actually searing with anger, he said very levelly and almost sweetly: "But aren't we neighbors? And aren't we all Hollanders?"

"I can't help that," she answered blandly.

Still more frigidly level he continued: "And aren't you a Christian, a church member?"

"Yes," she said.

He turned around and walked away. He whistled. He went past his house, past eight houses, all the way to the livery stable, where he filled the pail. Then he returned with the filled pail, looking without defiance, but with a steady hatred at the complacent women on the porches and behind shifting curtains in the houses he passed. He looked at the polished hydrants jutting from the two houses nearest his house. The Hollanders were clean, very clean, scoured clean, he told himself. Polished and glittering and cold and clean like their forbidden hydrants and like the golden streets of their heaven. But he was a kind man, and he was more mindful of Detjen than of himself. When he entered the house, therefore, he explained, with his voice entirely free of chagrin, that their landlord had made arrangements with the livery-stable people for them to get all the water they wanted there, and since that was quite a little walk, it might be well to think up some plan by which he would be able to supply her with all the water she needed before he went to work in the morning — that is, if he should get a job.

She looked at him silently, and when she filled the kettle with the water he had brought, she cried a little. Outside, the children shouted over their game with the beer-bottle tops.

The next day two things happened.

Just before noon Rolf was carrying a pail of water from the livery stable. An old disheveled woman beckoned to him from her house, which was the one next after those with the two polished hydrants. She smiled at him and, thinking he knew no English at all, designated her water-tap, which was not polished, but looked dull and green. She smiled winningly at him and was surprised when he answered her with as much English as he could muster. Then she beamed and asked him to wait. A little later she came out of the house with half a can of white syrup and some fried cakes, which were a bit dry, and patted his hair and touched his rosy cheeks and told him once more, meticulously, that he could have as much water as he wanted any day.

He felt uncomfortable, but he liked her. When he brought the gifts home to his mother, she smiled, and Gerda forced him to go with her at once and visit the nice old lady. (Some days later the Dutch children on the street told them that the old lady was crazy, and that she was an American. After that craziness became almost synonymous with kindness. It did not matter. They got the water five houses closer, and the other neighbors could stare all they wanted, with their hard, hostile eyes. The Idemas all liked the old woman and accepted her gifts. At least, she did not try to sell them any old, outmoded and threadbare outfit at an exorbitant price, as the neighbors soon started to do. And long after, they learned that the old woman was not in the least crazy.)

Two hours later on that same day Harmen Idema found a job. All day he had wandered over the city, looking at names on carpenter shops and on houses under construction. The city seemed to be filled with Hollanders. When the names were Dutch, he would ask for employment. He hated all this, but he knew that he had to put aside all pride and feeling. Steadily he went from one place to another and was turned away, or even laughed at because he was so green. By noon he had found three employers who had been civil. He could almost be thankful for that. Then, very far from home, he found another shop, a large one, from which emerged a lantern-jawed man and looked him over.

The man explained he would have to learn the trade from the bottom up, because American ways of construction were different and so superior to Dutch ways. Idema no longer protested; he listened. He no longer explained that he had been a master builder, that he had erected hundreds of homes and schools and churches, that he had been his own architect, and that he could figure out any plan, no matter how intricate. There was no longer room for truth and pride and boasting. There was no patience for his own opinions. He was silent and listened and acquiesced. And when the man offered him twenty cents an hour as if he were doing him a favor, and went on to impress upon him that he would be of little use the first few days except to sweep up the shavings and carry in lumber, he again accepted, without haughtiness, but also without a trace of cringing. As he walked away, the man shouted to him: "Tomorrow morning at seven." And when he had taken a few more steps, the man called him back once more and asked: "You belong to a church, don't you?"

He nodded. "Yes," he lied.

"All right. At seven."

Then he walked slowly home through the heat. At seven, for twenty cents an hour, nine hours a day, he figured tiredly, interrupting other thoughts which rose again and again, cutting into a vast drone of bitterness which seemed to hum through his whole being. For the house they lived in they had to pay fifteen dollars a month. Mr. Kuiper had to be paid off so much each month, besides the rent. The figuring was simple enough, and Idema tried desperately to come to some numerical exactness, but he could not. By the time he was near home, he was almost calm, however. He had to be calm, for a wife and four children depended upon him absolutely, in a strange land, with hostile people of his own nationality. There was no longer room for his own opinions and his own ideas. "Not yet," he told himself grimly. "Not yet, not yet, but some day."

When he entered the house, he looked buoyant, and when Detjen's face fell at the mention of the twenty cents, he assured her that certainly he would get more soon. Then, while she listened and did not believe him, he continued, against his own convictions and against his whole being, telling her that they should make the best of things, that they should try to get along with their hostile neighbors as well as they could, that they should even think kindly of Mr. Kuiper.

But they never did. When several weeks later they learned that Mr. Kuiper was paying their landlord only twelve dollars' rent while he pocketed the other three, which they needed so desperately, they had not yet learned to think kindly of Mr. Kuiper, so that this truth came with hardly any shock. To Idema it seemed as if he had vaguely expected it all the time.

But the first two days had passed away and he had been promised a job. . . .

[The children] had come to the conclusion that, apart from the Dutch people who lived here, America was a marvelous place. The Negroes astounded them, they worshiped them after Rolf told them about Eliza's

David Cornel DeJong's younger brothers, Meindert and Corneil
Archives, Calvin College

flight over the ice in *Uncle Tom's Cabin.* The Italians and Polish were wonderful, even though they smelled very strong. And above all there were simply dozens of crazy people, idiotic and imbecile. These were the most wonderful and incomprehensible. And perhaps the most interesting was Bessie, who also had a son who was not quite all right. Lately they had decided that perhaps all these people were not quite crazy. Perhaps they were just nice and harmless and only seemed crazy because they were kind in contrast with the Hollanders, who were sane and unkind. . . .

Suddenly they heard a loud shouting from the street. They saw a large crowd of boys coming toward them, shouting: "Dutchman, Dutchman," throwing tin cans and clods. Rolf grabbed Ka's hand and they fled to the end of the yard, where they crawled through the bushes. The boys had reached their sand castle and trampled it down, kicking the sand aside. They stood behind the spiraeas and watched them, Ka on the verge of tears, Rolf grim, Ger muttering: "Those are those Dutch boys from the other alley."

But they were discovered. They ran on again, frantically, because Ka could not go fast. They crossed yards and flower-beds, while all the time the shouting grew louder. They ran on. On Carter Street, with its street-car, they hesitated, because they could not cross. Then Ka shouted joyfully: "Look, look, there comes father!" They ran toward him.

Harmen Idema walked down the street. He was tired and hungry. It had been a hard day in the hot sun, putting a roof on a house. He was not used to the new work yet, and it was not easy to get on with the other carpenters and the stupid superciliousness. Listlessly, he thought about the heat, about the future, and walked on. Then suddenly he saw his children, and behind them a group of shouting boys. He grew furious, but when Ka tumbled against him and grabbed his hand, he quieted himself. Ger took his other hand. When he saw that she turned around to stick out her tongue, he was going to scold her, but he did not. "Are they after you again?" he asked bitterly. "Come along. Stay with me."

Ger explained everything, and Ka clutched his hand more firmly. When he noticed how hot her hand was and how she panted, he lifted her and carried her. The boys followed behind them, about twenty paces away. First there was silence, but then they sang in unison:

> "Dutchman, Dutchman, belly fulla straw,
> Can't say nothin' but ja, ja, ja."

They walked on in silence, without turning. People looked unconcerned from porches or smiled vague, pitiful smiles. They walked on. "Can't you chase them, father?" Ger urged impatiently.

He shook his head. "They won't do anything now." They went on, and the shouting and singing followed. Mrs. Idema opened the door and looked out. She scowled, but when she saw Mrs. Jansen complacently smiling behind her screen door, she let them in, hastily, and shut her own door. More boys came and also girls. They sang in unison and threw pebbles and dirt against the door. Then they dribbled away, slowly.

Ger explained again about the castle, about everything. But Dirky crawled to the screen door and sat down on the mat to play with the little red engine Rolf had found. Then he sang, imitating the boys as closely as he could:

"Dutchman, Dutchman, belly fulla straw,
Can't say nothin' but ja, ja, ja."

Ka came and scolded him for that. Then he cried a little, because Ka had been so angry, but soon after that they all sat down to eat.

Boyhood — and Beyond

Gerald R. Ford

Gerald R. Ford, Jr., was the 38th President of the United States, as well as its 40th Vice President. He was the first person to be appointed Vice President under the terms of the 25th Amendment, and when he became President in August 1974, he was the only President in U.S. history to fill that office without having been elected either President or Vice President.

After graduating from South High School, where he was captain of the undefeated state championship football team, Ford attended the University of Michigan. He was the center on the Wolverines football team, which was undefeated (and won national championships) in 1932 and 1933. Ford's No. 48 jersey has been retired by the school. Following graduation, he turned down pro football contract offers from the Detroit Lions and the Green Bay Packers in order to go to law school at Yale. After obtaining his law degree and then serving in the U.S. Navy during World War II, Ford, who had supported the 1939 Neutrality Act, returned to Grand Rapids a confirmed internationalist and became active in Republican politics. Some supporters urged him to take on the Republican incumbent, Bartel J. Jonkman, an avowed isolationist, in the 1948 primary. Though nobody gave him a chance to unseat Jonkman, Ford won that 1948 primary two to one, and then won the general election to represent Michigan's 5th District in the House of Representatives for the next 24 years — until President Nixon appointed him Vice President in 1973.

As a political leader, Ford described his philosophy as being a "moderate in domestic affairs, an internationalist in foreign affairs, and a conservative in fiscal policy." He was elected by his Republican peers to be the House Minority

Leader in 1963, and President Johnson appointed him to the Warren Commission in 1964. After Ford succeeded Nixon in the White House, his most controversial presidential action was to pardon Nixon for his part in the Watergate scandal; historians believe that the controversy was one of the major reasons Ford lost the 1976 election to Jimmy Carter, who won with a mere 50.1 percent of the popular vote (Ford had reduced a 34-point Carter lead to a two-point margin in the three months before the election).

As an indication of how much opinion changed on the Nixon pardon, Ford was presented with the John F. Kennedy Profiles in Courage Award in 2001 precisely for his decision to pardon Nixon. He was also awarded the Presidential Medal of Freedom by President Clinton in 1999. In 1981 he opened the Gerald R. Ford Museum in Grand Rapids and the Gerald R. Ford Library in Ann Arbor, Michigan. Ford died on December 26, 2006. The following narrative is excerpted from his autobiography, *A Time to Heal.*

My mother, Dorothy Gardner, was born in 1892 in Harvard, Illinois. She attended high school there and a girls' finishing school, then spent one year at college. In 1912, when she was twenty years old, she met a wool trader named Leslie Lynch King, who lived in Omaha, Nebraska. After a whirlwind courtship they married, and on July 14, 1913, I was born. My parents christened me Leslie L. King, Jr.

Apparently, my parents quarreled all the time — later, I heard that he hit her frequently — and in 1915 they decided to divorce. Mother's parents were living in Grand Rapids at the time, so we left Omaha and stayed with them in their large, comfortable house near Garfield Park.

Following her divorce, Mother fell in love with and married Gerald Rudolf Ford, a paint salesman for the Grand Rapids Wood Finishing Company. (Years later, he took out formal adoption papers and renamed me Gerald R. Ford, Jr.) For the first three years of Mother's marriage we lived in a rented two-family house on Madison Avenue, S.E. My recollections of that time are vague. I still have a faded photograph of myself as a youngster dressed like an early frontiersman, with a coonskin cap on my head. One of our neighbors was a salesman for the Franklin "air cooled" automobile. All the children in our neighborhood were fascinated by it.

Another local attraction was Firehouse No. 7, several blocks away. It was the last in the city to rely on horse-drawn equipment. Whenever there was a fire, the bells would clang, the sirens would scream, the station house doors would swing open, and the teams of horses would come charging out. The sight was spectacular.

I went to kindergarten at Madison Elementary School, a block and a half from home. It was an old three-story building with a gravel playground in back. Even at that age I recall playing softball and football and coming home with a dirty face, torn clothes, and skinned knees and elbows. In July 1918, my half-brother Tom was born. When he was still an infant, he came down with scarlet fever. In those days, if someone had scarlet fever, the family was quarantined; a big sign on the door warned visitors away. Our family physician was Dr. John Wright, a friendly, heavy-set general practitioner who had scraggly white hair and drove a fancy car. He made house calls frequently, and somehow Tom pulled through.

One day when I was five years old, I had a terrible stomach ache. My parents rushed me to Butterworth Hospital, where the doctors diagnosed my problem as appendicitis and decided to operate as quickly as possible. When it turned out that my appendix hadn't been infected, my parents were furious.

In 1919, shortly after the end of World War I, we moved to more prosperous East Grand Rapids and bought a home — the first my parents ever owned — on Rosewood Avenue; and I attended the East Grand Rapids Elementary School. My stepfather was making headway as a salesman at the Grand Rapids Wood Finishing Company, and soon he got into the coal business with his oldest sister's son, Harold Swain.

As a child I had a hot temper, which Mother taught me to control — most of the time. A strict disciplinarian, she would ridicule me and show me how foolish I looked when I got angry and said stupid things. She also used to twist my ear. Even more effective was her habit of sending me up to my room with orders to stay there until I was ready to come downstairs and discuss rationally whatever I'd done wrong. One time she gave me the poem "If" by Rudyard Kipling. "Read this and profit from it," she said. "It'll help you control that temper of yours."

Despite all the discipline, I never once doubted her love. A stout, big-boned woman with an attractive face, she was the most selfless person I have ever known. Because she made other people's problems *her* problems, she had thousands of friends. The Grace Episcopal Church Guild, the Grand Rapids Garden Club, the Daughters of the American Revolution — she was engaged in one church or civic activity after another. And when she wasn't attending meetings, she was busy baking bread or sewing clothes for needy families. Having the family together for major holidays like Thanksgiving or Christmas would fill her with joy, and she wasn't shy about expressing it. And if a relative or neighbor suffered in any way, she would be reduced to tears.

Although my stepfather didn't display his emotions quite so openly, I know he felt them just as deeply. At six feet one, he was a handsome man with jet-black hair parted in the middle. He kept himself in excellent physical shape and had the straightest shoulders I have ever seen. Tragedy had entered his life at an early age. His own father had been killed in an accident when he and his three sisters were very young, leaving his mother without funds. As a result, he was forced to leave school after the eighth grade to support the family, working first for the local electric railroad, then for the Grand Rapids Wood Finishing Company. Although he knew that formal education opened the doors to success, he never felt sorry for himself. Instead, he did what he could to help others in need. He was a vestryman in church, a devoted Mason, a Shriner, an active Elk, and a strong supporter of the Boy Scouts.

As a disciplinarian, he was every bit as strict as Mother. A man of impeccable integrity, he drilled into me and my three half-brothers (Dick was born when I was eleven; Jim when I was fourteen) the importance of honesty. In fact, he and Mother had three rules: tell the truth, work hard, and come to dinner on time — and woe unto any of us who violated those rules. This is not to say that my stepfather couldn't laugh or have a good time. Even when I was a toddler, he'd toss baseballs and footballs with me. In the summer, he and Mother would drive us to Ottawa Beach on Lake Michigan, thirty miles away. Along with three other men, he owned a cabin near Bitely, on the Little South Branch of the Pere Marquette River. He'd take me there to fish and share in a wide variety of outdoor activities. He was a marvelous family man. Neither of my parents could be described as "secure" economically; but emotionally both were very secure, and if I retain that characteristic today, I owe it to them.

At about this stage in my life, I developed a stuttering problem. Some words gave me fits and it would take me forever to get them out. I don't know what caused the problem — eventually, at the age of about ten, it went away — but it may have been related to my ambidexterity. For as long as I can remember, I have been left-handed when I've been sitting down and right-handed standing up. As strange as this may sound, I'd throw a football with my right hand and write with my left. It seemed perfectly natural to me. My parents and early teachers, however, became quite concerned and tried to make me use my right hand all the time. After a while they gave up, and I continued switching hands as I'd done before.

In 1921, my stepfather suffered some financial setbacks. The bank foreclosed on our Rosewood Avenue mortgage, and we were forced to move to a rented home on Union Avenue. The house was large and clean, and we boys all had chores to do. Between 6:00 and 6:30 every morning, I had to remove the ashes from the furnace and put in the day's supply of coal. Every night, I banked the furnace before going to bed. During the summer I cut the lawn and often had to clean out the garage. All of us had to make our own beds and take turns cleaning up the kitchen and washing the dishes after every meal. No one complained — chores were a matter-of-fact part of everyday life.

In the mid-1920s, Grand Rapids was known as a strait-laced, highly conservative town. The large number of Dutch immigrants and their descendants were hard-working and deeply religious. Almost everyone attended church, and a strict moral code was scrupulously observed. Like many youngsters my age, I was tempted to defy convention. In the rear of our rented property on Union Avenue stood a two-story garage, which resembled a barn. There, a group of us established a social club. We learned to play penny-ante poker and other games. It was a great hideaway because my parents wouldn't climb the ladder to get to the second floor — or so I thought. My stepfather, however, knew better. He caught us red-handed several times and reprimanded us severely.

By the time I entered seventh grade, I was becoming aware of the deep emotions that rivalries can stir. Sometimes the competition stemmed from an effort to win the attention of a girl; or it emanated from a natural desire to outperform others in sports. The fact of the matter was that several of my classmates hated each other. Because of this, I developed a philosophy that has sustained me ever since. Everyone, I decided, had more good qualities than bad. If I understood and tried to accentuate those good qualities in others, I could get along much better. Hating or even disliking people because of their bad qualities, it seemed to me, was a waste of time.

In my sophomore year at South High School, I played center on the city championship football team and was named to the all-city squad. Our coach, Cliff Gettings, used the double wing formation. He was a stern taskmaster, and I remember the hours I spent leaning how to center the ball with speed and accuracy. The T-formation center today looks directly ahead and simply hands the ball to the quarterback. But with the single or double wing, the center was forced to view everything upside down. The opposing lineman had the jump on you, and to carry out your blocking assignment you had to be very quick. You also had to perfect different types of snaps. If the fullback was coming into the line, you had to drop the ball softly in his hands as he was moving forward. The snap for a punt had to be on the kicker's right hip. If the tailback was running left or right, you had to lead him an arm's length in the right direction.

Athletics, my parents kept saying, built a boy's character. They were important, but not nearly as important as attaining good grades. My parents made sure I did my homework and pressed me to excel. In chemistry and other science courses, I received average grades. In Latin, which I disliked, it was a struggle to earn C's. Math was not too difficult. In the courses I really enjoyed, history and government, I did very well. At the end of my junior year, I made the National Honor Society and ranked in the top 5 percent of our 220-member class. My parents also insisted that I hold part-time jobs. I mowed lawns, handled concessions for Alex Demar at a local amusement park, and at lunchtime worked in Bill Skougis's restaurant, across the street from school. It was there, in the spring of 1930, that I received the first major shock of my life.

My job was to slap hamburgers on the grill, handle the cash register, and wash dishes. One day at noon, I was behind the counter in my regu-

Gerald R. Ford graduated from Grand Rapids South High School in 1931.
GRPL, Library Photo Collection

lar spot near the register when I noticed a man standing by the candy display case. He'd been there fifteen or twenty minutes without saying a word, and he was staring at me. Finally, he came over.

"I'm Leslie King, your father," he said. "Can I take you to lunch?"

I was stunned and didn't know what to say. When I was twelve or thirteen, my mother had told me that Gerald R. Ford, Sr., was not my real father, but we hadn't really discussed the situation at home. I knew that the court in Omaha had ordered my father to pay her between $50 and $75 per month for child support. He hadn't paid what he owed. His own father, my grandfather, had assumed that obligation. But when Grandfather died, the checks stopped coming in. Until now, my father had made no attempt to get in touch with us.

I looked him in the eye. "I'm working," I said.

"Ask your boss if you can get off," he persisted.

Bill Skougis told me it was all right. My father took me outside to a new Lincoln. A woman was sitting inside; he introduced her as his wife. They had taken the train to Detroit from Wyoming, where they lived, had purchased the car, and now they were driving home through Grand Rapids.

"Where shall we go for lunch?" he asked.

"The Cherry Inn," I said.

As we drove to the restaurant, he told me how he had located me. There were five high schools and one parochial school in Grand Rapids at the time. He had gone to the principal's office at South High and asked, "You have a Leslie King, Jr., in school here?" The secretary had said no. "Well, do you have a Junior Ford here?" They told him they did and added that I worked part-time in the restaurant across the street.

Our talk over lunch was superficial. My father knew I was an athlete, and he wanted to know how good the team at South High was. We didn't mention the divorce or anything else disagreeable. Leaving the restaurant, we drove back to South High, where my father handed me twenty-five dollars. "Now, you buy yourself something, something you want that you can't afford otherwise," he said. Then, with a wave, he and his wife were gone.

That night was one of the most difficult of my life. I don't recall the words I used to tell my parents what had happened, but I do remember that the conversation was a loving and consoling one. My stepfather loved me as much as he loved his own three sons. I knew how much he wanted to help me and how lacking in financial resources he was. Nothing could erase the image I gained of my real father that day: a carefree, well-to-do man who didn't really give a damn about the hopes and dreams of his firstborn son. When I went to bed that night, I broke down and cried.

During the summer of 1930, after my junior year, my parents scraped up enough money to buy an old house on Lake Drive in East Grand Rapids. The place was in terrible shape, and all of us spent nights and weekends trying to refurbish it. The house's location presented a problem of another kind. East Grand Rapids was four miles from where we'd lived previously. I'd been going to South High since the seventh grade. I was captain-elect of the football team, and I wanted to win my diploma from the school I'd attended for the last five years. Public transportation between Grand Rapids and East Grand Rapids was inadequate. That summer I worked at the Ford Paint and Varnish Company — which my stepfather had founded two years before — and earned 40 cents per hour cleaning smelly paint vats, mixing colors, and filling thousands of cans. I had some cash in the bank. So I exhausted my savings, and for the magnificent sum of $75, bought a 1924 Ford coupe with a rumble seat.

The car ran beautifully during the football season (we were undefeated that year and won the state championship), but then cold weather set in. One December day, the temperature fell below zero and there was snow on the ground. Because I didn't know much about cars, I hadn't bothered to pour antifreeze into the radiator. I parked the car at school, attended varsity basketball practice, and drove home for dinner that night. As I pulled into the driveway, I noticed clouds of steam rising up from the engine. I lifted the hood, saw that the motor was a fiery red and decided — incredibly — that what I needed was something to keep the car warm all night. Some old blankets were lying in the garage. I laid them on top of the engine and went inside to eat. Just as we finished the family meal, we heard fire engine sirens loud and close. We looked out the window, and my poor car was in flames. That was a serious loss economically (I didn't have any insurance), and the fact that my own stupidity had caused the fire made me feel worse.

I wish I could say that experience taught me all I needed to know about cars. In my senior year, my parents bought a six-passenger Chandler sedan. At the time, I was on the South High track team. We had a meet at Grand Haven, thirty-five miles away. The team had no money to pay for traveling expenses, so the coach suggested that several of us borrow our parents' cars for the journey. My stepfather agreed. We got to Grand Haven on time and won the meet. That's when my troubles began. Leaving the parking area, I backed the Chandler into a tree. The impact broke the clamp that attached the spare tire to the back of the car. We couldn't put the tire inside because six of us from the track team were packed in the car. No problem, I thought; I would simply tie the tire on the back. Not until I returned home did I realize my mistake. The heat from the exhaust had burned a hole through the spare tire, and my stepfather let me have it.

"Why did you back up without looking?" he fumed. "Look at all the damage you caused." Insurance paid the bill to repair the car, but the policy didn't cover the ruined tire. I had to pay for that.

Although Arthur Krause, the principal of South High, was an alumnus of the University of Indiana, he was an ardent University of Michigan fan. The Wolverines, he pointed out, were one of the finest teams in the land. They had boasted stars like Bennie Oosterbaan and Benny Friedman. Their former coach and present athletic director, Fielding ("Hurry Up") Yost, was a living legend, and their fabulous new stadium could accommodate crowds of nearly ninety thousand. I had captained the all-state [South High] squad that year, and it seemed natural to him that a boy with my record would want to go to the best college in the area. And Michigan was not only tops athletically; it had a fine academic reputation. Again the problem was money. My stepfather was busy raising three other children; he had no funds to spare.

That's when Krause came to the rescue. Learning of our family's strapped financial situation, he arranged for me to receive a $100 South High "bookstore" scholarship — a full year's tuition in those days. Whatever other funds I needed I could earn myself by doing part-time jobs. Which is precisely what I did as soon as I entered the freshman class at Ann Arbor in the fall of 1931. I'd saved $100 that summer working at the paint factory. For three hours every day, during the lunch period, I waited tables in the interns' dining room at the university hospital, then helped clean up the nurses' cafeteria. A wonderful aunt and uncle, Roy and Ruah La Forge, sent me a two-dollar check every week. And once every two or three months, I received $25 for donating blood at the university hospital.

If I had to go back to college again — knowing what I know today — I'd concentrate on two areas: learning to write and to speak before an audience. Nothing in life is more important than the ability to communicate effectively. As an athlete at South High, I'd attended a number of public functions and had had some experience speaking before large groups. But I was horribly unprepared for the challenge of my freshman English course. (South High hadn't taught me — or I hadn't bothered to learn — anything about basic composition.) Every weekend, I would labor over the one-thousand-word theme due on Monday morning. At the end of the year, I earned a C in the course — and I was glad to get it.

In the spring of my freshman year, I pledged Delta Kappa Epsilon fraternity. That fall, I moved into the Deke House, where I'd spend the next three years. In order to earn my board, I washed dishes after meals. Although these were Depression years, most of my fraternity brothers came from well-to-do families; only three or four of us had to work. Academically, the Deke House had a lousy reputation. Athletically, however, it ranked fairly high, and it was certainly no slouch as a party house. Because I divided my time between studies, sports, and part-time jobs, I seldom had time for parties and I guess I was naïve about alcohol.

My parents didn't drink and never kept liquor in the house. I had never smoked and hadn't had a drink until the spring of my sophomore year. The previous fall, when Michigan was the undefeated national champion, I'd injured my knee playing football, and I was scheduled for an operation. The night before I was to go to the hospital, Jack Beckwith, a friend and roommate, took me to the Spanish Club in Ann Arbor, where we spent hours drinking tequila and smoking long cigars. I woke up the next morning with probably the worst hangover I have ever had. I got to the hospital on time, but the doctors and nurses took one look at me and decided to postpone the operation until the next day. . . .

In my first year at Michigan, I had won the Meyer Morton Trophy — a silver football — awarded to the outstanding freshman player in spring practice. But I saw limited action as a sophomore and junior, playing behind our All-America center, Chuck Bernard. I took solace from the fact that the team was undefeated and won the national championship two years in a row. "A punt, a pass and a prayer — that was the way the sportswriters described the Wolverine offense and they had a point. The theory that Yost developed — and that coach Harry Kipke refined — was that if you had a good punter, a good passer and a strong defense, you would always win. If you won the toss of the coin, you always kicked off and gave the other team the ball. You counted on your defense to force them into mistakes. Inside your own 40-yard line, you always punted on second or third down. If you were near your own goal line, you punted on first down. If your punter did his job, you could pick up 10 or 15 yards with every exchange. Then, if your passer connected, you could score and score again.

Although we'd lost a number of first-string players through graduation, I felt confident as I headed into my senior year that our 1934 team would be on a par with its predecessors, perhaps even winning the national title again. Bill Renner was a fine passer, John Regeczi was an outstanding punter and our defense was strong. Then disaster struck.

Renner broke his leg before the first game and was out for the season. Regeczi injured his knee. Our defense struggled mightily, but we just couldn't score. We lost to Michigan State 16-0 and then to the University of Chicago — the great Jay Berwanger team — by the lopsided score of 27-0.

Team morale was low. Then something happened to give us a needed lift. One of the best pass receivers on the team was a black track star named Willis Ward. He and I were close friends — we roomed together on trips out of town — and our friendship grew even closer during our senior year. Our next game was against Georgia Tech, an all-white school whose coach threatened to forfeit the contest if Willis played. Michigan tried to work out a compromise whereby both Willis and some Georgia Tech star would stay on the bench. Because I felt this was morally wrong, I called my stepfather and asked what I should do.

"I think you ought to do whatever the coaching staff decides is right," he said.

Still unsatisfied, I went to Willis himself. He urged me to play. "Look," he said, "the team's having a bad year. We've lost two games already and we probably won't win any more. You've got to play Saturday. You owe it to the team." I decided he was right. That Saturday afternoon we hit like never before and beat Georgia Tech 9-2. . . .

Looking back, I realize I was lucky to have competed in sports. As a football player, you have critics in the stands and critics in the press. Few of them have ever centered a ball, kicked a punt or thrown a touchdown pass with 100,000 people looking on, yet they assume they know all the answers. Their comments helped me to develop a thick hide, and in later years whenever critics assailed me, I just let the jibes roll off my back.

The Times of My Life

Betty Ford (with Chris Chase)

Betty Bloomer Ford grew up in Grand Rapids from the age of two, graduated from Central High School there, and also studied dance at the Calla Travis Dance Studio, where she graduated in 1935. She then attended the Bennington School of Dance in Bennington, Vermont, for two summers, where she studied under Martha Graham. Graham was a demanding teacher who took Bloomer on for further study and shaped her life. Bloomer then moved to Manhattan's Chelsea section and worked as a fashion model for the John Robert Powers firm to pay for her lessons with Graham. She was chosen to be in Martha Graham's auxiliary troupe and got to perform at Carnegie Hall.

When Bloomer returned to Grand Rapids in 1941, she became fashion coordinator for Herpolsheimer's department store, and she organized her own dance group and taught dance at various sites in Grand Rapids. After her first marriage ended in divorce in 1947, she began dating a college football star and graduate of Yale Law School named Gerald Ford. The couple got married in the middle of Ford's first political campaign during the fall of 1948, just days before Ford was elected to the U.S. Congress for the first time.

Betty Ford was one of the most candid and outspoken First Ladies in the history of presidential politics. Her openness to speak tolerantly about marijuana use and premarital sex, for example, and her advocacy of the Equal Rights Amendment and legalized abortion caused some conservatives to demand her "resignation"; unfortunately for them, her overall approval rating was at 75 percent. Her honest approach to her breast cancer and mastectomy while in the White House helped raise the visibility of a disease that Americans were not accustomed to talking about. In 1978, after she had left the White House, Betty Ford was open and honest about her treatment for chemical dependency, and she established the Betty Ford Center to deal with substance abuse and recovery in Rancho Mirage, California. She tells the story of the center in her book *Betty: A Glad Awakening,* published in 1987, the same year she was inducted into the Michigan Women's Hall of Fame. In 1999, President Gerald Ford and Betty Ford were jointly given the Congressional Gold Medal "in recognition of their dedicated public service and outstanding humanitarian contributions to the people of the United States of America." The following excerpt comes from Betty Ford's 1978 autobiography, *The Times of My Life.*

I always wanted to be called Elizabeth, but it didn't happen. Once in a while my parents, hoping to make an impression on me, delivered both barrels: "Elizabeth Ann, you stop that!" and my husband, when he's trying to hurry me along because I'm late, will occasionally say, "Ee-liz-a-beth, come on now," but mostly I've been Betty or Bet or Bets.

I was born in Chicago on April 8, 1918, a year brought to my reluctant attention in March of 1977 by my daughter, Susan. She telephoned and said, "Well, you're going to have a birthday pretty soon," and I said, "Yes, I'll be fifty-seven," and she said rudely, "You'll be what?"

"I'll be fifty-seven," I said.

"Mother," she said, "get out a piece of paper and a pencil and subtract eighteen from seventy-seven and find out how old you're really going to be — "

Obviously, I did not care to be fifty-nine, so I had lost a couple of years. It didn't do me a bit of good. No sooner had I hung up on Susan than I got a whole load of birthday greetings sent to me by a very nice fifth-grade class. Their teacher wrote that they had been studying the Presidents and their wives, and had thought it would be a good idea to send me cards, and every darn one of those cards said 59 on it. If it didn't say 59 once, it said 59 in all four corners, or it had a cock-eyed picture of a big cake with what looked like 150 candles on it.

When I was a baby, my family lived in Chicago and Denver, but we came to Grand Rapids when I was two, and my memory starts there.

My mother's name was Hortense Neahr Bloomer; my father's name was William Stephenson Bloomer. He worked for the Royal Rubber Company, and he traveled, selling conveyor belts to factories. My mother wrote him every single night. I can remember coming downstairs after my homework was done, and my mother would be at the desk writing to my father. Jerry and I are the same way: we've always communicated daily; the only difference is we've used the telephone.

One of my father's favorite pastimes was fiddling with an old crystal set. I can see him sitting hunched over that crystal set, earphones on, and all of a sudden crying, "Wow! I got Chicago, I got Chicago, come listen to it," and we'd all run and take his earphones and listen to WKMG or whatever that famous old station was in Chicago.

I had two older brothers, Bill Junior and Bob, for whom I felt sorry because I didn't believe any girl would marry a man named Bloomer, despite the evidence that my adored mother had done so.

(There aren't too many Bloomers around the country. After I got over being embarrassed about the name, I started trying to uncover a relationship with Amelia Bloomer, who'd invented the divided skirt. I never could find a connection, but for years, when I traveled anywhere, I'd look in the phone book to see if there were Bloomers in that town.)

My brother Bill was seven years older than I, my brother Bob five years my senior, and I think I was an accident, the result of an unplanned party. Mother, who was thirty-five or thirty-six when I came along, always said I'd popped out of a bottle of champagne. I liked that idea.

My mother was an attractive woman, my father was a good-looking man, and I was a fat little kid. We had a cottage up at Whitefish Lake, where we went every summer, chugging off in an old Cole Eight touring car.

We left for the lake the day school let out, and we didn't come home until school started again, so we had dozens of friends up there. (It wasn't until I was a teenager, and my brothers were grown, that we began to lose interest. By that time, the Depression was on, and we all wanted to work during the summers, and our cottage was sold.)

I can still feel my mother's arms around me, holding me, as she stood out on the porch and we watched a storm come rolling in across the lake, waves swelling, thunder crashing, lightning slicing the sky, and my mother telling me how beautiful it was. I found out later she was scared to death, but she taught me not to be afraid; I was safe in those arms.

Almost forty years later, I tried to do the same thing for Susan. It didn't work. She's twenty-one now, but at the first crack of thunder she goes straight down into the cellar with a candle. I thought Mother's method was good; maybe I wasn't so strong-willed as Susan.

There was a hotel near the cottage, Hart's Hotel, which featured picnic grounds. Being a baby who liked to wander, I'd find my way to the picnic grounds — there's a snapshot of me out there in my rompers, with the Dutch-boy bob many children sported in those days — and I'd stagger from table to table, and everybody had a cookie or a piece of cake or some ice cream for me. I just got fatter and fatter until finally my mother hung a sign on my back. It said, PLEASE DO NOT FEED THIS CHILD.

I much preferred the cuisine at the picnic grounds to eating at our cottage, because my father was a great fisherman. He spent his entire vacation fishing, and we were served fish and fish and fish until I hoped I would never see fish again. To this day, I don't like it. Once in a while in a restaurant I'll order Sole Véronique, with the grapes, but I won't prepare fish. They say it's good brain food, but I don't know how they know.

Brain food notwithstanding, we passed wonderful months at Whitefish Lake. When I was tiny, I had to go out on a snipe hunt. The older kids take the little ones into the woods in the dark and say they're going to catch snipes, which only come out at night. And all day long the older kids have been working, setting up booby traps and scary things to pop out of the bushes at you. Once you've been on a snipe hunt, you're considered a veteran, and you can join the group and torture some other little kid.

In Grand Rapids, we lived at 717 Fountain Street, right in the middle of the city. The house had a front porch and vines and a hanging glider. It was frame, as were most of the buildings in town. When I moved East, I was surprised to find so many houses were brick. In Michigan, the furniture industry flourished because of the plentiful supply of wood. At one time, lumber barons stripped the northern part of the state of its trees, flattening out acre after acre, and where they went through nothing came up again but scrub oaks and pines. Now it's changed, the forests have been replanted, and there are beautiful woods, just as there used to be.

Named for the mile-long rapids in the Grand River, Grand Rapids grew out of a trading post founded by a French Canadian named Louis Campau who wanted to barter with the Indians. The year was 1826. By 1836, there was already a cabinet shop in the village. Dutch woodcarvers came to settle, and the thrifty, hardworking Dutch were largely responsible for the stable character of the developing city, in which every factory worker seemed to have his own neat little house with tulips planted out front.

We used to brag that Grand Rapids had more privately owned houses than any other place in America.

I recall our house as being filled with light, probably because I was happy there. Certainly the furniture wasn't light; in that period, they used a lot of heavy oak. Many of my friends' parents had done well in the furniture business; they had couples working for them, and chauffeurs to drive their cars, but I was never made to feel inferior.

I started dancing lessons when I was eight years old. I'd have liked to study the piano, too; but although we were reasonably comfortable, there was just so much money to go around. As it was, I tried to play the piccolo in the school band. That was the instrument they loaned me, and I lasted about two weeks. I think I learned to play "America, the Beautiful," and got bored. I wasn't born to be a piccolo player.

I was a terrible tomboy and the bane of my big brothers' existence. I trailed them around and tried to make them let me play football and ice hockey with the guys, and sometimes they had to babysit me, and I was always interfering in their fights. When they got to rolling on the floor, I'd be trying to pull off the one who was on top. It didn't make any difference which one was on top; I was for the guy on the bottom.

We didn't have a bathroom for every bedroom at 717 Fountain Street — not many people did in those days — and I had to share one with my brothers. For years I darted across the hall in my birthday suit. Finally my mother said I couldn't do it anymore. "You've got to start putting something on."

I couldn't understand what she meant. We'd grown up together like puppies, and it didn't make sense to me. "Well," she said, "you never know when the boys are going to have friends over, and they may be coming up the stairs or out of their room, and you don't want to be caught running around bare nekkid."

She put me into a robe, but I thought she was being foolish. My daughter, Susan, having also been brought up with older brothers (we threw them into the bathtub together), has, for better or worse, equally unconventional ideas about what constitutes propriety. "I'd rather have a guy see me naked than in curlers," she says.

My children speak their minds in a way that might have surprised my mother. She was a rather formal woman, and whenever she took me shopping, I had to wear a hat and white gloves. If I said that my friends weren't made to dress this way, Mother pointed out that she had lived in big cities, not only in Chicago and Denver but also in Seattle, and her mores were not necessarily those of Grand Rapids. She'd loved Seattle, even though it had rained there just about every day. "You carried an umbrella, that's all," she would say.

Mother was particular about table manners too. You weren't permitted to butter an entire slice of bread at one time, and if you wanted to eat an apple, you were banished from her hearing. "You sound just like a horse," she would say. "Go into the kitchen or go to your room." Same thing with gum. If you insisted on chewing it, you were asked to go off by yourself.

We tend to think we're more easygoing than our parents, but I was imprinted with some of my mother's prejudices. I could never stand to see anyone chew gum either.

Because he was gone so much, my father came home bearing gifts, trying to make up for his absences, and when I was little he seemed to me to be a cornucopia from which stuffed animals poured. He brought me a teddy bear, which I fastened onto and dragged everywhere. He was just a typical brown teddy bear, but I thought the world of him. In fact, I thought all the stories I read about teddy bears were true; that bear was alive to me.

It's funny, I swore all the time I was growing up that I would never marry a man who traveled, but it must have been in my stars. My first husband traveled and then Jerry ended up being gone from home two hundred days a year throughout much of the time when our kids were growing up. "I love my father, but I didn't know I had a father until I was ten or twelve years old," Susan says. "Everybody was supposed to be home for dinner Sunday night because Daddy always made a point of being home for Sunday-night dinner. Well, it meant nothing to me. Just a man sitting there at the table."

In the play *The Glass Menagerie,* the absent father is characterized as "a telephone man who fell in love with long distances." I've known a few men like that, and they didn't all work for the telephone company.

As a child I did a bit of short-distance traveling myself. The little girls I knew liked to weekend at one another's houses (what kids today call sleepovers). Mary Adelaide Jones and I invented a game we thought was hilarious. We would stand in the shower in her house and stick our bottoms under the hot water, to see who could outlast the other and get her fanny reddest.

Mary Adelaide's mother, whom I called Auntie Flo, was a stunning woman, very strict. I revered her. I guess I liked the discipline. The Joneses' house had a ballroom in which we children weren't permitted. It held a grand piano and a few throw rugs, and the floor was waxed so shiny you could see the electric lights reflected in it. Auntie Flo did not want us walking across that floor with our muddy feet.

Auntie Flo Jones was only one of a vast circle of aunts and uncles who were not really related to me at all. One night, when I was staying over at the Jones house, and Mary Adelaide and I were saying our prayers under her mother's supervision, I was going on and on about God bless Aunt Gussie and Uncle Armand, and God bless Aunt Leona and Uncle Arthur, and God bless this other uncle and that other aunt, when Auntie Flo said in some wonderment, "Betty, where do all these aunts and uncles come from?" "Oh," I said, "my mother gets 'em for me."

My actual family was small. All the grandparents had died before I was born, but I have pictures of them. They look like they were fun. They smile out of photograph albums, the women in skirts down to the floor and high button shoes, the men in bathing suits with sleeves and stripes. I don't know how they ever swam in those things.

We were all demon swimmers up at Whitefish Lake. It was a tight-knit community; most of the people we knew there have held on to their families' cottages, and today they go up with their grandchildren. The members of my generation feel a closeness that comes of our parents' having been friends, and of our having shared long summers when our world was as green as our hopes. Mostly we haven't seen each other for years, but if by chance two of us meet we start right in to chatter as though we'd been together yesterday.

Home from the lake each fall, we'd find, or make, new mischief. On Halloween, instead of trick-or-treating, we'd go on a rampage called "garbage night." We tipped over everybody's garbage pail, whitewashed everybody's porch, soaped everybody's windows. We did things so terrible I would be furious if my children had ever tried them. One Halloween night, my brother Bob and his friend Bobby Bill Roe waited until the trolley car had stopped to let some people off, and then they ran out and pulled the trolley off the line, breaking the electrical contact. The conductor had to get down out of the car and come and wrestle the thing back into place.

I'm grateful it's different now. You just buy candy and hand it out, or moppets come around with UNICEF boxes, and that's a pleasure. We were really nasty kids.

Fountain Street was regal, with beautiful old houses and huge old trees, and in the fall, after the raking, there would be great piles of leaves to jump in. People were still permitted to burn leaves then, and the smell was gorgeous. Even today, when I think of Grand Rapids, I think of fall and the things that go with fall — the wood smoke, the crunch and smell of the leaves, the pumpkins, and the football games.

When the stock market crashed in 1929, my dad lost a lot of money, and after that my mother said we had to cut back, and she became chief cook and bottle washer.

Still, there were few shadows over my childhood. Even our animals led charmed lives. We had a German shepherd named Teddy, a dog I believed to be brilliant. By the time he was fourteen years old, he was so slow crossing the street we were afraid he was going to get hit by a car; he'd wander out with perfect confidence, like those ancient ladies who hold up one imperious hand to stop the onrushing traffic. So we gave him to friends who lived in the suburbs. Once these friends took a ferryboat across Lake Michigan from Muskegon to Milwaukee, and they dropped Teddy off in a kennel on the Milwaukee side, some sixty miles from the pier, and then continued on a motor trip. When they returned some days later, Teddy was missing. He'd leaped the wall of the kennel. They felt awful, but there was nothing they could do, so they drove back to the ferry, and there was Teddy waiting, his poor feet blistered. He'd traveled the sixty miles on foot. That dog was a genius. Or at least he had a good nose.

All of us in the gang I grew up with went to social-dancing class together. We started, as I mentioned earlier, when we were eight years old. The girls wore white gloves and ankle socks and black patent Mary Jane shoes. (Funny how that never changes. In the seventh grade, for her Junior Assembly, my daughter Susan still wasn't permitted to wear stockings; it was socks, Mary Janes, and white gloves all the way.)

Our dancing teacher was named Calla Travis. Calla was an old woman even then — she lived to be ninety-three — and we were the great-great-grandchildren of her first students. (Considering that I began giving lessons when I was fourteen, I probably could be teaching the great-great-grandchildren of my first students. Bill Seidman, one of the advisors my husband brought with him to the White House, was always telling everybody I'd been his dancing teacher, and I could have killed him for it.)

Calla kept us under control with castanets. I can still see her shaking her unnaturally red hair, flashing those clattering castanets, calling boys and girls to order and attention.

Every year she put on a show featuring her pupils. The recital came in the spring, and for the big event Calla took over the stage of the St. Cecilia Society's building. My debut there was not auspicious. A bunch of us were skipping around the stage, sand buckets from the five and dime decorated to look like baskets of flowers in our hands, and I dropped my basket, which went clunk, clunk, clunk down toward the footlights, while everybody in the audience roared. My mother decided then and there that I was a total flop, and might as well give the whole thing up.

It was after one of Calla's shows that I got my ring from Bud Wilmarth. I was ten years old, and my girlfriends and I were already engaging in romantic rivalries. The big thing was to get a boy to give you an engagement ring. The ring had to come from a good Woolworth's, one that carried the finest ten-cent jewelry, and it had to have something that looked like a diamond in it. A lot of girls were after Bud Wilmarth, but it was I he promised the diamond ring. He said he would bring it to the recital at St. Cecilia's. We dressed in the rest rooms — there were mobs of children to be costumed — and then you had to walk through a tunnel to get to the stage. That tunnel, black as a coal bin, was where I elected to wait for Bud after the recital, I guess so that nobody would see if he stood me up. Outside, my poor mother was sitting in the car, wondering what was keeping me, but I had no intention of leaving until Bud showed up with the ring.

When I was in fifth grade at the Fountain Street Elementary School, I got my first kiss from a boy. We were taken on a class picnic, a bunch of us piled onto the back seat of a car, and John Sears got me under a blanket and I felt a peck on my cheek. I was stunned. I thought, Oh my heavens, this is really big stuff.

At twelve, I went to my first dance with a boy. He was a friend of my brothers, and as it turned out, I married him when I was twenty-four. Those were the days of the big bands touring the country. Wayne King had come to Grand Rapids, and I was thrilled to be asked to go. I think my mother permitted it only because my brothers were also going, and she felt they would be keeping an eye on her baby. Little did she know that all they wanted to do was lose me.

I wore my first long dress, pink net with little rosebuds on it, and a full, scalloped, tiered skirt. It wasn't nearly sophisticated enough to suit me; I wanted one of those that were slit to the waist in the back. But my mother was firm: either the pink number or nothing, take it or leave it. I took it.

When you say you've had a sunny childhood, the assumption is that you're smart enough to know you've been lucky. I did know it. But, for even the most fortunate, there are intimations of mortality. A friend just my age died when we were both so small the grownups wouldn't tell me what she died of. That frightened me. And my mother was president of the Mary Free Bed Home for Crippled Children — run by a group of ladies who raised funds to support it — and I would go there with her and see babies who'd had polio, or who were in casts for some other reason. By the time I was a teenager I found I could entertain them. We'd bring all of them into one big room, and I'd work with a record player and beat out rhythms. If the children's legs were in casts, but their arms were free, they would clap. If their arms were crippled, sometimes they could tap their feet. Denied normal movement, they exulted in whatever movement was possible. I would dress up in a leotard and long skirt and try to make the whole event festive and dramatic, and the children would work very hard and laugh very freely.

I was one of the fortunate people who slip into adolescence easily, turning from tomboy to girl without paying any particular price. Teddy the bear and Teddy the dog had been the cherished companions of my childhood, but as I came into my teens, I was looking around, figuratively speaking, for Teddy the boy. And, even more fervently, I was looking ahead to a career as a very important dancer. I had aspirations, but I wasn't smart enough to have fears.

Fourteen was a watershed year for me. For one thing, my mother stopped making my clothes. Up until then, I had been able to think of nothing that would be more fun than to have a store-bought dress. Store-bought dresses weren't as nice as what my mother made me, but when you're brought up by a fine seamstress, you don't appreciate handwork. I barely got through sewing class in school. (It was a required subject in the seventh grade. The boys had to take shop and the girls had to take cooking and sewing. Miss Gillette didn't think much of my seams, and I certainly didn't care.) It skips a generation. Susan sews beautifully.

When I was fourteen, I chose to be confirmed an Episcopalian. I'd been christened, but not confirmed. My father was a Christian Scientist, my mother an Episcopalian, and I liked the Episcopal services. I also had a couple of friends whose father was dean of the church, but that didn't affect my decision; those girls were devils. Like sewing, piety seems to skip a generation; I wonder if my grandchildren (Mike's as yet unborn babies) will be hellions just to pay their daddy back for being a minister.

I was one of those goody-goodies who liked school, and Central High was one of the best schools in Grand Rapids. I knew very few students who went away to boarding school; from Central, you could get into almost any college without taking college boards. I particularly admired my Latin teacher, who was stern (again, my liking for discipline), and I was fond of my French teacher and also the guy who taught math and coached the Central High football team.

Every afternoon, right after school, I went to dancing class. Because I'd loved the social-dancing classes, I'd persuaded my mother to send me to Calla's studio for other kinds of instruction. Calla offered a complete program — Spanish dancing, ballet, tap, acrobatic — with excellent teachers, and I signed up for everything. I adored it all.

I dreamed of going to New York to ballet school until I encountered modern dance. I think Calla herself had first heard of the Dalcroze System of modern dance during a visit to the University of Wisconsin, which was one of the few colleges that taught it. I immersed myself in books about Mary Wigman in Germany, and Ruth St. Denis and the Denishawn dancers. I loved the freedom of movement they preached. In ballet, each jeté, each arabesque, was totally prescribed, and I was probably the worst ballet dancer who ever came down the road. I couldn't get my knees straight enough. When I had to do a solo ballet number — you couldn't complete Calla's courses and become a full-fledged teacher until you did a solo ballet number — I wisely designed my own costume. Instead of a tutu, I wore a thing with scarves hanging down and covering my knees so you couldn't see whether they were bent or straight. I got out there and pirouetted to the "Waltz of the Flowers," and presto, I was a professional.

There was no kind of dance that didn't fascinate me. I'd hear about some boy who'd been out West among the Indians and learned a rain dance, and I'd go to him and make him teach it to me. I was insatiable.

Last year I heard Beverly Sills on a television show. "I don't sing because it's my career," she said. "I sing because it's my happiness."

Dance was my happiness.

The year I turned fourteen, the Depression was in full swing, and from then on I worked at various jobs, trying to contribute to my upkeep. Saturdays, at lunchtime, I made three dollars working as a teen-age model at Herpolsheimer's Department Store. I would wander through Herpolsheimer's tearoom wearing an outfit from stock, and ladies at the tables would stop me — "Just one moment, dear, let's look at that" — and I would say, "Twenty-five ninety-five, third-floor sportswear." I'd leave my paychecks with the cashier for a month or so, and by the time I went to collect there would be enough to amount to something.

Saturday afternoons I gave dancing lessons. Having gone into the business of teaching social dancing to tykes, I naturally had to charge less than Calla, the master. Calla got a dollar, so I think I charged fifty cents. Our house didn't have a room large enough for classes, and I rented Auntie Flo Jones's basement. Her ballroom was still out of the question — she wouldn't permit all those Mary Janes on her satin-finished floors — but the recreation room was okay.

She took a dollar from me for the use of the hall. "It isn't the money," she said, "but if you're going into business, you have to start right, and understand how businesses are run." I paid Wally Hook a dollar too. He was a good piano player. And, once in a while, Walt Jones, Mary Adelaide's brother, would sit in and blow his saxophone or bang his drums. On those days, we felt we had a really classy band. My pupils learned the foxtrot, the waltz, and the Big Apple.

In Central High, we all belonged to fraternities and sororities and had to go through the pledge business of being scouts. If an older member told you to crack yourself like an egg and scramble, you had to knock your head on the edge of a chair and get down on the floor and flail about. Two weeks of this; it was the snipe hunt all over again.

My sorority was Gamma Delta Tau, but we were called The Good Cheers. When I told Sis Hall (now Mrs. Benjamin Fisher) that I was going to write a book, she offered me only one piece of advice: "Don't forget The Good Cheers," she said. Nowadays, sororities and fraternities aren't too highly regarded, unless they have a purpose like debating clubs or French clubs. I think schools are trying to get away from pupils' feeling of being excluded — and maybe that's a better way, but the societies were big in my day.

When my brothers' friends began looking at me with calf eyes, asking if they could take me to the movies — again, I date this pretty much from my fourteenth year, despite a couple of previous long-dress parties — my brothers were put out. Why, instead of pole vaulting, or playing tennis, were these heretofore perfectly sensible guys suddenly mooning over dopey Betty Bloomer?

I loved it. And I was bad. I would set my cap for somebody and work at it until I got his fraternity pin. As soon as I'd got it, I was satisfied, and I moved on to the next victim. I was scrupulous about giving the last fellow's pin back, that's the only good thing I can say for myself.

Betty Bloomer Ford attended Grand Rapids Central High School in the early 1930s.
GRPL, Library Photo Collection

Sometimes there was a boy who wasn't interested, and that annoyed me. I had crushes on boys I couldn't get dates with. I actually fought with another girl over a boy named Dick May. Dick May just didn't care. Once he did something to me that his father considered rude, and Dick was made to ride his bicycle up to our house and bring me a box of candy. That didn't help our relationship either.

Bud Wilmarth, who'd given me the diamond engagement ring, was sent away to Howe Military School, and when he came home on holidays, his family would throw parties. The whole crowd from Calla's ballroom class would go, and we'd be so impressed with Bud in his uniform and his brass buttons. We'd dance in the dark — the lights were turned out, but you didn't stay with one partner all evening, you kept changing partners — and you could always tell when you were dancing with Bud; you could feel those brass buttons against your chest.

The boys of my youth.

Bud Wilmarth.

Walt Jones.

Jack Stiles, who went to a different high school and had a beautiful silver car, and who would sometimes come by Central and pick me up and drive me home.

Monty Welch, who was a prankster. He took me to a birthday party where the ice cream was frozen very hard, and he was so determined to conquer it he cut through the ice cream and kept right on going through the china plate. Everybody else thought it was funny, but I was completely mortified.

Louis De Lamarter, whom I dated but who — thank the Lord — hadn't invited me to go with him when he went down to the Majestic Theatre where they were showing a Boris Karloff movie and took a duck or a goose in under his coat. Just as Boris Karloff was climbing out of a well, his great dripping hands looming up out of the darkness, Louis let go with this duck or goose or whatever it was off the balcony of the theatre, and it fluttered down and landed on a woman, who practically had a heart attack. Louis had to go to court. Somehow he managed to get off with a reprimand.

We girls didn't have steadies — I wouldn't have gone steady for the world, looking forward as I was to my big career in New York — and mostly we double-dated. The truth is you were glad if your date was driving because then you didn't have to rassle in the back seat with a boy who had more hands than you could control, when you weren't in the mood for going six rounds.

We did play kissing games (I played Spin the Bottle, and my children after me played Spin the Bottle) and we listened to the radio (there wasn't any television, of course) and kept notebooks in which we wrote down the words to popular songs like "Smoke Gets in Your Eyes." Just about every weekend a name band would come to town — they traveled from school to school — and we'd go to the dances and sigh over the vocalists. There was one fellow with Fred Waring who had a divine voice.

Once in a while, the De Lamarter family took me to Ann Arbor to a football game, and since my father worked out of Chicago, where the

Royal Rubber Company had its main office, I sometimes got over there to see a dance performance in a theatre.

We had lots of snow in Grand Rapids, which is just a bit south of the snow belt, and I was used to ice skating and tobogganing. We'd hold toboggan parties at the country club on nights when the hills were covered with crunchy powder. We'd go out in the moonlight, build jumps, then pile maybe six people onto one of those long flat sleds with their runners curling up in front. The more people who got on, the faster it went, and we'd go whizzing over these jumps, half the time flying off and landing in a drift. It was very exciting, and afterward we'd go in and sit by the fire and drink hot chocolate.

I've said I had a sunny childhood. I also had a wonderful girlhood. Then, the year I was sixteen, my father died of carbon monoxide poisoning. He had gone out to the garage to work on the car; it was a summer day, very overcast, very humid. The garage doors were open, he had the engine running, and he'd got under the car to fiddle with something.

A couple of friends from Detroit had stopped by the house to visit and Mother went out to the garage to get Dad to come in, and she found him. The ignition was on, but the motor wasn't running anymore. The car must have run out of gas, and the air was so heavy.

They called an ambulance and took him to the hospital, but it was too late.

I'd been out with Ev Thompson, a girlfriend who had her own convertible, and we came wheeling up to my front door with the top down on this hot, hot day. Ev was honking the horn and we were waving and yelling and showing off the way sixteen-year-olds do, and my cousin Shine, who was the same age as my brother Bob, came racing down the front walk to the car and said, "Shh, just calm down." And I said, "Why? What's wrong? What's happened?"

"Well," Shine said, "they had to take your father to the hospital."

She didn't tell me he was dead. Maybe she didn't know.

Growing Up in Old Lithuanian Town

EDWARD V. GILLIS

Edward Victor Gillis (Edvardus Bartholomeus Victoras Gylys) was born in Lithuanian Town, Grand Rapids, in 1920. His father, Bartholomeus, had come to Grand Rapids in 1904 to avoid conscription into the Russian Cossack army. Edward was a lifelong resident of Grand Rapids, where he had a successful career in the tool and die and precision manufacturing industry, holding various supervisory positions for forty-five years. During World War II, he served as a professional diver for the U.S. Army Amphibious Engineer Corps.

But Gillis was better known for his avocations. He was president of the 700-member Michigan Archaeology society and received its Award of Excellence during his ten-year tenure as editor of the *Archaeological Journal Newsletter.* He participated in archaeological excavations of the Aleutian Islands and Old Fort Michilimackinac. He was also a scholar of Native American culture and was cofounder of the Grand Valley American Indian Lodge. As editor of the Lodge's newsletter for fourteen years, Gillis won a national award for "Outstanding Journalism." Until his death in 1999, he was an avid collector of patent medicines, Indian crafts, turtle models, postcards, and music. The following memoir is an excerpt from his book *Growing Up in Old Lithuanian Town,* published by the Grand Rapids Historical Commission in 2000.

Of the several areas in and around Lithuanian Town that were available for ice-skating, Richmond Park, with its warming shelter and a place to change skates, probably ranked as number one. The Grand Rapids Recreation Department also created another rink, along the eastern edge of Harrison Park, by damming up a rectangular parcel of land and flooding it. Here parents would bring their very young children for their first wobbly ice-skating lessons. But these were not places where we could really rough it up on the ice. So many of us skated on the frozen-over shallow swamps that were north of Ann Street and west of Turner, on either side of the north-south railroad tracks and extending almost to Comstock Park. Here we could find areas of open, windswept ice that were great for playing hockey or "crack the whip." The only drawback was the many stick and brush muskrat "houses" we had to skate around. Another skating spot popular with teenagers was a section of cleared ice on the Grand River, just in front of the present Holiday Inn North and between Ann Street and the Grand Trunk railroad bridge. We would scrape and hand plow the snow from a 20 × 40-yard area along the shore and play hockey with our homemade tree-branch hockey sticks. Sometimes I think we hit one another's shins more often than the puck, which was usually a squashed Pet milk can. We frequently hollered "time out" to reattach our clamp-on-style ice skates, which unfortunately had a way of tearing off the soles and heels of our shoes, prompting our fathers to become do-it-yourself shoemakers. The few kids who owned shoe skates were the envy of the gang. By January or so, when the ice was good and thick in most places, we would speed skate some four or five miles upriver, heading for Stoney Reef, about two miles above North Park Bridge. Almost without fail, at least one of us would break through the thin ice that formed where water passed over river boulders. But the water at Stoney Reef was shallow, and a dip was only waist deep. We would make a fire on shore and dry out our clothes, especially the long johns that kept us warm. Not trusting that the long johns alone would do the job, my mother would give me a small glass of wine to drink as she wrapped a large, homemade scarf around my neck. "Now that will keep you warm," she'd say.

When we weren't skating or playing hockey in the winter, we were having snowball fights, building snowmen and snow forts and making icy "sliders" on the sidewalk. We also had the opportunity to go bobsledding at night when the snow was good. According to the late Bill Krem, someone owned a huge bobsled, equipped with four sets of runners, that could seat forty adults and children. The sled, which made three or four runs a night, would start at the top of Richmond Park Hill and coast all the way to Alpine Avenue, about a half a mile away. Then everybody, including the kids, had to pull the heavy bobsled back up to the top of the hill. Another bobsled that operated a few blocks south, on the Crosby Street hill, also coasted down to Alpine Avenue.

The "sweet science" of boxing was another pastime that found favor among Lithuanians, particularly those "toughies" who used to march up and down Leonard Street or hang around Harrison Park, according to one oldtimer, looking for a fight. Al Kukta, coach and promoter of the Lithuanian Athletic Club boxing team, was one of the better-known Lithuanian fighters of the 1930s. An annual participant in the local Golden Gloves matches held at the downtown Civic Auditorium, Al reached the state finals twice and was a state finals winner at least once. Other top amateur boxers who made names for themselves in Golden Gloves included Shorty Navicki, John Beaver (Vainavicius) and Pete Gregaitis.

Boxing was a much talked-about and argued-about sport in the Lithuanian community's social halls, especially during the 1920s and 1930s, and many of the men followed it closely, cheering for fighters of Lithuanian origin. Even though Lithuanian-American great Jack Sharkey (Juozas Zukauskas) was not from Grand Rapids, the men of Lithuanian Town gathered eagerly to listen to the broadcasts of his matches on the neighborhood's first radio, owned by Adolph Zigus. Local pride certainly overflowed in 1932 when Sharkey defeated Max Schmeling of Germany to become the heavyweight champion of the world. It was a proud day for Lithuanians the world over. . . .

Just as golfing had its caddies, bowling had its pin-setters, and many Lithuanian boys who started as pin-setters developed a lifetime interest in this indoor pastime. In those days, bowling was quite affordable at 20 cents or so a game, and two bowling alleys, Chinnicks and the Fanatorium, operated in downtown Grand Rapids. Wenger's Bowling Alley, still in business today, was located right in Lithuanian Town, on Leonard Street near Muskegon Avenue. As a pin-setter myself in the 1930s, I worked at the Wenger alley for about five or six years. To this day, I hold an unofficial city record for having set two alleys at a time for 16 hours straight, from 9 a.m. to 1 a.m. At five cents a game multiplied by 166 games, my earnings for the day came to $8.30, almost what my father earned in a whole week. . . .

Even when the boys of Lithuanian Town were not playing organized sports, they managed to have a good time. The games they played in the years before they were old enough for part-time jobs were often rough and tumble, many of them relying on the wooden six-shooters carved by ten-year-old Joe Savickas, the best weapon maker in the neighborhood. Whatever the props, the games themselves always had an element of bravado and an "I-dare-you" attitude that prompted the players to take foolish risks. There was a spot at Indian Mill Creek, for example, where a seven-foot-high concrete retaining wall lay opposite a sandbar on the north side of the creek. The idea was to jump the 12 to 15 feet from wall to sandbar. If you didn't make it, you landed in the creek and got a good soaking. But if you succeeded in going the distance, your landing on the water-packed sand was hard enough to jar your teeth.

The Richmond Hill sand jump was likewise risky business. Just about where the hill curves to the northwest was an open area of soft, loose sand extending to the foot of the hill. The name of the game was to get a running start and leap off the crest of the hill, jumping 20 feet horizontally in order to drop 30 feet vertically into the sand and tumble down the hill. Needless to say, the soft sand made for a hard landing.

As if these dangerous pastimes weren't enough, we also played tag among the lumber piles at the old Haskelite Wood (now Evans) Products plant. Stacked about four feet apart, the piles were of different heights, and we jumped from pile to pile as we played. Stumbling or missing a jump made for many bruises on our elbows, ankles, and chins, but I don't recall that any of us broke any bones. Some kids were not so lucky. Local legend has it that, some time before 1920, a Lithuanian boy was playing around an empty tank car parked on a siding between Myrtle and Webster. Apparently, he lit a match to look inside the top of the tank car, and the thunderous explosion that ensued killed him and blew out windows in many neighborhood homes. Three Lithuanian boys under the age of ten came to grief when they tried to dig a cave into the south bank of Indian Mill Creek. The resulting cave-in buried two of the boys alive; the third one ran for help, but it was too late.

Looking back on the days of my boyhood in the early 1930s, I remem-

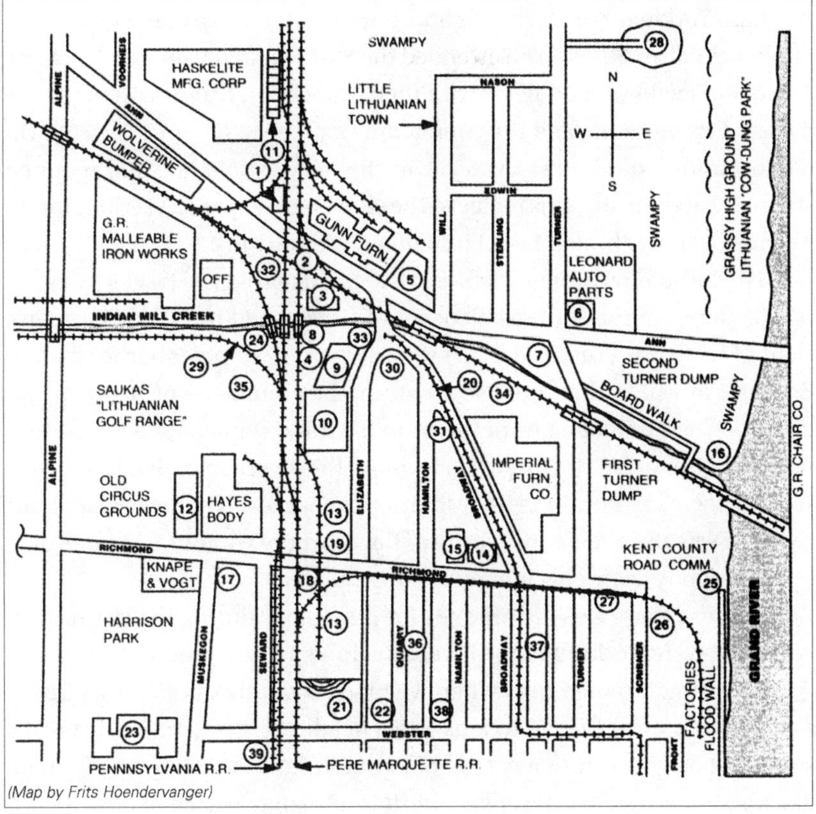

(Map by Frits Hoendervanger)

Northern Old Lithuanian Town, where Edward Gillis grew up in the 1920s and 1930s

Map by Frits Hoendervanger, courtesy of Grand Rapids Historical Commission

ber that we all belonged to gangs. Not to be confused with the criminal gangs of today, these were simply groups of boys who lived in the same immediate neighborhood, were approximately the same age and spent their free time together. I also recall that by the time we reached the age of eight, we no longer played with girls lest we be labeled "sissies." And those were fighting words in Lithuanian Town. So were the slurs hurled back and forth between Lithuanians and other ethnic groups. But a little bit of pushing, shoving and wrestling between adversaries usually restored the peace.

John Yurkinas recalls rock fights between Lithuanian kids who went to public school and those who attended the SS. Peter and Paul parish school. The open neighborhood fields with their hillocks and gullies provided the perfect battleground, and the combatants gave each other no quarter. On one occasion, Joe Dauksza was hit in the head by a stone and required stitches. Later on, BB guns replaced the stones as weapons. A serious injury to one boy finally brought the Lithuanian civil wars to a halt. . . .

The Lithuanian Town stockyards, located across the tracks from the pickle plant, on the southeast corner of Crosby and the Pere Marquette right of way, also exercised a certain fascination for neighborhood boys. En route by rail to their final destination, the animals — pigs, sheep and cattle — were unloaded from the train in Grand Rapids for exercise and feeding. After a day or two in the feedlots they were reloaded into open-slat stock cars to continue their journey to market. What we liked about the spot was the decidedly "western" flavor where we could imagine ourselves cowboys as we wandered among the pens.

Because there was little money for playthings during the Depression years, we were nothing if not ingenious in using the materials at hand. Charley Daugin remembers when we made scooters out of 2 x 4s, roller skates and a shiny tin can to look like a headlight. Pete Draugalis recalls stomping our heels into a couple of Pet milk cans and clippety-clopping like horses along the sidewalks. Another must-have piece of growing-up equipment was the slingshot, which we made from tree branches, inner-tube rubber and a small piece of leather. Targets included sparrows, squirrels, bottles — and the occasional house window. Even our Christmas gifts were quite modest, often consisting of the assorted nuts, candy, an orange and a banana that filled one of our knee-length socks hung near the kitchen stove.

Although we could buy a kite kit for 29 cents and have a better-flying product, homemade kites were especially fun on a windy day. Homemade stilts were also popular at times, despite the risks of walking three feet off the ground. During our annual spring pollywog hunt, we used tin cans and homemade nets to capture our prey and then put them in quart-sized mason jars from home. As soon as the pollywogs began to grow, my father would ask, "How would you like to grow up in a jar?" Our answer would be to take them back to the pond.

Our favorite spot for hunting pollywogs was Pollywog Pond, located between Webster Street and the south fence of Braudy's junkyard. Braudy's itself, although it was supposed to be off-limits, was probably our favorite playground. Enclosed by a seven-foot, red-painted fence, the property covered about two city blocks and was separated by Richmond Street into a south yard and a north yard. Metal was processed daily in the north yard, so our playground was in the south, or storage, yard. Sneaking in on weekends by means of several loose fence boards, we had a virtual scrap Disneyland at our disposal. All kinds of old machines filled the space — room-sized ventilators, huge pipes, an endless variety of mechanical objects, even genuine doughboy helmets from World War I that somehow came into our possession.

One glorious day there appeared four old steam locomotives to be cut up into scrap. Just sitting in the engineer's seat, one hand on the throttle and leaning out the window, came close to being the ultimate boyhood dream. But we wanted more, and one particular weekend saw about twenty of us try to get one of the engines going. While some of the gang carried five-gallon buckets of water from the pond to pour into the 8,000-gallon tender, others gathered wood for the firebox. But with no steam draft to force the smoke up the chimney, we had more smoke coming through the cab windows than out the stack. The big brass bell had already been removed, so we couldn't ring that, and, worst of all, we couldn't even get the whistle to blow. Finally, reluctantly, we decided to give up.

Railroads were such a continuing source of fascination that a fair number of kids took to hopping freight trains. Three major railroads passed through Lithuanian Town. The Pennsylvania Railroad and the Pere Marquette were north-south lines that ran between Elizabeth and Seward avenues. The Grand Trunk Western Division of the Canadian National line passed east and west along Indian Mill Creek and Ann Street, the northern boundary of Lithuanian Town. All three lines intersected at Fuller Junction, just west of where Broadway used to cross the creek, and it was there that all the locomotives took on water.

Many hobos rode the rails, especially during the Depression years, and often large numbers of them set up transient camps or "jungles" near Fuller Junction. They were always friendly toward us kids, and we loved to hang around listening to their stories and watching them make soup in coffee cans. Sometimes we would even filch food for them from home. In 1936, the summer I was sixteen years of age, a friend and I succumbed to the lure of that wailing whistle in the night. "Going on the bum," we hopped a freight and made it all the way out to Seattle. We worked at odd jobs during the one-month, 4,000-mile round trip, including farm work, which paid a standard dollar a day with a noon meal included. I came home with $12 in my pocket, a dollar more than I had started out with.

Just as some of us were fascinated by steam locomotives and captivated by the romance of the rails, Tony Lucas (Lukshas) treasures his memories of the old Fire Engine Company No. 9 on the northeast corner of Leonard and Quarry. Because he lived only a block away, he spent a lot of time hanging around the old firehouse waiting for the excitement of an alarm. As soon as the fire bell sounded, the white fire horses would be brought out of the stalls and hitched up to the engine while the fire in the boiler was being stoked into life. As it emerged from the fire station, the horse-drawn, steam-powered engine would belch black smoke, on its way no more than one or two minutes after the sounding of the alarm.

The changing seasons brought their own delights. Indian Mill Creek was an idyllic spot of natural beauty that for us Lithuanian kids was a bit of summertime heaven, a place to skinny dip, fish and crab and while away the summer hours in our own little world. We had favorite spots at Indian Mill Creek back when the brush-covered banks afforded all the privacy we needed. Although we knew better than to dive into the shallow creek, we certainly splashed a lot and we held contests to see which of us could stay underwater the longest. Once, to make a deeper swimming hole, we built a dam in the creek west of Alpine, but a flooded field was the result and the farmer made us tear it down. One of the best places was along the west bank of the Grand River, about a mile above the Ann Street Bridge. We called this spot the "high banks" because we could get a running start and dive into the water. But we couldn't swim there on Friday afternoons because the Comstock park tannery drained its tanks that day and the river ran red along the west bank for hours.

Another place we swam was at the mouth of Indian Mill Creek and the Grand River, wearing the clinging cotton bathing suits we used to buy at the dime store for about 59 cents and whose cheap dyes washed away in about two weeks. We called this small public beach "Bloodsucker Beach" because of the leeches that clung to our legs there. The beach was equipped with a bathhouse and a diving raft about twenty feet offshore. This was the very place where Benny Dubinska's twin brother, Anthony, dived shoreward from the raft instead of into deep water, broke his neck and drowned. Sometimes, for a change of scene, we headed up to the eight-foot-high flood wall, about where the Kent County Road Commission garages are today, and dived off into the river, which was about six or seven feet deep at the time. Today, the spot is so silted that the water is only about one-and-a-half feet deep.

Living in Lithuanian Town, we also had easy access to the Harrison Park swimming pool, built around the turn of the century, where I earned my swimmer's pin when I was seven or eight years old. Torn down in 1932, shortly after the Richmond Park pool was opened, the Harrison Park pool was drained each Saturday night and filled each Sunday. By Friday the water was so polluted that it burned our eyes red. Girls used the pool in the morning and boys in the afternoon, or vice-versa, but there was no coed swimming.

Crabbing in Indian Mill Creek was yet another summertime pleasure, and so were the epicurean crawfish its waters yielded up to us kids. Since none of us wore shoes in the summer, we would simply wade into the creek at the Pennsylvania Railroad bridge and walk upstream to around Alpine Avenue, turning over stones and debris on the creek bed and grabbing the crawfish as they tried to scurry away. On a good day, we could just about fill a one-gallon lard pail. Afterwards, we built a fire and cooked them until they turned red and ready to eat. Other kids sometimes cooked their crawfish haul in the hot water that poured out of a pipe emerging from the Malleable foundry.

Fishing in Indian Mill Creek, in the days before it became heavily polluted, was another summer pastime. Just above the old Alpine iron bridge, a huge rock protruded from under the retaining wall, causing the current to scoop out a three-foot hole in the creek bed. This was a favorite spot to fish, and my brother Ted had great success in catching brook trout and brown trout.

Each year during the 1920s and 1930s the gypsies came to town and set up camp about a half mile north of Ann Street between Turner Avenue and the river. In the earlier years, they came by horse and wagon and had their horses reshod at Baker Blacksmith Shop on the northwest corner of Leonard and Muskegon. By the late 1930s, they no longer came by wagons, but had large touring cars instead. We always begged our mothers for discarded costume jewelry to use as small trinkets in exchange for having our fortunes told. And we believed everything the gypsies told us.

Medicine shows began coming to Lithuanian Town as early as 1915, setting up in an open field, and remaining for a week or so, or until the sales artists felt their pitch was wearing thin. The shows had a vaudeville air about them, and many people came to hear the spiels. Each year, my father spent a dollar for a bottle of "snake liniment" for his back. Other folks were fascinated by the twenty-foot tapeworm preserved in a jar of brine. Tapeworms were a common problem in those days because of poorly inspected meat, and the tapeworm medicine always sold well. So did the 10-cent boxes of taffy candy with their worthless little gifts inside.

Grand Rapids was also a stop for the Barnum and Bailey Circus, which used to unload at the railroad siding north of Leonard Street. The entire company — animals, performers, and the loud, attention-getting, steam-belching calliope — would parade west on Leonard to Alpine, then north on Alpine to Richmond, finally turning east to a big open field where the Pitsch Lumber and Wrecking yards are now located. Here, the circus would remain for a week, providing ample time for curious boys to hang out among the exotic animals and colorful performers. All too soon, the circus train would reload alongside Seward Avenue between Richmond and Webster and head out for its next destination.

Summers from 1918 to 1924 were the occasion for free outdoor movies sponsored by the city recreation department and shown at Harrison Park before the school was built. The movies, mostly comedies and cartoons, were projected onto a twelve-foot-square cloth stretched across a wooden framework, and the audience, mostly kids, sat on the grass. The old Turner School, at the southwest corner of Turner and Eleventh, showed free movies in its gymnasium in the late 1920s and early 1930s. During the same years, the Berkey and Gay Furniture Company offered Saturday morning movies in its auditorium on Ottawa as a gesture of goodwill towards the community. We got the coming attractions from those fathers who worked there, and we were happy to trek across the river for ninety minutes of serials, cartoons and comedies.

In January of 1929, Lithuanian Town got its own neighborhood movie theater, called, appropriately enough, Our Theater. Built by the firm of Willer and Boshoven and located on the northwest corner of West Leonard and McReynolds, the building was unusually large and opulent for a neighborhood movie house. Among its more unusual features was a machine that projected moving white clouds across a high, curved, sky-blue ceiling. As a nine-year-old when the Our Theater opened, I had as much fun following the clouds across the "sky" as I did watching the movies.

Until the advent of "talkies" in 1932, the only sound heard in the theater was organ music, before, during and after the movie. The Our Theater instrument was a $25,000 Paige organ, made in Lima, Ohio, and played by Russell Thrall, an exceptionally talented musician. As my mother used to say, "I don't know much about the movies, but his music was so beautiful."

During the summer months, the movies were not the theater's only attraction. When the weather turned hot, people flocked to the Our Theater to cool off, for this Lithuanian Town cultural gem, unlike most other movie theaters of the time, boasted the luxury of an early but effective version of air conditioning. Owner Allen Johnson piped cold water from a deep backyard well into radiators equipped with fans to disperse the cooled air throughout the theater. Then he piped the "spent" water into outside sprinklers used to cool the roof. The system worked so well movie patrons hated to leave the theater. In 1936, in fact, during one of Grand Rapids' hottest summers, many people stayed to see the show twice. The Our Theater was eventually one of three movie houses on Leonard and in the early 1960s became home to Grand Rapids Civic Theater.

The boys of Lithuanian Town always joined eagerly in Fourth of July celebrations. Back in the days when carbide lamps were still in use, we would put a small chunk of carbide and a little water into a quart-sized paint can, clamp a lid on and use a nail to punch a small hole in the bottom. After acetylene gas built up in the can, we put a match to the firing hole for an explosion that would propel the lid 75 feet away. We also saved up our nickels and dimes to buy factory-made fireworks, readily available in our neighborhood at Urban's Confectionary, on the northeast corner of Leonard and Muskegon. . . .

Two gangs stand out in Lithuanian Town's historical memory. One, the "Galoshes," committed armed robbery, and its members went to jail for their misdeeds. The other, the "Red City" Gang, were teenagers who hung out together for several years, gave their parents more than a few gray hairs, but steered clear of the law.

Inspired by the lawlessness of the Roaring Twenties, the five Galoshes Gang members, all young Lithuanians, armed themselves and decided to make some easy money. The gang got its label from newspaper articles noting that the miscreants wore galoshes to disguise their footprints in the snow during winter jobs. For several months, until they were brought to justice, the Galoshes Gang had the entire West Michigan region buzzing about the heists of several West Side businesses. Among their most sensational hold-ups was the Grand Rapids Packing Company job. Entering the building at night, after workers had left, they overpowered the night watchman, bound and gagged him, and broke open the company safe. Obtaining an undetermined sum of money, they made their escape without detection.

Even more sensational was their armed robbery of the Villa Tavern on North Alpine Avenue. Entering the tavern armed with sawed-off shotguns, they forced all the customers in attendance to surrender their money, along with the cash in the establishment's till. The tavern was full at the time, but no one was hurt during the robbery. For a time, the Galoshes Gang led local police on a merry chase, but the only crime wave in Lithuanian Town's history ended when police gathered enough information to arrest all five gang members. Once in custody, they were quickly convicted and sent to prison for terms of up to seven years.

Aside from the work of the Galoshes Gang, there seems to have been a relatively low incidence of serious crime in the Lithuanian community, but it would not be accurate to imply that only angels held forth. Just as in other neighborhoods, young men found ways to create minor trouble.

They stole fruit from street vendors and orchards, hopped coal trains and threw off big pieces of coal, and "salvaged" salable scrap metal from industrial outdoor storage areas. For the most part, however, those were not considered serious crimes as long as no one got caught. . . .

Like some youth of today, Lithuanian teenagers with too much time on their hands formed a gang. In the early 1920s, they began gathering around the grassy, tree-shaded eastern part of Harrison Park, along Muskegon Avenue, sometimes sleeping overnight in the park. Although he was never formally "elected," Red Waitkonis, a good-natured, affable, tough guy, became the gang leader. In time, the group became known as the Red City Gang. Members were looked upon as a pretty tough bunch of Lithuanians, and although they never went looking for trouble, those who knew them had no doubt they could more than take care of themselves. A household word in the 1930s, the Red City Gang ultimately broke up as members turned their attention to such adult pursuits as marriage and family, and World War II intervened.

During the gang's glory days, its members frequently headed for Fuller Junction, just a few blocks from their hangout. All northbound freight trains stopped there, making it easy to hop aboard one of the empties. These free rides courtesy of the Pennsylvania and Pere Marquette lines brought them to a variety of destinations, including Traverse City, Petoskey, Big Rapids, Cadillac and Mackinaw City. One evening an argument developed about something up in Traverse City, 140 miles away, and without further ado the gang jumped aboard the 11 p.m. Pere Marquette freight train and took off to settle their dispute. . . .

One of the Red City Gang's notable pastimes was playing cards, and poker was the game of choice. The second most popular activity was to argue about almost anything. An argument developed one day over the ballistics of firing a man out of a circus cannon. Typically, several gang members sought some way to prove their point. Lacking a cannon, they climbed a small tree, tied a rope near its top, and slowly pulled the top branches towards the ground. The 16-year-old who volunteered to be the human cannonball could not have been more surprised when his friends let the rope go. Witnesses said he flew in an arc 45 feet high and hit the grass hard enough to cause bleeding from his mouth and nose. Although he ended up sore all over, miraculously there were no broken bones. His friends took him home in a cart, and he told his mother and father that he fell out of a tree. A few weeks later, he was back to hanging around the park, none the worse for his cannonball flight.

The Red City Gang called a small section in the northwest part of Harrison Park the "lumber camp." There, before the advent of chainsaws, gang members sawed, chopped and split logs into kindling size, selling some and keeping the rest for their families. Gang members also spent one summer logging a three-to-five-acre woodland area in what they called the North Woods, now known as Richmond Park, which was scheduled to become the Lithuanian Freedom Cemetery. The Lithuanian Freedom Cemetery Association acquired the property, just east of the SS. Peter and Paul parish cemetery, because non-Catholics were not permitted burial in the Catholic cemetery. Once the trees were cut, other gang members hauled the logs to the lumber camp on a horse-drawn four-wheeled wagon owned by John Yurkinas's father. John estimated that they lumbered at least 75 to 100 trees during the unauthorized two-to-three-month timbering project, with the end product divided among the crew.

One of the regular visitors to the gang hangout at Harrison Park was Grand Rapids police officer Ernie Bockheim, who almost nightly cruised the park area on his motorcycle. Bockheim impressed the youths with his knee-high leather puttees, uniform jacket and sunglasses, and they would jam around him with a lot of teasing and joking. Always in parting he would, in unpoliceman-like fashion, roar away, much to the pleasure of his Red City Gang fans.

Yesterdays in Grand Rapids

JOHN THOMPSON

In 1969, *Harper's* magazine began a new series entitled "Going Home in America," in which it published essays by notable American writers on their memories of and return visits to their hometowns. Poet, novelist, and critic John Thompson inaugurated this series in the May 1969 issue with the essay reprinted here. Some of the others that followed were editor-in-chief Willie Morris's essay on Yazoo City, Mississippi, Midge Decter on St. Paul, Walker Percy on New Orleans, John Hollander on New York City, and Marshall Frady on Gary, Indiana.

Thompson was also the author of *The Founding of English Metre* and *The Talking Girl and Other Poems.* His short story "Jack Frost" appeared in the November 1968 issue of *Harper's.* During Morris's tenure as editor-in-chief, Thompson was the bimonthly book critic, alternating issues with Irving Howe. He taught English at the State University of New York at Stony Brook.

I used to be coming home, not going home. I would sneak in like a thief in the night. I came on the train then, up from college in Ohio through the flatlands and into Southern Michigan, a real milk train. It stopped often and they loaded the domed forty-gallon milk cans from the racks where the farmers left them by the roadbed. There was an engine and sometimes a mail car and the milk car and a passenger car that was like a caboose, with a coal stove in the middle. I remember once the engineer or the fireman saying something to a man in a buffalo-check mackinaw by one of the milk platforms and the man said, Oh, he had forgotten — with the engine throttled down you could hear them easily. Their voices were like lettering in the air. It was a clear cool day, probably Thanksgiving vacation. After a while the man came back with two boxes of eggs and handed them to the cab. The Iron Horse snorted and we rattled on to the next place. Retired railroaders used to deadhead on that train just for something to do, and they were about the only passengers. They wore vests and looked at their chained watches a lot, as trainmen used to. It was thirty years ago.

Coming in to Grand Rapids we went through Cutlerville and past the new General Motors plant and Plaster Creek and past the sidings of the gaunt old brick furniture plants, then dead or dying, soon to be as otherworldly as Roman aqueducts, to the marshaling yards, past blown smoke and those junk-fenced backyards with dead holly-hocks and sunflowers that line all American railway tracks, and two-and-three-story wooden tenements with washings on the back railings where the outside stairs go up, and past the asphalted truckline parks where the herds of trailers rested, twice as big as boxcars and already carrying more goods than the rails did, and into Union Station.

It would not really be night and I would not really be sneaking in like a thief, because my father and my two sisters and my brother-in-law would be there to meet me. I was more like some uncaught criminal who had to go back again and again by daylight to the scene of the crime. I didn't know what the crime was. All I knew was that there was something I had to hide and that it was shameful to be that way. Now I think that what I had to hide, what I had to hide so hard it almost killed me, was that I loved them.

Union Station had a big humpbacked shed that could take six or eight trains under it. It was cold and full of the sweet smell of coke. They met me there. For that milk train, there would be no crowd, but years later after the War when I used to come in on the Pullman off the Wolverine with Dilly and maybe Robie Macauley and Joe Brewer, also going home from New York for Christmas, and the train full of college kids, all of them somebody's friends or relatives, there might be big crowds with many people one knew. There were suitcases, and eyes darting everywhere, hands waving, glad cries, hugs, jostlings, steam hissing from the

The Grand Rapids Union Depot viewed from Ionia Avenue (looking north), shortly before it was razed in 1961
GRPL, Library Postcard Collection

airbrake couplings and everybody's breath white in the cold air of the shed, everybody talking at once, laughter, and my older sister Kathryn and my father standing there at the edge of a bottomless pit where I would fall. I could never get used to discovering again that I was taller than she, to say nothing of him. She would smile with that look on her round face that I believe now was, for the moment, simply an expression of the kind of love and pride that anyone, any woman at all, is entitled to feel for her brother who has grown up and gone away and who comes home. My father fidgeted beside her, eager but shy, grinning, ready to be told he was doing something wrong. There were, at that moment, no tears in my sister's eyes. Someplace deeper than Hell yawned at my feet and I walked straight across it on nothing but the rickety scaffold of my own loud laughter and blabber, looking around, sideways and back, counting them all, bumping suitcases, collecting and being collected, herding and being herded through the crowd. I was a steer in the slaughterhouse chute. The façade of the station was two or three blocks long, brick with tall sort of Italian Renaissance arched windows and for the main entrance a pediment with four enormous sooted Ionic pillars, and then up behind the pediment a dome with clocks in it. Union Station has been torn down now for the Expressway, which is no wonder because like so many American towns Grand Rapids by the middle 1950s had already become impossible to get to on the train.

All hometowns are like Troy, of course, and we all believe with the accurate faith of Heinrich Schliemann that the true Ilion, "seventh of nine settlements on the same spot," still lies there under the mere huge windy tumulus of the present. The Ilion of our childhood has little but its geographical location in common with what stands there now; and that great place established as if by the gods expressly for us to grow up in had little to do with what may have stood there before. Before? Except for Southerners and for some New Englanders, there is no Before for American children. Past, present, and future are all there in that seventh city of Ilion and not only can we excavate it easily and completely but, when we do, it all switches on like some toy city, the lights, trolleys, automobiles, people, all begin to jerk about, there are sounds, whistles, horns, songs; and all those poor little persons, switched back to life, loom once more into their Homeric order, lifting stones such as twenty men couldn't budge today. They rule our lives, rising before us shining or baleful with an intensity far beyond the weak abilities of any other time; they are as irreplaceable, they are as inimitable and yet as potent in stamping with their typed identities all mere mortals who follow them as were the ranked deities of Olympus. . . .

— When I grew up here the Negro community was —

— Black. Let's say Black.

— I know. I'm old-fashioned I guess. Even my students have to remind me sometimes to say Black.

— Yeah. You know, as long ago as when I was a kid I never liked that word Negro. It sounded — well, I guess even then it sounded like a euphemism.

— For Nigger. Or as they say down South, Nigra.

— Nigra. You can't mispronounce Black.

— With my friends, you know, in New York, you're a Spade.

— Yeah, that's a little in-group word. It's getting kind of old now. You were to say that to the kids these days, it's bad news.

We talked about Small's Paradise and the Red Rooster in Harlem where, as I explained, I don't feel much at home anymore. Reggie Gatling, executive director of the Kentfields Group Rehabilitation Center in Grand Rapids, combed the splendid bush of his moustache and laughed, tilting back behind his desk. Clearly he was a very busy man and yet one so secure, even so comfortable in his total occupation — in charge not only of his Rehabilitation Center for youths, with, he says, the lowest recidivist rate in the country, but obviously involved far beyond that, a very busy executive and organizer — so comfortable that like good generals in books he knows how to live at ease in constant crisis. He can turn off his telephone and send his assistants away, if he feels like it, to chat for most of a morning with an inquiring stranger.

Reggie Gatling was amused by what I said about the old self-contained community with its ghetto and its churches and its own regulation of a complex social life under its own Captain Coe of the Grand Rapids Police Force, and amused by what I posited as the disruption of that system by waves of immigration.

— That's not it at all. That's not what it's all about. You're all wrong. What's changed is just Black Power. We are not going to have our children destroyed anymore by white racism. We are for Black Power by any and all means whatsoever. By all and any means whatsoever. . . . Vietnam? Hell, I hope that war goes on forever. When our boys come back from there, they're trained. And they understand. They're for the Cong, all of them. . . . Sure, sure, I know. These liberals come around with their Planned Parenthood. And we run 'em out. It's genocide. We want Black babies. We told them to go to hell. You say we're ten per cent. I say we're more like forty-nine per cent and it won't be so long before we take over. . . . Elect? Sure, we can elect a few niggers here and there. Can't elect a Black man, yet. . . . They can't find Black teachers! Of course they can't. They wouldn't know a teacher if he bit 'em. I can find Black teachers with all the qualifications you can name, right down the line. . . . Look, I know my phone's tapped. I know what happened to Eldridge and Malcolm and LeRoi. . . .

He admires the young people today. He hadn't had that kind of nerve, to stand up to a cop and say Pig.

In music class at Sigsbee School we sang "Old Black Joe" and *Down in the cornfield, hear that mournful sound, all the darkies are a-weepin, Massa's in de cold cold ground.* Charles Molson, small Black — not "black" of course any more than I am "white," I can see his face now, round smiling, the color of polished slate; he grins among us as we all tag along up Fuller Avenue one afternoon after school, walking Dorotha Riekse home, the belle of the sixth grade. We walk not exactly with her but in our eleven-year-old loutishness we skulk a few paces behind her where she strolls with two or three attendant maidens of her Court of Venus. Dorotha had come to us in the fifth grade from some unknown elsewhere, tall, sophisticated, in a fascinating way horse-faced, and bearing under her cashmere sweater the first pair of breasts we had ever seen on a contemporary of ours. We all fell head over heels in love with her. We sat behind her every Friday night at the movies and had a soda with her afterwards at Dutmer's, and sometimes, as we are doing on this afternoon, we walk her home: Ben Litscher, Ruben Frost, Guy Dygert, a couple other fellows. Charles Molson is with us.

Someplace along the way, Charles drops off, and it is at this moment I look into his eyes. I too will drop off at my corner, so will each of the other boys, wishing probably each of us that we might be asked to continue on along but not expecting it. I was never in my life inside the door of Dorotha Riekse's house, never was invited to her birthday parties.

Yet when Charles dropped off there, attired in a hideous mustard-and-raw-sienna diamond-patterned sweater just like the rest of us, with corduroy or blue-serge knickers, sagging knee stockings and high tennis shoes, just like the rest of us, when he dropped off it made somehow a picture to remember always.

He is not saying anything. His round cheeks, color of polished slate, bulge in a slight and terribly complicated grin. There must have been a moment we looked at one another, a look that petrified the air along the line of sight between our two faces into an eternal rod like an iron crowbar. Dorotha and her entourage prattled on along the sidewalk under the maple leaves, and then he was gone, in this one moment that I recorded to last as long as I live. He drifts on across the street, westerly where the houses are one size smaller and less adorned with front porches and bay windows, over there where in the section of some forty or fifty city blocks the Dutchmen live and then past that the niggers.

Chuck Molson was recklessly brave in football. He wrote for our mimeographed Annual the account of the great Henry School game. *Bob Palmer got the ball and made a remarkable run which brought the ball to within five yards from their goal and Charles Cadey carried it over — Sigsbee 6 — Henry 0.* Chuck Molson made the second, and, as it proved, the winning touchdown. He wore the same clothes we did and talked just like the rest of us, the way people in Michigan talk, a standard enough accent distinguished only by the peculiar slow sort of ironic intonation many of us have. In the "Jokes" section of our Annual he is immortalized thus:

Molson: "Yes, sah, I'm a great singah."
Boy: "Wheah you all learn to sing?"
Molson: "I graduated from correspondence school."
Boy: "Boy, you suah lost lots of your mail."

In high school, where we still sang "Old Black Joe" and "Massa's in de Cold Cold Ground," and where we put on a blackface minstrel show in which my girl's brother Ernie sang "Chloe," strutting in blackface with enormous painted red lips and a gold-headed walking stick, to our applause (even though stagefright pinched off most of his noisy bass voice), there, in Ottawa Hills High School, our best athlete was also Black. It was impossible for him to make any movement that was not totally a flowing forth of the most delicate grace and the most overwhelming power. My girl said she didn't care about basketball as a game but she just liked to see him move. I remember that very clearly, where, and when, and what it smelled like in the crowded balcony of the gym. He was our black panther.

And I remember as perfectly as we remember all those trivial things that somehow stir up our ignorance, that transfix and dismay the circuits of our memory like some unwelcome surge of voltage beyond their capacities, I remember that at one of those games some friend in judicious approval told me to note how carefully Bernard, when the water boy brought the one towel to the five gasping and sweating players at a time-out, how carefully but casually Bernard would flip the towel on along around the ring, and managed always to use it last. He went to college and flew a P-47 against the Germans and survived that and became a lawyer. I don't know where he is now, nor where you may be, Charles Molson, Chuck, who won the game against Henry School and whose eyes I met one afternoon on the east side of Fuller Avenue just south of Bemis Street when we were eleven years old.

Reggie Gatling recommends for the Hong Kong flu, which has me halfway down today and all the way down some other days, plenty of Scotch. We talk about this and that, and then, Well, maybe, he says, maybe he'll just go to Africa and die. . . .

A few weeks ago, I went up Glenwood Avenue again for the first time in years (I don't know why going south was going up, on that flat street, and north was down, but it was) — when I went up and past our house, that whole world, all of it, both those two blocks, had shrunk to a fraction of its former scale, as anyone would expect. For a few years, of course, that street was not only Grand Rapids but the world. Any trip away from there carried me over distances as weird and empty as Space to land me somewhere as strange as the moon. . . .

The street itself had shrunk, the houses had diminished themselves, the yards where I used to roam as in vast pastures had all but disappeared, they had become nothing really. The little houses stand shoulder to shoulder, with space between them only for a narrow driveway to the garage at the rear of a backyard you can scarcely turn around in: big enough once for a baseball game.

If I want to know anything about these houses, even about our house, my house, my father's house, I cannot simply look at them from the window of my rented car and recall who lived here. Nobody every lived in these dingy dollhouses! No, I have to call back from its buried depths that seventh level of Troy, and look at that lost city in my mind's eye, where it is restored to its full size and color and mystery and terror, and then how clear and simple it is. That is the O'Neills', on that side there the empty lot with the big apple tree that was Jack O'Neill's to climb by his whim and favor (they built a double house there, goodbye apple tree, and Myron Kozman moved in upstairs), then there are the Bowmans', the Geisslers', McIntyres', Kendricks', Wolffs', and on the corner of Sherman Street the Schwanks' later to be the Logies'. So much for that side of the street.

Let me mention only one house on our side of the street. In some summer before I was old enough to go to school they built two houses in the vacant lot next door to us. The second of these houses had a hipped roof and blue shutters. Don Webber moved in and he was my age. But one day I was walking past the house, when it was brand new, with my mother. She walked slowly and there was a nurse with us. We walked up to the corner where there flourished a magnificent fountain-top elm, an old forest giant some farmer had spared. On the way back from the corner, my mother said as we passed the new house, "That's a storybook house." I remember that because I didn't understand it, which is why we remember so many things. My mother was smiling and holding the nurse's elbow. I don't have many memories of my mother. She said, "That's a storybook house." It was a sunny day, maybe early in autumn, and I would just as soon I had died that day as any other.

In almost every house on the street there were children, nearly of an age. When Chuck and Don Webber and I invited Jack O'Neill to come along while we played Doctor with — I suppose even now it is not fair to give her name — with a little friend of ours, he declined because his was too big and might hurt her. It was Donald who instructed us in these things. He had come to the neighborhood from someplace else, into that new house the other side of Hake's, and he was full of strange lore, much of it about girls. He even claimed that Muriel across the street, who was as old as my older sister, had hair growing between her legs, but this I found unbelievable, and I still to this day think of him as some kind of crook. There is a certain sort of swindler, a glib, plausible, sexual, handsome variety of fellow you run into here and there, likely to be redolent of foreign places and of the couches of more than a few famous ladies: he is always Donald.

In a recent visit to Grand Rapids I took Susan for a drive up that street which was my world for five years, and then down around Wilcox Park where Ben Litscher lived before the Depression, and around the block at Sigsbee School, my world for seven more years. Then we drove around and looked at the houses where my friends lived, past Johnny Nind's on Woodward Lane (another and later casualty of the Depression), and Ottawa Hills High School, up where Dave Evans lived, and we drove along all the streets I had walked all those years in high school, and back over to Sigsbee Street where my girl lived (in front of her house a Black man was shoveling his walk). I had set off with some idea that I was taking Susan on a great expedition. What happened was that even though I did a lot of doubling back it was all over before I knew it. If I hadn't managed to get the Hertz car stuck in the snow as I tried to show her the circle by Reeds Lake in Hodenpyl Woods where in the back seat of a Buick I first got laid, if I hadn't done that the whole trip would have been over in fifteen minutes. We saw everything there was to see in fifteen minutes. Such has it come to, the vast and monumented city of my youth.

The real Grand Rapids is not mine. The real city is there, it actually exists, with 177,000 people in its central limits, the seventy-first city in the United States, just above Springfield, Massachusetts, and Nashville, and just below St. Petersburg and Gary. This real city has the problems of all American cities, people have moved out to the metropolitan areas, downtown is blighted, shoppers go to the great interplanetary shopping centers out on the Belt Line. It costs a fortune to get enough water, to get rid of the sewage, to build enough schools for the kids. The Black citizens want this and that. (The words "Grand Rapids" leap right out of any page of print for me, often enough in error when my glance has caught some other collocation of words with a capital G and a capital R, but now and then this flick of recognition is accurate. How strange to read, in the New York papers, about riots in Grand Rapids.)

It is often said that Grand Rapids has taken care of many of these things better than a lot of other cities. Of course there are stories about the money made off the first Lake Michigan pipeline, but the pipeline was built; and they built us a Civic Auditorium in the very depths of the Depression. There have always been capable people willing to pitch in and get these things done, and we must not take them for granted. These things get done in some parts of the world and do not get done in others. There are plenty of places on earth where they can't figure out how to bring clean water in or how to get rid of their own shit.

Rich people in Grand Rapids, unless they have some really enormous pile of inherited loot, so big it takes them two quarts of gin a day to stay on top of it, unless they are in these extremities they tend to go in for some sort of civic enterprise. And the factories are booming, printing, metals, furniture, and there is a big transport business, and the city does the banking for a large part of Michigan, and buys and sells. There are lots of jobs. You can spin along north, south, east, or west on the new expressways. Lower Monroe has been cleaned out, the old nineteenth-century buildings are gone, those odd old Germanic brick structures so pilastered and corniced and silled, replaced by parking lots and various city buildings, miniatures of the bronze Seagram Building or of some other clean-cut cube on stylish stilts. . . . When I was a child, the Hearst papers on Sundays often had full-page pictures of the world of the future, with big highways zipping around through the sky like spilled ribbons and shiny buildings all over. And just such a vision our renewals all over America have confirmed. Only we never guessed how scruffy it could get down there under the expressways, how easily concrete gets shabby, how monstrous the long long ramps can be. They are nothing like those marvelous structures, real bridges over water, as we might have supposed they would be. Hearst's artists drew those aerial ribbons without underpinnings, and they didn't have to worry about litter. We never guessed that those big open spaces would have to be filled with autos. And most of all, we never guessed at the disorientation these settings can induce. They're all just like going to New Haven. Whisk, you're off the New England expressway, and though your car slows down, your head is still going seventy miles an hour. The sign says "New Haven" all right, but what the hell is this? Is it supposed to be finished? Is this the city, or an airport, or what? What are those strange buildings standing isolated and at such peculiar angles to one another? Are there people in there? What is all this space, space, space? How do I get out of here? The urb has been Renewed by an Expert. But in Grand Rapids, maybe it will look nice. You can't say they didn't try. . . .

"His adolescence, each one's homeland," said Delmore Schwartz. Any of us could carry on forever about our high-school years, and yet those years have almost no literature worth mentioning. *The Catcher in the Rye* never seemed very real to me. Nor, I must admit, does what I observe of actual high schools seem very real. How impossible to believe that these kids we see now, fifteen or sixteen years old, our own children perhaps, are living as we lived then in a turmoil of pain and discovery and elation, living in a world of heroes and heroines, gods and goddesses really, and learning the language and customs of that country, acquiring the ways of feeling and acting which will never be lost no matter what passports we acquire and what other lands we may come to inhabit. There is never another girl like the first real girl, never such friends, never such necessary teachers.

It is a time like that period of our infancy when, so we are told, we acquire suddenly the capability of language, and toddling at our mother's apron strings we master the unbelievable intricacies of human speech, so complex in their structures and transformations that no grammarian has even been able really to describe them. It is the greatest intellectual feat of our lives no matter who we are. If a child should miss that, if he should somehow be shut away from people when he is three and four years old, then that mysterious quickening of the lobes of his brain would be all for nothing: this is our one chance and it cannot come again.

So it may be for us in our adolescence. Yes, some people get through these years without goddesses and without gods, without much love or much dread. And I believe I recognize them, too. *Who, moving others, are themselves as stone, Unmoved, cold, and to temptation slow. . . .* Yes, they are the ones, *they are the Lords and owners of their faces.* And, I believe, it really is they who inherit heaven's graces. The rest of us, those who found adolescence to be an entire world, well, many of us were lost there and it can take years and years to get out.

There was my girl. There was my teacher, "the Chief," Mary Baloyan, fierce, generous, dark-eyed, noble, her profile that of her ancestors who wielded scimitars in Asia Minor. She taught me to read poetry and made me write things, and made me an actor in our school plays; she was so good to me, a savior of the order which can only be called that of absolute necessity. There is Dave Evans, who taught me to be a Socialist and to drink like a gentleman. I did once believe in both those noble attainments, and again it was necessary that this should have been. But I have no friends left from that age. They are still boys and girls in my archaeologist's Troy. I do not go back home to them and while I have not forgotten our clubs and our dances and our huddling in frozen automobiles it would not amuse me to recall it now. The scars of my accent still show where I came from, but that country no longer exists and I have denied it.

There was another Grand Rapids, too, this time almost the real one. Out of high school, I was still around for a while. The town was poor then. And like so many who grew up in the Depression, we never expected we would ever have real jobs. There was no place for us in the world. It was depressing. . . . Then the war came, and then after that Grand Rapids, like all of America, was flooded by the great overflowing and unreceding Nile of prosperity. My hometown was gone forever, gone for good.

The city I knew later, with Dilly and our children, when we came for so many years to wonderful homely old Gun Lake, this was no longer my hometown. It was someplace else. Oh, I could talk about it, but it was someplace else and not my hometown.

LONG-SMOLDERING FEUD IGNITES GVSC FRACAS

By Robert Alt

Grand Valley State College may be growing up.

Last week, a feud that had been brewing for months between Ottawa County officials and GVSC students erupted with the closing of the student newspaper, *Lanthorn,* and the arrest of its editor by the Ottawa County prosecutor's office. The prosecutor charged that the paper was obscene.

Friction between students in social organizations such as fraternities and those students who traditionally reject fraternity-sorority life increased.

JOHN THOMPSON

> While the Ottawa County police action may be unprecedented in Michigan, the feud between town and gown is traditional as is the friction between students associated with fraternities and those students highly critical of fraternity life.
>
> *The Interpreter,* December 11, 1968

. . . In our adolescence we live in another city, big, pristine, all stretched out for us. Here we search for Man, Woman, Table, Chair, and so on. How often we think we have found them, only to see that this one we have fastened on is not really Man, is not really immemorial Woman. That is not true chair nor this true table. But perhaps we do find them. . . . Perhaps we find the gods and goddesses and the wise one, the Sybil, as I found Dave Evans and my Bernice and found Mary Baloyan; and then, the next thing we know, from that city we are exiled, no sooner do we learn our way round in it than we are pushed out. Joe McGee! It took me two or three minutes to remember his name. He was a senior in high school when I was a sophomore. I think he hadn't much money, but he was desperately handsome, belonged to a classy club, and danced with all the most beautiful girls. One day, later on, by what chance I don't know, I was eavesdropping around the fringes of some talk he was having with his peers, in the drugstore or someplace. How well I knew what he meant when he said, "What am I doing? I'm savin' up my money to go back to high school." You see what happened to Joe McGee.

Others, as I said earlier, do not conduct this search for avatars, or do not find them, or cannot remember the images of infancy so as to know how to look for them — and these, as I have said, are the lords and owners of their faces. They conduct the governments of our cities, they solve the very real and unquestionably fascinating problems of water supply, sewage disposal, fire protection, law enforcement: never doubt that these affairs demand anything less than a very alert intelligence and a determination to finish a job, never doubt that it is worth a man's time to do them. More loftily, they meet payrolls, they buy and sell, they gamble in the great game of American capitalism, they propose and they dispose. This is the real city; gods do not haunt it and no one would look there for Man, for Woman, for Chair or Table.

I have described three cities, three levels of our Troy. But what have I said about the third city, the real city, the actual Grand Rapids, Michigan, where every living man has to get up the rent and bring home the bacon, where there are payrolls to be met and children to be fed and housed and hauled in station wagons to ski slopes, where fortunes and careers are to be made — where, for the citizens to contemplate if ever they go downtown, and for convention visitors to buy pictures of on colored postcards in the Pantlind lobby, there will be mounted an assemblage of sheet steel costing $100,000?

Neil Munro told me about this city. Of course I knew it was there but I didn't really know it until he told me. Neil is around thirty years old, very modern, editor and publisher of the new weekly, *The Interpreter,* and his Grand Rapids is not the Grand Rapids of the Depression, when there were no jobs, no money, no girls — when there was no Neil Munro either with whom to have a very long and very wet lunch. But then what? Neither of us can remember who it was that said America is the only country that went directly from barbarism to decadence without every passing through the stage of civilization.

John O'Hara, Neil says, is the only writer this city makes him think of. Nobody else says anything about this kind of town. Neil is right. John O'Hara's people live all of them haunted by nothing more than the ghost of their first love affair. After that there is no place to go, and the work and the banks offer them nothing but a flat success and, rolling in money, they don't know what is wrong. And yet we still think of the American Midwest as though it were Winesburg, Ohio. In my day, or perhaps it was really only in my own sunken place, my dullness or inactivity, my dejection, my depression — in my own city, yes, there were the lovelorn, the mute, the unequipped, the unsponsored, and the uninstructed, the frightened, a young man could hardly get laid, the girls were all married or crazy virgins who went to church. Now it's like everyplace else.

We interrupt ourselves, Neil and I, and we remark how the Grand River is about the size of the Arno, that the wealth of Florence under Lorenzo de Medici and of Grand Rapids under — but we no longer have our old city boss, Frank McKay — under whatever constellation rules it now, are not dissimilar. This is not a happy thought and we look around the dark restaurant, packed with steak eaters and bourbon drinkers and gin drinkers and think for a moment about Florence, of frescoes and bell towers and bronzes. Well, why not? Why not indeed. It is enough to make you want another martini. . . . But at least it is no longer Winesburg, Ohio. . . .

This third of my cities, the real Grand Rapids, with its pavements and payrolls and sewers and school bills, its money and its jobs, its money, this city will never be real to anyone who has even the vestigial ghost of a memory of having once inhabited that first city of childhood. A city begins in dreams, or, in order that I should not sound too much like those brochures on the charms of Grand Rapids, it begins in nightmares, which are the same thing. Dreams, nightmares, they are built of the past but they are about the future. If the real city denies these, then it is not real.

Was it a good hometown? Was it? I would not have thought to say so before I began writing this, but yes, it was. I think it is a better town for Reggie Gatling's boys than it ever was for me, though. They will succeed, no doubt in ways they don't expect, but I never really tried. I thought it should be some kind of Florence, some kind of Athens, some kind of city connected with my mother's face and with Dave Evans's bitter sense of justice and with Mary Baloyan's passionate conviction that expression must be true, but I couldn't think of anything to do about it.

I don't care now, and I am surprised, really, that I can remember so much. Most of your people, Grand Rapids, are less frightened, from day to day, than most people in most places or most times have been. They are not threatened by starvation nor by whips nor by enemy swords, as most of mankind has always been threatened. If they have the supreme threat of hydrogen dissolution hanging over their heads day and night, hanging by a hair plucked from the head of Richard M. Nixon, well, we all live with this (how do we?) and who is to say that this is your fault, or who is to say that anyone knows better than you what to do about it? You are not deliberately cruel, except to yourself, as you say over and over again, "I must be ignorant, I must not aspire, I must not cast doubt, I must bring home the bacon." And yet you know as well as I do what was said in that little volume which has been one of my favorite books for as long as I have been able to read, the one from which I cribbed the title for this procession of dim reveries. In its narrow green cover it stood between the bookends under the tasseled lamp of our "library table" on Glenwood Avenue, *The Yesterdays of Grand Rapids.* Its author, Captain Charles E. Belknap, still poses in his bronze Boy Scout uniform with his bronze moustache in the little park named for him at the fork of Fulton and Lake Drive. He was a wonderful writer gifted in natural comedy and thus he was unafraid to know tragedy when he saw it:

"Although Grand Rapids was a good-sized town when I came here, the islands were still in the river. . . . I was somewhat older before I really appreciated the great sycamores at the water's edge, the island plateau of giant water elms, the almost tropical mass of grape vine that festooned the trees, and in every depression the wild plum and crabapple that crowded the elder bushes and sumac. . . . But even then the three islands were almost without a blemish. Indians never built a fire at the foot of a tree and the high water that flooded the islands each year washed them free of all refuse of their camps. The heavy covering of grass and plants prevented washing of the soil. The prevailing west winds wafted the odors of trees and flowers over the village.

"May not an old man of today be forgiven for a longing that this beautiful playground of his boyhood might have been spared for his great-grand-children? Only men of deep thinking can tell you how long nature was in creating these islands, but any schoolboy with a piece of chalk can figure how long man was in obliterating the last trace of them."

Those islands in his dream city had actually existed, rooted in earth and watered by our river and flowering magnificently in the bright real air as well as in his dreams, but we know what he was talking about. He was talking about the city we have all destroyed, cowards, dirty cowards, our hometown of justice and truth where I was born in Grand Rapids.

Technicolor Paddy

Roger Wilkins

Roger Wilkins was born in 1932 in Kansas City into a family legacy that is legendary in the civil rights movement. His father, Earl Wilkins, was, until his death from tuberculosis when Roger was not yet nine years old, the business manager of the prominent African-American newspaper *The Kansas City Call.* After the family was in New York for about three years, his mother, Helen, a well-educated and dynamic professional woman, married Grand Rapids physician Robert Claytor. She played a key role in desegregating the YWCA and was a prominent citizen of Grand Rapids for over sixty years (1943-2005). His uncle, Roy Wilkins, was the longtime Executive Secretary of the national NAACP (1955-1977). Wilkins himself grew up to be Assistant Attorney General of the United States in the Johnson administration, a Pulitzer Prize–winning columnist for *The Washington Post, The New York Times, The Washington Star,* as well as National Public Radio, and an outspoken advocate for civil rights of all kinds.

After graduating as president of the student council at Creston High School, Wilkins completed his B.A. and J.D. degrees at the University of Michigan, interning with Thurgood Marshall at the NAACP's Legal Defense Fund. Already in his early thirties, Wilkins was Special Assistant to the administrator of the Agency for International Development (AID), Assistant Director of the U.S. Community Relations Service (1964-1966), and Assistant Attorney General of the United States (1966-1969). After leaving the federal government at the end of the Johnson administration, and after a brief stint at the Ford Foundation, Wilkins joined the editorial staff of *The Washington Post,* where he is perhaps best known for his role as one of the journalists to expose the Watergate scandal. Along with Carl Bernstein, Bob Woodward, and Herbert Block, he earned a Pulitzer Prize. He later was a columnist for *The New York Times,* where he also served as the first African-American on its editorial board.

Wilkins's books include *Jefferson's Pillow* (2001) and *A Man's Life* (1982), from which the following segment has been excerpted. He is also the publisher of *Crisis,* the journal of the NAACP. Wilkins is currently the Clarence J. Robinson Professor of History and American Culture Emeritus at George Mason University and a network radio commentator for NPR.

Some time early in 1943 [my mother's] work with the YWCA took her to Grand Rapids, Michigan, where she made a speech and met a forty-four-year-old bachelor doctor who looked like a white man. He had light skin, green eyes, and "good hair" — that is, hair that was as straight and as flat as white people's hair. He looked so like a white person that he could have passed for white. There was much talk about people who had passed. They were generally deemed to be bad people, for they were not simply selfish, but also cruel to those whom they left behind. People who could pass but did not, on the other hand, were respected.

She saw this doctor again in the spring and they exchanged visits in the summer. By the time he came to New York, I knew that he was important to my mother and to all of us. He and my mother were married in October 1943, when I was eleven years old. My father had been dead two and a half years. . . .

I was once more on a train with my grandmother, heading toward Grand Rapids and my new home. . . . We left New York on the New York Central's Wolverine, which we boarded at the 125th Street station, after it had come out of a hole in the ground at 96th Street and Park Avenue. As the train moved slowly north, across the river at 138th and then smoothly up through the Bronx, I could look back across the Harlem River, up over the Polo Grounds up there on the bluff for what was perhaps the last time and see the great high, light-sand-colored hulk that was 555 Edgecombe Avenue. And as it faded out of sight and later became fuzzier in my mind farther and farther back down the Hudson Valley, the tension in my stomach began to ease. There was anxiety about the unknown, to be sure, but the terror I had gathered in the Harlem streets over the past three years began to subside.

The train went on up the Hudson to Albany, then over to Buffalo, then across the dull Canadian plain to Windsor, then under the river to Detroit. As I sat on that train, staring out the window hour after endless hour, sitting next to my grandmother, I felt glad that Harlem was behind me. But my relief had been purchased at a real and quite substantial cost. Though I was not again to know such terror, I had also, at the age of twelve, moved beyond the last point in my life when I would feel totally at peace with my blackness.

When we reached Grand Rapids, my mother who had preceded us by a month to set up housekeeping, and my stepfather — whom I, with my mother's help, had decided to call Pop, in distinction to Daddy, whose place could never be taken — met us at the station.

To me, my Pop's car was quite grand. It was a dark-green 1941 Chrysler Royal four-door sedan. The grillwork looked like two sets of matching swords laid end to end coming to a point where the tips touched. Though it was 1944 and the car was three years old, it was one of the last generation of cars produced before Detroit went to war. Though the car was a good omen, I felt the tension flowing certainly and swiftly back into my stomach as Pop swung the car out of the station lot and headed toward my new home.

I didn't know what Grand Rapids was. A tiny sliver of Manhattan had become my reality, and I could not imagine a life without dilapidated buildings and the hard, black youths who lived in them. As we drove through the seedy blocks surrounding the Grand Rapids railroad terminal, my terror returned once more.

But then we drove past that into the city's squatty little downtown and on beyond that to my new home in the north end of Grand Rapids, a neighborhood every bit as white as the Minneapolis one in which my mother had lived as a twelve-year-old a quarter of a century before. This would be the place I would henceforth think of as home. And it would be the place where I would become more Midwesterner than Harlemite, more American than black, and more complex than was comfortable or necessary for the middle-class conformity that my mother had in mind for me.

The driveway ran all the way down the right side of the property as you faced it from the street. The lot was about 150 feet deep and 50 feet wide. There was a backyard with grass, and near the alley there was a two-car garage and a little storage shed just behind that. It was very different from New York, but not totally alien, because there were faint echoes of Kansas City — except that all the people you could see wherever you looked were white. That was different from any place I had ever been in.

When we got out of the car, I saw a bicycle leaning up next to the house. It had a big maroon-colored frame, skinny wheels and a seat with a shaggy sheepskin cover, not the popular balloon-tired type. I looked at Pop and he smiled and nodded. He had gotten it for me, because he knew I couldn't ride in New York where the traffic made it risky. The bike was out of step, like him and me. I had a new home, a strange bike and a different father. . . .

Robert [Claytor] was not used to having a boy around the house, and certainly not a middle-class city boy whose life had mainly been spent under the direction and comfort of a number of female relatives. Nevertheless, he tried to be fatherly. One day he came home with a new baseball glove and a ball. But it wasn't a big brown Rawlings glove with the kind of pocket I could grease lovingly for hours. It was a small puffy gray thing with no discernible pocket at all. I was polite and tried unsuccessfully to be enthusiastic as we played a pitiful game of catch along the driveway in back of the house. He threw in a stiff, almost formal way and I kept dropping the ball because that mitt wasn't made for catching. We never played catch again.

From time to time on Sunday he'd take me over to Valley Field — the best baseball park in Grand Rapids — to see the local black semi-pro team play. Ted Raspberry was the organizer and the entrepreneur of the enterprise. Mr. Raspberry was a jolly dark man who smiled a lot and had gold teeth in his mouth. Raspberry's team was pretty good and generally won. The infield chatter was sheer ecstasy.

"Come *on* baby, bump it past this motha!"

"At's okay, baby, this cat's momma didn't give him no eyes."

And after a pitcher had slipped a third strike past a batter:

"Way to go baby, you humpin' better than you did last night!"

After the games people would come up to Pop and say, "Hiya Doctor, how you doin'?" "Glad to see you out today, Doctor." "That your boy there, Doctor? Yea? Well, he's a fine-looking boy."

Pop knew I liked those games, so he took me out as often as he could.

And he was always generous and thoughtful. Because, though he didn't know just what kind of glove to buy or what sort of bike I wanted, his groping to please me all signaled a life that was very different from any I had ever known before.

Grand Rapids was pretty single-family houses and green spaces. The houses looked like those in *Look* magazine or in *Life.* You could believe, and I did, that there was happiness inside. To me back then, the people seemed to belong to the houses as the houses belonged to the land, and all of it had to do with being white. They moved and walked and talked as if the place, the country and the houses were theirs, and I envied them.

When we were settled and I could ride, I rode my bike east out along Knapp Street, past [Fuller], past the cemetery and into the country, and I rode west, down Monroe and over the Ann Street Bridge over the Grand River and into the west side. The neighborhood was different there. It was a mixture of older houses and industrial buildings. The lawns were smaller over there, and the paint was peeling on some of the houses, and on some of the others it was worn away altogether. Those were the wind-beaten gray houses with the spot-sized yards that were all brown and rock hard, beaten by large feet and small into brown ugly places where broken tricycles and half-gutted Teddy bears were strewn about. The people who lived in those houses on the west side of the river were called Polacks, and they went to Union High School and played fantastic football.

One day, I rode north. By now I was gaining confidence. I knew I could find my way home and I began to think about things other than landmarks as I rode. I began, for instance, to look at the people I would pass, and they would look back at me with intense and sometimes puzzled looks on their faces as I pedaled by. Nobody waved or even smiled. They just stopped what they were doing to stand and look. As soon as I saw them looking, I would look forward and keep on riding.

I explored the north for several days. Finally, well into my second week in town, I headed south. I rode down Plainfield Avenue for a few blocks, past Creston High School where I would be enrolled in September, past Creston Heights, a few blocks on — our neighborhood shopping center, where the local branch of the Old Kent Bank was located, and then on south for miles. Grand Rapids was mainly south of where we lived, and this day I was going to find it.

I rode for miles, down and up and down again, until Plainfield changed into Division Avenue and I was again in Grand Rapids' squatty little downtown. And I rode on past the Division movie theater and farther south until I began to see some Negro people.

I had long passed downtown and its large stores and I was now in an area where there were small commercial buildings, warehouses, small, flat factories and second-rate store fronts with people living in the rooms upstairs. Down the side streets, there were big old run-down houses and people walking around or sitting on the stoops. There were black men and women and some girls, but it was the boys I was looking for. Then I saw a group: four of them.

They were about my age, and they were dark. They were walking toward me on the sidewalk on the side of the street where I was riding. Though their clothes were not as sharp as the boys' in the Harlem Valley, they were old, and I took the look of poverty and the deep darkness of their faces to mean that they were like the hard boys of Harlem.

One of them spotted me riding toward them and pointed. "Hey, lookit that bigole skinny bike," he said. Then they all looked at my bike and at me. I couldn't see expressions on their faces; only the blackness and the coarseness of their clothes. Before any of the rest of them had a chance to say anything, I stood up on the pedals and wheeled the bike in a U-turn and headed back on up toward the north end of town. It took miles for the terror to finally subside. Harlem had really put white fear into me.

Farther on toward home, there was a large athletic field that was ringed by a quarter-mile track and had a gridiron laid out end to end and a baseball diamond too. As I neared the field, I could see some large boys in shorts moving determinedly around a football. When I got to the top of the hill that overlooked the field, I stopped and stood, one foot on the ground and one leg hanging over the crossbar, staring down at them. All of the boys were white and big and old — sixteen to eighteen. They were wearing football cleats and shorts, and some of them wore tee shirts that said "Creston Polar Bears." They would assemble, bend over, then run very hard in the same direction. Sometimes they would throw the ball and they had the biggest thighs I had ever seen. I had never seen a football workout before, and I was fascinated. I completely forgot everything about color, theirs or mine.

Then one of them saw me. He pointed and said, "Look, there's a little coon watching us."

I wanted to be invisible. I was horrified. My heart pounded, and my arms and my legs shook, but I managed to get back on my bike and ride home.

When I came home my grandmother asked if I had had a good time and I said, "Yes." She asked me what I had done, and I said, "Rode my bike around some." She asked me if I had made any new friends and I said, "No."

"You will," she said. "It just takes time." Then she went back to her cooking and I went on upstairs and lay across my bed.

But it wasn't many days later that I was on my bike, standing still next to the curb sitting on the saddle and watching some boys playing on a playground not far from my house when somebody came up from behind me and said, "Hi." I looked around and saw a blond boy with blue eyes. He was sitting on a bike smiling at me. He spoke again. "My name's Jerry," he said. "Jerry Schild. What's yours?"

We shook hands, rode down to the river together, and began to talk a little.

"I know what house you live in," he said, "because I deliver your paper. Everybody in the neighborhood knows about your family moving in. There was a lot of talk. And I've seen you around, on your bike. I never saw you talking to anybody and you're new, so I thought I'd talk to you."

I didn't know what to say for a minute, so I kept throwing stones at things in the river. Then I said very carefully, "Yea. When you're new, there's nobody to talk to at first." He looked thoughtful for a little while and finally he brightened and said, "Say, why don't we take a tour of some of my favorite places around here. Places I bet you've never seen." We mounted our bikes and took off down the street. It was the happiest day I had had in years.

That night at dinner, I suppose I talked more than I had at any time since we moved to Michigan. I told my family everything I knew about Jerry and about where we had been and where we would go the next day. My mother remembered paying him for the paper a few times and remarked on what a polite, efficient person he seemed to be.

Then I told them that Jerry had said that everyone in the neighborhood knew where we lived and had talked about it. My stepfather gave my mother an imperceptible nod and then she said: "You know how we've told you about the neighbors getting upset Poppa bought the house we lived in on South Franklin. Well, it was pretty much the same here. When Pop bought the house here, the seller didn't know he was a Negro. Your Pop didn't say whether he was or he wasn't and the man didn't ask."

I glanced at my stepfather, whose green eyes were glinting amusement and then turned back to my mother. "Well, at some point they found out that he was a Negro and the neighbors started to have meetings about our moving into the neighborhood. There was even some talk about burning a cross or something, but everybody thought that was crazy except the wild man who suggested it. And so they decided that the thing to do was to try to buy the house back and they tried. But Pop told them that he had bought a house for his family and he needed it and he didn't intend to sell it. They told him that he would be happier with 'his own people across town,' but he told them that he hadn't found a house across town good enough for his family and that he assumed that the people around here were Americans and that those were 'his own people' so he didn't feel uncomfortable. They tried a couple more conversations, but then they gave up. They all seem pretty reconciled to it now except Mr. Stuits across the lot. But he doesn't do anything but bang his lawnmower into the fence. And since it's his fence that's fine with me."

That night I thought about Stuits and the other people on the block. Our house was just about the biggest in the neighborhood, and we had a nicer car than anybody on the block. I was pretty sure that none of the other men was a doctor and that the women probably hadn't even gone to college, much less been Phi Beta Kappa. And, though that bit of social calculus was somewhat comforting, when it was all done, the other people were still white and I was still a Negro. There was no getting around it.

Jerry was true to his word. The next day at midmorning, he rode up and we took off on our bikes on another day of exploration of all the wonders the north end of Grand Rapids held for a couple of twelve-year-olds. When it was time for lunch, Jerry led me to the sparsely stocked store in the large ramshackle building two blocks from my house. "Why're we going here?" I asked. "To get something to eat," he replied. "My folks run this store. My mom mainly. And we live upstairs."

I didn't say anything. I just laid my bike against the front of the building and followed him into the store. His mother, a large pleasant woman, greeted us warmly and gave us Spam sandwiches with mayonnaise for lunch. Afterward, Jerry took me around the back and up the outside stairway that led to the living quarters above. I met his three younger siblings, including a very little one toddling around in bare feet and a soiled diaper.

While Jerry changed the baby, I looked around the place. It was cheap, all chintz and linoleum. The two soft pieces of furniture, a couch and an overstuffed chair, had gaping holes and were hemorrhaging their fillings. And there were an awful lot of empty brown beer bottles sitting around, both in the kitchen and out on the back porch. While the place was not dirty, it made me very sad. Jerry and his family were poor in a way I had never seen people be poor before, in Kansas City or even in Harlem. But, if Jerry minded, he didn't let on and, of course, neither did I.

Jerry's father wasn't there that day, and Jerry didn't mention him. But later in the week, when I went to call for Jerry, I saw him. I yelled for Jerry from downstairs in the back, and his father came to the railing of the porch on the second floor. He was a skinny man in overalls with the bib hanging down crookedly because it was fastened only on the shoulder. His face was narrow and wrinkled and his eyes were set deep in dark hollows. He had a beer bottle in his hand and he looked down at me. "Jerry ain't here," he said. He turned away and went back inside.

But if I didn't find him that time, it was one of the few times during those weeks when I didn't. We filled up our time together. I even got up at dawn sometimes to help him with his weekly collections. I would get a little pocket money and a lot of company.

Then one day our front doorbell rang and I could hear my mother's troubled exclamation, "Jerry! What's wrong?" Jerry was crying so hard he could hardly talk. "My father says I can't play with you anymore because you're not good enough for us."

My mother looked at both of us in horror, then she attempted to comfort Jerry by saying soft soothing things. When the worst of his sobbing finally eased off, she brought him a warm washcloth so he could wash off his face. "It's not fair," Jerry said. And my mother agreed that it was not fair and that it wasn't right either, but she told Jerry that she didn't see how she could tell him to disobey his father. Then she suggested that maybe if Jerry let a little time pass and then talked it over with his father again, he might come to a different conclusion. Jerry said no, he didn't think so and that she didn't know his father. My mother has a very sweet face, and sometimes an almost beatific smile, but at that moment, I saw her smile tighten into pure steel. "Oh yes," she said gently to Jerry, "I know your father all too well."

And Jerry didn't talk about it again to his father as far as I know. He'd just sneak and see me and hope the old man wouldn't find out. But it was different. And school was about to start.

Creston High School was about a mile away, and served all the children from the north end of Grand Rapids from the seventh grade up. It was all white and middle-class. Nobody talked to me that first day, but I was noticed. When I left school at the end of the day I found my bike leaning up against the fence where I had left it with a huge glob of slimy spit on my shaggy saddle cover. People passed by on their way home and looked at me and the spit. I felt a hollowness behind my eyes, but I didn't cry. I just got on the bike, stood up on the pedals, and rode it home without sitting down. And it went that way for about the first two weeks. After the third day, I got rid of the saddle cover because the plain leather was a lot easier to clean. Sometimes when I was riding home, standing up, people would yell, "Nigger, why don't you go back where you came from." And that's about all they did, except for one day when some large boys threw apple cores and stones at me.

Roger Wilkins attended Grand Rapids Creston High School and was elected president of the student council in 1949.
GRPL, Library Photo Collection

But even then, the glacier was beginning to thaw. One day I was sitting in class and the freckle-faced kid with the crew cut sitting next to me was asking everybody for a pencil. And then he looked at me and said, "Maybe you can lend me one." Those were the best words I had heard since I first met Jerry. This kid had included me in the human race in front of everybody. His name was Jack Waltz.

And after a while, when the spitters had subsided and I could ride home sitting down, I began to notice that organized football practice was being held on the athletic field, and that little kids my size were playing in pickup games in the end zones. It looked interesting, but I didn't know anybody and didn't know how they would respond to me. So I just rode on by for a couple of weeks, slowing down each day, trying to screw up my courage to go in.

But then one day, I saw Jack Waltz there. I stood around the edges of the group, watching. It seemed that they played forever without even noticing me, but finally somebody had to go home and the sides were unbalanced. Somebody said, "Let's ask him." And they did and I accepted.

As we lined up for our first huddle, I heard somebody on the other side say, "I hope he doesn't have a knife." One of the guys on my side asked me, "Can you run the ball?" I said yes, so they gave me the ball and I ran three quarters of the length of the field for a touchdown. And I made other touchdowns and other long runs before the game was over. When I thought about it later that night, I became certain that part of my success was due to the imaginary knife that was running interference for me. But no matter. By the end of the game, I had a group of friends. Boys named Andy and Don and Bill and Gene and Rich. We left the field together, and some of them waved and yelled, "See ya tomorra, Rog."

And Don De Young, a pleasant round-faced boy, even lived quite near me. So, after parting from everybody else, he and I went on together down to the corner of Coit and Knapp. As we parted, he suggested that we meet to go to school together the next day. I had longed for that but I hadn't suggested it for fear of a rebuff for overstepping the limits of my race. I had already learned one of the great tenets of Negro survival in America: to live the reactive life. It was like the old Negro comedian who once said, "When the man asks how the weather is, I know nuff to look keerful at his face 'fore even I look out the window." So, I waited for him to suggest it, and my patience was rewarded. I was overjoyed and grateful. . . .

I didn't spend all my time in the North End. Soon after I moved to Grand Rapids, Pop introduced me to some patients he had with a son my age. The boy's name was Lloyd Brown, and his father was a bellman downtown at the Pantlind Hotel. Lloyd and I often rode bikes and played basketball in his backyard. His basketball wasn't like the ones up in the North End. Up there were orange hoops hung on garage backboards. Here the basket was made out of four pieces of wood like a wastebasket with no bottom and it was hung on a tree in the backyard. We didn't dribble on a smooth concrete or black-top garage entrance, but on the uneven dirt in the backyard.

After a while, my mother asked me why I never had Lloyd come out to visit me. It was a question I had dreaded, but she pressed on. "After all," she said, "you've had a lot of meals at his house and it's rude not to invite him back." I knew she was right and I also hated the whole idea of it. . . . I didn't share Lloyd's limitations. I looked at him and his life from the north end of Grand Rapids as if I were seeing him through a telescope turned backward. And though I could join him temporarily in that small place, I had escaped those constrictions peculiar to Negro people and I didn't want to be forced back on a permanent basis.

And I wasn't sure my escape was permanent. With my friends in the north, race was never mentioned. Ever. I carried my race around with me like an open basket of rotten eggs. I knew I could drop one at any moment and it would explode with a stench over everything. This was in the days when the movies either had no blacks at all or they featured rank stereotypes like Stepin Fetchit, and the popular magazines like *Life, Look,* the *Saturday Evening Post,* and *Colliers* carried no stories about Negroes, had no ads depicting Negroes and generally gave the impression that we did not exist in this society. I knew that my white friends, being well brought up, were just too polite to mention this disability that I had. And I was grateful to them, but terrified just the same that maybe someday one of them would have the bad taste to notice what I was.

It seemed to me that my tenuous purchase in this larger white world depended on the maintenance between me and my friends in the North End of our unspoken bargain to ignore my difference, my shame, and their embarrassment. If none of us had to deal with it, I thought, we could all handle it. My white friends behaved as if they perceived the bargain exactly as I did. It was a delicate equation, and I was terrified that Lloyd's presence in the North End would rip apart that balance. But my mother, either driven by manners or by a deep and subtle understanding of her son's psyche, seemed determined to press the issue. . . .

I am so ashamed of that shame now that I cringe when I write it. But I understand that boy now as he could not understand himself then. I was an American boy, though I did not fully comprehend that either. I was fully shaped and formed by America, and America was both powerful and racist. White people had all the power in sight, and they owned everything in sight except our house. Their beauty was the real beauty; there wasn't any other beauty. A real human being had straight hair, a white face and thin lips. Other people, who looked different, were lesser beings.

No wonder, then, that most black men desired the forbidden fruit of white loins. No wonder, too, that we thought that the most beautiful and worthy Negro people were those who looked most white. We blacks used to have a saying: "If you're white, you're all right. If you're brown, stick around. If you're black, stand back." I was brown. . . .

America told us that we were inferior, and most of us believed it. I had never had to confront much of that in segregated Kansas City or in Harlem. I was color-conscious, of course. It was in the air, and I absorbed it like oxygen. But until I lived in Grand Rapids among all those white people I had never been forced to confront the enormity of the inferiority that America had slammed into my soul, and despite the fierce pride as human beings my family had, I couldn't help but accept it. . . .

So, I was ashamed. I was ashamed of myself, my whole being. I was ashamed of my color, my kinky hair, my broad nose and my thick lips. I didn't look like my friends, and I didn't have their heritage. Parents didn't tell Negro children in those days of the heroism, intelligence and courage that it took for their slave ancestors to survive during that brutal time. "We didn't like to clank our chains," as my mother once said to me. And what we knew of Africa came from Tarzan movies and the story "Little Black Sambo." So, living in Grand Rapids, when I was a teenager, was like having been born with one eye in the middle of my forehead. . . .

It was not that we in my family were direct victims of racism. On the contrary, my stepfather clearly had a higher income than the parents of most students in my high school. Unlike those of most of my contemporaries, black and white, my parents had college degrees. Within Grand Rapids' tiny Negro community, they were among the elite. The others were the lawyer, the undertaker, and the other doctor.

But that is what made race such exquisite agony. I knew that other blacks were targets of harsh job and housing discrimination; but, though being a Negro did pose some inconvenience for us, those major life-numbing blockbusters were not present in our daily lives. I did have a sense that it was unfair for poor Negroes to be relegated to bad jobs — if they had jobs at all — and to bad or miserable housing, but I didn't feel any great sense of identity with them. After all, the poor blacks in New York had also been the hard ones; the ones who tried to take my money, to beat me up, and to keep me perpetually intimidated. Besides, I had heard it intimated around my house that their behavior, sexual and otherwise, left a good deal to be desired.

So I thought that maybe they just weren't ready for this society, but that I was. And it was dreadfully unfair for white people to just look at my face and lips and hair and decide that I was inferior. In high school, I thought I was doing my bit for the race when I served as student council president. By being a model student and leader, I thought I was demonstrating how well Negroes could perform if only the handicaps were removed and they were given a chance. But deep down I guess I was also trying to demonstrate that I was not like those other people; that I was different. My message was quite clear: I was *not nigger.* But the world didn't seem quite ready to make such fine distinctions, and it was precisely that fact — though at the time I could scarcely even have admitted it to myself — that was the nub of the race issue for me. . . .

One Saturday evening after one of our sandlot games, when Creston wasn't playing at Houseman Field, I went over to Lloyd's. Lloyd's sister Bobby and all the rest were there. I had hurt my leg making a touchdown so I limped a little and talked a lot.

Somewhere around the third elaboration of the story, Lloyd said mildly that he'd like to come up and play some Saturday. I kept on talking, but all the time my mind was repeating, Lloyd wants to play. He wants to come up to the North End on Saturday. Next Saturday. Next Saturday. I was trapped.

So, after the final story about the final lunge, when I couldn't put it off any longer, I said, "Sure. Why not?" But, later in the evening, after I had had some time to think, I got Lloyd alone. "Say, look," I said. "Those teams are kinda close, ya know. I mean, we don't switch around. From team to team. Or new guys, ya know?"

Lloyd nodded, but he was getting a funny look on his face — part unbelieving and part hurt. So I quickly interjected before he could say anything, "Naw, man. Naw. Not like you shouldn't come and play. Just that we gotta have some good reason for you to play on our team, you dig?"

"Yeah," Lloyd said, his face still puzzled, but no longer hurt.

"Hey, I know," I said. "I got it. We'll say you're my cousin. If you're my cousin, see, then you gotta play. Nobody can say you can't be on my team, because you're family, right?"

"Oh, right. Okay," Lloyd said, his face brightening. "Sure, we'll say we're cousins. Solid."

I felt relieved as well. I could have a Negro cousin. It wasn't voluntary. It wouldn't be as if I had gone out and made a Negro friend deliberately. A person couldn't help who his cousins were. . . .

I would sometimes lie on my back and stare up at passing clouds and wonder why God had played such a dirty trick by making me a Negro. It all seemed so random. So unfair to me. To *me!* But I never doubted the goodness of America. It was better to be American, even a Negro American, than anything else. And segregation was so stupid, its proponents so ignorant and the surge of good in the world so powerful, that things would have to change. The future belonged to America and to all of us who lived in it, including me.

But still, I wasn't white in the pervasive whiteness of my wonderful country. The mayor and the senators and all the other important people were white. And all the big kids and important athletic heroes and all the pretty girls in my school were white.

In school I was gaining more friends, and the teachers respected me. It got so that I could go for days not thinking very much about being Negro until something made the problem unavoidable.

One day in history class, for instance, the teacher asked each of us to stand and tell in turn where our families had originated. Many of the kids in the class were Dutch with names like Vander Jagt, De Young, and Ripstra. My pal Andy was Scots-Irish. When it came my turn, I stood up and burned with shame, and when I could speak, I lied. And then I was even more ashamed because I exposed a deeper shame. "Some of my family was English," I said — Wilkins is an English name — "and the rest of it came from . . . Egypt." Egypt! Well, it was in Africa, but only barely. . . .

There began to be a cultural difference between me and other blacks my age, too. Black street language had evolved since my Harlem days, and I had not kept pace. Customs, attitudes, and the other common social currencies of everyday black life had evolved away from me. I didn't know how to talk, to banter, to move my body. If I was tentative and reactive in the North End, where I lived, I was tense, stiff, and awkward when I was with my black contemporaries. One day I was standing outside the church trying, probably at my mother's urging, to make contact. Conversational sallies flew around me while I stood there stiff and mute, unable to participate. Because the language was so foreign to me, I understood little of what was being said, but I did know that the word used for a white was *paddy.* Then a boy named Nickerson, the one whom my mother particularly wanted me to be friends with, inclined his head slightly toward me and said, to whoops of laughter, "technicolor paddy." My feet felt rooted in stone, and my head was aflame. I never forgot that phrase.

I have rarely felt so alone as I did that day riding home from church. Already partly excluded by my white friends, I was now almost completely alienated from my own people as well. But I felt less uncomfortable and less vulnerable in the white part of town. It was familiar enough to enable me to ward off most unpleasantness. . . .

And then there was the problem with girls. In the early days in Grand Rapids, my mother had a woman come in once a week to do the washing and the heavy cleaning. She was a scrawny white woman with lank brown hair, dead blue eyes and the drawn and wrinkled skin that in later years I came to associate with excessive use of both alcohol and cigarettes. Her name was MacEarlin and she came from a poorer part of the North End about seven blocks away from our house.

I didn't like Mrs. MacEarlin, because most of her teeth were gone and her gummy mouth looked horrible, but my mother said she was a good worker. The first-baseman on our high-school baseball team lived near Mr. MacEarlin in one of those faded-out frame houses in that end of town and he had a pretty sister named Shirley. She was a grade ahead of me and had olive skin and a rich deep body.

One day I came home after school and my mother told me that Shirley had been talking to Mrs. MacEarlin about me. My breath got short and I asked her what Shirley had said.

"She told Mrs. MacEarlin that she liked you," my mother said.

"Yeah. Really, did she say that? Really?" I asked.

"Yes," my mother said. "She said she liked you because you know your place."

I didn't say anything and my mother looked at me, waiting. Then she said, "Isn't that funny? She likes you because you know your place. Can you imagine that?"

"Yeah, that's pretty funny," I said, but I didn't forget that girl's big gaunt colorless house, the deep eyewells framing the rich brown eyes or the way I first felt when I found out how she thought about me. . . .

They were everywhere, the girls. They all had budding bosoms, they all smelled pink, they all brushed against the boys in the hall, they were all white, and, in 1947-49, they were all inaccessible.

There were some things you knew without ever knowing how you knew them. You knew that Mississippi was evil and dangerous, that New York was east and the Pacific Ocean was west. And in the same way you knew that white women were the most desirable and dangerous objects in the world. Blacks were lynched in Mississippi and such places sometimes just for looking with the wrong expression at white women. Blacks of a very young age knew that white women of any quality went with the power and style that went with the governance of America — though, God knows, we had so much self-hate that when a white woman went with a Negro man, we promptly decided that she was trash, and we also figured that if she would go with him she would go with any Negro.

Nevertheless, as my groin throbbed at fifteen and sixteen and seventeen, *they* were the only ones there. One of them would be in the hallway opening her locker next to mine. Her blue sweater sleeve would be pushed up to just below the elbow, and as she would reach high on a shelf to stash away a book, I would see the tender dark hair against the white skin of her forearm. And I would ache and want to touch that arm and follow that body hair to its source.

Some of my friends, of course, did touch some of those girls. My friends and I would talk about athletics and school and their loves. But they wouldn't say a word about the dances and the hayrides they went to.

I perceived they liked me and accepted me as long as I moved aside when life's currents took them to where I wasn't supposed to be. I fit into their ways when they talked about girls, even their personal girls. And, indeed, I fit into the girls' lives when they were talking about boys, most particularly, their own personal boys. Because I was a boy, I had insight. But I was also Negro, and therefore a neuter. So a girl who was alive and sensuous night after night in my fantasies would come to me earnestly in the day and talk about Rich or Gene or Andy. She would ask what he thought about her, whether he liked to dance, whether, if she invited him to her house for a party, he would come. She would tell me her fears and her yearnings, never dreaming for an instant that I had yearnings too and that she was their object. . . .

The yearning for a girl, however, was not susceptible to evasive strategies. There may be few more powerful obsessions than a teenage boy's fixation on a love object. In my case it came down to a thin brunette named Marge McDowell. She was half a grade behind me, and she lived in a small house on a hill. I found excuses to drive by it all the time. I knew her schedule in school, so I could manage to be in most of the hallways she had to use going from class to class. We knew each other, and she had once confided a strong, but fleeting yearning for my friend Rich Kippen. I thought about her constantly, night, morning and afternoon.

Finally, late one afternoon after school, I came upon her alone in a hallway. "Marge," I blurted, "can I ask you something?"

She stopped and smiled and said, "Sure, Roger, what?"

"Well, I was wondering," I said. "I mean. Well, would you go to the hayride next week with me?"

Her jaw dropped and her eyes got huge. Then she uttered a little shriek and turned, hugging her books to her bosom the way girls do, and fled. I writhed with mortification in my bed that night and for many nights after.

The rest of my days in that high school were spent pretty much in that atmosphere. In my senior year, I was elected president of the Creston High School student council. It was a breakthrough of sorts.

Grand Raptures

Jim Harrison

Jim Harrison's latest novel, *Returning to Earth,* was published in early 2007. He is also the author of five volumes of novellas — *The Beast God Forgot to Invent, Legends of the Fall, The Woman Lit by Fireflies, Julip,* and *The Summer He Didn't Die* — as well as eight novels — *True North, The Road Home, A Good Day to Die, Farmer, Warlock, Sundog,* and *Dalva.* He has also published eight collections of poetry, including *Braided Creek,* a collaboration with former United States Poet Laureate Ted Kooser, *The Shape of the Journey,* and, most recently, *Saving Daylight.* He has three works of nonfiction out: the memoir *Off to the Side* and two essay collections, *Just Before Dark* and *The Raw and the Cooked: Adventures of a Roving Gourmand.*

Harrison is the winner of a National Endowment for the Arts grant, a Guggenheim Fellowship, and his work has been published in twenty-seven languages. *The New York Times Book Review* has said that his work is "a big, wet, sloppy kiss Harrison continues to plant on the face of life itself," and the *Dallas Morning News* has called him "one of our finest living writers."

Jim Harrison now divides his time between Montana and Arizona, but much of his fiction is set in northern Michigan — both the northern Lower Peninsula and the Upper Peninsula. He grew up in Reed City and Haslett, near Lansing, and he spent a month in Blodgett Hospital in Grand Rapids recovering from an accident that blinded him in one eye. He wrote the following memoir about that episode specifically for this book.

A serious eye injury brought Jim Harrison to Blodgett Hospital in Grand Rapids in 1944.
GRPL, Library Photo Collection

Permit me inaccuracies on this little voyage with no compass but memory. Naturally we remember what is memorable rather than the effluvium that covers us like lint and falls all too generously from the media heavens. In the Upper Peninsula years ago I showed a retired commercial fisherman a satellite photo of the Superior coastline from Munising to the Soo and he said, "They got it all wrong." He had spent fifty years on Lake Superior and was plainly not interested in a space vehicle's idea of his home water.

When I was growing up in Reed City in the 1940s, Grand Rapids was our capital city, perhaps partly because our daily paper was *The Grand Rapids Press* and it was the place to go to get work, or for major fun, or for a major illness or injury. The latter was my downfall when one spring afternoon towards the end of World War II, I was playing games with a girl in the woodlot behind the Reed City Hospital and she poked me in the left eye with a broken bottle for unclear reasons. My sight and a great deal of blood leaked out on my shirt.

Within an hour my parents took me off to Grand Rapids in hopes that a specialist, Dr. Dewar at Blodgett Hospital, could save my eye. I stayed there for nearly a month, and for the first ten days both eyes were kept covered, an ideal situation for fear to take residence. The most frightening thing of all was the sound of the horn of diesel trains which at that point hadn't made their way north to Reed City. I could only imagine an immense dragon wallowing its way up the Grand River which I had observed on the way into town. Another fear in the children's ward was a severely burned girl who made a lot of noise. In my darkness I could hear visitors praying for her. She didn't make it.

When my bandages were taken off the doctors were still not sure if my eye could be saved. One day I was visited by a salesman of glass eyes. Later in a poem I said,

> His case was full of fishy baubles
> against black velvet, jeweled gore.

I spent a great deal of time looking out the window and sixty years later I can feel a tremor when passing the Byzantine dome of the Greek Orthodox Church.

Finally I was released though I had to spend an extra week because the children's ward was quarantined. The Blodgett folks and good doctors saved my eye though it is basically sightless. It "jogs like a milky sparrow in its socket," I observed in another poem. We made a number of trips back to Grand Rapids to see Dr. Dewar, after which I got to eat a hamburger in a restaurant, a rare treat as we were a family of modest means, my dad being the agricultural agent for Osceola County, and there were eventually five children. When I heard at the time that our big, old house in Reed City had cost three thousand dollars I was stunned at the fortune life cost and my father's ability to support us.

The texture of the times somewhat mitigated the trauma of my injury. Our main family worry was whether my uncles, Walter and Arthur, from Paris, Michigan, would return from World War II. They did return, though in somewhat damaged shape, and helped my dad build a cabin (for nine hundred dollars) on Wells Lake near Leroy. This was a time when the world was truly imperiled and everyone in Reed City had to turn their lights out during air raid warnings and people kept track of their ration stamps.

In my teens my family moved south to Haslett near East Lansing and I recall when some members of our football team made a few ignoble trips to the brothels on Pearl Street. Of course I was only the designated driver.

Later on while living in Leelanau County I became fast friends with the famed bird hunter Nick Reens who grew up in Grand Rapids in a family of eight fine children. In thirty-five years of hunting together and exploring the taverns of the great north I was able to relive a childhood not my own by listening to Nick's stories.

I also met Dan Gerber Jr. at Michigan State all too long ago and we became lifetime friends. Back when we edited a literary periodical called *Sumac* in Fremont we were always inventing reasons to drive to Grand Rapids to visit Schuler's Bookstore and also get something good to eat. And I also clearly recall the cold foggy mornings we departed for New York City, England, Russia and Africa from the Grand Rapids airport.

I felt very good when my collected literary papers and manuscripts were purchased by Grand Valley State University through the Meijer Foundation. Part of the deal is that I'll spend a week every October at Grand Valley. In my off time I'll sit in the Kentucky Suite at the Amway Grand Plaza and look at the much-changed urban landscape I viewed sixty years before. I'll stare down at the Grand River and perhaps see a dragon swimming there or at least recapture the smell of the polished wood floors at Herpolsheimer's. I hope I won't smell the iodine in the halls of Blodgett Hospital. Hospitals don't smell like that anymore.

Being Rent in Twain

GLEN PETERSON

Glen Peterson was born and raised in Grand Rapids. After attending Christian schools, including Grand Rapids Christian High and Calvin College, in 1959 he moved to New York City and lived there for more than five years. He first worked for a church and community center in Harlem, then taught 6th grade at P.S. 144 Manhattan, and drove a taxicab. After that he traveled extensively in Europe and worked picking pears at Kibbutz G'vat in the Jezreel Valley in Israel. Back in the United States, Peterson became involved in the civil rights movement and participated in the march from Selma to Montgomery, Alabama.

Peterson returned to Grand Rapids to work for ten years in the marketing department of Eerdmans Publishing Company. In 1975 he went on to graduate school to complete a Ph.D. in clinical psychology, and subsequently established a private practice in Grand Rapids, doing individual therapy and marital therapy. He also started a consulting business in which he worked with more than a hundred law enforcement agencies to evaluate police officers for psychological suitability and fitness for duty. Peterson has done professional writing in police psychology and has made presentations at numerous conferences in that field.

Peterson is an opera enthusiast, traveling nationally and internationally in search of the opera experience, and he has volunteered extensively for local opera causes. He has lectured frequently on the subject of opera; he created the radio program "All About Opera," which ran for two years on a west Michigan classical music frequency; and he has made frequent public appearances as a board member of Opera Grand Rapids and as past president of Friends of the Opera. He wrote the piece that follows for this book.

Glen Peterson

A few years after the American Civil War, a sluggish coal-fired steamship — one of many — pushed off from Rotterdam with a full load of emigrants headed for the New World. Among the passengers was a handsome widow who stood at the rail with her fourteen-year-old son. They looked ahead, to the west, where the sun was not so much setting as simply disappearing into the gray sky and water. They looked behind, where the ship boiler's black clouds blurred the last visual memories of their known world.

Antonia DeKorne must have taken some comfort in knowing that she would be accepted into the small but growing Dutch settlement in western Michigan. But she probably also wondered on that trip how she would survive when they got there. On the other hand, her resourceful son, Boudewyn, was already surviving quite well. At fourteen he was an accomplished woodcarver, and on the voyage he used his time to finish carving an exquisitely detailed knife handle: it featured four delicate, twisted columns holding up a pedestal, on which stood a pair of yoked oxen — his memory of the Dutch landscape. The ship's captain offered to buy this unusual work of art, but Boudewyn wanted to keep it. Instead, he agreed to carve a duplicate for the captain, which he did before the ship reached New York.*

In the New World, Antonia met a widower in Zeeland, Michigan, and she remarried. Her son, Boudewyn DeKorne, eventually settled in the Grand Rapids area; he started up a furniture/woodcarving business, and he married Kate Roest. Those two were my Grandpa and Grandma DeKorne. They bought a house on Grove Street, where they raised their twelve children, of whom my mother, Bertha, was third from the youngest.

My Grandpa Peterson lived alone on Virginia Street, between Diamond and Eastern, and I never saw him without a shirt and tie, a suit and vest, and a watch fob decorously looped from his vest. He smoked eigh-

* The name of the "Antonia DeKorne Family" is on the American Immigrant Wall of Honor at Ellis Island. The knife handle is still in the possession of one of Boudewyn DeKorne's thirty-four grandchildren.

teen cigars every day, claiming that smoked meat lasted longer. He smoked his final cigar of the day in his upstairs bathroom, where he had placed a straight-backed chair under the light so that he could read his Bible every night before going to bed.

Grandpa Peterson had worked in the printing business. His son William was also in that business, working at the Dean Hicks Book Bindery, when he met Bertha DeKorne. Their courtship lasted seven years and included frequent outings to the Boat and Canoe Club on the Grand River in North Park. They took the Interurban Trolley to get there, and they placed a wind-up Victrola between them, in the center of my father's canoe, so that they could listen to music on the river. They were married at the very beginning of the Great Depression, the same year — 1929 — that Grandpa DeKorne died. Grandma DeKorne, who had continued to live alone in the house on Grove Street, grew older and deafer, and then she needed regular help. At the same time, my parents needed a bigger place to live, which they could not afford. So my mother and father came to raise their family in the same house where my mother was raised. I was the fourth and last child of William and Bertha Peterson, born the year our family moved into that home on Grove Street. I attended the Creston Christian Grade School on Leonard Street, east of Plainfield, the same school my mother had attended thirty-five years earlier.

That Grove Street house was the repository of a good number of DeKorne family memories. Grandpa's woodworking tools were scattered around our musty Michigan basement, and the attic had boxes of old photographs. A portrait of Antonia DeKorne hung on the wall in the living room. Even the barn held scraps of wood that Grandpa had begun to carve. Grandma died when I was eight, but up until that time — and often afterwards — the house was a gathering place for the DeKorne relatives. As they had prospered, most of them had moved out to better neighborhoods, but they would come to our house for coffee on Sundays after church. Balancing Grandma's china on their knees, they would nibble brown bread and windmill cookies and talk about the achievements of their children.

That house was in an old neighborhood of Grand Rapids that featured small hills, alleys, and uneven streets running at odd angles, which created backyards and vacant lots that were shortcuts to other parts of the Creston neighborhood. The railroad tracks and adjoining yard barns at the bottom of Grove Street Hill, just east of Taylor Avenue, were defining landmarks of my world. Slow-moving steam engines coughing up volcanoes of soot and embers and pulling empty boxcars were sources of creative play for the neighborhood kids. We could jump onto the steel ladders leading to the tops of the boxcars and ride until a responsible adult chased us off. We stuck pennies on the tracks with wads of spit and watched from a few inches away as freight trains pressed them into foreign medallions. The yard barns provided hiding places from imaginary railroad detectives.

It was a hard-working neighborhood. The fathers were gone a lot, working at low-paying jobs, and the mothers swallowed curses as soot from the trains descended on their Monday morning clotheslines. In one sense, the neighborhood was culturally diverse. Though there were neither African-Americans nor Jewish families, the second-generation immigrants of the Creston neighborhood were more diverse than the Dutch families of my Christian Reformed church, school, and extended family. This neighborhood was the source of an education that I would not get at church or school.

Even though my parents never socialized with the neighbors, neighborhood kids had no trouble blending in with each other. One neighbor was a former miner from West Virginia. He looked like Li'l Abner, and his wife looked like Daisy Mae; and they lived emotionally, waving around guns when they were mad at somebody. They had a fenced-in back yard, where the father stalked and beat his naked Dogpatch children with a leather razor strop. Blood seeped from the welts on their backs and legs. Their screams roused a neighborhood too afraid to intervene. There were also neighborhood boys who used guns to rob a store, and they went to prison. Jim, another neighbor, drove a stock car on summer Saturday nights at the Speedrome. For a short time there was a family of Latvian refugees who did not speak English. We also had a neighborhood bully named Zeke, and I still think about him with revenge in my heart.

The diversity of the Creston neighborhood was reflected in a variety of colorful shops that were a contrast to my monochromatic church and school. On the west side of Plainfield, just north of Grove Street, a lighted sign with one large "B" blinked "Bowling Billiards Beer." On hot summer evenings, I could stand just inside the back door of this marvelous place and watch the smoking, sweating pinsetters work those Brunswick pinsetting machines. Across Plainfield was a small shop that sold and traded new and used comic books. Bertha, the owner, had the same name as my mom, but this Bertha kept a gambling game board under the counter. Sometimes my hard-earned dimes would disappear quickly, even though I knew it was a sin to gamble. I committed a similar sin at the two pinball machines at the Choo-Choo Grill on Plainfield near Leonard. Playing a pinball machine was gambling.

Creston was an active neighborhood, and everything a family needed was within walking distance, including doctors and dentists, not to mention piano lessons from Miss Spoelstra. She had a large Victorian house on Plainfield across from Charlie Gierman's garage. On the way home from piano lessons I could treat myself to a jelly donut at the Betty Lou Bakery. On Saturdays we went to John Oosterhaven's meat market on Coit Avenue, where my dad always bought a chuck roast for Sunday dinner.

On autumn Saturday afternoons, our family would go to the Farmer's Market, which was north of Leonard between Front Street and the Grand River. There were several long aisles, and farmers sold not only produce but live chickens, geese, and rabbits. One time my dad bought a Flemish Giant rabbit, which later grew to huge proportions, and my sister entered it into a pet contest at Briggs Park.

For an evening's entertainment, if I had earned some money, I could join other neighborhood kids at the stainless steel Bastian-Blessing soda fountain at Hoxie's drugstore, on Plainfield and Caledonia, and order a "dead man's phosphate" — one shot of every flavor mixed with soda water. Or, if I had a lot of money, I could get a banana split. We would dip our straw wrappers into the whipped cream and blow the wrappers up to the tin ceiling, where they would stick. When my older sister started working at Louie's Ice Cream Shop across Plainfield, I would go there instead of Hoxie's. My sister was nicer to me than I ever was to her, and I could usually figure on getting an extra large amount of ice cream for my money.

Most of my memories are summer memories. We went swimming in the Briggs Park pool on Knapp Street, but there was too much chlorine in the water, and it was also so crowded that the best you could do was find a spot to stand in the water and hope some other kid didn't jump on you. So when we got a little older, we rode our bikes way out Plainfield past Three Mile Road to go swimming at either Softwater Lake or Lamberton Lake, both of which had public beaches. At Softwater there was a swing that you had to hold in one hand while climbing up some slippery wooden steps to a platform; from the platform you could swing out over the deep water and let go. Lamberton Lake had a high dive that was too high for me. But my friend Henry could go off that high dive and swim under water way out past the raft, where nobody could see him come up. He wanted people to wonder if he had drowned. Another friend, Clifford, always wore a funny porkpie hat, even while swimming. He could go off the high dive at Lamberton with a cigarette in his mouth. He had a way of holding it with his tongue and curling it back into his mouth without burning himself, so he could come up with his hat still on and puffing the cigarette. Even the adults who disapproved of children smoking had to acknowledge the genius of that. With such an achievement at the age of twelve, he must have become a famous adult.

The firemen at the original Engine House Number Five on the corner of Leonard and Monroe were always friendly to me, and, for a real treat, they even allowed me to slide down the fire pole a few times. Every summer that department would put on a demonstration of their skills. They would arrive with lights on and siren blaring, and they would park a ladder truck near Spencer and Plainfield. Then some firemen would jump out of an upstairs window of a building — into the net held up by the other firemen on the sidewalk. Then the guys with the net would walk away, and the firemen in the building would toss a dummy out of the window, which would crash to the street where the net had been, and the people who had not seen that joke the year before would scream — and then laugh.

Sometimes in the summer we would just watch people working. Off an alley called Grove Place there was an auto repair garage worked by two greasy mechanics, and they didn't mind having boys hang around and watch them work. Grant, the owner, frequently worked with a cigarette hanging out of his mouth, even as he cleaned carburetor parts in a porcelain pan of gasoline. Sometimes he would even douse the cigarette in the pan of gas — just to shock us. Grant's favorite toy was a large steam-powered tractor that he would fire up every spring and then clatter up and down the alleys. You only have to see something like that once, and you understand the basic principles of a reciprocating steam engine.

Several men of the Grove Street neighborhood had good mechanical skills. My dad had a machine repair shop in the barn behind our house. With a few tools and a simple instruction from him, such as, "Remove anything you can from this machine," my brothers and I received an education in how to fix things. Watching our neighbor Jim tune up his stock car also made the concepts of auto repair relatively simple. It was easy to see how shaving the heads on a V-8 increased compression. One of my older brothers bought a 1928 Chevrolet that had to be started with a crank. One day he decided he would rather have a convertible, so he and some friends cut off the top of the car with a hacksaw. But this created structural problems. The car had a rotting wood frame beneath the steel, and the sides and doors of the car sagged outward. He solved that problem simply by tying the sides together with a rope. My brothers always had interesting cars, which regularly needed fixing. One of them was a Nash, which apparently rested on coil springs, but without shock absorbers; even when it was parked, a slight wind would make that car rock like a cradle. There was also a getaway car with running boards and spare tires in wheel wells on the front fenders.

It was a short bike ride to the main city dump, which was just north of Ann Street, on the west bank of the Grand River (large sections of the dump were actually in the river). This was a great source of parts for making things. For example, starting out with an orange crate from Thiebout's grocery store and a plank from behind someone's barn, we could find wheels and axles in the dump and have the basic materials for making a soapbox racer (we called them "scrammies"). We learned how to wrap clothesline around a broomstick steering column, and run the cord through pulleys borrowed from my dad. Once I learned the hard way that a scrammy racing down Grove Street Hill also needed reliable brakes.

I was comfortable hanging around in the Creston neighborhood. In my memory, adults would patiently answer questions asked by a curious and impatient boy. The mechanic Grant was a good example of that practice. I watched him, and grew up wanting to be a mechanic. Another good example was Mr. Winter, who would, in his tiny, cramped shoe repair shop on Plainfield, answer questions about how and why things were done the way they were while he worked at his belt-driven lathe. The railroad men sitting in the small tower next to the train tracks on the corner of Leonard and Plainfield didn't mind if I climbed up the ladder and visited with them. They liked to talk about trains, and they didn't ever seem to be doing anything else. Whatever railroad workers did for work, these guys were not doing it. Sometimes they would give me a railroad flare, which I could save for the Fourth of July.

So I was educated by the Creston neighborhood. While the church and Christian school were laying a foundation of guilt and shame, the Creston neighborhood was slowly eroding the protective layers of Dutch Calvinism and exposing me to alleged evils that sometimes turned out to be rather banal. For example, I was content to play with my Catholic friend Butchie, who went to St. Alphonsus on Carrier Street. But the minister of our church condemned Catholics for worshiping idols and praying to Mary instead of to Jesus, as they were supposed to. I asked Butchie if she worshiped idols; she said she didn't, and I believed her.

In the competition between the teachings of the church and my experiences of the real world, the church didn't do very well. The church and Christian school sort of lost me with the Old Testament stories of God's wrath. God was always ticked off. And even when he was not angry with his chosen people, he was angry with someone else — always wanting the Israelites to kill off more Midianites or Amalekites or Philistines. It just seemed so unfair. We were taught the Bible story about a gang of boys who laughed at the prophet Elisha's bald head. That made Elisha mad, so he asked God to do something about it — and God did. God sent two she-bears out of the woods, and they killed forty-two of those boys. Now that was overkill.

I was usually respectful, but sometimes I participated in some very similar mockeries. For example, the crazy lady who lived on the corner of Page Street and Plainfield might have been a prophetess. And it probably was not nice of me and my friends to make a mockery of her — but I don't think I deserved to be rent in twain by a she-bear for it. In a moment of uncharacteristic assertiveness, I once got into an argument with a marginally competent Sunday school teacher about the injustice of it all. I wasn't much of an arguer, but I think maybe I was identifying with the underdog.

I was aware that my family was poor, because I could see the cars and houses and possessions of the other more upwardly mobile families from the church and Christian school. But I learned early about the advantages of being resourceful. At one point I came up with a novel idea: I took my wagon to the railroad tracks, where large lumps of coal had bounced off the coal cars. I loaded the coal lumps into my wagon, took them home, and put them down our coal chute. One day my mother saw me doing this work, and she stopped me. She said that we were not that poor — that I did not have to collect coal for our furnace. I became aware that my mother was embarrassed about our being poor. It was the first time that I thought about being poor as something to be embarrassed about. From then on, I only collected coal when my mother was gone — or not watching.

The church delivered a mixed message on the subject of poverty and riches. On the one hand, the minister seemed to glorify poverty and the spiritual value of not worrying about the future. Jesus was poor, which seemed to be an ingredient of his godliness: "It is easier for a camel to go through the eye of a needle than it is for a rich man to get into heaven!" On the other hand, it was clear to everyone that the members of the church with professions, excellent jobs, and the trappings of wealth were often highly respected. Financial success seemed to be equated with general wisdom. Wealthy men got respect that extended to every aspect of their lives. Their wealth gave them not only social position but status in the church hierarchy. So it was difficult to know how we were to think about this.

We did some fun things in childhood, but there were a lot of things to worry about, and I learned to worry at an early age. Besides that, pure joy was a very suspect emotion in a Dutch Calvinist family; and it was the joy itself that smacked of irreverence. I learned that lesson one summer at the DeKorne cottage on Glen Lake, which Grandpa and Grandma DeKorne had bought and which was shared by all their children and grandchildren. We usually spent a week or two at the cottage every summer, and those are some of the best memories of my childhood. However, we were not allowed to swim on Sundays. That was Grandma's rule.

One Sunday morning I saw my Uncle John, a holy man, go down to the lake for a swim — in total violation of that inexplicable rule against swimming on Sundays. (He was a missionary in China, but was back in Michigan for a vacation.) Breathless with excitement, I ran to my mother and asked her if I could go swimming, too. "Uncle John is going swimming!" was certainly an irrefutable argument. But my mother hedged, claiming that Uncle John was just going in the lake to take a bath. "You see, he has a bar of soap."

"I can do that, Mom. I can take a bath in the lake!"

But nothing would persuade my mother to get past the rule that Uncle John had, by his actions, just called into question. Finally, running out of her stock of inadequate explanations, she spoke the truth, identifying the true source of the sin.

"You can't go in the lake, because if you went in the lake, you would just have fun," she said. Well, she had me there — and she was right about that. Having fun on Sundays was the sin. Not swimming. Having fun.

Speaking of fun, sex education was nonexistent for a Christian Reformed boy — even one with two older brothers and an older sister. A Christian doctor came to our school once, but I was too embarrassed to ask questions. The mystery of sex just merged with the mystery of guilt and shame. I couldn't figure it out. In early adolescence, I was playing with a worldly-wise older neighbor girl in our secret camp down by the railroad tracks. She had sparkling black eyes, but she didn't have any brothers, and she wanted to see the thing I peed with. In exchange, she would show me the thing she peed with. Naturally, I was not prepared to deal with this development. So, in a posture of righteous indignation, I stalked out of our secret camp and decided to go shoot some baskets instead. She never made that offer again, which, of course, I came to regret.

The Dutch Calvinist work ethic trumped everything else. Work always came first — before extracurricular school activities or sports. Not working was never an option. Collecting coal was the early beginning, but by the age of ten I had a decent income from my other entrepreneurial schemes. It was always easy to make a little money by going around the neighborhood and picking up newspapers and magazines in my

Still part of a viable business district, the Plainfield and Coit intersection was the heart of Grand Rapid's Creston neighborhood in the 1950s.

GRPL, Library Photo Collection

wagon. I took them to the recycling station on the corner of Coldbrook and Plainfield, where they paid cash for recyclable materials. My brother told me you could get into the Creston Theater with an old aluminum pan, but I never dared to try that — because it was a sin to go to the movies. When I found aluminum at the dump, I turned it in to the recycling station on Coldbrook.

However, my real source of income was door-to-door selling. My best product turned out to be figurines that I created from a kit I had bought at the D & C five-and-dime on Coit Avenue. I poured plaster of Paris into inverted rubber moulds to make a variety of animals, which I then painted. My dad helped me make a box with compartments for the finished products, and helped me fit the box onto my bicycle for traveling to the better neighborhoods. That box also became a display box with a strap that went around my neck when I went door to door. At one house on Dale Street, an interested man liked the dog, but the figurine for sale was the wrong color. The man said he would buy one if it were the color of his dog. I took notes on the coloring of the man's dog, made another figurine with my dog mould, painted it to order, and made an easy 25 cents for the effort. After that I made moulds of several different kinds of dogs. Then I went looking for houses with dogs, took notes, and when I went to the front door a week later, I was prepared to sell a plaster-of-Paris figurine that looked exactly like the dog barking at me.

On Saturday mornings men headed north on Plainfield Avenue to go fishing at the lakes north of town. On Friday nights I collected night crawlers by climbing over the fence at the Kent Country Club with my flashlight and a can. Early on Saturday mornings I was set up on the corner of Knapp and Plainfield with several cans of live bait, a sign, and a box to sit on while waiting for customers. I collected the profits of these ventures and brought them to the Old Kent Bank that formed the triangle between Coit, Plainfield, and Quimby. I handed the coins over to Mr. Dielman, the manager, who put the money in my savings account. If Mr. Dielman wasn't there, I went back home. I wouldn't turn over my money to anyone else.

I was about ten years old when the Stadium was built out on Turner Avenue, near Comstock Park. The Quonset-style building was remarkable for two reasons. First, because the roof began to sag dangerously right after the building opened, they had to build a large frame on top of the roof to hold it up. When it was safe, they opened it up again for the main reason it was built: it was an ice rink that was to be the home of — and this was the second remarkable thing — a new professional hockey team, the Grand Rapids Rockets. The team manager, Lou Trudell, had been imported from Canada to put together a winning team. Besides being a very pleasant man, Lou was a man with a vision: he started hockey leagues for kids in Grand Rapids. The Pee Wee Rockets were for boys of twelve to fourteen, and the Junior Rockets were for older boys who might develop into potential players for Lou's professional team. Every team had a corporate sponsor, and I proudly wore my Meijer's jersey.

The Pee Wee Rockets practiced on Saturday mornings, and we played our games on Saturday nights — just before the professional Rockets played. I was small for my age, and not a very fast skater, but my quick reflexes served me well as a goalie. In fact, the stats suggested that I might be the best goalie in the league, but that was a matter of debate. My stats *were* good, but I thought it was perhaps because our defensemen were the best. I secretly believed that McKay, another goalie in the league, was better than I was. However, nobody could deny that my performance was nothing short of brilliant the night I stopped "Kramer's breakaway slap shot."

A slap shot is an aggressive slap at the puck that is intended to get maximum speed on the shot. It is also very intimidating for the goalie. The shooter, of course, has less control with a slap shot, so sometimes the line of fire is as much a surprise to him as it is to the goalie. Nonetheless, it is always scary. A breakaway shot is a situation in which the offensive wing or center has a clear shot at the goalie, with no defenseman in between. The trick is to have your hottest center or wing man screaming down the ice toward the enemy goalie, and to get the puck to him just as he hits the blue line at supersonic speed. That's a breakaway. There is no defensive player between the shooter and the goalie. It's just the two of them.

Kramer was the hottest center in the league, and maybe I was the best goalie. Kramer always wore a bright chartreuse knit cap, and he must have been six feet tall even as a Pee Wee. He was all legs and elbows — sort of awkward — but he had a slap shot to scare the crap out of every other kid on the ice. And on this Saturday night at the Stadium, Kramer got a breakaway shot at me. My coach had taught me to always stay tight in the crease (the rectangle painted in the ice in front of the net), unless someone came at me with a breakaway shot. "If someone gets a breakaway on you," he said, "you stay in the crease up till the last split-second, and just as he gets ready to fire, you skate out at him, which cuts down his angle." So, just as Kramer yanked his stick back in the wind-up to his terrifying slap shot, I skated out on him.

I don't know what gods manage these things, but they were with me that night as I thrust my taped-up goalie stick in front of Kramer's slap shot. The smoking puck spun to lifelessness about ten feet to the right of the net, where I dropped on it just as Kramer was preparing to kill me — a Pee Wee Rocket drama that brought the cheering crowd to its feet.

My interactions with the adult Rockets team members were another source of an education that I couldn't have gotten anywhere else. Their dressing room, which they had to share with the Pee Wees, provided some of the sex education that I had foolishly forfeited with the black-eyed beauty just a year or two earlier. Some of the Rockets were loud and bawdy. Some had missing teeth and ragged scars that they wore as badges of honor. Most of them were French Canadians, and they taught the Pee Wees to sing French drinking songs: "Ooooooo . . . Ahhhh lou etta, gentile ah lou etta. . . ."

One of those adult Rockets was a great artist, and the walls of the dressing room were decorated with anatomically correct drawings of men and women doing astonishing things. I studied those pictures. My raucous adult male role models might have caused a riot if they had ever entered the narthex of Broadway Avenue Christian Reformed Church. But to me there was something very attractive about their violence and disobedience. I enjoyed identifying with that world of fighting and spitting and swearing, even though I never dared to do any of those things myself. I was worshiping some of those crude, bloody men on Saturday nights at the Stadium when I should have been home taking a bath and cleaning my shoes for Sunday morning. I was collecting stray pucks and the broken hockey sticks of my heroes, shattered swords that I would tape up and caress with more reverence than I had ever shown in church. This was sacred stuff. At times there was negative publicity about one or more of the Rockets who were getting into trouble — usually related to alcohol or fighting. But I was a Pee Wee Rocket, and it was easy for me to discount the significance of their sins.

At the age of fourteen, children were allowed to get a "work permit," and this enabled me to apply for regular jobs. I landed two important jobs that shaped my future. I began working for a short, gum-chewing Armenian-American named Dick, who was the concessionaire at the Welsh Civic Auditorium. He always wore one of those paper hats that you would expect to see in a Norman Rockwell painting of a cook in a diner. I worked at Dick's concession stands selling popcorn, candy, and drinks for events booked at the Civic Auditorium. This also gave me free access to those events, and that opened my eyes to a world far beyond the Creston neighborhood. There were symphony concerts, Golden

Gloves bouts, basketball games, and the circus, among other events. But the best part of this education was the Grand Rapids Light Opera Company. When the student prince jumped up on the table and lifted his stein with the fake froth and led his fellow Heidelberg students in a rousing drinking song, I was so smitten that I forgot to breathe. I saw many operettas, including *The Merry Widow, Carousel,* and *Desert Song,* and I was drawn into that world with the comfort of coming home. "O, Rose Marie, I love you. I'm always thinking of you. . . ."

While working at the Civic, I frequently stopped in to see Red, the owner and cook of the Butterwagon, the mobile restaurant parked next to the Welsh Auditorium on a street that no longer exists. Red's sign boasted: "Every Burger Cooked in a Pound of Butter," and there was some evidence that it was actually true. After I was done working, I would always spend some of my earnings on one of Red's burgers, and then find my bus in the late-night lineup of buses preparing to make their final runs from Lower Monroe out to the neighborhoods.

My other important job at age fourteen was at the new Meijer Supermarket on the corner of Fuller and Michigan, the very same Meijer supermarket that had sponsored my hockey team and paid for my uniform. Even though I was a scrawny kid, the manager, Bud Clark, agreed to take a chance on me — probably because my dad knew him. To get to work, I bought a Whizzer motorbike. I started out sweeping floors, stocking shelves, and carrying out sacks of groceries. Soon I moved to the produce department, where I continued to work for several years.

It was not the first Meijer market in the Grand Rapids area, but the Fuller-and-Michigan store was built to accommodate their main offices. Fred Meijer was a strong presence, always involved, and he knew everybody's name, including mine. This was an experience of simply knowing when I was in the presence of greatness. I was devoted to that company and worked hard for them. My job at Meijer's supported me through high school and college.

By the time I entered Christian High School on Franklin Street, I had developed a confusing blend of beliefs and disbeliefs. The church, school, and family prevented me from giving voice to my beliefs about an unfair God. And my identification with the underdog grew stronger as more information came out of the South about the shocking injustices forced on African-Americans. One of my friends in high school, Norman, told me he was planning to enter an oratorical contest during our senior year, and he talked me into doing the same. I signed up, and I decided to speak about racial injustice. There was a first prize, a second prize, and two honorable mentions — four citations and only five students who had entered the contest.

Now perhaps the reason I was the only person not to get a prize was the subject matter of my oration, which I was presenting to a conservative Christian Reformed high school full of kids whose parents were Republicans, including mine. I'd like that to be true, but it wasn't. The truth is, even though I was a fairly intelligent kid, my insecurities always trumped my intelligence. I was so nervous standing up to speak that I lost my place. I didn't have my speech memorized well enough, and I was too insecure to just speak from what I knew. So I was the only one of the five speakers not to win anything. My friend Norman won first place, and he became a minister.

But it never occurred to me that my Dutch Calvinist background had limited me in any way. After graduating from Calvin College four years later, I drove my 1954 red-and-black Mercury hardtop to New York City and parked it on the corner of 122nd Street and Seventh Avenue — in central Harlem. I had arranged to work at a Christian Reformed Church and community center there. I was primed for the 1960s, a college graduate, and ready to help save the world. I was still a virgin. At this point, if I had ever met a Jewish person, I was not aware of it. And also at this point, I had never met an African-American person. But I was in Harlem, and that was about to change.

Rocky and Me

Max Apple

Max Apple grew up in Grand Rapids listening to the stories of his grandmother, Gootie, about whom he wrote one of his books of nonfiction, *I Love Gootie*. Apple went on to graduate from the University of Michigan, and after that entered a writing program at Stanford University. But his father died while he was there, and he returned to Grand Rapids. When he went back to graduate school, it was the University of Michigan again, and he lived in Ann Arbor during the anti-Vietnam War protest years with his 95-year-old grandfather, Rocky. This experience was the source of his book *Roommates,* from which the memoir below has been excerpted. Apple also wrote the screenplay for the 1995 film of the same name.

Apple has also published two collections of stories, *The Oranging of America* and *Free Agents,* as well as two novels, *Zip* and *Profiteers.* Two screenplays that he wrote, *Smokey Bites the Dust* and *The Air Up There,* have also been made into movies. Five of his books have been *New York Times* Notable Books. His stories and essays are widely anthologized and have appeared in *Atlantic, Harper's, Esquire,* and many literary magazines, and in *Best American Stories* and *Best Spiritual Writing.* His essay "The American Bakery" was selected by the *New York Times* as one of the best to appear in the first 100 years of the *Book Review.*

Apple has received grants from the National Endowment for the Humanities, the National Endowment for the Arts, and the Guggenheim Foundation. He has given readings at many universities, and has taught at the University of Michigan, Stanford University, New York University, Columbia University, and Rice University, where he taught for twenty-nine years and held the Fox Chair in

English. His Ph.D. is in seventeenth-century literature. Since the autumn of 2001 he has been teaching fiction and nonfiction creative writing courses at the Kelly Writers House at the University of Pennsylvania in Philadelphia.

Our bond began, I think, in January 1936, five years before my birth when my grandpa Rocky, his son Max, two female cousins, and his son-in-law, Sam, who was my father, were in Max's black Chevrolet returning to Grand Rapids, Michigan, from a family wedding in Detroit.

It was about nine p.m., and Max was at the wheel. He was twenty-three and not too experienced at highway speeds, but his car was new and he enjoyed driving. He wasn't going too fast — he couldn't. The wind blew blinding snow at the car, and beneath the snow lay the dangerous black ice of Michigan winters.

Somewhere near Lansing, the Chevy skidded on one of those ice sheets and began to cross the median. Max hit the brake, the car spun off the road into a healthy elm tree.

The passengers were all thrown from the car. The steering wheel kept Max inside, but the pointed Chevrolet insignia penetrated his chest.

When the first ambulance arrived, the driver and the attendant left the two women where they were. They had been killed instantly. Rocky and my father were battered but conscious. They watched the two medical workers load Max onto a stretcher.

The ambulance, because of the treacherous weather, had to travel far slower than usual. The emergency medic put oxygen over Max's mouth and held a stethoscope to his heart. A few minutes from the hospital he removed the oxygen. "I'm sorry," he told Rocky, "he died." Rocky pushed open the door of the ambulance and tried to jump out. The medic and my father barely kept him from doing so.

Rocky never told me that story, never mentioned his son at all. What I know of my uncle Max comes from my grandmother, who never stopped mourning him, and from my mother, who even years later during my childhood still visited the cemetery so regularly that tombstones with Hebrew lettering are my earliest memories.

In many families there is a single defining event that changes everything. This was ours. Five years later, at my birth, my parents, grandparents, and my two sisters were all living together — a band of survivors. My arrival, I think, finally turned them toward forgetting. No one could replace their loss, but I entered the world loaded — they named me Max, and everyone had an equal share in me. I was born two generations deep.

In a big gray clapboard house in the industrial district of Grand Rapids my family began, like many immigrants, to put all they had into their children. In our case the grandchildren were the children as well.

At home we spoke Yiddish, but at school my sisters and I hung on to English like the life raft it was. Once we had the language we polished it. The girls become paragons of fluency, high school debate champs. They brought home gilded trophies that thrilled us.

Around the kitchen table it was the nineteenth century. In Yiddish the adults talked about the czar and pogroms — but in the dining room only the issues of the day passed my sisters' lips as they practiced debate before a large gilded mirror.

They quoted from *Time* and *Newsweek* and kept all the old magazines in stacks under their beds. My mother almost swooned when she looked up from washing dishes or cooking to see her debating daughters gesturing with their arms and using big words. My grandma thought their padded bras were a clever way to keep warm. My father carried their trophies in his truck to show them to the purchasing agents and plant managers in northern Michigan who sold him scrap steel and metal.

"You'll be a speaker, too," my mother promised me, but I didn't think so. I gravitated instead to an older set of debaters who didn't say "Excuse me" or interrupt in allotted two- or three-minute bursts. These debaters, Rocky and my grandma, weren't practicing, either. They wished upon one another cholera and ague and what they had, a life in exile among the goyim. If anyone gave out trophies for Yiddish cursing, they would have been daily winners.

Gootie, my grandma, was a short, large-boned woman who made the kitchen her kingdom. She entered the living room only on special occasions — like Monday night to watch "I Love Lucy." She had to think about her movements ever since she fell from a freight train in Russia during the First World War. Her broken leg, never properly set, left her dragging a stiff limb for the rest of her days. The disability made it necessary to plan her movements in advance. She did the same thing psychologically. Slow and careful in everything, she was the exact opposite of her speedy husband. They were the marriage of thought and action, and in constant conflict.

Rocky was a whirlwind and the family pioneer. He came to America on his own in 1914 and began immediately to work sixteen-hour days so he could bring his wife and two children, Bashy and Max, to Michigan. During what he called "the first war," none of his letters were answered. He didn't know where his family was or even if they were alive. But he saved his money and he kept writing.

After the war, when Gootie, my mother, and Max returned to their village from the big city of Odessa where the Russian government had shipped them, their house was a ruin and their German and Lithuanian paper money worthless. A few letters were waiting for them.

In Michigan Rocky went to night school, where he learned to read and write English. The only thing he did at less than top speed was sign his name. When he had to do so, usually on some kind of official form, he did it the way a good basketball player shoots free throws: he concentrated on mechanics. He braced himself with his left hand on the writing surface, checked the position of his thumb and forefinger on the pencil or ballpoint, and then executed the curves of "Herman," the slightly ridiculous American name that an immigration clerk gave him because "Yerachmiel" was too hard. The men who worked beside him at the American Bakery were smarter. When they couldn't say Yerachmiel, they called him Rocky, the name that stuck.

I never missed an opportunity to watch him sign "Herman." It was regal. He should have used a quill and a blotter. He always gave it a quick double check before he put the pen down. When I learned cursive in fourth grade I filled Palmer method notebooks practicing writing between the big lines and small lines with my name and his. Max Apple never got beyond a scrawl, but I could do "Herman Goodstein" like a master forger.

Gootie never learned English. That lack kept her housebound more than her lame leg did, but she made immobility a strength. She liked the rest of the family to report our experiences to her, and she rewarded us with her ironic commentaries on what we told her. A coffee cup always in front of her, her bad leg propped on a stool, she made her spot at the kitchen table the center of the household. She analyzed things and passed judgments. She kept a big white rag beside her to blow her nose and to wipe her eyes, which regularly leaked tears of laughter. She had two big things to laugh at — America and her husband.

What she knew about America she learned from looking at pictures in the newspaper, watching people on the street, or picking up the news and gossip that the family brought to her. Her longest field trips were our walks to the supermarket. She liked to go with me because I had the patience to read labels and explain what was in the cans and packets that were new and usually amusing to her.

I could read by five and liked to show off. We were quite a pair in the supermarket. I read the labels aloud in Yiddish, then together we tried to translate subtleties — things like the difference between tomato paste and tomato sauce. We spent a lot of time on such matters at the neighborhood A&P, while all around us gentiles roamed, loading their carts with what we knew were slabs of pork and shotgun shells.

We didn't go to the A&P to buy — my parents did that once a week in our dark green Pontiac — Gootie and I went to the store for entertainment. The aisles of the A&P were our movies. She liked to watch people load up on absurdities like tissues and deodorant. She could look at the shopper, and the contents of the cart, and then imagine the life. She had no experience with romance but liked it above all else. When we saw a couple call one another "honey" or "sweetheart" and exchange a little kiss near the door, she mimicked them. At home she would pause near the refrigerator, give me a soulful look, purse her lips, and call me "sveetheart honeydear" until neither of us could stop laughing.

She was comfortable at the A&P because in Lithuania her parents had a small store where she had sold bread and produce and liquor by the glass to barefoot peasants. I thought of her as a clerk in a Lithuanian 7-Eleven doling out vodka like change. She wanted me to own a store someday — her son, Max, when he died, had already been a partner in a clothing store.

"You'll have more than a store," she told me. "Someday you'll have two stores."

This was a subject of dispute between my grandparents. Rocky didn't want me primed for storekeeping. He had bigger plans. On my outings with him he took me to various teachers, men who he said knew what to teach a boy like me. He would regularly lead me to the apartment of one of these sages, usually a dingy three or four rooms near a gas station. He introduced me in the same way to each of the wise men: "Do something. Teach him. He's growing up like a goy."

I don't know what any of these men might have done. As I think of them now, they were probably bigger disappointments than I was. The itinerant teachers and rabbis who passed through western Michigan in the late 1940s would no doubt have preferred to be elsewhere. How he found so many amazes me. The easiest for me to sidestep were the bearded old men, the meshulachs, who appeared at our doorstep before Rosh Hashanah to collect money for widows and yeshivas. They were the traveling salesmen of Jewish charity, their eyes on richer prey than Rocky. I had no problem with them: a quick blessing and that was that. While they talked to me they read bus schedules.

The younger teachers who tutored me for weeks at a time made up a kind of circuit, a pony express of teachers who alighted for a while in the provinces. They would lead a service in Kalamazoo, perform a wedding in Niles, teach a class in Muskegon, all the while doing penance for their mediocrity in the seminary and praying for a better life in a big city. Most of them got their wish, but not before Rocky brought me in and made his plea.

I would sit beside a Hebrew book and a glass of tea, while a wispy man in his thirties would say, "So we'll begin."

We never got beyond beginnings. My heart was too American. While they helped me read and translate Hebrew and Aramaic prayers, I was thinking of baseball. The three or four teachers whom I remember specifically were decent men. They were not very worried about me or my failure; they had their own problems. I remember one young man who was thinking of taking a permanent job; after a few minutes of teaching he quizzed me about rentals in the area. Another was learning to drive. He drew diagrams of a car in traffic and narrated his moves to me. As I stumbled over the Creation and Noah and Abraham's early life, the teachers were as bored as I was. If they had a choice, and the proper training, they would have preferred to be killing chickens.

Rocky didn't take out his anger and disappointment at me, but it became part of the constant feud with Gootie — not that they needed a reason to argue; it was a daily event. There was no suspense in their disagreements: when Rocky and Gootie argued, Rocky always lost.

My father stayed out of all the squabbles, but my mother had inherited Rocky's quick temper and used it against him. She inevitably sided with Gootie. Because the war had separated her parents, when my mother came to America at twelve, someone had to tell her who the dapper fellow in brown-and-white shoes and a gold pocket watch was. She never understood him. In a way, her father remained more a stranger to her than to my sisters and me, who had known him all our lives.

If the argument with Gootie was serious enough, Rocky responded by storming upstairs. The house was a triplex. We lived downstairs, and there were two apartments above. The heat from the coal furnace was erratic on the first floor, almost nonexistent on the second, although with a wall heater, the back apartment was warm enough to rent.

Rocky slept in the front apartment. I don't know when he and Gootie stopped sharing a bed, but my guess was that Max's death had ended that part of their life as well. Sleeping in the empty apartment gave him the privacy he needed to keep his hours, to bed at eight-thirty, up at four.

To get upstairs you had to walk through a long unheated hallway and then up a dark staircase. To go from the warm crowded downstairs filled with the noise of my sisters and their girlfriends and the TV and the bustle of the kitchen to the cold empty upstairs seemed to me a terrible punishment. Usually, after an argument with Gootie, he would retreat to his bedroom but return in an hour or so. When his anger didn't abate, the big job of my childhood was to coax him downstairs, back into the bosom of the family.

Gootie never stayed angry. Sometimes I thought she argued for sport, just to rile him up. When he didn't come down for a meal, she worried. So did I.

I would put on my coat and go upstairs. He was usually sitting at a wooden table covered with a white crocheted cloth, reading the Talmud.

At four and five I was like a little lawyer going to question the prisoner in his cell. On the first trip I would merely listen — let him get out his rage and state the justice of his case. On the second trip, maybe an hour later I would bring food prepared by his enemy wife. He would refuse to touch it.

Then my work began. I had to charm him into eating. He was stubborn and not always hungry. Sometimes I failed.

Depending on the severity of the argument — how injured he felt — he would stay upstairs for hours or even carry on the dispute the following day.

On one occasion it stretched into a second, and then a third, and a fourth day. That battle concerned a housepainter. Rocky had promised the job of painting our house to Ed — one of his Polish co-workers at the bakery. Gootie had struck a deal with Mr. Cooley, a retired man who lived across the street. She had made the deal in Yiddish — I had translated, so I felt partly responsible. Mr. Cooley got the job. I witnessed the handshake.

For Rocky more than honor was at stake. At that time, he clung tenaciously to his part-time job. Ed, his candidate, was one of three people who could squeal to the union. The "bastids" from the union had forced Rocky to retire. He continued to work, secretly. His cousin Phillip, who owned the American Bakery, kept him on part-time. Rocky knew the danger, but he always wanted more hours. Going to the bakery with him was a kind of espionage mission. The union spies we knew might be anywhere. He had only joined the union when he had to, and then, in a matter of months, the union work rules forced him to retire.

Phillip was taking a big chance, Rocky told me. If they caught him, the union could shut down the bakery. I never went in without looking around for the union men, whom Rocky described to me only as "bastids, cokesuckers, and son of a beetches."

While he worked, I would have a doughnut and a glass of milk and all the time keep a lookout. I ate at a little rest area Rocky had set up for me, a stool and some soft flour sacks to lie down on if I wanted to take a nap. I didn't bother him while he worked. I knew better.

There were two other bakers, Joe Post and Ed Wizneski, the one who moonlighted as a painter. Joe weighed over two hundred pounds and tossed seventy-five-pound sacks of flour like marbles, but when he decorated a cake he held the long tube of artificial color delicately, like a paintbrush, and made tiny green and red flowers even when he was looking across the table at Rocky, yelling at him to go faster.

Ed teased Rocky about turning him in to the union. Rocky took it seriously.

"What's your hurry?" Ed would say, "You're not even working, you're not here, you're retired." Rocky tried to ignore the taunts, but he worried that Ed, who also moonlighted as a drunk, would tell the union. He probably considered the housepainting job as a kind of bribe. I tried to explain all of this to Gootie and my mother — it didn't help. They wanted him to retire. Even part-time he was still working thirty hours a week. I understood more than they did how much he loved the bakery.

Usually I had to wait in the salesroom, but when he let me come into the back I could watch the process, sometimes the whole thing, from flour, shortening, water, yeast, and eggs to those crisp shiny breads that emerged.

I watched the rising of the bread like a cartoon. Rocky knew exactly when it was ready for the oven and when to take it out without a clock or a timer.

On cake days he stayed late. Rocky and Joe Post were both cake men. They used a different kind of flour, and on cakes, even Rocky slowed down. They waited until all the breads were done, then readjusted the oven temperature. When they made fresh frosting I always got a taste.

"You gotta know what you're doing when you bake cakes," Rocky said. "Cakes aren't like cookies or doughnuts."

When there was no one else to do it, he made doughnuts, but he hated it. "Doughnuts," he said, "is not baking — it's frying."

I knew them as frycakes. The American Bakery made only one kind, no topping, just fried pieces of dough with a hole in the middle.

Rocky drew the line at cookies. I'd seen him storm away once when Phillip asked him to make ten dozen coconut spots.

"You want cookies," he said, "you don't need a baker. He can make cookies."

He pointed to me. Phillip looked my way. I was excited, I thought he was going to let me do it.

"Don't be so stubborn," Phillip said. "Just ten dozen, how long will it take you?"

Rocky took off his apron and threw it on the table. "C'mon," he said to me. I waited a few seconds in case Phillip decided to ask me, then I ran to catch up.

At home we never made cookies, either. "If you're going to eat all that sugar," he said, "eat something good, a pastry or a cake."

In the front, while I waited for him, I would read a book or have a snack, but when he allowed me in the baking room I watched, riveted by the process before me. I never got tired of it. Staying home couldn't compare with the bakery.

"I'm on your side," I told him. "I want Ed to paint the house."

Downstairs, I lobbied Gootie. She was ready to give in, but my mother hardened her heart: "If you'll stop bringing his food to him, he'll come down when he's hungry," she said. "Just leave him alone."

On the fifth day of the dispute, when he wouldn't even come down to watch "The Original Amateur Hour," my mother gave up. "Tell him that Ed can paint the house," she said. "I can't stand it anymore, he's wearing me out."

I ran upstairs without a jacket to tell him the good news, but he wouldn't budge. His anger had separated itself from the cause, it had taken on an independent life. I couldn't reason with him.

It was only about eight o'clock, but he had already hung his trousers and jacket over the chair at the foot of the bed. Propped on the huge pillow that kept him almost a third of the way to sitting while he slept, he told me he was never coming downstairs again. I believed him.

I went downstairs and returned with my pajamas, two Archie comic books, and my pillow. Later my sister helped me carry up one of the feather beds that Gootie had carted from Russia. He told me to go downstairs, but I refused.

The bedroom had been a kitchen and still was. A porcelain sink separated two mahogany beds. I settled in across the sink from him. Even though the room had some heat, I could still see my breath. In a few minutes Rocky snored. I was about seven years old, almost asleep myself, when I heard from behind the kitchen wall — the tenants.

I saw them every day as they crossed the yard to the back entrance that led to their apartment. They were newlyweds. She was a small brunette about twenty. I don't remember her name, but his is embedded forever. I heard her moan "Roger" over and over. I wasn't sure what they were doing, but I understood that it mattered.

In the morning Rocky ordered me downstairs. “It’s too cold for you up here,” he said.

“I like it,” I told him, and the next night I was back.

When he saw that I meant business and wouldn’t budge, Rocky relented. He let me carry messages back and forth. For two days the bargaining continued. Then we reached a settlement. Ed would scrape the house, Cooley would paint. As chief negotiator, I named my price and I got it. I stayed upstairs. Rocky had a roommate.

While I lingered in the old world, my sisters went headlong into the melting pot. Years before debate, they figured out democracy by joining clubs. Maxine rose to captain of the Turner School Safety Patrol. Bailey became a junior high student council officer. Encouraged by their examples and my second-grade teacher, who thought that I didn’t play enough, my parents urged me to take a big step into America. Reluctantly, I became a Cub Scout.

Mrs. Clark came to our class to recruit for a new den. I knew her. She was the cashier at the Red and White, a small grocery store on Front Street, four blocks from our house. It was the only store that stocked the big brown chunks of root that Rocky ground up for horseradish.

Mrs. Clark was a very heavy woman with blond hair and red lipstick. Her son John was in my class. On the playground he was always the captain of one of the teams, and I was happy to be on his side whenever he chose me.

John had been a Cub Scout the year before in another den and liked it so much that Mrs. Clark wanted to offer all of us the same opportunity.

She asked John to stand in front of the class. He wore the full blue uniform.

“But here” — Mrs. Clark pointed at his right shoulder — “here you can see that there’s nothing written in for his den number. Next week we’ll have a number that John will wear — so will all of you. Cub Scouts,” she said, “is not like school, but it’s not like recess, either. It’s organized. You’ll have fun, and you’ll learn things without even realizing that you’re learning.”

SS. Peter and Paul Church, where Max Apple learned kite-making, is a well-known West Side landmark.

GRPL, Edward Gillis Collection

I joined, but there was only one problem. Our den would meet at the Church of St. Peter and St. Paul. Rocky forbade me to go.

"A Jew," he said, "doesn't go to a church."

I argued. "It's not a church, it's a meeting room in a church."

"That's the same thing."

"It is not," I said. "It's just a room with chairs and tables like a school. And there's no priests or nuns, just Mrs. Clark, the den mother."

"First they tell you den mother, pretty soon they'll start talking about a Holy Mother. I know, it was like that in Lithuania."

"They didn't have Cub Scouts in Lithuania," I argued.

"You're right, we didn't waste our time on such things. We studied."

He refused to give his permission, but with my parents and sisters and even Gootie encouraging me, I stood my ground.

"You want to go to a church," Rocky said, "you'll go without me."

I did. My father drove me to the meeting in his truck. I didn't even tell Rocky I was going. I walked up the steps and into the yellow brick building as wary as if I were entering a prison.

I remember that it didn't smell right to me. I walked past stained-glass windows and didn't look up. I headed for the room number that I had written down. I knew it was in the basement, so I just looked for stairs. When I saw them I ran, and when I found the room I opened the door and saw only Mrs. Clark and a few boys in uniform and not a room full of nuns and priests as I half expected. I relaxed. There were chairs and a blackboard and on the table a kite-making display; everything looked like school.

"Hi," Mrs. Clark said, "I'm glad you could make it." She knew, I think, because I had bought only a cap and a compass instead of a full uniform that I was on shaky ground. "You like kites?" she asked. "I hope so. We're having an interesting demonstration."

"Outside?" I asked, hoping it would be so I could tell Rocky that the whole thing took place outdoors and not even mention that I had entered and gone downstairs.

"No!" Mrs. Clark said. "Right there at the table, but next week, after everyone makes one of his own, we'll go outside together and fly them. You'll really like that, everyone does."

She waited until all fourteen boys arrived, then we pledged allegiance to the flag, holding our caps against our hearts, and recited a Cub Scout pledge. Mrs. Clark read a letter from the district director, welcoming us as a new pack. She wrote our number on the blackboard so we could write it down and buy shoulder patches.

"You're in for a special treat tonight," she said. "I told you when I made the announcement at school that we'd be doing kites, but I didn't tell you that we'd be learning from a master kite maker who has been making his own designs for more than twenty years. Let's give him a big Cub Scout welcome."

We did. I clapped as hard as anyone until the side door opened and a bald priest walked in.

"This is Father Dembrowski," Mrs. Clark said. "I know some of you boys go to church here and know him very well. We appreciate your coming in to spend some time with us, Father."

"It's my pleasure, Mrs. Clark," the father said. "I like Cub Scout groups, and I want you to know that all the church grounds and facilities are open to you. But when you start flying your own kites, please stay off the parking lot on Sunday morning or I'll probably lose my job."

I recognized him from the bakery. He was a heavyset bald man about fifty. This was the first time I'd heard him speak English. In the bakery it was always Polish. Rocky had talked to him lots of times. He was one of three or four priests who gave the American Bakery a lot of business. I looked down in case he might recognize me. It felt strange to hear him speaking English.

"Kite-making," the father said, "is a challenging and wonderful activity. As Mrs. Clark said, I've been doing it for many years. A well-built kite can give you hours and hours of pleasure, so let's get started."

He walked to his worktable, where there were sticks and paper and string.

While he demonstrated kite making I kept my eye on Mrs. Clark to see if she would put on a nun's habit. When she noticed me staring she motioned with her hand for me to watch the father.

I did. He had fast, nimble fingers. We all watched as he tied the plywood and then stapled thin paper to the wood. It took him only a few minutes.

"When you make them at home," he said, "don't worry about the stapling — I can do that for you here. Just pick whatever design you want and cut it to size."

He held up a simple brown kite. "There's about a nickel's worth of material here," the father said, "and if you're careful, you can fly it all year. Can't beat that, can you?"

Each of us got a little kit, plywood, string, and paper. A gift from Father Dembrowski. I snuck mine into the house and put it into the drawer where my shirts and Rocky's long underwear lay side by side. It was the only drawer long enough to hold the sticks. I hid the packet at the bottom of the drawer and took it out only when I was sure I would be alone.

I wanted to make a good kite and was sure that I could. The priest's instructions were clear. But every time I put the two pieces of plywood on the floor and started to tie one against the other, I didn't see a kite, I saw a cross. The more solidly I tied the sticks, the more guilty I felt. I angled first one stick a little, then another. The shape I finally tied into place was much closer to an X than a cross.

Rocky didn't mention the Cub Scouts. I think he assumed I had never gone. The next week I snuck the kite out and walked to the church. Mrs. Clark had my hat and compass waiting for me.

"You can order the rest of the uniform whenever you want," she said, "there's no hurry. This is enough to make you official." She put the hat on me. I remained a proud Cub Scout for about fifteen minutes.

When I brought my frame to Father Dembrowski for stapling, he shook his head. "You'll have to redo this," he said. "It will never fly. Don't you remember what I showed you last week?"

His fingers went at my knot, and before my eyes my kite became a crucifix. I ran for the door.

"What's the matter?" Mrs. Clark called out. "Don't you feel good?"

I was up the stairs and out of the church before she could move her big body from the chair.

At home, I found Rocky cleaning the birdbath. I confessed.

"I went to church," I said, "but I didn't make a cross."

He put down the hose and stopped scrubbing the ceramic bowl. I told him about Father Dembrowski and the kite.

"You became one of them?" he asked. I had forgotten that I was wearing my blue beanie.

"Just a Cub Scout," I said, "not a goy."

"And you want to do this?"

I nodded. "Everyone in my class is in the den."

"C'mon," he said.

We walked to the Church of St. Peter and St. Paul. I wouldn't go in. Rocky did.

"I thought we weren't supposed to go in," I reminded him.

"We're not," he said, "but if you're wearing a hat, it's not so bad."

I sat on the steps and waited for him. Mrs. Clark came out first. She put a big arm around me. "I'm so sorry, honey. I didn't know. Your grandpa and Father D talked it all out in Polish. Father D didn't mean anything about religion — he was just talking about kites."

She waited on the steps with me until Rocky and Father D came out. They were still talking Polish. Behind them marched my den, everyone carrying a kite. John Clark handed me mine, bent back to the X I had originally made.

We flew the kites on the church parking lot. My misshapen one got into the air, but as I ran to give it space it sank and stuck on the antenna of a 1947 Plymouth, the priest's car.

After that we met at Mrs. Clark's house. She and John lived in three rooms above the Red and White. We met at the store and watched while she locked the door; then we followed her up the steep staircase to her three-room apartment for our snack. She carried two wet glass bottles of milk. Her body took up the entire width of the staircase. She passed the banisters the way semi trucks pass each other on a narrow highway.

We were seven years old, a time when everything is funny, especially fat people. But I don't remember anyone ever laughing about Mrs. Clark. She had great dignity and character. So did John. I didn't know what to call it then, but I knew John was someone you could always trust.

She passed out milk and cookies, then John collected the cups and washed them. They didn't even have a television set. The only decoration in the room that barely held all of us was Mr. Clark's picture on the wall. We saw him in his uniform, and we knew he'd died in Europe defending his country. We were little boys in blue beanies drinking milk in the apartment of a hero. It made me feel as if I were serving my country, too. A few weeks later I bought the trousers and shirt and an official whistle. That year I made a straw broom and a lamp, and I learned to climb a rope hand over hand. But I never forgot the kite. The next year, when it was time for Boy Scouts, I stayed home.

When I was twelve Rocky gave up on my intellect. My approaching Bar Mitzvah made him face reality. I would become a man, but not a rabbi.

Tenderly, he gave me the news that was not news to me. "Not everyone can do it," he said. "In Europe you would have had a chance."

"In Europe," I reminded him, "I would have been dead."

He had an alternate plan. He believed in apprenticeships. "You can be a professional man," he said. "You'll never have to work nights."

He walked with me to the Rexall drugstore a block from our house. I waited at the soda fountain while Rocky talked to the pharmacist, a man I knew only as Doc. Doc had two gold teeth like fangs when he opened his mouth wide, warning us not to read the comic books.

A tall man on level ground, Doc was a giant when he stood in the elevated pharmacist's booth and looked out at his goods, his eyes more observant than today's electronic cameras.

He stepped down from his perch — he and Rocky walked toward me. I sat on a round stool, staring straight at a tube of Unguentine, trying to look as professional as I could.

"Your grandpa tells me," Doc said, "that you want to be a druggist."

Rocky had coached me in advance. I had a line. "If he asks you something," Rocky had said, "just say, 'I'm ready to work.' That's all."

I nodded.

"Can I trust you around the comic books?"

"I'm ready to work," I said.

"A lot of sick people come in here, you know that," Doc said. "You'll be exposed."

"I'm ready to work."

"You may be ready," he said, "but you're too young. It's against the law."

"Sonofabeetches," Rocky said. "The unions are ruining him, too. Give the boy a chance, Doc. I want him to be something."

"I told you, Rocky, I can't hire him, but . . . maybe. . . ." He stared at me.

"I'm ready to work," I said.

"You can hang around," Doc said. "You can learn the ropes."

He walked behind the soda fountain to the stainless-steel surface where the soda flavorings and the milk shake machines were. He handed me a damp red rag.

I held it in two hands as if it were a money belt.

While I wiped the sticky surface of the soda fountain, Doc went back to his druggist's perch and Rocky, accepting my failure and my limitations, walked to the American Bakery satisfied that he had done what had to be done. I would be a professional man.

At the Rexall store I also swept the floor, straightened the shelves, and stayed alert for learning the secrets of the druggist's trade.

"If you're a good worker," Rocky had told me, "he'll take you in the back and show you how he makes the medicines. Once you know that, you'll understand science."

I waited, but science eluded me. Doc didn't fill that many prescriptions. Most of the time he worked crossword puzzles from some of the magazines on the rack. After tearing out the puzzle pages he'd put the magazine back for sale.

"Nobody'll miss it," he said. Though I was careful not to risk my job by reading the comic books, Doc didn't seem to mind if I read the newspaper or the magazines. Since I was about to become a scientist myself, I began to notice how often Albert Einstein appeared in the news. I read everything I could about him in *Life* and *Look* and *Colliers* and *The Grand Rapids Press,* and reading about the great physicist whetted my appetite to understand prescriptions.

One day I finally asked Doc when he was going to show me the compounds.

"Okay," he said. "You wanna know medicine — I'm gonna show you."

He told Jerry, the fountain worker, to watch the entire store. He led me, not just behind the counter, but into the back room, where there were boxes full of cigarettes and candy and toothpaste and Vaseline alongside the glass bottles of medicine.

"There's two big things wrong with the world," Doc said. "One is war, the other is the clap."

He opened a bottle and put a blue-and-orange capsule into my hand. "Look at that," he said. "Know what you're holding?"

I didn't know. "Penicillin," Doc said.

He took the capsule out of my hand and dropped it back in the bottle. "I've seen you reading about Einstein in *Life*."

I nodded.

"It's all baloney. I mean, he might have invented the atomic bomb all right, but it wasn't the bomb that saved us — it was penicillin.

"The Germans had a plot to give everybody the clap. You're too young — I'm not gonna tell you how, but once they knew we had penicillin they called it off. So what do you think is more important, the bomb or penicillin?"

"Penicillin," I said.

"Don't forget it," Doc said.

I tried not to, but all the magazines had pictures of the flash of light and the mushroom cloud. Doc's blue-and-orange capsules couldn't compete with all that power.

When I read that Einstein didn't believe in God and never went to synagogue, it strengthened my own resolve. I became absolutely certain, in spite of Doc, that I liked Einstein even more than penicillin. The great scientist gave me confidence. One Saturday when Rocky was hurrying me to get ready for synagogue, I dropped my own atom bomb. I refused to go.

He left without me, and that afternoon we had it out. With Einstein in my corner I denounced religion.

Rocky called me an *apikoros,* the Hebrew version of the Greek epicurean, and he stopped talking to me. He didn't wake me, he didn't take me to the bakery with him, he didn't bring pastries home. When I came into the living room to watch baseball or wrestling with him, he left.

The rest of the family wisely stayed out of it. It complicated matters that at this time I was actively preparing for my Bar Mitzvah. Whatever I believed, I certainly intended to go through with that. I wanted the presents.

"Call off the Bar Mitzvah," he said. "An apikoros doesn't need a Bar Mitzvah."

I refused, and my family backed me up.

"Go ahead," Rocky said, "have a Bar Mitzvah, but I won't be there."

We went down to the wire. My parents, the rabbi, nobody could convince either of us to give in. I said it was science versus faith, a phrase I read in *Life* magazine. More likely I was getting even for all the years of stale tutoring. Ten days before I became a man, the drugstore got its first shipment of 3-D comic books. There had been rumors that they were coming for months, and other than the Bar Mitzvah nothing excited me more. Sharkey, who distributed magazines and tobacco, whetted my appetite. He had seen one. "Superman looks like he's flying off the page to punish you," he said. "You've never seen anything like it."

There were already 3-D movies. I had seen ads for Bwana Devil, but it was downtown at the Majestic and too expensive. I had to wait until it came to the Town on Bridge Street as part of a triple feature.

In the weeks of my apprenticeship at the Rexall store, I had never, while on duty, opened a comic book. The day the 3-D's arrived, I couldn't resist. I bought one for a dollar, ten times the price of a regular comic. There were five 3-D titles, but Mighty Mouse did me in. I wanted to see the red line that signified his speed in three dimensions.

When Doc caught me, I had opened the cellophane packet that contained the red-and-blue three-dimensional glasses and I was sitting on a pile of Police Gazette issues, holding the comic at an angle to feel the full force of Mighty Mouse coming off the page.

Doc yanked the comic out of my hands. I held on so tightly that one of the pages ripped in half. He pulled the glasses off my face.

"Get out," he said. "You know the rules."

I ran home and went to my bedroom before I started to cry. When Rocky came in I was really sobbing. He still wasn't talking to me. He left the room, but in a minute he came back. He sat down beside me.

"What happened?" he asked.

"Doc kicked me out," I said. "I'll never be a druggist." I told him why.

Later, Jerry, who worked at the fountain, told me what happened. Rocky walked to the back, into the employees-only area, where Doc was mixing a prescription.

"He went at Doc with his fists," Jerry said. "It was the funniest thing I ever saw. The old guy wanted to fight. Doc didn't want to hit him, so he just kept running around the Hallmark card display and finally he yelled for me to watch the store and he ran out the door."

I was still crying when Rocky came home.

"It was his fault," Rocky said. "The druggist put Einstein into your head. I'm glad you won't be a druggist."

He rubbed my back until I stopped crying.

At my Bar Mitzvah he sat in the first row and motioned for me to sing louder. He corrected my four mistakes in the Hebrew reading. I gave my speech in Yiddish, a language that only my family and a few of the old people understood. I spoke about what was on my mind, the atomic bomb. I compared it to the Flood in Noah's time and reminded my audience that nobody promised rainbows after bombs.

After the Bar Mitzvah, I didn't flaunt Einstein and Rocky was equally discreet about God. For prescriptions we went to the Cut-Rate store on Leonard Street.

The Memory of Cells

JOHN OTTERBACHER

John Otterbacher grew up in the working-class neighborhoods of northeast Grand Rapids. After an extended time at St. Joseph's Catholic Seminary in Missouri and Wisconsin, he graduated from Aquinas College in 1966. He completed the M.A. and Ph.D. degrees in clinical psychology at St. Louis University, and he did additional graduate work in urban studies and human relations at St. Louis University and the University of California.

Otterbacher first became politically active in the efforts of Dr. Martin Luther King, Jr., and in the political campaigns of Robert F. Kennedy. After returning to Grand Rapids as an assistant professor and clinical psychologist at Aquinas College, he was elected to the Michigan House of Representatives and the Michigan Senate for eight years. In 1978 he ran unsuccessfully for the Democratic nomination for the U.S. Senate.

During the 1980s and '90s, Otterbacher had a full-time private practice in clinical psychology. In 1998, he and his wife, Barbara Craft, took their two youngest children to sea, spending the next six years sailing the Atlantic (four crossings), the Baltic, the Mediterranean, and the Caribbean. During those years he began writing seriously. Since returning once more to Grand Rapids in 2004, Otterbacher has divided his time between a limited private practice and writing. His work has been published in *Cruising World* and *Sailing and Yachting Monthly* (England), and, his first book, *Sailing Grace,* is being published in early 2007. He wrote the following narrative expressly for this anthology.

John Otterbacher

The historical sense involves a perception,
not only of the pastness of the past, but of its presence.

T. S. Eliot

Highland Park is my home away from home.

It awaits three dusty alleys from our home, alleys full of mischief and adventure. Garages with doors sagging at odd angles from rusted hinges, overflowing with the flotsam of backyard life: push lawnmowers, garden tools, spare lumber, dated Fords, Chevrolets, and Dodges, some up on Hollywood blocks, coiled hoses, wagons and tricycles, the dead dog's doghouse, broken swing-sets, exiled — "I can fix it" — household appliances, the detritus of the working class in the early 1950s.

Stray animals migrate from garbage can to garbage can. Stray children linger, flailing away at patches of overgrown weeds with "weapons" discovered on the prowl, pounding the ground in boredom. A gauntlet to run on some days, more often a fidgety saunter, mouths a-run, all elbows and skinned knees, and enough scuffling to ensure tonight's banishment to the bathtub.

The last abbreviated alley ends abruptly at a flimsy yellow-and-black-striped barricade, the Street Department's thin protection from a steep decline that opens out beyond, down a vertical path, sliding and bracing, tumbling sometimes, through several decades of unattended scrub growth — thirty treacherous yards maybe — then out into the green expanse of Highland Park.

Loosely administered by the Parks Department, a majority of the sprawling acres attempt to be a nine-hole golf course. Golfers are few and far between in these confines. Irish, German, Polish, and Dutch mothers and fathers, on the other hand, are pumping out children well beyond their scrawny yards' capacity for confinement. In the absence of golfers, the fairways double as football fields in autumn, baseball fields in spring, and a place to gather year around. The steep incline leading to the second green becomes "sled central" with any snow cover. Less steep inclines spill down onto the first and fourth fairways for the younger kids.

A poor excuse for a creek separates the golf course from the rest of

Highland Park and its adjacent golf course were popular recreation areas on the West Side.
GRPL, Library Postcard Collection

the park. An above-ground public swimming pool anchors a play area sprinkled with swing sets, sliders, teeter-totters, and an overused horseshoe pit. The creek disappears inconspicuously into an ancient concrete sewer duct at one end of the park, affording us ample opportunity to test our nerve with flashlights. We roll up our pant legs, as if we won't get wet.

Each spring, when the snow melts and the runoff overwhelms the city's sewer system, the creek backs up. It sprawls brown and oily over its banks, out over great swatches of fairway, ushering in a short season of wading with makeshift nets and containers "borrowed" from those open-doored garages to hold the harvest of this year's catch of tadpoles and frogs, even an errant fish or snake. Whatever our preoccupation at the time, we all head for the park when it floods. It is as close as nature gets to acting out in an urban environment.

As light fades on this particular evening, several of us, probably late for dinner, collect our wares and head in the direction of home. We straggle across the last fairway to where the path leads into the woods and snakes up the ridge. Off to our left, a knot of boys swirl around the fifth green shouting and swinging sticks at a shadow on the ground, darting this way and that to escape their mayhem. My friends drop their nets and containers and race to the action, keeping whatever poles and sticks they have. Without knowing why, I do not follow, instead moving quickly toward the path up the hill. As I hurry by the green, I see that it's a rat they are attacking — driven out of the sewer and into the open by the flood. Already injured, he is dragging his greasy left hindquarters behind him helplessly, fair game for the hacking and stabbing. They descend on him, bellowing ferocity and excitement. I shout a disbelieving "Stop!" but nobody listens. I turn away as they close in.

I drag the picnic basket out to where the "new" car sits. It's a used Nash, black and bulbous with a flat, angled trunk. My father stands in front of it, hands on his hips, grinning at it appreciatively. It shimmers in the late afternoon sun, the last drops of a hose-off still running off a windshield wiper.

"She's a beauty," he says to no one in particular, then glances down at me for confirmation.

"Sure is, Dad. And so black."

"Now get the kitchen chairs and we'll hit the road."

Hitting the road is what my father lives for — and the rest of us too — on that Thursday each week that he has off work. He struggles with his latest house project while we are at school. At 3:30, rain or shine, we pile into whatever "new" car he is driving and head for the city limits. To everyone's amazement, he has torn out everything behind the front seat of the car, right down to the steel frame floor, and into the trunk compartment.

"Going to build in a great back seat for the kids," he explains to my disbelieving mother. She says nothing, but her eyes widen when she glances down at us kids.

This is a drill we are all familiar with. Diane and I file back into the house, through the backroom to the kitchen, and rustle up the battered white wooden kitchen chairs. We lug them through the backroom, down the steps, and across the backyard. Mr. Derham, working on his flowers across the street, furtively summons his wife to the front door. They stand on the porch in a trance, watching the procession of children with chairs out to the car.

My dad opens the side door, slides the front seat forward, and angles the chairs into the steel-framed compartment where the imagined backseat will someday reside. The chairs sit unevenly on the exposed metal floor. Diane and I climb up onto them tentatively, looking at each other and giggling, our version of Mom's disbelief. Dad and Mom slide the seat back and climb in. Jim, the youngest, sits on Mom's lap. Diane and I reach up to hold the back of the front seat when we are underway. Our chairs shift with each corner we take.

"It's good to be on the road," Dad beams as he glances back reassuringly. "Time's awastin'."

For fifty weeks a year "the road" takes us to an undetermined site, surprise being part of the bargain. Most often we end up at a beach — Lake Michigan on hot days, an inland lake if not — or a wooded state park. Hotdogs and hamburgers will sizzle on the grill at some point, Dad in full command.

"Isn't this great!" he'll exclaim to anyone within earshot, grinning his way out beyond my sister's crushing hospital bills, the tedium of his job, and the demands of a worn-out house.

And it *is* great, an island of time together in the unforgiving procession of weeks where he is asleep when we leave for school, home for an hour at dinner, and back to work until midnight. "Hitting the road" is synonymous with time with Dad, that thin slice of the week when Mom seems genuinely happy, a happiness that spills over onto us kids. It is her temporary reprieve from the low-grade depression that came with losing her teaching career to a conventional marriage and kids, her man to a manager's hours at the Kent and Center Theaters.

If Thursdays are a bright spot in the week, vacations are nirvana. Dad gets out of work at 11:30 p.m. and drives our already packed car home. We leave within minutes of his arrival, filing in our pajamas, teddy bears under our arms, out to the waiting car. He will drive all night — "no sense wasting valuable time" — into a fourteen-day marathon that will not have us back home until midnight on the last night. Into these compressed days flow the most truly happy times in a childhood where absence gives "responsibility" a bad name.

John Otterbacher

Judy Thomor opens the floodgate in the third grade. She leans away from the ruler-wielding boy up the aisle, eyes flashing playfully as she does. With her right hand she reaches back to protect herself when he persists. The tips of her fingers are flushed, the nails a pale pink. She arches away when he prods again, a bobby-socked saddle shoe sliding out from beneath her desk. Her calf, and her persistent good nature . . . the stray wisps of hair at the nape of her neck, unbridled by the rubber band that clasps her pony-tail . . . the bright smile, her teeth and just a glimpse of her tongue.

I am too shy to talk to her. But I do talk to everyone else. When Sister Mary Catherine, exasperated by my intransigence, moves my desk up beside her, facing the class, I try not to be too obvious with my glances at Judy. Both calves now and bobby socks, the red suggestion of a playground fall on the knee that peeks out beneath her uniform skirt. Legs like a pony, fingers to match, pinched tightly around the pencil with which she is completing a class exercise. I want to touch the lightly veined underside of that wrist.

By spring, Sister Mary Catherine is running out of punishments. Banishment to the principal's office yields nothing except a growing fascination with the Indian chief bust that Sister Regina has on the cabinet behind her desk. She will give it to me on the last day of school, six decompressed weeks after Sister Mary Catherine fails to return from Easter vacation.

In a last desperate attempt at child control before she goes, Sister Mary Catherine actually wedges me under her desk for several hours, lecturing from there so that she can keep me jammed up against the inside front of her desk with her knees. I am more or less face-down on the tightly laced tops of her shiny black shoes, unable to twist my head far enough to look up under her robes.

When I crane my head as far as I can in the other direction, however, I can see out to where my classmates' feet fidget beneath their desks. At the very top of my range of vision — this is really uncomfortable! — are the shoes, socks, and legs of Judy Thomor. Her shoes are contentedly quiet on the floor. Sister Mary Catherine is droning on about something or another, irregularly hitching her chair in closer, tightening the cage she has fashioned around me. But she can't touch me now, so long as I can breathe, for I can see Judy Thomor's legs. Both of them — her socks, her scuffed saddle shoes.

She moves a foot now, rocking it over on the side. What this does to her calf, how the muscle jumps out, the shadow it creates in the indentation along her shin. What the late afternoon sunlight, angling through the bank of windows across the room, does to the fine sheen of hair on her leg. . . . I gulp what little air Sister Mary Catherine allows and hold it as I twist my neck still further. The pain is impossible as I reach the edge of Judy's skirt, that formless shadow down between her thighs. I almost pass out with what I cannot see, dousing myself later with Catholic guilt for trying. Desire is the same as action, I am told.

I make regular visits to the principal's office over the next several years, as often as not for incessant talkativeness. The sentences I squeeze out to Judy Thomor, however, are few, hesitant, and labored. She renders me almost entirely mute on those rare instances when we are alone together. She may not even know that I am crazy about her, although I drop ham-fisted clues with cringing regularity: a box of candy slipped to her mother one afternoon — "Don't tell Judy who left it" — and a rose on Valentine's Day in the sixth grade.

The closest we come to physical contact — tag on the playground aside — happens one sunny afternoon at the end of the school year. A group of us have been climbing trees out in back of Ray Soper's house. When he and the Thomor girls get called in for lunch, I stay in the tree, awaiting their return. Judy comes back very quickly, before anyone else, and climbs up into the tree, more slowly and shyly as she makes her way up to my branch. She sidles out to where I am swaying, striking a pose, one hand holding the branch above her, the other lingering invitingly in her blue-jeaned lap.

Take it! I am instructing my hand. *Or put your arm around her. Reach over and kiss her, for cripes sake. Do something. Anything!*

But my body, quite detached from my brain, cannot move, not even an inch. So we sit there, both flushed with perspiration and deepening shades of red — we do nothing but blush and sweat. We can't even laugh, or fall out of the tree, or anything — only sit there and die together, paralyzed and mute. It is not death in its entirety, for we go through the motions when the others return. It may be the worst thing I have ever *not* done.

Judy cures a paralysis of another kind the following fall. I am twelve years old now, going on nine sexually. The closest I have come to a prurient adventure is an awkward turgidity when I wake up in the morning. To my mother's considerable annoyance, I sometimes miss the toilet bowl altogether. Even the most romantic ruminations I can muster — dancing with Audrey Hepburn, kissing, actually kissing Judy Thomor — call nothing to hormonal attention. Until vaccination day.

The long line snakes down the hall and into the nurse's quarters, as I try to quell the torture of knowing they are going to hurt me, and resolve not to be cowardly, or worse yet, to get sick and pass out. Then there's the poke itself, sleeves rolled all the way up — "Leave it that way" — and back to the classroom. Soon Miss McCann is conducting an oral exam, quizzing us to keep us awake, acknowledging the waving hands of those with the correct answers.

I sneak a glance across the aisle to where Judy sits. She is, as usual, waving her hand cheerfully, for she is smart too, only this day with her blouse sleeve rolled up over her shoulder. My eyes fixate on her armpit. White, the shadow of a shave mark, the suggestion of an underlying muscle. White and secret, the slightest hint of goose bumps, a soft undulation with each wave of her arm. Judy Thomor exposed. I can't take my eyes off her. I want to bury my face in her armpit, breathe her in.

Miss McCann is pacing back and forth across the front of the classroom, oblivious to the joys of the flesh. The throb in my groin is increasing, finding resistance at the underside of my desk. Something altogether amazing is happening here, but I cannot pry my almost full attention away from the pale invitation that is Judy Thomor's armpit.

I exhale when somebody's answer drops Judy's arm back to her side. And I eagerly wait for another question, with its happy probability that Judy will know the answer. Nothing else matters. Nothing else exists.

When recess is announced, Andy Reilly nods down at my pants. "Nice, John," he says and laughs out loud, prompting my quick positioning of a notebook in my lap. I sit there until the others file out of the classroom, feigning an unnatural interest in the mysteries of the handout sheet on my desk. When they are gone, I inspect myself with a mixture of embarrassment and pride, and slink off to the restroom, holding my schoolbooks awkwardly at belt level.

Within months, the same Andy Reilly dispatches me to Butterworth Hospital with torn ligaments in my left knee. I spend six long weeks on crutches, deep into the basketball season. My obsession with Judy continues, nurtured by her regular solicitations about my knee. On a few miraculous afternoons she carries my books as I limp home. We talk to each other now, a great leap forward in our tentative relationship. I go looking for her on the afternoon my doctor finally liberates me from the crutches. "No running for a while. No jumping or twisting. Take it *very* easy on stairs, going up or down."

When I return to school, I don't see her in the parking lot. "She's staying after class," someone says, "cleaning the blackboards for Miss McCann."

The school door is locked from inside, a stern janitor barring reentry. I must see her, must show her. I climb up onto the brick wall next to the steps and work my way out along the narrow ledge that borders the front of the building. Slowly, carefully, I edge my way out, clinging to the protruding bricks as I go.

"Jeez, John" — Andy Reilly talks that way when he is impressed — "You're going to kill yourself."

Encouraged, I let myself smile ever so slightly — *hold on, hold on* — and keep edging out, sliding my right foot ahead, then easing my left along. I am almost to the outcropping beneath the window frame — *thank God the window is open* — reaching around the corner, grabbing the open window frame, and pulling myself across to where I can see Judy, resplendent in a red sweater, putting the erasers on the tray below the blackboard.

She's gonna love this.

"Judy!" And she does, her eyes widen with surprise, a broad smile just starting to break over her face. I never register the full smile, as excitement overrides caution, and — *Oh damn!* — I lose my grip and drop over backwards, down through the hedge and onto my left heel — "Oh damn, oh damn!" — the knee giving way. Judy's head appears out the window above me, her hand across a smile at first, then alarm at my writhing, my torn left knee clasped in both hands.

It's not easy to win the girl, or to keep her. For another two months she lingers, until I can, for a second time, hand in my crutches.

An uncoupling occurs over summer vacation. Nothing is said, really, only a kind of unavailability that becomes chronic. "Judy went skating with a friend." "Judy is visiting her aunt and uncle in Muskegon." "Judy is spending some time at her cousin's cottage."

I look forward to returning to school, re-entering her orbit. But when we get there, I discover that she has been growing while I languish in shrimpdom. Always a little taller than me, she now looks down from so high that I have to step back to de-emphasize the difference. Other differences appear as well: her breasts against her cotton blouse, a bra that now serves as more than show. There is also a new resonance in her voice, the speech slower, almost sophisticated. This while my own voice lingers an octave above those of my peers. I feel like a little kid around her. I still *am* a little kid.

Judy Thomor is slipping away from me, lapping my elongated childhood. I am losing her, and there is nothing I can do about it. I lie awake at night, trying to will my way into growth.

The end comes with harsh abruptness one afternoon when I have been detained after school. I straggle down into Mary Waters Park, along the cyclone fence that divides the playground from the playing fields. Glancing to my right through the fence, over by the monkey bars, I can see Jimmy Groel, the quarterback of our football team, hovering over Judy, playfully pinning her wrists to a bar above her head, holding her there with his left hand. With the trigger finger of his right hand he is circling the outline of her breast beneath the blouse, flicking at what can only be her nipple. Far from being distressed, she is smiling, squirming away halfheartedly, and laughing — fresh light in her eyes. If she sees me, she doesn't show it, not now and not later. Nothing is ever said. She simply moves on, the object of my first great ache of longing.

Decades later, after years of abundance and attrition, I have a wry appreciation for the stickiness of early experience. While we are all ultimately responsible for *how* we respond to history, it does leave its fingerprints all over us. The unresolved dramas of childhood — and memory's imperfect transcription of them — do color everything that happens later, yielding up order and disarray.

Yesterday lives within today, just as today will imprint itself on tomorrow.

Grand Rapids never goes away.

Beneath the layered husk of my life, down in the memory of cells, a rat still scurries, seeking higher ground. White kitchen chairs shift and rattle with every turn the car makes, the luster of the open road. And Judy Thomor stands at the door, bobby-socked and angled and just out of reach, smiling and holding up the mirror.

Sins and Misdemeanors on the Southeast Side

Reinder Van Til

After graduating from Calvin College in 1967, Reinder Van Til spent time as a G.I., a cabdriver, a house painter, and a substitute teacher in the Grand Rapids Public School system. He then spent four years studying comparative literature at Ohio University, before joining the editorial staff of William B. Eerdmans Publishing Company in 1974. Between 1978 and 1987 he was a freelance writer and editor in St. Paul, Minnesota, and served as editor-in-chief of the Minnesota Craft Council's quarterly publication, *Craft Connection.*

Van Til has collaborated with William Brashler in writing, under the pen name Crabbe Evers, five Duffy House murder mysteries, including *Murderer's Row* and *Bleeding Dodger Blue.* His nonfiction books include *Lost Daughters: Recovered Memory Therapy and the People It Hurts* and a centennial history of the Michigan Veterans Facility (Grand Rapids). He has written more than a hundred articles for publications such as the *St. Paul Pioneer Press, Chicago Tribune* Sunday magazine, *Michigan History Journal, The Twin Cities Reader,* and several art museum magazines. Since returning to work for Eerdmans Publishing in 1987, he has been an academic representative and editor. He wrote the following memoir for this book.

Saturday mornings in autumn during the 1950s would often find my father, a respected professor of theology and a minister of the gospel, prowling our Grand Rapids backyard with the bloody hands of a man slaughtering animals. He had grown up on farms in Indiana, and there did not appear to be any city ordinances at midcentury that prohibited a city backyard from functioning as the equivalent of a barnyard once in a while. A rooster crowing in the morning, something you never hear in the city anymore, was fairly common then. Our neighbors had a large coop that represented respectable accommodations for a rooster and several hens, especially since a small door gave them access to the interior of a spacious red barn. People for the Ethical Treatment of Animals was in the distant Orwellian future, and ethical animal husbandry and butchery in city backyards simply meant killing the animals you were going to eat as quickly and efficiently as possible.

On a designated autumn Saturday, we would get a delivery of several crates of chickens. My father, who had been busy sharpening his hatchet on a whetstone in the basement, would emerge from the outside trapdoor that covered the steps descending into the cellar. He had set up an old tree stump as his chopping block at the very rear of our backyard, between the two garages, under the box elder tree. We boys would watch from a safe distance — probably my kid sister, too, because she was a tomboy — delighting in the sight of those white-feathered fowl dashing around insanely until the phantom message that their brains, such as they were, no longer had an attachment to their bodies had gotten through to their nerve endings, when they would abruptly and spastically lurch forward and collapse in the grass. Shortly after they had become inanimate, my mother — also raised on a farm — would yank them up unceremoniously by their scaly legs and dump them into scalding water for the feather-plucking stage of the operation.

We also raised rabbits for the family larder. They mostly lived in cages in the backyard, but we gave females who were nesting and bearing young the upper room in our garage. Most of these urban rodents were white with pink eyes, and they were all destined for the dinner table, so we were told not to become attached to them. When their time came, Daddy tied their back feet together and strung them, a half dozen or so at a time, upside down along a bar he had attached to two trees. He pulled down on their ears with his left hand, and with his right hand gave them a quick whack at the base of their skulls with a multipurpose household weapon: a chair leg whose hollowed-out core had been filled with lead. (This also became the designated weapon of deterrence against intruders after he had given his rifle away to a hunting friend.) The rabbits would expire instantly and virtually painlessly (at least I never heard a sound out of them). Then he would quickly gut them and skin them.

I don't know whether the dean of Calvin College, where my father taught Reformed doctrine, would have been appalled to come upon his associate professor on one of those bloody Saturdays. But it was certainly less out of the ordinary at that time than it would be today. Actually, I never thought of my father much as a professor; to me he was a warm and animated man who wielded a club and knife expertly in his enormous hands. Because his study door was usually closed — after all, he did have a half dozen kids bouncing off the walls of that small house — it was not often that I saw him at his real work in those early years. When I did interrupt him in his study to ask one of my boyhood questions, I would see a studious man lift his head out of a book and peer at me over his reading glasses.

The lone rabbit to escape our dinner table was Thumper, a huge male who stuck around as my pet after all the others had become part of the food chain. I always thought Thumper got his name from the way he would "thump" on his hindquarters in his cage; but perhaps it was actually my father who had named him on the basis of other talents he possessed. He was not confined during the day, and he was allowed into the cage of any female who was in heat — which was about as often as the old breeding-like-rabbits cliché would dictate. Thumper was very domesticated: I could let him out of his cage in the morning with no fear that he would wander off. He had it too good there. He would hop around the yard in his dignified way, nibbling at clover by my mother's feet as she hung out the wash.

Because Thumper was my pet, I watched the rabbit-butchering only two or three times. Somehow, though the chicken beheading was always a melodramatic spectacle, the sacrificing of rabbits was a little difficult to swallow — even though their behavior could be peculiar and I never did become attached to the others. Fowl are at a greater remove from our species than mammals are, and thus they are regarded as suitable for the dinner table in almost every culture of the world. We don't tend to make pets of them, and perhaps that's why Americans tend to eat far more chicken than they do rabbit or lamb, and why they are appalled by cultures that eat dogs. People on this continent do use roosters in cockfights and dogs in dogfights, but I've never heard of people betting on rabbit fights. I remember, though, the strange and exciting scene of two buck rabbits squaring off. They would stand a few paces apart, catapult forward, and smack their heads together as if they were mountain rams — then fall off to the side somewhat dazed. What I did not realize at that young age is that the air in our backyard must have been thick with hare estrus.

The Neighborhood

We lived on Hancock Street in southeast Grand Rapids, a street that runs parallel to and one block south of Hall, and is only three blocks long. Its western terminus is Eastern Avenue, where it runs dead into the Oak Hill Cemetery, which seemed so vast to us kids that we couldn't conceive of Hancock continuing on the other side. Its eastern terminus is Kalamazoo Avenue, which runs through the southeast side on an angle and, as far as we knew, continued all the way to the city of Kalamazoo.

In winter we would sled down Marshall hill, starting at the top at Hall and making a sharp turn at the bottom so as not to slide out onto Hancock. Some of the bolder sledders would sometimes go into the street, and cars had to be careful not to hit them when the snow was hard-packed and icy. I loved to sled down on the backs of the neighborhood's big boys, just on the edge of danger, seeing how sharply they could turn without falling off and how close they could come to going into the street below. Sometimes, under their influence, I would violate my family's boundary rule and cross Eastern to sled in the cemetery. It was more daring than Marshall hill because there were tombstones to dodge. One time, I was flying through the cemetery on the back of one of the big boys when we hit a tombstone with such force that it shattered my sled. The momentum carried me off his back and into a faceful of snow. I can't recall what lie I used to explain how the sled got busted on the far side of Eastern — to conceal my violation of the territorial commandment — nor whether the lie worked.

It was a small but magical world. The backyards of our territory seemed huge at the time, and there were few fences of any kind, let alone privacy fences; most yards simply opened onto the gravel alley, so you were always aware of what your neighbors were up to. Fire was a favorite motif for us young boys. It was not illegal to burn anything in the city then — trash in the alley, autumn leaves at the curb, and so forth — which brought out the budding pyromaniac in a lot of boys. In our neighbors' barn, the part-time habitat of the chickens, there was, next to the old, unused Model-T Ford, a tank of fuel oil. I would periodically slip in there, draw some oil into a small coffee can from the spigot on the side, and splash it into a smoldering trash barrel in the alley — bringing out the lady across the alley in alarm at her suddenly dramatic barrel fire.

On Saturdays we would hear the familiar clip-clop of the vegetable peddler's horse, blinders and feedbag on, as the two of them moved from house to house. Peddlers didn't use the manure skirts favored nowadays by downtown tourist horse-and-buggies. So they would leave our street spattered with road apples and wet with a stream of water that leaked off the block of ice, mingled with torrents of horse urine. Watching that horse do his business right on our street was endlessly fascinating. But the world of transportation was changing: at the age of nine, I was the first on our block to see the new 1955 Chevrolet as it turned onto Kalamazoo Ave. from Hall Street. It was the fall of 1954, and the newly designed Chevy was the classic two-tone color of Thousand Island dressing and gun-metal grey. What a beaut!

The coal storage room in our basement, when it was cleaned out during summers, was where my buddy Larry and I, both eight years old, set up our cigarette-making operation. We gleaned cigarette butts from friends' homes or off the street, sliced off the old paper, and rolled that old tobacco in Sears catalog pages. Longing to be like the grown men we observed, all of whom seemed to smoke unfiltered Camels, Lucky Strikes, Pall Malls, and Chesterfields, and tiring of the acrid taste of our own clearly inferior butts, we were constantly on the lookout for the real thing. One day we came upon a metal slug that was just the size of a quarter, a valuable commodity to a boy who seldom had a denomination of legal tender that large on his person. It happened that the car wash on the corner of Eastern and Evergreen had a cigarette machine where packs were a quarter. So when I was sure that all the adult attention at the car wash was diverted, I slipped that metal slug into the machine's slot, pulled on the knob that said Pall Mall (my uncle's brand), and rejoiced when I heard that pack of cigarettes thump into the tray. Larry and I quickly left the scene of the crime on our bikes — for another crime scene, behind the playhouse his father had built for the older girls and their dolls, a secluded spot surrounded by lilac bushes; after some unsuccessful attempts, we succeeded in lighting up our Pall Malls and inhaling our first real cigarette smoke — just as we had seen it done by our uncles and the big boys.

I would have been all right if Larry had not turned green and gone into the house with his tail between his legs. There followed an examination by his mother, which revealed the strong smell of tobacco smoke. Later, a parental delegation came to speak with my mother, which in turn prompted an interrogation by my father. I can't remember the punishment, but I'm certain that there was one; yet the strong exhortation not to smoke had its desired effect for only a few years. Because so many of the adult males we admired smoked cigarettes or cigars, smoking held its seductive allure, and we never had warnings in school about the dire effects of tobacco. After all, many of our teachers smoked. The prohibition seemed to be based solely on one's age, since it appeared inevitable that we were going to smoke anyway.

Harm and Danger

Our family had a car (a 1949 Studebaker), but it was mainly for trips out of town, not for driving around town. It stayed in the garage most of the time because, as my father declared ominously, "It costs fifty cents every time we take that car out of the garage." He wouldn't think of driving to work at the college (a mile away) or to church (almost a mile in the other direction), and we rarely took it out to go shopping. Everything we needed was within walking or biking distance. There were no supermarkets or malls. We bought all the commodities of daily life at separate small establishments, most of them spread out along Kalamazoo Avenue. The produce that we didn't get directly from farms we bought at

Kingma's stand; we got our milk and cottage cheese at Burt's Dairy, and our canned products and dry foods such as cereals, flour, and sugar at Korfker's store on the five-corner intersection where Kalamazoo crosses Hall. There must have been a bakery nearby as well, but Mother baked all our breads, pies, and other pastries. I remember riding in the car only to get meat from our locker in Madison Square. Families would buy a quarter of a steer and have it butchered and stored at the locker. The refrigerators of the day (then called "iceboxes") had only tiny, ineffective freezers, and we couldn't afford a free-standing freezer. Years later I wondered what quarter of the steer my family was in the habit of purchasing, because steaks were very scarce and there always seemed to be more of liver, tongue, and ox tails than would account for 25 percent of any normal animal.

In the early 1950s, delivery of daily milk in glass bottles probably cost a few cents extra per month. My father had calculated that those few pennies were a cost he couldn't justify since he had able-bodied children around. Thus it was my job to ride my bike to Burt's Dairy, where the coins that had been doled out to me in a little leather pouch were just enough to cover two quarts of "homo" (14 cents a quart), two quarts of "skim" (11 cents), and two quarts of "regular" (13 cents), the last of which had the separated cream sitting at the top. I would then load the wire basket holding the glass quarts into the wire basket on the handlebar of my bike and ride home, careful to avoid big cracks in the street or sidewalk. One day while on this mission, I lost my concentration for a moment and hit a piece of heaved-up pavement. My Roadmaster shuddered and went down, with me going over the top and onto the pavement with the milk bottles. The broken glass bottles cut me, and soon the blood from my hand was mixing with the milk from the broken bottles to form a pink rivulet flowing toward the storm sewer.

There were other temptations and dangers that came with growing up in that part of Grand Rapids — for example, the train tracks that crossed Kalamazoo Avenue at the lumber company. If we followed the railroad tracks west, where we weren't supposed to go, there were above-ground manholes that would occasionally be uncovered. At nine or ten I was fascinated by what might be happening below the city; so I enticed a friend to climb down the iron-looped steps with me into one of those manholes. From the last rung we dropped into an enormous underground concrete pipe that must have been the height of a man and had a small stream of water flowing down the middle. We could straddle that stream by shuffling along with our feet wide apart. But when we saw two large rats moving our way along that water flowage, we retraced our steps and scrambled back up that ladder.

The dangers we sought always posed a dual peril: the hazard to life and limb of the adventure itself, and then the punishment at home if our parents got wind of it. There was an ambivalence to our naughtiness: we loved to fly under the radar of adult attention, but we also enjoyed stirring adults out of their sedate lives by flouting the rules once in a while. And even though our parents prayed fervently every day for God to keep us from "harm and danger," we were fascinated by dangerous wrongdoing. There seemed to be so many things we were supposed to be reverent about, and so many activities that were proscribed, that we always had an overwhelming need to be irreverent and to do one of the prohibited things.

Old man Foster was the neighborhood hermit and tippler (judging from his backyard) who also had "Stevenson for President" signs in his front yard in a Republican city in 1952. He had heaps of beer and liquor bottles in the far back of his yard that were not picked up by garbage trucks; nor did he haul them off to the dump. We delighted in sneaking under the lilac bushes and smashing those bottles against the rocks and concrete blocks that were also part of the rubble there. We relished the pure, sharp tinkle of shattering glass.

It was always difficult to tell whether anyone was home at Foster's place because the shades were drawn even in the middle of the day; so we often acted as though no one was there — until the day Foster himself came out on his back porch with his shotgun and threatened to shoot us. I got my brother and friend over the fence — plus my own rear end — just in time to escape Foster's pursuit. I had fully expected that tender portion of my anatomy to be pierced by birdshot.

That evening at home, there came a heavy, insistent knock on the door — a knock my guilty conscience fully expected. We were in the kitchen when my father answered the knock, but a peek told me it was Mr. Foster. I pulled my brother under the dining room table, so we'd be out of sight. The man was ranting and blustering, shouting at my father that he had a shotgun ready for those boys the next time they came on his property. Well, our father would certainly have been in Mr. Foster's camp on the issue of keeping children under control. But as soon as Foster issued the threat to shoot "those boys," he lost any advantage he might have had with Daddy, who was a big man with the broad shoulders and huge hands of a former farmboy. (He had told us of youthful competitions that would feature picking up the rear ends of horses — a "foolish" activity he cited as the origin of his hemorrhoids.) Mr. Foster was short and slight, and when Daddy laid hands on his coveralls, from our view under the table, Foster's feet seemed to levitate off the porch.

"Don't ever threaten to shoot my children again, you understand?"

Foster sputtered. This was not the response he had anticipated. When he had his feet back under him, he beat a hasty retreat back to Butler Street. But even as the door closed on Foster, the book was not closed on us.

"Now where are those boys?" The question boomed from just above us as we watched Daddy's trouser legs pivot. We might have wished for a little birdshot in our cherubic backsides from old man Foster's 12-gauge after what we got from our father. I remember getting double what my brother got because I was older and had led my younger brother into sin.

Biblical and Western Themes

Although our family did have a car, we did not have a television. TVs were certainly available, but still an unmistakable luxury item for our family budget. More to the point, my father was adamantly opposed to a TV in the house because of the seductions that he admitted it posed for *him.* Television in the early 1950s offered a steady diet of Westerns, of which Daddy was enamored. Having done a great deal of work in his youth with horses, he was still in love with those animals. If we had a television in the house, he figured, he would watch too many Westerns. And he couldn't find enough time as it was to read the things he wanted to read. This, he figured, was a sound principle for his children as well. So it was no TV in our house as long as he was alive. Of course, we knew how to find a TV set in one or the other of our friends' homes, and my favorite shows were *The Lone Ranger, Sky King* (brought to us by Ovaltine), and *The Range Rider and Dick West.*

It would be understating the case by quite a measure to say that my family was devoutly religious. We prayed and read the Bible at every meal; we even sang hymns at the conclusion of dinner in the evening, and then we'd listen to more Bible stories at bedtime. Because the Bible was my main source of literary narrative, its stories informed my imaginative sense of the world around me. An empty lot along the alley was in my imagination the field of Ramoth-Gilead. Not far away, in a double lot that one could ride a horse through, stood a pear tree, which to me was where Absalom got hung by his hair as he tried to escape his father's men. The barn behind us was the temple which Samson, the Middle East's first suicide bomber, pulled down by its pillars, killing hundreds of Philistines along with himself. The ark of the covenant traveled on one of the neighborhood's horse-drawn vegetable wagons, perhaps below the canvas that was usually covering a block of ice — as it was being secretly moved, I imagined, to another location. Across Hall Street — the forbidden terrain — was the land of the Philistines.

As I got older, I was more drawn to the stories of "cowboys and Indians." My early reading heavily favored historical fiction from America's pioneer days, a favorite novel being *Indian Drums and Broken Arrows,* which I must have read a dozen times. As we got more adventurous, and our authorized territory grew, we would pack for a day's journey, dreaming of the lives of those early settlers. We had been told — probably at the Grand Rapids Public Museum, with its dioramas of early Indian and animal life in the Grand River valley — that Kalamazoo Avenue was originally the trail of the Potawatomi and of white settlers after them. It angled through the woods following ancient animal routes, and the street that was descended from that early path still meandered against the grid the city had imposed on itself. It must have originated at the Grand River in the beginning, but we only knew its northern source as Franklin Street.

Imagining that we were settlers taking our horses down an Indian trail, we wore cowboy boots and hats and packed sandwiches in big farmers' handkerchiefs, which we tied to the end of a stick. This was how Huck Finn and other adventurers were depicted in the juvenile novels and the *Illustrated Classics* comic books that I couldn't afford but made sure to inherit from older, better-heeled cousins. The baskets on our handlebars carried other crucial items, such as bows and arrows, plus anything of value we found en route.

Our journey took us southward on that slanting urban trail, past the drugstore and barbershop at Alexander Street, down the hill and across Hall, and then past all the familiar shops, through the lumber and hardware district and over the railroad tracks, past Kingma's and Boston Square, past Hope Reformed Church and our own church, and finally past the greenhouses and fire station at Burton Street. By that time we knew we had put real distance between ourselves and home, that we were getting closer to "the country." Past Burton the residential and commercial neighborhoods were replaced by a more industrial region. There were some factories on the west side of Kalamazoo Avenue, including the Michigan Bread Company near Alger (where the Range Rider and Dick West showed up to do their schtick in person one Saturday in midsummer). On the other side was a heavily wooded cemetery and another set of railroad tracks — a passenger line that would sometimes drop off people at trackside even though there was no station there.

After Alger the land really became rural: a large meadow and then woods on the west side of our trail, the back nine of Indian Trails golf course on the east, a last vestige of civilization in that part of the city. Kalamazoo Avenue, still angling, had become a country road. On and on we pressed our "horses," to 28th Street, which was the end of Grand Rapids as we knew it. (The first superstore outpost of the Meijer empire, Thrifty Acres, had not yet been built on that corner.) Beyond that was a forest and Plaster Creek — and the swamps resulting from its overflow. We took our bikes down the footpaths until we could go no further; then we propped them up against trees, slung our provisions over our shoulders, and set off down the narrowed trail. I was reading a good deal of James Fenimore Cooper in those days, so I instructed my white braves on how to proceed down the trail with all the stealth of our native predecessors — careful not to snap a twig that might alert enemies to our presence. Our early attempts at making bows and arrows out of branches and twigs were not very successful; but we did occasionally discover a real treasure — an authentic arrowhead (at least we believed so).

Sins of Thought, Word, and Deed

As I approached puberty, there were larger territories and other sins to explore. I was hanging around with older boys, an activity always fraught with the thrill of imminent peril. If you were fast carrying the football, as I was, you could get into the bigger kids' games. Some of those boys seemed a whisker away from the juvy home; it probably wasn't quite that close, but I felt like I was living dangerously. It seemed irresistible to me to make fun of some of the bigger boys whom my peers deemed worthy of mockery; but that would in turn require that I be adopted by an even larger friend, who would then be my "protection," in case I dropped my guard around one of the kids who hadn't forgotten a taunt — or his urge to beat me up.

One day a protector of mine, Pete, asked me whether I wanted to go over to Dale's house, where — he said with a wink — friends were working on model cars. I was flattered. Ordinarily I was only allowed to fall in with them in one of their outdoor sports; it was a rare treat to be invited to an older boy's house. We cheerily greeted Mrs. Van Dyke when we entered the back door and proceeded upstairs. As we reached the top of the stairs, I saw a sign on Dale's bedroom door that said: DO NOT ENTER! WORKING ON CARS!

"'Working on cars' is code," Pete whispered to me conspiratorially as he rapped a secret combination of knocks on the door, also apparently part of the code. When the door was first cracked and then opened to let us in, there were no model cars in evidence — only several boys who looked as though they were members of a cult.

"What's *he* doin' here?" one of them said.

"He's a friend of mine," said Pete.

That flattered me again and seemed to satisfy them, because they all put their hands back into their pants. What they were up to was beyond my ken at that time, though I quickly figured out what the code word "cars" in the phrase "working on cars" referred to. But I had not yet reached puberty, much less been involved in such a group endeavor. What I did know for sure, though, was that this was one of the prohibited things. I abstained. I had the feeling that, since I had no idea what I was doing, this moment could be one of the most embarrassing of my young life, and I didn't want to risk that.

Whether it was a coincidence or a lingering result of that incident's suggestiveness, not long thereafter I did have the first stirrings of priapic enthusiasm in my nether regions. I had injured myself running through the nursery on the corner of Hall and Neland on my way home from Oakdale School. The nursery had lines of thin metal wire, stretched tight between posts at about five feet high, to support Christmas trees. These wires were invisible against a gray and rainy sky. Of course, I wasn't supposed to be cutting through the nursery in the first place; but I'd been detained after school, and I didn't want my mother to ask questions. So I was running full tilt when I caught one of those wires right at eye level and went down with a gash across my eye, the eyelid sliced open. When my mother saw me walk in the door, my face covered with blood, I had the gratification of seeing her faint for the first time. When she revived, we went on my first of many subsequent trips to the emergency room at Blodgett Hospital, where I was sewn up without any further trauma.

After a few days, I went to a doctor's office to have my stitches taken out, a procedure that did not require the doctor. As I sat alone in the clinic's sterile room, a lovely nurse entered wearing glasses with black "cat-eye" frames. She was all white and starched in her nurse's uniform, including the perky white cap and the sheer white hose — a vision of professional loveliness. And when she bent over to examine me, her uniform bunched out at the button line to reveal a décolletage worthy of Marilyn Monroe. As she snipped away at my eyelid, the smell of her and her bosom gently brushing against my head were intoxicating. I began to imagine ways that I could get injured more often, wounds that would not cause permanent damage or even hurt too much — but that might require stitches.

Franklin Park

Franklin Park (now Martin Luther King Park) lay halfway between our first house on Hancock and the one on Dunham where we moved when I was eleven. It had a pool and a pavilion on the south end and tennis courts and lawn bowling on the north. Between the pavilion and the hill up to the tennis courts were a large diamond for baseball (where high

The pavilion and swimming pool at Franklin Park were crowded with the youngsters of the Southeast Side.
GRPL, Swanlund Postcard Collection

school and even college teams played) and two smaller ones for softball and the minor leagues of Little League. Along the Benjamin Avenue side stood a grove of oaks and maples.

A large area in front of the pavilion was flooded in winter to make a sizable ice-skating rink. I got onto that rink as soon as my ankles were strong enough to hold me up on skates. My mother had dyed an old pair of girl's skates black to save me embarrassment — which, of course, didn't work. My best Christmas ever, when I was eleven, I received brand-new hockey skates, not somebody else's hand-me-downs. It's odd that we never played hockey at Franklin Park, but I learned from the big boys how to skate fast, skate backwards, to stop with a flourish of shaved ice, to "crack the whip," and, of course, how to skate with girls. Even without hockey, skating fast had its risks, and one day I came home from a tumble onto the ice with my thumb bone sticking out of the skin at the first joint, occasioning another trip to Blodgett's emergency room.

In midsummer the heat seemed to rise off those baseball diamonds that were ice in midwinter as if they were skillets, the air reeking of the oil sprayed on the fields to keep the dust down. We played endless innings with a skeleton crew: half an infield and outfield, no catcher (the batter had the cyclone-fence backstop behind him), and no first baseman either, so it was "pitcher's hands is out."

When we got really heated up, we'd leave our gloves, balls, and bats under a tree and go to the swimming pool. Downstairs in the pavilion you could put your clothes in a basket for a nickel; you had to take a shower before going in the pool, and then as you emerged from the showers into the pool area, a lifeguard on a bench would record your entrance with a number clicker and have you spread your toes — looking for athlete's foot. Those checkers, lifeguards forced to do unglamorous toe inspection, were authority figures to us: they were high school students with a serious demeanor and a power complex around smaller kids. They could send you back to the showers if your feet were too dirty.

My social world expanded rapidly at Franklin Park: it was common ground for black kids from west of Fuller and south of Alexander and white kids from the north and east. It was my first experience of integration. I swam and played ball with black kids and got to know them as peers and fellow athletes at Franklin Park: we undressed together (for swimming), compared the shades of our skin, raced each other, and shared lunches. And that was where I met Buster Mathis. Buster was very large and very black — yet withal a gentle giant who never tried to intimidate us smaller kids. In fact, a favorite game was for a bunch of us to accumulate our nickels and dare him to do a cannonball off the high dive. Indulging us for his payday of nickels and his moment of notoriety, Buster would spring high off the board, wrap his huge body into a ball, and hit the water like a runaway boulder plunging into a lake. The splash, as we hoped, would always shower cold water on the lifeguard sunning himself on his elevated perch, and this would inevitably lead to Buster's expulsion from the pool. The bear-like teenager would slowly go over and pick up his pile of nickels, grin at us, and leave the pool for the day, a grand and heroic spectacle for those of us who had paid for the show.

Buster was surprisingly agile, as he showed on the basketball courts in Franklin Park pick-up games with his quick hands and feet, even before Muhammed Ali's "float like a butterfly, sting like a bee" mantra. Later he became one of the best boxers in the history of a town known for its pugilists. In fact, he went on to hold the heavyweight championship of the world briefly — sometime during that ill-defined era between Leon Spinks and Mike Tyson. Even as a pro he had that huge hulk of a body, the somewhat incongruous figure of a very dark overstuffed pillow mounted on a couple of walking sticks.

Franklin Park was a second home to me. The pavilion had an old basketball gymnasium upstairs that smelled of decades of kids' sweat; its wood floor creaked with every player's movement. It was where I saw legendary local hoopsters such as Annel Simpson and Maurice Calloway play during long Michigan winters. Years later, when I was a senior in high school, I even got into a pick-up basketball game with Ottawa Hills' own Mickey Stanley, the Detroit Tigers' centerfielder who played flawless defense when he was switched to shortstop for the 1968 World Series.

Faith-Based Street Theater

My devout parents talked much about "worldliness" (what later became known as "secular humanism") when I was an adolescent. This did not mean merely a prohibition of the church's specified "worldly amusements" of dancing, movie-going, and card-playing; it meant that we should not be people *of this world,* whom I understood to be those who didn't need to go to church twice on Sunday — could perhaps even play ball or watch the Lions on Sunday — people who had TVs and drove convertibles, who wore cashmere sweaters and listened to rock 'n' roll music. Ironically, when we moved to within a block of my father's place of work, Calvin College, where we would have expected to be enveloped by coreligionists with the same compunctions about "the world," it instead broadened my exposure to white people who were not Dutch Calvinists. There were only one or two such families on the new block, where, along with WASPish Methodists, lived Polish Catholics and next door the first Jewish people I had ever met; there were widows and widowers, teachers, three judges, and a few folks who were just plain comfortably secular. And after the red-lining that had kept blacks from residing east of Fuller Ave. was abolished, black people began to add pepper and spice to our neighborhood's whiteness.

I dearly wanted to be more worldly, but as I broadened my social contacts and savored the worldliness around me, my father sought to temper those influences and keep his brood focused on the "life of faith." For instance, we had never been allowed to go trick-or-treating because, as Daddy exhorted us, "We don't believe in Halloween!" We weren't pagans, he explained; and we weren't Catholics either, so we didn't observe All Saints Day. To my father — the theologian of everyday life, always on the lookout for ways to "redeem the time and glorify God" — October 31st was Reformation Day, a Protestant high holiday that commemorated the date in 1517 when Martin Luther nailed his "95 Theses" to the door of the Wittenberg church. But since the natives in his family had become restless, Daddy knew he had to come up with a creative alternative to trick-or-treating.

So on the evening of October 31, 1957, while all our neighborhood friends were going around from house to house in their store-bought outfits, we were dramatizing the story of Luther's rebellion against the Church of Rome on the stage of our own backyard. Daddy had written a skeletal script and stage directions, and since he was aware of the attraction dressing up held for young males, he allowed us to spend a couple hours that afternoon rummaging in the attic, a repository of old clothes, robes that could be customized, period hats, and costume possibilities from a wealth of relatives. The *dramatis personae,* customized by the improvising dramaturge for this occasion, were four characters played by me, my younger sister and brother, and a school friend I had hornswoggled into participating in this alternative Halloween. Being the oldest, I naturally chose the role of Martin Luther for myself; my friend Dave, who was not clear on the theological issues, became Luther's friend and colleague Philipp Melanchthon. My younger sister and brother were fellow dissident monks, with my brother doubling as the messenger from Rome who delivered the "papal bull" into Luther's hands.

As the lion-hearted hero, I nailed the 95 Theses — on a kind of scroll that my father had fashioned — to the front door of our garage. Daddy, who had some pyromaniacal tendencies of his own, supplied Luther and Melanchthon with torches he had made by wrapping kerosene-soaked cloth diapers around the ends of two-by-fours that were sitting around in the garage. With these we made our way through the dark passageway between the garages into the moonlit alley in back. Along with our fellow robed priests, we were fleeing the wrath of the established church when a messenger from Rome rode up on horseback (my father supplied both the background narration and the horse impersonation). After reading the condemning judgment of the papal bull aloud, Luther put his torch to it and threw it into the trash barrel, which had also been prepped with a touch of kerosene so that a dramatic conflagration ensued. After declaring that we were all now free from the corrupt Church of Rome, and throwing in a few Latin phrases such as *sola Scriptura,* Luther led his minions back to the house for apple cider and *olie bollen* (the Dutch treat that was my mother's specialty — deep-fried, apple-studded dough balls rolled in sugar).

My father's eye and ear for the dramatic and his generous sense of fun gave this concept legs for a couple years. By the time I was fourteen, however, I was trying to get out of the house as often and for as long as possible. So that year I made certifiable and parent-sanctioned plans to be at a friend's house for the evening of October 31 well in advance. I made sure I was with a friend whose parents had no overly religious or dramatic tendencies; in fact, I made sure I was with a friend whose parents were a good deal more worldly. In that transitional period between trick-or-treating and dating — and only one year removed from Reformation theater — we did what came natural to teenage boys: from the lilac bushes in an alley about four blocks from his house, we lobbed eggs from our mothers' refrigerators and rotten tomatoes from neighborhood gardens at passing cars on Fuller Avenue.

The 1950s saw the early flourishing of much of the art, entertainment, and popular culture icons and traditions that we have come to identify as authentically American, primarily because of the growth spurt of television — which, like us, was still in its adolescence. My own home had only classical and church music to listen to. But as I got out of the house more often, both literally and in the larger sense of venturing into frowned-on popular culture environments, I wanted to experience the music, literature, and art "of this world." I secretly savored Elvis Presley's "Jailhouse Rock" and "Hound Dog," Sam Cook's "Don't Know Much about History," and the hits of our own Del Shannon. Jazz had freed itself from the big band era and was beginning to make its way into the Midwest hinterlands. Dave Brubeck and his quartet were respectable enough to play the Civic Auditorium in Grand Rapids, and my first experience of one of their concerts when I was fourteen opened up a world of music that became a lifelong passion.

It was 1959, the last year of what has often been caricatured as a gray decade; but it was a time that I had experienced in full color, and at fourteen I was just on the edge of savoring life in my hometown. Indeed, it was not long after this that we did indulge in all the church's banned activities — the "worldly amusements" of movies, cards, and dancing — without giving it much of a second thought. I still had most of the important things in front of me: driving, drinking, athletic endeavors, real sex, and almost all of my reading of the classics of literature. But what was definitely behind me, along with headless chickens and model cars, was my career in faith-based street theater.

Half a Chance to Prove Myself

Al Green

The Reverend Al Green started singing professionally at the age of nine, when he and his brothers formed a gospel quartet, the Greene Brothers (Green dropped the final "e" of his last name when he went solo), in their hometown of Forest City, Arkansas. They continued to perform, now with their father, after they had moved to Grand Rapids. They sang in churches on tours throughout Michigan and the northern part of the country — ranging as far away as Canada and New York. Al's father kicked Al out of the gospel group when he caught him listening to Jackie Wilson.

At sixteen, Green formed a pop group, Al Greene and the Creations, with high school friends; they released a single record, "Back Up Train," in 1967, which climbed to No. 5 on the national R&B charts. Shortly thereafter, Green signed up to record with Willie Mitchell's band and in his studio, and together they shaped a sound that defined its own place in pop and R&B music. Between 1969 and 1976 they recorded eight albums that sold 20 million copies worldwide. Eight of his hits were million-selling singles, including "Let's Stay Together," "I'm Still in Love with You," "Tired of Being Alone," and "Look What You Done for Me."

In 1976, Green felt called to the gospel ministry and was ordained as the pastor of the Full Gospel Tabernacle Church in Memphis, where he serves to this day. Over the next decade or so, Green recorded nine best-selling gospel albums. He returned to the secular music charts in 1987 with "Everything Is Gonna Be Alright," and a year later his duet with Annie Lennox on "Put a Little Love in Your Heart" gave him a Top 20 pop hit. Green has won eight Grammy awards, and has been inducted into the Rock and Roll Hall of Fame (1995) and into the Gospel Music Hall of Fame (2004). In 2002, Green received a Grammy Lifetime Achievement Award. The following memoir is excerpted from his autobiography, *Take Me to the River.*

It was my brother Walter who laid the way for us, the year before we pulled up stakes, when he'd gotten married and moved out with his bride to Grand Rapids, Michigan. And sure enough, he got a job right away, working on the assembly line in a refrigerator plant, with a salary that paid the rent on a little two-room apartment and a good time on a Saturday night down around Division Street and a TV and a vacuum cleaner and a washing machine out on the porch, all for no money down and easy monthly payments. He'd even been able to put a little extra aside and that summer sent for Mama and brought her up for the first vacation of her life. She'd come back with a new hat and hairdo, telling tales about a city full of black folks putting on airs and while Daddy sniffed and acted disapproving and said Walter was good for nothing and shouldn't have left, what with us so short of hands at harvesttime, I guess somewhere deep inside a hook got planted, one that pulled and tugged until it finally reeled him in.

I got my first look at Grand Rapids that gray November morning as we rolled into town at dawn, and it seemed to me nothing like the stories Mama had told of a fine and fancy place. People, more people than I'd ever seen, were hurrying on to their jobs, bundled up against the bitter cold and dodging icy water splashed up by passing cars. Snow sprinkled with soot was piled up everywhere and the air was so thick with the smell of the city you could hardly breathe it in. The buildings were big, just like Mama said, but through the windows I got glimpses of tiny rooms and the cramped lives inside. The open fields of Jacknash, the endless sky, and the deep pine forests suddenly seemed more distant than ever, a fading memory on the far side of the world.

I looked up at Mama with tears in my eyes. "I want to go home," I said, and she turned to me with a wordless look that set me to crying even harder as Daddy turned the corner down a block of ramshackle row houses, looking for the address off the scrap of paper he clutched in his hand. "I want to go home," I said again before Mama shushed me and looked over to her husband like he might know how to tell a little boy that his home, for the moment, was right where he was sitting, inside a truck with Arkansas plates driving down Franklin Street, smack down the middle of Grand Rapids, Michigan.

Walter's wife had people in the area, and for the first few weeks, we somehow managed to squeeze in with them. I can't say I recall too much about those first days in Grand Rapids, aside from a confusing swirl of strange faces in a crowded apartment, the hustle and crush of the streets, and a cold that seemed to seep in through every crack and crevice right to your bones. I clung close to Mama day and night, wrapped in her arms for warmth and comfort, and I do remember a kind of fear mixed in with shame that always comes from having to depend on the kindness of strangers.

Daddy was gone most days, scouring the city for work and trying to find his family a more permanent place to live. He quickly discovered that the opportunities supposedly around every corner in Grand Rapids seemed instead to always be just out of reach. The first job he applied for was at a foundry; it was also the first job he was turned down for. The first of many. Seems like landing one of those good-paying spots on an assembly line depended less on a man's willingness to work hard than on who he knew and what kind of strings he could get pulled. The line formed at the rear, and there was a whole lot of other displaced dirt farmers with no prospects standing directly in front of Daddy.

Somehow, through a combination of odd jobs and a little help from Walter, we managed to rent an apartment across the hall from where we'd been staying and eventually moved farther down the block on Lafayette Street. The square footage wasn't a whole lot more than what we'd left behind, and after a few days, the walls felt to me like they were starting to close in. Back home, we had all the outdoors to roam free, and that was a liberty I'd come to take for granted. Now suddenly I'd lost my connection to God's creation and was too frightened to even open the front door and face those hard and hostile streets.

But of course, I couldn't stay cooped up in that tiny, two-room flat forever and, as those first fearful days turned to weeks, and the weeks to months, I slowly began to find my way around that strange landscape of sharp corners and concrete, through the constant rumble of traffic and across the frozen maze of city streets that stretched in every direction as far as I could see. And what I found was a whole lot of other folks in the same boat that we were in — black families from Mississippi and Georgia, Arkansas and Alabama — all come to the promised land on a wing and a prayer and all wondering what happened to the pot of gold at the end of the rainbow. The few lucky ones, like Walter, who'd been able to get hold of a weekly paycheck, seemed to be making everyone else envious and uneasy, like he knew something they didn't. But it sure wasn't Walter's fault that his wife had family in Grand Rapids who'd been able to put in a good word for him. And it wasn't his fault that he couldn't turn around and help his own family up the ladder. In that struggle for survival, it was every man for himself.

For me, the struggle was in just trying to keep connected to the things that had made my young life worth living. Cut off from the glory of the natural world, lost in the shuffle of our uprooted family, feeling as forlorn and lonely as I could ever remember, I began to turn inward, losing some of the spontaneous joy that had always made the world seem bright in my eyes, and with it, that childlike innocence that trusted and believed the best in everyone.

It was my feelings about my brother Bob that most clearly marked the change that was taking place inside me. In our family, the kids pretty much tended to hang together in pairs, according to age. Walter and William were a team and so were Mary and Odessa. Among the younger kids, Margaret and Maxine took up together, followed by Larnelle and Cluster. My partner was Bob and, back home in Jacknash, we shared the same chores, swapped the same clothes, and played with the same toys. It was a connection that just came naturally, and the closeness I felt toward my brother was something I never thought twice about.

But in Grand Rapids, all that started to change. Like Walter being the only one with a good job, the rules of our new life seemed to come down to a single hard fact: You were on your own. As a family, our fates were still tied together, if only because you could never get away from each other in that cramped apartment. But the fact that we were all packed in together like sardines was actually beginning to drive us apart, each one trying to find some private space inside themselves to block out the clamor and confusion that kept us all so nervous and on edge. So I guess it was only natural that simple bonds of kinship that brought us together, in pairs and as a family, would begin to tatter and fray. It wasn't long before I found myself avoiding Bob altogether, leaving him to fend for himself as I tried to stake out my own boundaries. Looking back, it seems as if those days marked the beginning of the end of my childhood, a time when I began to wonder who was on my side, who I could trust, and who was looking out for me.

The only person I could be sure of anymore was the one who looked back at me in the mirror. *I* was the only one I could really depend on, I decided, and it was up to me to make sure that Al Greene got what he needed to get by. It may seem like a sad state of affairs when a nine-year-old boy comes to the conclusion that he's only got himself to lean on, and the truth was that Mama and Daddy were doing the best they could to keep the family together: not only with food and shelter, but also with the everyday kindness and love that are every bit as necessary for survival. We were all adjusting as best we could to the new realities of city life, but the sad fact was, some of us were more adaptable than others. I couldn't tell you, for instance, whether Bob ever had a second thought about his new life, or the one he'd left behind. The fact is, it was as if he just hunched up his shoulders, ducked his head, and pushed his way through from one day to the next.

But for little Al, the change was almost too much to bear. Where was the sound of singing birds? Where was the warm caressing wind blowing up from the Gulf of Mexico? Where was the tender, patient murmur of Mama's voice, singing about how Jesus loved the little children as she rocked me to sleep?

Without those things as part of the regular rhythm of my life, I began to dry up and harden deep down inside, and it wasn't long before that sadness started turning into anger. It made me want to strike out at all the cruel and uncaring circumstances that had cut away at my happiness, and for the first time, a mean and vindictive streak came to the surface like the marks of a pox.

After a few months, we kids were enrolled in school, and it was there, in the classroom and the playground, that I got my first brutal lessons in the law of the ghetto. At first, I did my best to keep off to myself, not bothering anybody and hoping that no one would bother me. But there's something about a loner that always seems to attract the wrong kind of attention, and I'll never forget that day after school when I was surrounded by a gang of hard-core street kids who wanted to see just what this raggedy country boy was made of. It wasn't the first time I'd had to face the taunts and torments of a bully, but these guys made Shorty back in Jacknash look like a choirboy. They started pushing me back and forth between them, knocking me around like a rag doll, and when they saw that I couldn't defend myself, the biggest and meanest one laid into me with a terrible vengeance. I remember being knocked down onto the frozen hard dirt of the school yard with him standing over me, kicking at my ribs, and a whole crowd gathering around, shouting and screaming like they wouldn't be satisfied until I was dead. Finally, I guess everyone just got bored with me laying there and taking those licks and I managed to crawl away, dragging myself back home, where my mama cleaned me up and held me in her arms, like old times, as I cried myself to sleep.

But the tears I shed weren't so much from the bodily pains I had suffered as from the humiliation and rage that was boiling up inside of me like a fever. And the comfort I found that night wasn't from resting my head on Mama's soft breast. It was from my new-found determination that no one was going to treat me like that again. I swore it to myself — a childish oath all the more terrible for the cold conviction in my heart.

The next day on my way to school, I ducked behind the alley of a corner grocery store where the owner piled up his empty soda bottles until the delivery truck came with a new shipment. I don't know if that heavy glass Coca-Cola bottle was the first thing I'd ever stolen, but I can sure tell you it wasn't the only sin I intended to commit that morning.

I arrived at the school yard early, lurking around the corner of the cafeteria until I saw the boy who'd gotten such pleasure with every punch and kick he'd landed on me. Moving quickly up behind him, I raised that Coke bottle and brought it crashing down on his head, sending him staggering up against the wall while his posse just sort of stood back, wide-eyed. I hit him again, right across the face, and I remember some part of me wondering why that bottle didn't break as I rained blows down on him until he dropped down to his knees, his face covered with blood pouring from his nose and from a nasty gash over one eye.

I let up then, stepping back, still holding that bottle and looking around for anyone else who might be foolish enough to cross me. While I'm not proud to say it, the fear and awe I saw in the eyes of those kids gave me a nasty feeling of satisfaction. In that moment, it was as if I'd unlearned everything I'd ever been taught in Sunday school or my mama's Bible lessons. God may love a humble and contrite heart and blessed he may be who turns the other cheek, but on a grammar school playground on a cold morning in Grand Rapids, Michigan, it was might that made right, and only the strongest and fiercest and most brutal would survive.

In the months that followed the Coke bottle confrontation, my reputation as a badass dude spread through the school and the neighborhood. Although I never really cared a nickel for sports, I made a point of trying out for the football team. And I also made a point of getting kicked off the team a month later after repeated warnings for unnecessary roughness. It got to where I could hear kids whispering about me as I walked down the hallway and I felt proud of myself, a feeling that fed the dark certainty that I only had myself to depend on.

It would have been easy enough to guess where I was heading — a poor kid in the ghetto, trying to prove he's a man. That's a surefire formula for an incarcerated life. It was only a matter of time before my tough-guy attitude would take its course and I'd end up as another sad statistic of the urban black "crime problem." . . .

Back then I might have fooled everyone else with my mean and menacing demeanor — everyone, that is, but myself. I'd taken care to hide the sensitive, vulnerable spirit that was so much a part of my childhood, but it was always there, just below the surface, crying for attention and seeking expression. And the best way — the *only* way — I could give voice to that deepest part of me was, as it always had been, through music. . . .

I sought out every opportunity I could to sing, and if anyone thought it was strange that the toughest kid on the school yard also had the sweetest voice in the school choir, well, I guess they didn't dare say a thing about it. All in all, I wasn't much of a student and just couldn't seem to get my mind around history, geography, and math. It wasn't that I was stupid. In fact, most of my teachers were quick to tell me that I had what it took if I'd only *do* what it took. I just couldn't see the point of learning a lot of facts and figures that I couldn't ever imagine having another use for again.

And, of course, that was an attitude that quickly caught up with me. After my grades started scraping bottom, it was decided that I was a candidate for "special education" classes. . . . But before I was transferred, the principal of the school pulled me aside and laid a little wager on the table. "I'm betting that you're smarter than you're letting on, Albert," he told me. "And I'm going to put my money where my mouth is. I'm going to give you a brand-new hundred-dollar bill if you make straight A's in all your classes for the next two months. No B's. No B+'s. It's gotta be all A's or you don't get a dime."

I could hardly believe my ears. I'd never even seen that much money, much less been able to pull it out of my own pocket. And you can be sure, from that very afternoon on, I was paying the very strictest attention to my lessons. I remember coming home after school, making myself a peanut butter sandwich, and heading back to my bedroom to study for the rest of the night. And sure enough, I was able to rack up two solid months of top grades to get that $100. And, sure enough, once I had it safe and sound, I was back to my same lazy ways, with all those A's turning back to C's and D's.

But through it all, I never got less than top marks in choir, all throughout my grammar school years, going from the soprano to the alto to the tenor sections as I grew and my voice continued to develop. For a long time, I was the youngest kid in the choir, thanks to my constant singing. It didn't really much matter where I was. I always seemed to be humming one tune or the other, and it wouldn't be long before I'd forget myself entirely and start giving it everything I had at the top of my voice. The school had a rule that you had to be a certain age to try out for the choir, but they overlooked the requirement in any case after I got caught singing alone in a classroom one day, waiting for the bell to ring and the lesson to start. I don't think I even realized what I was doing until I turned around and saw a whole crowd of people gathered in the doorway, looking at me in a way

After moving to Grand Rapids in the mid-1950s, Al Green attended Franklin Elementary School and South Junior High (here in his seventh-grade class picture).
GRPL, South High yearbook, 1959

I'd never quite experienced before. I can't say I was comfortable with them staring at me, but I can't honestly say I was *un*comfortable, either. The truth is, I didn't mind the attention, even though I pretended to get mad and told them all to get on about their business.

But I guess word got around, because before I knew it, I got called up before the choir master, a sweet, gentle man named Mr. Nelson. He tried me out on a few tunes, accompanying me on his piano, and the next day I was told to report to choir practice. It seemed like a good way to get out of doing all that reading and writing, so I went along, even though I was more than a little worried about how it might affect my rough and rambunctious image. But by the end of the first morning, I had no thought to keeping up appearances. I'd found something I truly loved to do . . . and was truly good at.

I looked forward to nothing more than arriving early each morning for practice, the sunlight breaking through the dusty windows of the school auditorium with its high, echoing ceiling and listening to the sound of our young voices bouncing off the walls and coming back around until it seemed like the whole room was filled with an invisible chorus of cherubs and angels. I was proud of being singled out as a soloist for the Christmas program or spring pageant or those special evenings when all the grown-ups would gather to hear us perform our selections of popular and patriotic tunes, clapping and carrying on like it was a command performance at Carnegie Hall and I was the star virtuoso, taking my curtain calls in the bright spotlight.

In those moments, I was worlds away from those dirty streets and dangerous playgrounds and crowded tenements. The music transported me, and the sound of my own singing was another kind of power, far different from the violent bullying that I used to keep the world at bay. Up on that stage, raising my voice to the rafters and feeling the notes fill me up from some abundant, radiant joy deep inside was a way of marking my place in the world, of standing firm and proclaiming loud and clear, "My name is Al Greene, and I am *somebody!*"

If it hadn't been for that school choir, I don't know but that I might have ended up locked in prison, brought down to the gutter, or buried deep in a pauper's grave. And I have to thank Mr. Nelson for giving me the first real opportunity I had in life to make something of my musical gift. Without his encouragement and the way he kept at me to improve my technical skills without ever letting me lose touch with the pure pleasure of singing, I don't know where I'd be today. You could say that music was an escape from the grim realities I faced every day, but it was more than that: Music *was* my reality.

And music was everywhere in those days. The late fifties was, of course, the Golden Age of American pop music, and so many of the sounds that would shake, rattle, and roll the world were just beginning to burst the bounds of the tired old Tin Pan Alley scene. It seemed like great tunes were pouring from every open window and every passing car, with most everyone's radio tuned to WCHB, blasting west across the state from Detroit. The fuse that would spark the Motown soul explosion had yet to be lit, but there was no doubt that something powerful and potent was in the air, getting ready to break out of the narrow bonds that had for so long defined "race music" and take its liberating message to a huge young audience, black and white. From Ivory Joe Hunter to Frankie Lymon; Nat "King" Cole to Clyde McPhatter; Chuck Berry to Little Richard to Fats Domino and beyond . . . everything you heard in those days was like nothing you'd every heard before.

As proud as I was to be front and center in our little school choir, I was prouder still of my family connection to the great R&B and blues that was the sound of the era. I had a distant cousin Herman on my daddy's side who used to live not far from us in West Memphis, Arkansas, and went by the name Little Junior Parker. I think my daddy, with his stern admonitions against worldly music, must have felt a little ashamed of his link to the down-and-dirty sound that was Little Junior Parker's stock in trade, but I also suspect that, if you'd asked him, he might have confessed to being at least a little pleased that one of our own had made the big time. . . .

By the time we moved to Grand Rapids, cousin Herman had relocated from Memphis to Houston, where he recorded some even bigger hits for Duke Records including his signature tune, "Next Time You See Me," and classics like "In the Dark," and "Annie's Got Your Yo-Yo." I made a point of following his career in the pages of *Rhythm & Blues* and other music magazines and traced his itinerary across a map when he toured with his all-star revue, Blues Consolidated, sharing the stage with Bobby "Blue" Bland, Big Mama Thornton, and so many others. The road show would roll through Detroit and Chicago but never seemed to get even close to Grand Rapids, which isn't surprising, considering that the city wasn't exactly known for a hot and heavy music scene.

Not that it would have made a difference even if it had. Daddy wasn't about to let me loose to scorch my ears with the sound of hell's own house band. In the days since his secret — and not-so-secret — visits to the local honky-tonk [in Arkansas], Daddy had gotten steadily more strict and set in his ways. And to his way of thinking, there was God's music and the devil's music . . . nothing in between and no two ways about it. Maybe it was the fact of having moved his family from that simple, set-apart life on a farm to the bright lights and dark corners of the big city that made him all the more determined against exposing his children to the sinful influences of secular music. Maybe he wanted to atone for his own attraction to the backbeat bump-and-grind of raunchy blues at its best. Or maybe he believed that a sanctified soul must be saturated daily in praise and worship.

But I don't think so. I think Daddy discouraged us from tuning in to the world beyond our four thin walls because he was still bound and determined to make a name for himself in gospel music and didn't want anything interfering with that goal. As soon as we'd gotten ourselves more or less situated in Grand Rapids, Daddy began blowing on the embers of his old dream, herding us kids into practice sessions in the front room and working us ragged with renditions of every gospel chestnut he could pull from the hymnbook.

And I must say, we weren't half-bad. My brothers and I were all a little older, and as we matured, our voices started to blend together with that smooth and polished four-part harmony that was essential to any self-respecting vocal group on the church circuit. I got a more prominent part in the lineup, doing background tenor parts and an occasional lead, and, like the day in class when I attracted all that attention, I didn't mind a bit when folks would hear me sing and set to stamping their feet and clapping their hands and shouting out praises to the Lord. It was only too easy to imagine that they were making all that fuss over *me*.

And just like in Arkansas, the Greene Brothers started working a regular circuit, doing our act and taking up offerings in little churches all around Michigan, from Benton Harbor to Pontiac to Lansing, making the run every time Daddy could grab a few days off from work and hoping, always hoping, that a talent scout from one of the big gospel record companies — Peacock or Specialty or Gotham — might just happen to be in the neighborhood and catch wind of our undiscovered talent.

And our repertoire kept growing to keep pace with Daddy's ambition. We could deliver as stirring a version of "Precious Lord," "How I Got Over," "Mary, Don't You Weep," or "I Looked Down the Line and I Wondered" as anybody this side of the Swanee Quintet or the Sensational Nightingales, and few could match our renditions of "Too Close to Heaven" and "Ain't Got Long Here." Daddy even tried his hand at a few original numbers, but when it came to that old-time religion, it was the tried and true standards that brought them out of the pews every time.

And for a while, it seemed like it was only a matter of time before we'd be getting that knock on the dressing room door and a dotted line would be just waiting to be signed. From [west] Michigan we started branching out, first east to Detroit, then over to Cleveland and Chicago, and eventually up into Canada and out as far as New York City.

Looking back, I can recognize what a rare opportunity it was for a young boy to see the width and breadth of this country. Those long nights on the road, sharing a sack of burgers, and harmonizing to the hum of the tires . . . those are some of the most precious memories I have with my family. The natural bond between brothers was strengthened on those long trips and cramped quarters, and whatever we had lost between us by trying to find our own way in a strange new land we almost made up for when we stood together, grouped at the altar of some church we'd never been to and would never see again, lifting up our voices high and proud. We were the Greene Brothers, and we were on our way.

Of course, it didn't quite work out like that in the end. The ties that bind a family together weren't strong enough to keep us from going, each off on his own way. My daddy's dream of gospel stardom would slowly but surely flicker and fade. And the sound of our voices, each one adding his harmony to the whole and all together celebrating the blood bond between us, would soon fall away into echoes and silence. But while it lasted, the Greene Brothers was the purest and sweetest and simplest way we each could find to say how much we loved each other.

Even if the Greene Brothers had never set foot outside the city limits of Grand Rapids, we could have had more than enough places to strut our stuff. The truth is, there are probably more temples, sanctuaries, and storefront churches per square block in that city than anywhere else I've ever been.

Within a block of our apartment, for example, we had no less than three full-time houses of worship, with packed-out congregations and anointed ministers of the gospel. It was a real spiritual supermarket. Right around the corner, we had the Baptist church of Reverend Gants. And not too far up the street was the African Methodist assembly of Reverend Cecil. And right next door to our building was Mother Bates's House of Prayer, which was where the Greene family could be found on a Sunday morning.

Mother Bates was one of those folks with a connection to God so strong and pure it was like a light shining all around her. I'm not saying she had a halo exactly, but the simple goodness and selfless kindness that showed forth in her life provided a beacon for our whole neighborhood. Folks can debate religion all they want, deciding all those fine doctrinal distinctions and denominational differences and making sure every "i" is dotted and every "t" is crossed. But when it's all said and done, the Christian life is lived out, day by day, by saints like Mother Bates, who take the Gospel at its word, preaching to the poor, caring for the orphans and widows, and loving their enemies as themselves.

For all the faithfulness of my own mother, who never missed a Sunday service and always had a Bible by her side, I think I learned more of what true faith is all about just by watching Mother Bates. There was no derelict drunkard so lost he didn't deserve a good meal; no ratty and worn-out streetwalker too forlorn to reach with a loving touch; no chip on the shoulder of a tough kid that wouldn't melt at her words of love or the promise of her prayers. It's no wonder that Mother Bates's storefront church was the hub around which the life of our neighborhood revolved. . . .

We hadn't been going to church for more than a few months when Mother Bates picked me out of the congregation to sing in the choir, and it was there that I could really let go, without having to worry about hitting the right notes for the Greene Brothers' harmonies or trying to sound just like Jackie or Sam or any other musical heroes I'd been drawn to on the radio. In those times, with two brothers behind me, banging out the rhythm on an old bass guitar and a snare drum, I was washed away in a flood of grace coming down from heaven, right through Mother Bates, and out across us all like a cleansing tide.

It wasn't too long before Mother Bates was taking me out with her on the revival circuit, stopping off at little churches and tent meetings all throughout the Midwest. I'd be up front singing gospel songs as the people filed in for the meetings, and afterward I'd sit beside Mother Bates as folks lined up to get her spiritual advice on their personal problems.

She'd be praying and ministering for hours after each meeting, and before the night was up, she'd be sitting in a pool of golden light, shed from the scores and dozens of candles the people would light and leave behind as an offering to the Lord. . . .

[In our neighborhood] we were all so busy trying to prove ourselves to each other that we never really saw how much alike we were — scared kids, staring down poverty and despair and a generally hopeless future, all trying to act like we had the world on a string. Gangs weren't as much of a substitute family for poor kids the way they are today. Which isn't to say that in the black 'hood of Grand Rapids, there weren't more than enough turf wars to make life dangerous. But in the late fifties and early sixties, the terrible social pressures that would come to tear black family life apart — drugs and broken homes and children having children and all the other plagues we've come to witness over the past decades — hadn't yet arrived full-blown on the scene. Gangs were a way for kids to work out their aggressions, not a whole lot different from playing cowboys and Indians. Young folks still had mamas and daddies, a place to call home, and a reason to stay out of trouble. And as hard as those times might seem in my memory, I know they're nothing compared to the trouble kids face today.

Still, like young folk everywhere, we managed to break out of our roles, find each other, and form lasting friendships. And I guess it will come as no surprise when I say that I found my best friends through music. And it's probably equally obvious that the music that drew us together was hardly the hymns of praise or choruses I was singing for Mother Bates or the Greene Brothers. Like just about every other teenager in America — black or white, rich or poor — I was tuned in to the rock & roll wavelength that was keeping the whole country in motion from ocean to ocean.

The year was 1964, and the sounds sweeping the nation brought with them the first hints of liberation from those tired old pigeonholes of race and class and style. By then *Billboard,* the magazine known far and wide as the "bible" of the music business, was lumping everything — black *and* white musical hits — into a Hot 100 chart. But the real sign of the times was what was on that chart. It seemed like the British Invasion and the Motown Sound were racing neck and neck to make music history, and between the Supremes warbling "Where Did Our Love Go," "Baby Love," and "Come See About Me" and the Beatles chiming in with "I Want to Hold Your Hand," "She Loves You," "Can't Buy Me Love," "Love Me Do," "A Hard Day's Night," and "I Feel Fine," there wasn't much room for anybody else. But of course, great singers and great songs always make a space for themselves and there was no shortage of key cuts that would go on to define the era: Mary Wells's "My Guy" and the Dixie Cups' "Chapel of Love"; Dean Martin's "Everybody Loves Somebody" and the Four Seasons' "Rag Doll"; Roy Orbison's "Oh, Pretty Woman" (a song I'd be proud to cover myself years later) and even Louis Armstrong with his unforgettable version of "Hello, Dolly!"

I loved it all and, to my eighteen-year-old ears, it all seemed to be coming from the same single source of fresh new creative inspiration. The musical explosion of the sixties, fueled by drugs and free love and the emancipation of our minds *and* our behinds, was still a year or so from its full bloom, but change was in the air, even in the cold, damp, and sooty air of Grand Rapids.

The truth was, the music I was hearing on the radio, like those singles I'd save up my lunch money to buy down on Division Street, had become a whole lot more appealing than the rusty old repertoire I did over and over again with the Greene brothers or down at Mother Bates's. Gospel music was lagging far behind pop, rock, and rhythm & blues and sometimes, standing up there singing to a lot of old folks in their stodgy Sunday best, I felt like I might go crazy if I heard them join in, flat and off-time, for one more chorus of "Savior, Pass Me Not" or "Standing in the Judgment."

And it wasn't just the music that was beginning to get up next to me. As I moved through those tumultuous teenage times, I was quickly losing patience with the messages I heard preached, Sunday in and Sunday out, in pulpits from Chicago to Cleveland, Brooklyn to Baltimore, anywhere and everywhere the Greene Brothers got a gig. Those preachers all seemed to be reading from the same playbook, telling us about how the meek shall inherit the earth and how God will exalt the humble and contrite of heart. "Be patient," they told us. "Wait on the Lord, and in due season, He will lift you up."

Meekness, humility, and long-suffering. That's the last thing any hot-blooded eighteen-year-old, with rock & roll echoing in his ears, wants to hear. All their sanctimonious Scripture spouting, their holier-than-thou attitudes and finger-wagging warnings about sin and damnation — church and church-going folk were starting to wear me out. I even took to avoiding Mother Bates, with those black shiny eyes that seemed to bore right through me like soul-scanning searchlights.

I took to spending more and more time away from home as well, where the crowded rooms and stifling smells of close-quartered living were pressing down on me like a suffocating wool blanket. Everywhere I turned — school, home, or church — the world was too small and too tired and just plain too *boring* to stand much longer. What solace I found, I found on the streets, which at that time seemed full of kids just like me, restless and rebellious and ready to break out — if only we could find a way.

And of course, the music was always there, spurring us on. My life-long love of Jackie Wilson became a burning obsession around that time and, to my ears, he was working at the top of his form just about then. From the moment his smash hit "Baby Workout" topped the charts in early 1963, it was as if a tidal wave of pure, jubilant energy had crashed down on top of us. And he just kept topping the stakes — and himself — with each subsequent song: "Shake! Shake! Shake!," "Baby Get It," "Big Boss Line," "Squeeze Her — Tease Her." Every time a new hit from Jackie exploded out of the little red plastic RCA radio I kept close to my pillow — I felt like *I* was going to explode. Sure, I yearned to sing like my hero, to make the notes bend and sway at my command, to let my voice soar higher and higher, and then, just when it was getting ready to break through into outer space, give it that patented Jackie Wilson rocket-booster soul shout that would send it right into orbit. And sure, I longed to strut my stuff as suave and continental, cool and sharp-creased as the Man himself, in a sharkskin, single-button tux and cummerbund, with my hair conked and my fine Italian shoes spit-shined and gleaming.

But more than anything, I wanted to get a taste of the life he lived, full of excitement and glamour, bright lights and beautiful women. I wanted to be the center of attention, the main attraction, the star of the all-star cavalcade. And somewhere along the way, I actually convinced myself it could happen. All I needed was half a chance to prove myself.

Opening a Door

Paul Schrader

Paul Schrader has been one of America's most respected screenwriters and filmmakers for almost three decades. After graduating from Calvin College, he earned an M.A. in Critical Studies at UCLA in 1970; the University of California Press published his thesis on the films of Ozu, Bresson, and Dreyer as *Transcendental Style in Film.* He was briefly the film critic for the *Los Angeles Free Press* but put criticism aside when his script for *The Yakusa,* a drama about Japanese gangsters, was filmed in 1975 by Sydney Pollack.

Schrader's landmark collaboration with Martin Scorsese on the noir psychodrama *Taxi Driver* (1976) started a durable creative relationship that also produced *Raging Bull* (1980), *The Last Temptation of Christ* (1988), and *Bringing Out the Dead* (1998). His notable screenplays for other directors include *Obsession* (Brian de Palma, 1976), *Rolling Thunder* (John Flynn, 1977), and *The Mosquito Coast* (Peter Weir, 1986).

In 1977, Schrader made his debut as a writer-director with *Blue Collar.* He has continued to develop his contemplative approach to often extreme material in *Hardcore* (1979), the unique, Cannes-award-winning film *Mishima: A Life in Four Chapters* (1985), *Patty Hearst* (1988), *The Comfort of Strangers* (1990), *Light Sleeper* (1991), and *Affliction* (1997), based on the story by Russell Banks. In 2006, Schrader completed production on *The Walker,* a conceptual progression of his 1979 classic *American Gigolo,* and in 2007 he will direct *Adam Resurrected,* based on the novel by Yoram Kaniuk. He has written the following reflections specifically for this anthology; the penultimate paragraph is excerpted from his interview with Garry Wills, first published in *Shouts and Whispers* (Eerdmans, 2006).

Opening a Door

My mother converted my father. From this single event sprang the consequences of my life. They were clerks in Muskegon, Michigan. My mother's parents, the Fishers (anglicized from the Dutch Visser), had emigrated from Friesland. My grandfather had secured unwanted swampland, diked it up, and started a celery farm. My mother's family belonged to the Christian Reformed Church; they still conducted services in Dutch on Sunday afternoons when I was very young. My father's father, a German, not particularly religious, had moved to Muskegon from Canada.

During their courtship my mother insisted that my father join the Christian Reformed Church. He did and, as is so often the case in those situations, became more devout than those who had been born into the faith. Before my older brother and I were born, they moved to Grand Rapids, where my father worked first at Michigan National Bank, then at Michigan-Ohio Pipeline. He had intended to go to Calvin Seminary, but times were hard and he had to drop out of college to support his family before he could even start the seminary.

We lived at various residences on the West Side of Grand Rapids because it made for a shorter drive to Muskegon, where we would go each weekend to visit my mother's family. It was something of an anomaly for us to live there because, at the time, the West Side was primarily Polish and Catholic; the South and East sides were Dutch and Reformed; those caught in the middle tried to keep the town running. We lived on Miller Drive, Escott Street and, later, Ducoma Drive. The house most vivid in my recollection was at 1405 Escott, just a block from Richmond Park and all the mysteries it held for a growing young man.

All the landmarks of my childhood have disappeared or changed function. Twelfth Street Christian Reformed Church is no long Christian Reformed. West Side Christian School, Grand Rapids Christian High, and the Franklin Street campus of Calvin College have all been sold and refitted as other institutions.

My parents, devout Calvinists, subscribed to the church's prohibition of "worldly amusements": these included dancing, drinking, card-playing, theater attendance, and the like. Sundays were reserved for

The swimming pool at Richmond Park drew those growing up on the Northwest Side during the summer months.
GRPL, Library Postcard Collection

church activities. No housework was to be done, nor lawn work or other chores. Sunday morning shoes were polished on Saturday night. Catechism lessons and Bible verses were memorized and tested at mealtimes.

My memories of this, surprisingly enough, are quite fond. Sunday afternoons, after the morning worship service, we would often convene at my grandmother's house (my grandfather had died) where my uncles, celery farmers all, would sit around the table and discuss the morning sermon, contesting the minister's exegesis of the text and his delivery of the sermon — before moving on to more mundane matters of farming and church gossip. The "young people" were allowed to sit at the table but not to join in the conversation. I was mesmerized watching these men, their Dutch faces red from the sun, their arms cross-hatched with scars from celery rot, arguing about predestination and throwing around terms like "prelapsarian" — and all the while the smells of cooking and the sounds of female laughter coming from the kitchen. When I consider the adolescence of my own children, whiling away countless hours in front of multi-channel televisions or video games, I have no doubt who had the better childhood.

The first crack in the well-maintained family-church edifice came with the advent of television. Our family, like other church families, did not have a TV. We were, however, only one of five or six families on the two-block stretch of Escott who were Christian Reformed. My street playmates, as opposed to our friends from West Side Christian School, were Roman Catholic — and they all had television sets. So, under the pretext of playing ball or such, my brother and I would slip over to the Swantacks' house to watch after-school kids' shows. But it would not be long before this leaked out. What galled my mother was not so much that we were watching television, but that the Swantacks had a plaster Madonna atop their television set. That was that. We soon got a TV of our own, in our living room, where my parents could monitor its use.

That crack became a fissure that was never repaired. Once the outside world — its music, jokes, and values — permeated Christian Reformed homes through the airwaves, hope for a cultural separation was a lost cause.

The dark side of those warm memories of sitting around my grandmother's table came out in the conversations my brother and I had with our father. Although he had been unable to enter the ministry, he was determined that his sons would. We would attend Calvin College, of course; that was a given. The issue was whether we would be pre-seminary students or not pre-sem. In a basement study that my father had filled with theological books, the arguments between father and sons would go back and forth — first with my brother, then with me. We won those battles, but not without a cost. The scars remained and were never healed.

That old environment of childhood never goes away. It doesn't matter how far or fast you run, you don't outrun your childhood. Those spiritual issues continue to nag until you find different ways to deal with them or *not* deal with them. And you just keep circling around it. John Wayne once said, "I don't like God much once I get him under a roof." I've really been very wary of institutionalized religion because I feel it has often been the enemy of spirituality. I do know, though, how I got out of Grand Rapids: the same way a bullet gets out of a gun.

For someone who spent twenty years in the fold of Grand Rapids and the Christian Reformed Church, I find myself reflecting remarkably little on those years. There is, however, a warm glow emanating from under the door to my childhood: memories of vacation Bible school, trips to Reeds Lake and the amusement park known as Ramona, sledding down Richmond Hill, door-to-door selling of flowers and candies, picking blueberries, collecting newspapers and salvage iron, nights in the church basement, bicycling with my ball and bat to Alpine Park and beyond. I can feel the chill on the doorknob: if I open the door, that glow will sweep away into the darkness beyond.

My Football Career

ROBERT VANDERMOLEN

After his storied athletic career at Union High School in Grand Rapids, Robert VanderMolen attended Michigan State University, where he graduated in 1971. He received an M.F.A. from the University of Oregon in 1973, and he taught briefly at Grand Rapids Community College during the 1970s. He has been a painting contractor ever since.

A member of the Grand Rapids Historical Commission, VanderMolen is a poet who has published ten collections of poetry, including, most recently, *Peaches* and *Breath*. Some of his recent poems have been published in *London Review of Books, Poetry, Parnassus, Driftwood, Sulfur, Epoch, St. Ann's Review,* and other poetry journals. He is married to Deb Stenman of Charlevoix, and they have two grown sons. He lives on the West Side of Grand Rapids. He wrote about his early football career specifically for this anthology.

I was eleven years old when I decided to play football. My father, like all the neighbor fathers, was a Detroit Lions fan. We watched games on TV on Sunday afternoons — sometimes the two of us, at other times with neighboring fathers drinking beer in our den. Occasionally we attended high school games at Houseman Field on Friday or Saturday nights. Until the age of eleven I was not a rapt or attentive spectator; I was often bored. But it was pleasant being part of a crowd at the high school games, especially in October, when nights grew crisp.

In elementary school I was the smallest boy in my class. During those years it seemed certain to me that my best bet in life would be to improve my wit. I wasn't likely to overpower bullies or attract girls with my physique — though my fantasy life was rich in those areas. Instead, I needed to be clever and amusing to find satisfaction in life. Precocious by day (or attempting to be), I practiced my alertness and timing by night. When I was left alone, trying to study or lying abed, I turned into a football hero — usually a running back zigzagging down a vast field with stocky Dutch and Polish boys falling over each other trying to catch me, the stands thunderous with stamping, clapping, and cheers. Standing in the end zone handing the ball to the official, humble in regard to my speed and pivots, my deadly stiff-arm, I was that old-fashioned Christian athletic type.

Eventually I cajoled my parents into buying me shoulder pads and a football helmet at Atlantic Mills. During tedious summer days I practiced charging across our West Side front yard, punching through massive defenses, the football tucked securely under my right arm. About all I had going for me, besides an effective dream-state, was agility. I was small but I was fast. I found neighbor kids to be an opposing team. But they were too young and easily distracted, and finally they grew tired of my stiff-arm. So I often played alone. Even my brother and sister headed somewhere else when they spotted me hoisting on my pads.

At some point, a cross-over occurred. Fantasy became intention. I would be a football player. Perhaps I'd be the smallest football player, but I was destined to be one of some regard. I worked on my running. I ran to school and I ran home from school. I ran through fields and woods. In the woods I zigzagged between the oak and maple trunks, leaping over small deadfall like a white-tailed deer.

During the evenings older boys played a sandlot game on the grass oval inside the parking lot at Covell School. They let me play outside receiver. I'd run furiously across the oval, but no one ever passed me the ball. On defense they pushed me to the end of the line, where nothing ever happened either. I suspect they were worried I'd be injured if I was anywhere near the action. Still, it was better than playing alone.

By seventh grade I hadn't grown a whit. Less than five feet tall, I weighed 75 pounds. But I signed up for the football team at Oakleigh School anyway. After two weeks I was the only seventh-grader left on the junior high squad. Every day I was beaten up. Just tackling or blocking the dummies knocked the wind out of me; of course, the older boys would push the dummy at the last moment to wreck the timing of my assault. I sensed there was a concerted effort to get me to quit. So I refused to. Besides, I grew up on stories about athletes overcoming enormous handicaps, and I was fitting myself into that mold. I never missed a practice; yet once scrimmages began, I found myself on the sidelines. My uniform didn't fit. The kneepads were around my shins, and the shoulder pads drooped like I was carrying pails of milk at the ends. I could spin the helmet around my head. My number was zero.

Every day I exercised with the rest of the team, went through the drills, practiced all the fundamentals. At home I worked out moves in front of the mirror on my bedroom door. Coach had told me, "You're small, so hit 'em with your body below their knees. You'll take 'em down every time." I practiced on my brother; he went down every time I could get him to stand still. After school with the team, however — out on the field, with bigger boys moving and jumping — I had more difficulty. Sometimes the wrong part of my body made contact. At home in the bathtub I was a small person with sore ribs, sore arms, sore legs, and a sore neck.

Eventually, when some of our players were out with injuries, the coach allowed me into scrimmages as a defensive end. One afternoon our lanky end caught a downfield pass that left only me between him and the end zone. I threw my body toward his legs along the sideline. Moments later, I awoke from my amnesia surrounded by the coach and the entire team. "That's how you do it," said the coach. Someone helped me to my feet. Thereafter, my teammates treated me as an equal, giving me pats and easy punches, tidbits of advice. It was my first experience of team. I hadn't known such a thing existed.

The coach that season at Oakleigh Junior High never allowed me into a real game, though I used to speak to him, standing near him on the sidelines, in the deepest voice I could muster: "Let me in, Coach." He would look down at me for a second, then sidle away with his clipboard.

The summer before I went into eighth grade, I grew a foot taller. I couldn't believe my good luck. I even started growing mustache hairs.

On the scale I found my weight edging up to 140 pounds. In September the coach established me as a defensive end. I never argued, though I was one of the quickest runners on the team and hadn't lost my ambition of being a running back, scampering for touchdowns amid the cacophony of the crowd. But again I remembered those stories of the lonely sports hero, the underdog biding his time. I could bide.

I was taught to keep the action along the line of scrimmage inside, keep the play from moving outside my position. That was how I discovered the delight of sacking quarterbacks, along with the dismay of "student-body-right" — a herd of buffalo coming at me.

My first big offensive opportunity arrived when Coach decided to experiment during a game at East Grand Rapids. He put me in as a deep receiver on the opening kick-off. I saw myself, gazelle-like, maneuvering downfield to the opposite goalposts. But it was a night game, and we had never played a game under the lights; we had never even practiced under lights. When the ball was kicked off, I lost sight of it immediately and it never came back into view. Some heartbeats later it bounced off the top of my helmet. East Grand Rapids recovered the ball on the one foot line. I stood there alone, my head ringing.

In the ninth grade we were introduced to a new coach. He was a younger man with a military bearing. After two weeks of drills and conditioning he installed me as a tackle (to play both ways). His pronouncement, in his office, was that I was too skinny for a running back. I had grown a few more inches but hadn't gained new weight. It seemed to me I was far too thin to play tackle. But, seeing my future slipping away, I kept after him. I memorized all the plays for tackles — but also for running backs and tight ends. Our formation called for a backfield consisting of a quarterback, a slotback (a blocking back), and a running back (combination fullback and halfback). One day in practice Coach grabbed my arm and pulled me into the backfield; then he yanked the running back into my position. I stayed in the backfield on offense; on defense I resumed my end position of the previous year.

Our first ninth-grade game was at home against Muskegon Heights. We were awe-struck when they clamored down the steps of the bus in front of school. They looked like a high school team. "Some of these guys must have flunked a few times," said Carl, our quarterback. We funneled into the basement ahead of our opponents. "Well," Coach said in the locker room, "let's see how tough you guys are." "Christ," said Carl, forgetting the rule we had about always showing team confidence. Coach scowled. He banged on a locker. We all banged on a locker. It was my first game as running back.

We were beaten by 65 points. But we made 21, and I ran for all three touchdowns. All afternoon I ran through two holes, tackle right and tackle left. Nothing else worked for us to get the ball across the line of scrimmage. Their two linebackers hit me over and over. I must have carried the ball thirty-five times.

That night my parents took me to the hospital because I was having difficulty breathing. I'd cracked ribs on both sides of my chest. The doctor wrapped me up in elastic tape, and I spent the remainder of that season on the sidelines in street clothes — near the cheerleaders.

In tenth grade I went to Union High School, the old red-brick square building between Broadway and Turner, and Third and Fourth streets, where a half-dozen players were vying for running back positions. Our first game was against Traverse City. I was on the junior varsity, and our match was played early in the evening, before the featured attraction. I didn't start the game, but I was sent in as a replacement in the first quarter. During the second or third play of that series I was handed the ball to run off-tackle. Over the summer, some of us had been getting together after work at Richmond Park to throw the pigskin around and practice some plays. I'd been refining a spin move, in which, as I hit a hole and it closed up prematurely, I'd pivot fluidly and set off in a new direction. Now, as I met the line of Traverse City linemen, I began my well-honed pivot to escape; but the wall of players collapsed on me before I had accomplished my maneuver. I was at the bottom of the heap, twisted like a corkscrew. I dragged myself off the Traverse City field, my ankle broken.

In the eleventh grade, my junior year of high school, not much happened. I was a reserve offensive and defensive end. Coach Milo Sukup didn't play juniors unless he had to. A couple of games I was run in when the score was lopsided in the fourth quarter. The only notice I received in *The*

Grand Rapids Press was when I lost one of my contact lenses. The game was halted briefly while we all crawled around on our hands and knees. We never found it. The *Press* said: "Rocky Rozema hit Bob VanderMolen so hard his contacts popped out." Rozema was all-state that year for Central High — with plenty of press.

My senior year I was made a starting outside linebacker — and a middle linebacker when a goal-line stand was called for. I was six foot three and 175 pounds. The previous winter I had dabbled with a weight-lifting program, but it was tremendously boring. By the end of January, I was only visiting the weight room occasionally. But I did eat more: to reach 175 pounds (and stay there), I had to consume five sandwiches at lunch every day; then I would plow through large dinners of meat and potatoes in the evening. In all of this my mother was extremely encouraging. I pushed down snacks before bed. I thought food: I ate when I was already full, and I ate again when I wasn't hungry. I concentrated on consuming calories. Still, I couldn't get past 175, and I was a skinny linebacker. I was also a skinny second-string fullback.

But I loved the game of football. I hated the double practices two weeks before school started. I hated the wind sprints, hitting the dummies, all the rituals of exercise and monotonous motion. For one thing, I always stayed in shape. I ran nearly every day, even on the hot and humid days. Furthermore, the fundamentals were second nature to me by this time; I'd had them down after my first season in the seventh grade. It was the crap of unsuited and noncontact practices I had to endure in order to reach the joy of scrimmaging.

I could lose myself in the play of football. All the concerns about pimples, girls, sex, arguments with my parents and teachers, and so on disappeared completely. It was a liberation. Plus, I had discovered a need for teamness, for being part of a group. It was an addictive thing. As a linebacker I was also part of a smaller unit, together with the defensive tackle and the end on my side of the center. The three of us ended up working so well together that we barely needed to talk. We played together instinctively, using waves and nods. I thought of us as a poised machine.

But football was also an extraordinary vent for aggression. I had ample amounts of teenage aggression, and football didn't mean that I wouldn't get into fights on weekend nights, in parking lots and side streets throughout the lower West Side, after a couple of beers with friends. We all did that. But I suspect that football curtailed wider ranges of violence. In both scrimmages and games, I played as intensely as I could. It made me relaxed, and it made me feel whole. I continued to hit low and hard.

When the season started, I looked forward so much to the games on Friday or Saturday nights at Houseman Field — that old grey place of moldering stone, which came alive under the lights, its natural grass a jungle green — that it seemed odd we didn't play more often. At the time it would have made sense to me to play Wednesday night games as well. It was marvelous, too, riding in the team bus, watching the crowds jamming both sides of Bridge Street, crossing the Grand River and marching up Michigan Hill toward the football game. I thought of it as a horde of West Siders moving across the river to sack the eastern segments of the city.

I hadn't given up fantasies of myself as a strong and flashy running back, though it occurred to me that, personality-wise, I was more suited to defense. I was good on defense, and our team was a strong defensive one. I took pride in it. Frankly, defense offered more freedom to a player, a freedom I wasn't certain I'd want to trade for the restrictions of offense. I did run the ball a few times as a fullback. In one game I managed a first down on three straight plays off left guard — my only first down in all of high school. But we also had a secret play that was designed for a goal-line situation. I don't remember the mechanics of it anymore, other than that I lined up at end. It was a trick play: one of the backs, after getting a hand-off from the quarterback, would in turn hand me the ball, and I would plunge over center. We didn't practice it on our field next to American Seating Company. I figured that was because Coach Sukup was wary of spies. Instead, Carl, our quarterback, the two other backs, Denny and Buzz, and I worked on the play in our school clothes at noon in the parking lot across from school. Coach would watch from a window. We worked on the timing. At night before I went to sleep, I'd run through the intricacies of the action, trying to picture how it would work in a game with an opposing team at the goal line.

The 1964 Union High School football team (Robert VanderMolen, number 53)
GRPL, Union High School yearbook, 1964

Then it seemed as if the coaching staff forgot about our play. Sukup said we didn't need to practice any longer: we had performed it as well as we were likely to. We played several games in which Coach never brought the trick play into action. It began to recede in my consciousness as well. But when we were behind by a field goal late in the Catholic Central game, Coach Sukup sent me in with the special play. It was third down, and we were on the 5 yard line. My hands were sweating. Houseman Field was a din of voices, of pounding and clapping. The band was playing, cheerleaders jumping. Steam rose into the lights on that crisp October night. But as the play unfolded, nothing looked like I had dreamed it in slow motion. After the ball was snapped, it became obvious that the play was going to take too long. Our line was sagging badly inward by the time I met Denny for the handoff. I was looking for some glimmer of an opening when the ball slipped right out the other side of my arms. The Catholic boys recovered, and we lost the game.

When I returned to the bench, I wondered whether Coach Sukup was going to punch me. I'd seen him hit other players — in the stomach, in the head, in the chest. Sukup was old school; he'd been a pulling guard for Tom Harman at the University of Michigan. He kicked helmets, and he kicked players, too. I wasn't afraid of him, but I wasn't certain what I'd do if he attacked me. I hoped he wouldn't. When I reached the sideline, Coach simply stalked off in the other direction. I liked to think he was a bit afraid of me. But it no doubt had more to do with the fact that, years earlier, my father once had been part of the coaching staff at Union. Coach Sukup never did hit me.

Walking the three or four blocks from school to our practice field the following week — my girlfriend, Mary, carrying my helmet on a warm afternoon in late October, almost like an illustration in an old book, leaves idling down, a faint whiff of the river dropping over the coffer dam, my cleats clacking down the sidewalk, small boys skipping along following the players and their girlfriends — all was forgiven. My father told me that, in West Side bars such as the Copper Top, which he would visit on occasion, all the talk was that Sukup had made up a stupid play. No one blamed me.

I won a scholarship to play football at Alma College the following year. I also won a scholarship to study English at Michigan State University. In September of 1965, I appeared in East Lansing, Michigan, wearing a herringbone sport coat, with a briar pipe in my mouth and an umbrella on my arm.

Wilma, Whitey, and the Tackers

William Brashler

After attending Grand Rapids Christian High School and three years of Calvin College, William Brashler left Grand Rapids and completed his B.A. at the University of Michigan, where he won a Hopwood Award in 1969. He then went on to earn an M.F.A. at the Iowa Writers' School.

Brashler is a journalist whose work has appeared in national magazines such as *Esquire, New York, Newsweek,* and *Sports Illustrated.* He has also been a long-time contributor to the *Chicago Tribune* and *Chicago Sun-Times* magazines. His sports profiles have featured many professional baseball, football, and basketball stars. He is the author of fourteen books, fiction and nonfiction, including *City Dogs, The Chosen Prey, The Don: The Life and Death of Sam Giancana,* and *Traders.* Perhaps his best-known novel is still the first one he published, *The Bingo Long Traveling All-Stars and Motor Kings,* a novel about a barnstorming Negro Leagues team, which was made into a motion picture starring Billy Dee Williams, James Earl Jones, and Richard Pryor. He has also written a book on the Negro Leagues for children and a biography of that era's greatest hitter, Josh Gibson.

Brashler has collaborated with Reinder Van Til, under the pseudonym Crabbe Evers, on five Duffy House mysteries, including *Murder in Wrigley Field* and *Tigers Burning.* He wrote the following narrative specifically for this book.

Wilma, Whitey, and the Tackers

On a fine day in 1946, on South Division Avenue, Richard Barlow, my maternal great-grandfather, decided to go out for some ice cream. He was eighty-six years old, a Dutch immigrant, a retired school teacher, and a favorite of my mother. A smart and articulate man who had been the principal of a one-room school in the south part of town, Grandpa Barlow once gave personal testimony in *The Grand Rapids Press* on behalf of a remarkable laxative and all-purpose tonic that gave him new energy and made him as regular as a clock. But on that day in 1946, his quest for a cool treat caused him to wade into the busy traffic on South Division, and he was struck by a car and killed. The driver, only eighteen years old, was not cited by the police. Grandpa Barlow's sudden death hit the family hard. My older brother Jim, who was only five, remembers that it was the first time he'd ever seen our mother cry.

A year later I was born, the fourth child of what would become a family of seven kids, and not long after that, our family moved into a house only a half mile away from the site of Grandpa Barlow's demise. Years later I could stand in the grassy, hilly field behind our house, in the uncluttered southeast side of Grand Rapids, and watch the unrelenting traffic on Division Avenue. If there was bad karma emanating from that thoroughfare, I never felt it. Yet I would one day have my own connection to the sad thing that happened there. Little did I know.

Although Richard Barlow was a man of letters, and my mother, Wilma, was a brainy, bookish, introspective young woman, my family was dominated by sheet metal. Her father, Albert Nydam, was a heating and sheet-metal contractor, a "tin knocker," who built a shop on South Division only yards away from where his father-in-law had been killed. Onto every furnace he installed, A. J. screwed a brass plate that read: "When Albert J. Nydam has done the job, it must be good. Sheet metal work and heating repairing done and repairs furnished for all makes of heating plants." My father joined the business after World War II, and for my entire childhood I knew intimately the smell of furnace filters and oil cans and the cold presence of sheet metal. Our house had tissue-box holders made of sheet metal, cat litter boxes made of sheet metal, shelves, brackets, and sandbox toys made of sheet metal. Even the grand, two-story pillars in front of our house were of heavy-gauge sheet metal.

If my mother chafed at the presence of such blue-collar, grimy-nailed relatives, she never admitted as much. She had gone to Calvin College to study chemistry, and of all the nerdy Dutch boys she could have fallen for, she chose a devil-may-care, blond-headed bean pole — he was 6′2″ and 135 pounds in college — from the Chicago area named Clarence "Whitey" Brashler. He had made it to Calvin by telling his mother that he would become a preacher. Instead, he played golf, worked on automobile engines in his dorm room, and courted the diminutive brunette from Grand Rapids. It was an odd match: Mutt and Jeff, long and lean versus short and compact, blond and brunette, bon vivant and student, a bookworm and a jock. But Wilma kissed him on their first date and the band began to play.

A deep scar that ran from his right eye to the top of his head gave evidence of what Whitey had been about. While a teenager during the Depression in Harvey, Illinois, he and a bunch of friends went joyriding in a jalopy. Whitey stood on the running board, and when the car tipped and flipped going over railroad tracks, everybody laughed, until someone said, "Where's Whitey?" Whitey was pinned underneath, his head ripped open like a ripe cantaloupe. It happened that the hospital they drove him to was the one where his sister worked as a nurse. She took one look at his bloody noggin and thought he was dead. She reportedly said, "If Whitey lives through this, Ma's gonna kill him."

He lived, and from then on sported that magnificent scar. One look at it, and a physician at a military induction center at the start of World War II declared him 4-F. Instead of going to war, he married Wilma and soon they were fruitful and multiplying. And multiplying. During the war my father worked in defense factories in Grand Rapids and Muskegon, and my mother took care of three kids in a small apartment on Eastern Avenue. At war's end, Whitey joined his father-in-law's heating firm. I don't think he much liked the old man and his stubborn Dutch ways, but he never admitted as much. By 1949 he and Wilma had five kids, including me, and needed a house. For $5,000, Whitey bought an old wreck of a farmhouse at 138 Alger S.E., only a half-mile away from the sheet metal shop on Division Avenue. Soon I would be running in the nearby fields and gravel pits, scaring up rabbits and pheasants and catching toads and garter snakes, and, by today's standards, risking my life.

Though my father was destined never to live in Illinois again, he remained a degenerate Chicago Cubs fan. He had played baseball in high school in Harvey, where he lockered next to future Hall-of-Famer Lou Boudreau: he played third base to Boudreau's shortstop. He always said he was as good as, or better than, Boudreau — and who were we to argue? The Cubs were a positively awful team during the 1950s, though they had been a powerhouse in my father's youth. Even so, he followed them over the static-filled airwaves of Chicago's WGN on his car radio. On summer days he would come home from work and sit in the car listening to the final innings from Wrigley Field while my mother implored him to come into the house.

Baseball and his deep-seated Dutch Calvinist traditions endured in my father's adult life. We belonged to the Christian Reformed Church, and he sent us to Seymour Christian School. It also meant I had catechism class after school one day a week. And Calvinist Cadets — a churchified version of Boy Scouts — one night a week. And Sunday school after church every Sunday . . . and Sunday night hymn-sings. The list went on and on. Calvinism, with its stodginess and social restrictions — no dancing, no alcohol, no movies, no Sunday purchases or events — was a nagging rather than a dominant presence in our house. We prayed before meals, but we did not quote Scripture, read *The Daily Manna,* or call God's wrath down upon each other. We did not shop on Sunday, but we did watch television — particularly professional bowling and football — as soon as we got home from church. We did not wear religion on our sleeves, but it was embedded somewhere in the fabric. We were, I later decided, Amish in polyester.

My mother went along dutifully; but as the years passed, I realized that she never completely bought into it. She never became a member of the church, which meant that she never took Holy Communion. My father sang to the rafters; she murmured under her breath. It was not a big deal, and I never remember either of them ever talking about it. Domestic tranquility was more important than fighting heresy or expressing iconoclasm. I also came to learn that my mother was a closet Democrat, a rare entity in conservative Republican west Michigan, and that she never thought very much of Gerald Ford, neither when he was a congressman nor when he was President. She may have been one of a couple dozen voters who pulled the lever for Roman Snow, Ford's perennial opponent.

But Wilma was devoted to Whitey, and she was a creature of her times, which meant she kept her religious and political rebellions to herself. Except during some of the raw days of the Vietnam War, especially when my brother John was overseas, I don't remember my mother ever baiting my father or moving him to rage over politics or religion. On Sunday afternoons the family often went for rides in the oily-smelling station wagon. My mother sat next to my father as if they were still dating, and her hand rested on the calloused one on his thigh as he drove.

Perhaps because there were five kids in the family, there seemed little opportunity for my parents to hover over any one of them. Our back door was always open, and my siblings and I ran in the back fields. In a nearby gravel pit there was a six-foot-deep frog pond in which we could easily have drowned. At the base of the gravel pit was a cement block company that regularly scooped gravel out of the hills only yards away from where we scrambled. We could have been buried alive. Plaster Creek, which was no doubt filled with toxins, flowed through the woods, and we waded and fished in it as if it were the River Jordan. My two older brothers owned BB guns, and we shot at just about anything that moved, including our cat, Fleabag. We nailed him many times. In return, he used to pee in our mitten-and-glove box. I once wandered too near a bunch of strange boys who were goofing off at the top of "our" hill, and as I turned away, one of them raised his BB gun and shot me in the back. Our neighbor, an older boy also named Bill — which made me "Little Bill" for many years — liked to make pipe bombs. He'd take a foot-long piece of galvanized pipe, fill it with homemade gunpowder, cap the ends, drill a hole in it for a fuse, take it to the back field, and light the fuse. We ran like hell and ducked behind a bluff until it blew. The pipe flew high into the air and came down like a piece of airline wreckage.

It has been said that those were simpler, happier times. I'm not sure about that. Crappy things happened. My first baseball glove was a Warren Spahn autographed model, a thing of beauty whose fingers had crisscrossed rawhide ties. After I had owned it for only a few weeks, it was stolen. Snatched off the handlebar of my bike like laundry off a line — and gone forever. Yet I do know that, even with all the opportunities for violence and mayhem — the guns, the explosives, the rough-housing, the

The lodge at Garfield Park, frequented by a young William Brashler
GRPL, Library Postcard Collection

rafting down the creek in leaky mortar tubs — no really bad thing ever happened. No Brashler kid ever broke a bone or needed stitches, got beaten up or went missing.

With one exception. I had a brief encounter with terror, or, at the very least, bonafide fear. It came not in the back fields of our house, but on a walk through the park. I was de-pantsed at gunpoint — when I was only eight years old. It happened on a summer day, in broad daylight, only blocks from my home. I was walking to Garfield Park's pool to swim with friends. I was blond, skinny as a stick, toting a rolled-up towel, and wearing only my swim trunks. My route took me through Burton Woods, a fenced-off square block of trees and bushes. Though surrounded by homes, the woods were quite dense and private. I'd walked the path through the woods dozens of times, usually whistling the theme song to "The Andy Griffith Show." That day I was suddenly confronted by a tall, severe boy of about fourteen who was wearing some kind of uniform and wielding a rifle with a wooden stock. He pointed the weapon at me and marched me off the path and deep into the woods. I was scared spitless. When we were out of sight of the main path as well as the homes surrounding the woods, the boy ordered me to take off my swim trunks. "Take off your swim trunks," I believe he said. I did so.

He kept the gun trained on me and my now naked babelaars, as diminutive as they were, and took the trunks and tossed them high into a tree, where they caught on a branch. Then he told me not to move or he'd shoot me. He didn't molest me or ogle me or do unseemly things with his rifle — he simply turned around and left. I stood there in my altogether, cowering like a lost puppy, afraid to move lest I get my ass shot off. Minutes passed, and finally I decided the boy was gone and I had to risk retrieving my trunks. I shinnied up the tree, looking like a hairless, albino monkey, and I managed to shake the branch and free my trunks. I put them on and sprinted home. When my father returned from work that night, he drove me around the neighborhood looking for the boy with the rifle. We didn't find him. I never saw him or his weapon again. But the damage was done. For years after that, I couldn't look at a tree without getting a chafing sensation in my crotch. I carried an ingrained suspicion of ROTC officers. And for decades after that, whenever anybody said that Grand Rapids was a great place to raise children, I responded, "Yes, if you don't mind having them stripped naked and terrorized by gun-toting bullies."

To be sure, over the years the event in the woods was grist for more laughs than trauma. At least my big brothers found it so. If there was any sexual abuse in my youth, it came in the form of the torture that religion infused into my being. From the moment I could read a Bible story in Sunday school, I was warned of original sin and the fires of hell. I was a sinner in the hands of an angry God. If I wasn't careful, I'd be the devil's workshop. The metaphors were mixed and vicious. I also learned early on — and this struck me like a spike in my forehead — that lust of the flesh would result in eternal damnation. Everywhere I turned, from age ten on, there was flesh and lust. The early days of television, in all its black-and-white blandness, offered the sight of models parading goods on stage on a program called *Queen for a Day.* I couldn't take my eyes off those women, and I knew I was sinning in doing so. I remember praying fervently that God would avert my eyes, cleanse my soul, and still the stirring in my pants. He never did.

At about the same time, my elementary school classmates and I began collecting stamps. My mother and grandmother were avid stamp collectors, and I spent hours poring over my own collection. My friends and I, all good Seymour Christian School boys, found stamps on discarded mail inside a dumpster behind a nearby shopping strip. But that's where we also found nudy magazines. Some wonderful man in the loan company was a connoisseur of glossy cheesecake magazines, and his monthly discards were our treasures. It was all tame stuff by today's standards, but bare breasts were bare breasts, and we sat in the low light of the trash bin and lovingly perused the spreads. Then we divvied them up between us.

The problem for me was what to do with my stash. I shared my bedroom with my two older brothers, so keeping porn there was out of the question. I finally settled on the inside ledge of the doghouse my father had built for one of his many hounds. That worked for months, until the doghouse rotted, and my dad and older brother decided one day to break it apart and burn it. I stood yards away behind a tree, trembling with anticipation, certain I was to be exposed for the collector of filth that I was. And yet somehow, perhaps by the grace of God, they missed my cache. They picked up the house and tossed the whole thing in the fire, nudes and all. It burned like the fires of hell. My relief was total, but I had no shame or penitence. Soon I was amassing another collection in another hiding place.

My older brothers were no help when it came to sex, either in my struggle to cope with my lusts or in my effort to understand them. When I was no more than eleven, my brother John once asked me if I "played with myself." I didn't know what he meant: the simple terms "jerk off" or "masturbate" would have sufficed, but John preferred to go with a euphemism. He went on to say that playing with yourself was wrong, and that if you wanted to be a good athlete, which I dearly did, you didn't play with yourself. "Do pushups instead," he said. He even made a sign for me to put on the wall behind my pillow. It hung right next to a color photograph of Floyd Patterson, the heavyweight champion and one of my heroes. "Do pushups instead," it read. My mother thought it was kind of strange and asked me what it meant. "Instead of tossing in your sleep," I replied. She shrugged.

My father was no help in the sex ed department either. I can't remember a time when he ever talked to me about girls or, God forbid, sex.

And yet, as the father of seven children, he had to have had some insight into the process. Years later he used to joke that, in his day, "safe sex meant a padded headboard." The Dutch Calvinist method of sexual education was either through osmosis or via the bad kid on the playground. My father was not profane or bawdy, so there was no opportunity for sex ed via a dirty joke or two. Even the men who worked heating and sheet metal were not wont to throw a good raunchy joke my way. As a wise-ass teenager working for my father, I once suggested that Nydam Heating could merge with nearby Godwin Plumbing and call itself Goddam Heating and Plumbing. The remark didn't go over well.

If there was one thing as alluring as the female form and the mysteries of sex in my early existence, it was baseball. Baseball consumed me. I don't remember a day when I did not awaken to live and breathe baseball. At age eight I played on my first park team, the South End Red Hawks, and at nine I made the cut with the Eberhard Giants in Little League. Eberhard's was a local chain of supermarkets. Our suits were green. I wore number 2.

We played our games at Palace Field, so named because it was at the end of Palace Street, not because it was anything close to regal. The field was a converted dump. The outfield was weeds that had been mowed flat, and it was flecked with cinders and clinkers dumped there from coal furnaces. The dugouts were cinderblock, the bleachers splinter-filled planks. But Palace Field, to me, was Tiger Stadium — we were all Detroit Tiger fans — and a glorious place. After all, it had a fence, unlike the fields at the public parks, and when you hit one over the fence you could prance around the bases. Never was there a feeling so grand.

When I was eleven, a home run hitter and a power pitcher with a killer curve that my father had taught me, I once struck out 17 of 18 batters in a six-inning game. We won city championships and played in state tournaments and all-star games. I fantasized about being Al Kaline, the great Detroit outfielder, and I was certain that one day I'd wear that uniform with the Corinthian letter D on its front. At the end of the season, a week or so before school was about to begin, I remember riding my bike down to Palace Field, sitting in the dugout alone, looking out on the field and realizing the season was all over, and crying my eyes out.

Then one day, during the summer I turned twelve, I felt a stabbing pain in my elbow. It hurt like hell and kept me from throwing hard for any length of time. I soaked the elbow, massaged it, even went to a sports store where they applied an electric vibrator to it. But nothing helped. I had suffered what came to be known as Little League elbow: the tendon had been pulled away from the bone from the stress of snapping off so many curveballs. After that, though I could still throw hard, I was never an effective pitcher again. Had I been a good Calvinist and suppressed my urge for the instant gratification I got with that curveball, I might have gone on to pitching glory.

What baseball — and sports in general — did for me was to open up my life to non-Dutchmen. My little corner of the world in the 1950s was all Dutch all the time. My schoolmates were Dutch (except for a lone immigrant girl from Hungary in 1956). My neighbors were Dutch. Everybody in my church was Dutch. I came to believe that Jesus and his twelve disciples probably were from somewhere in Holland, maybe Friesland. Only in Little League did I encounter kids who were not Dutch, and who were not, wonder of wonders, Christian Reformed. I played with Irish Catholic kids, Polish kids — our third baseman's name was Zibikowski — even a few black kids. I once broke off a curveball to Bobby Lovett, a black kid on the Foremost Insurance team. He turned his back, the ball didn't break, and I hit him in the butt.

No black families lived in my neighborhood in the 1950s. None were seen in Garfield Park unless they came with a team to compete. Blacks stayed north of Hall Street, and when they were ready for high school, they went to South High School. The local public school, Brookside, was as white as was Seymour Christian School. I don't remember this with any animosity, and I don't remember any meanness or hostility toward black kids when they came around to the park. They just simply were not a part of our lives.

My mother, however, was active in the Grand Rapids Urban League Guild. A mostly female social gathering, the guild arranged coffees and fundraisers, tutoring for children, and other events for blacks and whites in those pre–civil rights days. When she hosted meetings at our house, a bevy of soft-spoken, personable black ladies filled our living room. My father helped serve, and it was something to hear these women call out,

"More coffee, please, Whitey." And "thank-you very much, Whitey." "How kind of you, Whitey."

At about the same time that Little League elbow afflicted me, I became enamored of writing. I started writing stories and poems for my sixth grade teacher, a curmudgeonly lady named Mrs. VanKley, who inspired and haunted me simultaneously. But seeing my stuff in print in a school newspaper or literary review was very seductive. I entered short stories and essays in the Grand Rapids Youth Talent Contest and won first prize ribbons and $10 purses. And I got so heady with my Youth Talent success that one year I entered the music competition. I played the tuba, a tangled hunk of brass that, even with my silken embouchure, sounded like a foghorn. I carted it down to the Public Museum, on Jefferson Avenue, and competed with dozens of others in what turned out to be a local version of "The Ted Mack Amateur Hour." As I was performing, however, with the hoarse tones of my tuba causing little children to plunge their fingers into their ears, a thunderstorm knocked out power to the building. But it was a heartier era, and the judges, with the aid of candles and flashlights, told me to play on. I did so — valiantly, I think — but lost badly to an eight-year-old who sang "The Lord's Prayer."

But the writing bug bit deep, and it soon gained a status in my life next to athletics. Part of the appeal was the creativity of it all, and part of it was power. People read what you wrote. They responded, sometimes negatively, which made the exercise all the better. As I searched for things to write about, I realized that I couldn't pull much out of a tortured psyche, because I didn't have one. My childhood, but for that brief encounter with the crazed gunman in Burton Woods, was pristine. My parents had no rancid qualities, no toxic influences. They raised seven kids in Grand Rapids, Michigan, with no damage done. Had my father been a cad, a brooding drunk, or simply a monster, I'd have had more material. I would have been filled with resentment and rancor, some loathing and, best of all, a murky reservoir of excuses. Had my mother, battered or emotionally frayed, turned over in bed one morning and plunged an ice pick into my father's sternum, I'd have grist for a potboiler and an angst-ridden memoir rolled into one. But that was not to be. I had to invent my own miseries.

Or I had to discover hardship and struggle in others. That came about when I met the Tackers. The mid-1960s saw the formation of a semipro basketball league in the Midwest, and the Grand Rapids entry was the Tackers. The NBA was much smaller then, and many top college players never made the pro rosters. Their only option was with teams like the Tackers, playing on weekends in high school gymnasiums, making a few hundred bucks a game. Two of my friends and I volunteered to be statisticians and all-around gofers for the team, which meant we got into the games for free and had access to the players. The Tackers were hugely popular; the games were usually sold out, and we felt privileged to be insiders. Most of the players were black, with huge bodies and remarkable skills — and backgrounds totally different from us white-bread Dutch kids. They had names like Delton Heard, George Knighton, Herschel Turner, Billy "The Hill" McGill, Willie Jones, and M. C. and Ed Burton.

Delton Heard impressed us the most. A barrel-chested, knock-kneed, droopy-eyed, ball-handling magician, Heard once came onto the court with his shorts worn backwards. Heard's Globetrotters-like repertoire included a one-on-three fast break in which he would bank the ball off the backboard back to himself and stuff the rebound. I think the play was illegal, but we were amazed by it. As good as Heard and the others were — and we thought they were magnificent — they were ultimately frustrated, even depressed, players who were destined not to know the big time or the big money.

And therein I got my material. A few years later, while I was a college undergraduate seeking to impress my writing mentors, I put together a short story about a basketball player who had skill and finesse, and who still found real joy in playing the game, and yet was doomed to languish in the minor leagues. I mined everything Delton and Herschel and Billy "The Hill" had given me. It was a prelude to writing I would do later about Negro League baseball and great players such as Satchel Paige, Josh Gibson, and Cool Papa Bell, all of whom played in the shadow of major league baseball prior to Jackie Robinson's breaking the color barrier. They were the Tackers writ large, individuals who fascinated me because their lives and struggles were so foreign to anything I'd known growing up on Alger Street in Grand Rapids. They were the wellspring of my writing career, the material that I molded into *The Bingo Long Traveling All-Stars and Motor Kings,* the material that molded me.

And that's where things come together. After a pretty fair high school athletic career in baseball, basketball, and cross country, I was awarded a monetary college scholarship from the Tackers. It was an honor, and it helped pay tuition for my freshman year of college. I got my picture in *The Grand Rapids Press* with the other honorees. The owner and president of the Tackers was a man named Roger Lemmen, a rotund, bellicose businessman who alternately charmed and intimidated just about everyone he met. The Tacker players had respect but little love for Mr. Lemmen, especially when things were not going well for the team. But he was the boss, the owner, the mover and shaker, and without him there may not have been a team in town in the first place.

Several decades later, long after the demise of the Tackers and the passing of Delton Heard, I found myself rummaging through my mother's voluminous scrapbooks and journals. She saved everything. There, amid all that material, was the yellowed 1946 newspaper clipping of the accidental death of my great-grandfather, Richard Barlow, on Division Avenue. It was a straightforward, prosaic piece of journalism. But one fact jolted me to my core. The eighteen-year-old driver of the automobile that struck and killed my great-grandfather was none other than Roger Lemmen.

Mux at Ramona

SHERI VENEMA

Sheri Venema was born in Grand Rapids in 1947 and attended Seymour Christian School and Grand Rapids Christian High School before graduating from Calvin College in 1969. She taught English in the 8th and 9th grades at Millbrook Christian Junior High, and later was a substitute teacher in the Grand Rapids public school system. After working in real estate in Minneapolis, she completed an M.A. in journalism at the University of Minnesota.

Venema became a reporter at the *Norwich* (Connecticut) *Bulletin* in 1983, where she covered the U.S. Naval Base in Groton, as well as environmental news and city hall. After a brief stint at the *Baltimore News American,* she became a reporter for the *Hartford Courant,* where she covered a variety of beats and also spent three years as a bureau chief overseeing a staff of ten reporters. She started up a writing consulting business called Words & Work in Fayetteville, Arkansas, and later worked at the *Arkansas Democrat-Gazette* as associate editor of a new business section, where she covered the state's poultry industry, including the famous Tyson Foods.

Venema became visiting professor at the University of Montana's School of Journalism in 1999, and she accepted a tenure-track position in 2002. She teaches reporting and editing classes, mass media law, feature writing, and online news, and serves as the Journalism School's webmaster. She has won a fellowship from the American Society of Newspaper Editors and is currently working on a book exploring media coverage of the Church Universal and Triumphant, which is headquartered in Montana's Paradise Valley. She lives in Missoula with her husband, journalist and writer Michael Downs. She wrote the following memoir expressly for this anthology.

Sheri Venema

About the birth of my Aunt Mux and her twin sister in the midsummer of 1911, we know little. How long the labor lasted and which twin appeared first are lost to time. We do know that the twins were born at home on the southwest side of Grand Rapids two months before their due date. Together, the new babies weighed five pounds — about forty ounces each — their lungs weak bellows not expected to last a day. My Dutch immigrant grandparents thought it likely they would lose these tiny surprises wrapped in clean white rags; even so, they beseeched the Lord otherwise.

When God's answer came, it was from just across town, yet also from halfway across the world. It was a concept so exotic, so bizarre, that when it landed in my grandparents' ears and made its way past their disbelief and into their understanding, it was akin to being told to hoist their babies in a basket to the moon. Now, nearly a hundred years later, I have a tattered and dark copy of a clipping from *The Grand Rapids Press* about the trip my day-old twin aunts took to Ramona Park, an amusement park on the east side of town. The newspaper article, which misspelled my grandparents' name, appeared sometime in July 1911; it was carefully cut from the paper, probably by my grandparents. But the top right corner is torn. What I can see of the main headline is: "TO SAVE THE . . ."

> Tiny twins, weighing together only five pounds, or two and one-half pounds each, are being given a fighting chance for life at the baby incubator at Ramona. They are the daughters of Mr. and Mrs. De Ruyter of 368 Watson Court. When they arrived in the world two months before their time they were so tiny and frail that there was much doubt of their being saved. They were rushed to the incubator by Dr. Pyle and are reported as doing finely.

It had all the sob-sister elements of a story that newspaper editors and American readers love: babies near death, the breathless rush to safety, and, finally, a happy ending. But beyond that story is another in which not everyone does finely. That story is one of struggle, a choice between partaking of the world and hiding from it, a story whose themes have echoed through two more generations.

Like most Dutch immigrants who settled in Grand Rapids in the early part of the twentieth century, Roelof and Lammegien Ruiter believed that they rested securely in the hand of God. They were each just shy of twenty-eight years old when they left behind parents, brothers, sisters, aunts, uncles, and cousins in the Netherlands, arriving at Ellis Island in March of 1906 with three children, twenty-seven dollars, and their Dutch Calvinist faith. The strength of that faith is evident in a letter my grandfather sent back home a month later, describing the trip. Along with a young man's optimism about what lay ahead was an absolute trust that God would guide them through rough waters, both literal and figurative. The sight of a shipwreck in the North Sea as they sailed out of Rotterdam was a sobering reminder of the power of water and wind. "But it did not depress us or take away our courage," he wrote, "since we knew that without the will of our Heavenly Father, not one hair of our heads would be lost and we were safe with the Lord, even upon the deep waters of His sea."

On the second day of the crossing, a Sunday, he and my grandmother were astonished that only a dozen of their fellow passengers joined them in singing psalms at an impromptu on-deck worship service. So narrow was their experience of the larger world that they could scarcely imagine a life without psalm-singing on Sunday mornings.

Once they settled in Grand Rapids, my grandfather found work as a house painter. He and his young family joined a Dutch Calvinist community physically located in Grand Rapids but whose heart and soul had neither explored the city nor absorbed it. The isolation was intentional. Sixty years earlier, Albertus Van Raalte had led the first group of disaffected Calvinists from the Netherlands to the shores of Lake Michigan. They were fleeing persecution at home, where they found the state church too liberal. The state, finding them too zealous, had banned meetings of their new church, imprisoned its leaders, and fined its members. By the time my grandparents arrived, Grand Rapids was one of several Dutch Calvinist enclaves in America, highly cohesive settlements that worked to keep liberal theology — and the larger world — at bay. "In our isolation is our strength," they told themselves, and they built their lives around the church. Because they thought the angels in heaven spoke Dutch, church services were in Dutch as well. The Calvinists started their own schools, based on church doctrine, and eventually set up their own counterparts to many American institutions: hospitals, clubs, professional and charitable organizations, summer camps, even their own versions of the Boy Scouts and Girl Scouts. They shunned the sin of pride, as well as such worldly pursuits as dancing and gambling. They labored to be efficient and self-sufficient, and what they could not take care of, they believed, God would.

Imagine, then, the confluence of hope and horror that is churning in this small house on Watson Court that day in July 1911. The birth of the twins has brought the number of children in the house to seven, the oldest being ten. Another child, a girl just old enough to crawl, had died four years before. Now Tante Pylman, my grandfather's aunt who lives nearby, is about to appear with an idea that might save the twins.

Perhaps the new babies lie in a basket — or even in a bureau drawer. The house is hushed, the older children feeling the weight of family crisis without understanding it. My grandfather, a tall man with red hair, a handlebar mustache, and prominent ears, may be sitting in his reading chair, holding the Dutch Bible open on his lap. He prays. And perhaps he paces between the upstairs and downstairs rooms. He has been eager for the arrival of all his children, and in anticipation of this birth he has painted a bedroom and bought a new baby basket. My grandmother, whose own mother had died giving birth to her, rests in her bed upstairs. She has a theory about why the twins have come early, and it has to do with the trouble next door just a month ago. The neighbor woman was pregnant, though her husband had made it clear he wanted no more children — they had three already. Desperate and sliding into madness, the woman had spells of hysteria that often brought her husband knocking on my grandparents' door. "Help me," he'd say. "Help me calm her down." And Grandpa would go next door. Once, the woman tried to kill herself with a butcher knife. When her baby came a month ago, she abandoned the newborn boy in the backyard. The baby was saved and sent to a foster home, and his mother was carted away to a mental hospital. All of this has had my grandmother nervous and on edge.

Dr. Pyle is probably still at my grandparents' house. He lives only a block away, and he rushed over to deliver the twins. The minister is not here; he will be summoned later. One of the children, perhaps Nell, the oldest, has gone to tell Tante Pylman about the early birth. And now here comes Tante with an idea that could wrench the family from its safe Dutch harbor and thrust it into all the worldliness Grand Rapids has to offer.

Welcome to America! shouts the idea. Welcome to "can-do," to our belief that we can create anything, fix everything, show off while we're doing it, and brag about it later. Because over on the east side of town — *Step right up, ladies and gentlemen, boys and girls* — are the fleshpots of Ramona Park. Noisy glitz and glamor and vaudeville and dance halls and beer gardens. Ramona is raucous, rowdy, and enticing. And right there, on the midway at Ramona, is a sideshow that's a surefire draw for amusement park crowds bored by stage shows and fun-house mirrors. Real babies! The Preemie Show. *Right this way! Ten cents a peek!*

As it happened, Aunt Mux — she was called Grietje then, and her twin was Arentje — was born on the cusp of a new technology: baby incubators. And that summer, baby incubators were packing in crowds at amusement parks all over the country. The genesis of the incubator had been forty years earlier, after the devastating Siege of Paris during the Franco-Prussian War. Thousands of Parisians died — one estimate puts the figure at 47,000 — during the winter of 1870-71. Those who survived ate horses and dogs and rats and, eventually, the zoo animals. After the siege ended, French pediatricians joined a national effort to repopulate the country and began working to keep babies alive who might otherwise die soon after birth.

A pioneer in those efforts was E. Stéphane Tarnier, a Paris obstetrician beloved by his patients and admired by his pupils. He had saved the lives of thousands of women during childbirth by introducing antiseptic practices. In 1878, on a visit to an exhibition, he noted the use of a warming chamber for young poultry, and he asked the zookeeper who had made it to create a similar box for infants. Within two years Tarnier was using warm-air incubators in the Paris Maternité Hospital, nurturing babies in a false womb warmed to between eighty-six and ninety-two degrees.

In 1896, a young medical assistant at Paris's Maternité Hospital brought a new version of Tarnier's incubator to the World Exposition in Berlin. That young doctor was Martin Couney, a pediatrician with a showman's imagination. If we want people to notice the incubators, he reasoned, why not fill them with real preemies? He found them at Berlin's charity hospital, babies thought to have little chance of survival. With six incubators and six babies, the exhibit was mounted not in the science area of the exposition but in the amusement section, next to the Congo Village and the Tyrolean Yodelers. Couney called it "Kinderbrutanstalt" — the child hatchery. It drew gawkers in droves. All six babies survived.

Within two years, Couney had displayed premature infants at the Victorian Era Exhibition in London, bringing incubators across the channel as well as the babies to put in them (English doctors would not provide English babies). Copycat shows sprang up all over London, even at a Barnum & Bailey carnival, which put the famous British medical journal *Lancet* in a bit of a peeve. "[W]hat connexion is there between this serious matter of saving human life and the bearded woman, the dog-faced man, the elephants, the performing horses and pigs, and the clowns and acrobats . . . ?" the journal sniffed in an 1898 editorial.

That year, Couney brought his first show to America, to the Trans-Mississippi Exposition in Omaha. And by 1901 he had babies and incubators at the Pan-American Exposition in Buffalo. In each place, visitors paid to get in, usually a quarter. Parents of preemies paid nothing for their infants' care. The showrooms looked like hospital wards, with nurses and special feeding protocols. Still, fairgoers usually found the incubators somewhere along the amusement midway.

It was not much of a jump, then, from those early expositions straight to America's amusement parks. Baby incubators were still too experimental and too expensive for all but the largest hospitals. Couney, who moved to America in 1903, set up a perennial summer show at New York's Coney Island, and he later mounted shows across the country.

Copycat shows sprang up in other locations, including Ramona Park in Grand Rapids, a fortuitous coincidence for my twin aunts.

Grandfather might have agreed to send the babies to the park, and the older children might secretly have thrilled at the thought. But Grandma balked. Ramona Park? That wicked place? The place with the gambling and the bars and the dancing? And yes, probably prostitutes, too. What could Tante be thinking? And if this was the only way to save the twins, was it worth it? Could this really be in God's plan?

No, she declared. Nothing good could come of a godless place. The babies would stay home.

But Tante Pylman was determined. She huffed out of the house and down a few blocks to Grandville Avenue Christian Reformed Church, looking for the "dominee," the minister. Dominee Evert Breen is my hero in this story. He was born in the Netherlands, came to America, and graduated from Calvin Theological Seminary. By 1911, he had already been in the ministry — in Nebraska and Iowa and Illinois and now Grand Rapids — for twenty-two years. He spent only five years at the Grandville Avenue church, but he was there when my aunt needed him.

Tante Pylman might have known what he would say. A church photograph of Dominee Breen reveals a slight smile hidden between his mustache and the thin white beard that hangs far past his chin. The smile shows most in his eyes, which seem to know both joy and sorrow. Surely there was some dogma in him, some demarcation of black and white, of good and evil, but he must have seen many of God's gray areas during those two decades in the pulpit. He had probably been called, just a month before, to help the family that was unraveling next door to my grandparents. He might have helped place the child in a foster home. What was good and what was evil for that family? Dominee Breen had seen much pain and grief, and he must have known that God's will was not always comprehensible.

Now he and Tante Pylman hurry back to Watson Court, a short dead-end street off Grandville Avenue, to my grandparents' front door, one house from the corner. And this is what he tells my grandmother: "It makes no difference if those babies are under my *preekstoel* or in the incubators at Ramona." Mrs. Ruiter must send the twins to Ramona Park, Dominee Breen says, if it will save their lives. When my grandparents

A balloon race at Ramona Park on Reeds Lake, Grand Rapids' amusement and entertainment center for the first half of the twentieth century
GRPL, Library Postcard Collection

hear the word *preekstoel,* the Dutch word for pulpit, they also know that it means the authority of the church. What the dominee means is that, even if the reach of the church does not extend that far, God will guard the souls of those newborns during their sojourn in Ramona.

And so the babies go to see the world.

Grietje and Arentje joined the roller coaster and the carousel, the live stage shows, the dance halls, and the miniature railroad. The week they arrived, a new show started, featuring double jugglers, a short play ("The Coal Man & the Maid"), and an act called a "pianologue." It cost as much to see the preemies — 10 cents — as it did to see a matinee. Nurses decorated the twins' incubators with bright pink bows. There were other babies, too. The newspaper clipping mentions three of them, one an abandoned black child named Russell, who, at five weeks and three days when the twins arrived, was pronounced "cured" and was being offered for adoption. Russell and the other boys had blue bows.

For nine days Grietje and Arentje — their American names were Margaret and Angelyn — fluttered between life and death. And almost every day, Grandpa boarded the streetcar that would take him to his babies. Grandma was still recovering and went less often. On the ninth day, Arentje died in her little glass box. My Aunt Em, who was born three years before Margaret and Angelyn, and who was to become the family storyteller, recounts the next part of this story: "Your grandpa used to tell us about how he had to go by streetcar to Ramona Park to get the body of that little baby. You see, they didn't want a hearse there, because that would be a bad advertisement. And so, grandpa took the streetcar, and they placed this little baby in his arms, dressed, and a shawl wrapped around her, just like a real baby, a live baby."

Imagine now, my grandfather cradling his dead infant as he makes his way through the crowds at Ramona, out of the park, to the streetcar stop. He waits. He boards the streetcar with his burden. Do people coo over the child in his arms? Does he tell them, *Nee, overleden:* "No, she's dead"? Or does he pretend she's alive? How long those three miles, how hard the wooden mourner's bench on that streetcar journey from Ramona to the home of Zaagman the undertaker, just south of Franklin Street near Division Avenue, where he will leave her.

Later, in his grief, my grandfather makes a decision. He has prepared his home and his heart for another child, and he believes this is God's will. If Grietje also dies, he tells the family, we will adopt Russell, the abandoned black baby in the incubator show.

But Grietje thrives. The incubator show, which would normally shut down at the end of summer, delays its closing just for her. When she is ready to come home in late September, someone takes a picture of a nurse at Ramona holding her up to the light. At two months, she looks like a normal-sized newborn. To my grandparents, she must seem a miracle. Saved by God. Marked by destiny.

On her first birthday, Grietje the miracle baby — her family now calls her Margaret — is fat-cheeked and wide-eyed when my grandfather takes the family downtown for a photo portrait. Grandpa sports a straw boater. Grandma, newly pregnant once again, looks haggard. Four-year-old Em gazes at Margaret, as does my mother, Irene, who is almost three and sits on Grandma's lap. In the picture, it is Margaret on whom the light falls. Dressed in white and sitting securely on her father's knee, she looks startled.

Aunt Mux never seemed impressed with her start as a carnival sideshow. She wasn't curious about the machine that had saved her, or the bizarre circumstances, or even the other babies with whom she shared the stage. But the story has thrilled me since I first heard it. Had I been the one in that incubator, I always believed, I would have become a gypsy. Why didn't she? She grew up, but she was always small, birdlike. She rarely looked at the world head on. Instead, while her eyes gazed forward, she tilted her face toward the ground. Her family always called her Mux, a plain and flat nickname that replaced Margaret. There was so much she never did. Never married. Never learned to drive. Never had her own house. She and Em, who also remained unmarried, stayed in the family home with their brother and widowed mother and then, later, with just each other.

Mux stayed home in body and in spirit. By the time I was born, she was thirty-six, her choices diminished. She had gone to beauty school, and I remember that she gave me a fresh permanent every fall when I was in grade school. She clucked over me at the kitchen table as I handed her, one by one, the skinny pink curlers. If I said "Ouch!" as she wound my hair too tight, she'd tell me one thing she had learned, rhyming it in Dutch: "Die mooi wil gaan, moet pijn uitstaan" (To be pretty, you must bear pain).

If life had taught her that it hurts to be beautiful, Mux also learned that things are simpler for those who remain passengers, and that to chance more is to risk failure. I remember visiting her at Kent Dry Cleaners on Grandville Avenue, a few blocks from her home. I think she kept a bowl of lemon drops on the counter. That's the only job I remember her having, except for a week or so when she tried a downtown cleaners that paid more. But she couldn't walk there, and she didn't know the customers or any of her fellow workers, and so she went back to Kent.

She doted on her nieces and nephews, and there were many of us. She embroidered pinafores for me and my sister and sewed them onto our Sunday dresses. But even as she was a constant in my childhood, she was always in the background. While Em fussed over fancy desserts, Mux made the meat and potatoes. Em tied lavish bows on Christmas packages; Mux supplied the index finger that held the ribbon tightly against the box. I remember one Christmas, probably in the early 1960s: when Mux untied the bow on Em's gift that year, she found a new typewriter. It came with a book of practice exercises and a 33-rpm vinyl instruction record. Em, the older sister who had gone to college and to graduate school, who became a teacher and wrote poetry, was challenging her, daring her to step out of her incubator and into the world.

All those years ago, her parents had dared the ocean in winter. And although they wrestled mightily with it, they had dared the worldliness of Ramona to keep her alive. They lost her twin half, but Mux had survived the devil's playground. Maybe she had wanted to risk more along the way. Maybe she had wanted to put out one foot — or even a toe — to test the water. Maybe she told herself she'd learn to type. Someday. But I think she was satisfied with her life, even if Em was not. She had mastered the job at Kent Cleaners. She knew all the people whose arrival rang the little bell over the door. She knew their clothes — how much starch they wanted in their shirts and which buttons needed sewing. And they knew her. So she discreetly put the typewriter in the dining room closet and never touched it. It stayed there for years. No one talked about it again.

Mux had a quiet contentment and a knowledge of herself, even as she rarely stretched the boundaries she created. After her noisy public start at Ramona, she never engaged the world so vigorously again.

My birth was not as dramatic as Mux's. I was born in a hospital and grew up in Grand Rapids after World War II, the youngest of five children. We lived in the southeast part of town, where houses were newer than in what we considered the old Dutch district around Grandville Avenue. Still, most of our neighbors were Dutch. On weekdays my siblings and I walked to Seymour Christian School and later carpooled down Madison Avenue to Christian High. On Sundays, we went to morning and evening services — in English — at Burton Heights Christian Reformed Church.

Founded in 1905, that church was just the third English-language Christian Reformed congregation in Grand Rapids. By the 1950s, when I was a child, it was overflowing with meetings, clubs, and classes for its 1,200 members. The rooms and the sounds of that dark red brick building on the corner of Jefferson and Burton color all my childhood memories. Even now I can see the designs carved into the wooden pulpit and the communion table; they reminded me of bananas with the peelings curving away. I remember the rose and green of the carpets, the pictures in the stained-glass windows, and the graceful, undulating march of the organ pipes behind the pulpit. The building, in all of its ways and seasons, is part of my bones. All my changes were there, as Neil Young sings. In the sanctuary I was baptized as an infant and married as an adult. My father's casket lay there on a cool sunny day in April. The upstairs Sunday school room, where I played "Onward Christian Soldiers" on an upright piano, is also where I attended catechism class on Wednesday afternoons.

I adored the minister at Burton Heights when I was young. Rev. Leonard Greenway, a tall, lanky man who seemed to galumph into a room, made us giggle through our Wednesday afternoon catechism lessons, even as he drilled us in Bible names and places. He'd challenge us to find the name Eunice in the Bible, or the story of the loaves and fishes, and we would scramble through our New and Old Testaments to win the contest. "Give that girl a cement bicycle!" he'd roar to the winner. He delighted in us, and we in him. I thought he represented God; therefore, God must delight in me as well. I loved hearing him preach, I loved singing the hymns, and I loved feeling secure, embraced by that carefully constructed world.

When I was about nine or ten, I decided I would be a missionary. I chose a Margaret very different from my aunt as a role model: Margaret Dykstra, a missionary sent by Burton Heights Church to save souls in Nigeria. From Sunday school we took home tiny brown plastic television sets with a photo of Margaret Dykstra where the screen would be. Through the slot on top we were to push our nickels and dimes to fund God's work in this faraway land. When Margaret Dykstra came home on leave and spoke in church, her life seemed exotic, thrilling, and purposeful. I, too, wanted adventure in a foreign country, but only if it had a lifeline to home and church.

Shortly after that, Rev. Greenway left to become the minister at another church. For me, a fifth grader, it felt like being abandoned by God. The minister who followed him lacked mirth and adventure, and suddenly God did as well. Religion seemed full of constraints that chafed. I no longer looked forward to church. I dreaded the long Sunday afternoons, when most fun was prohibited: no bike riding, no playing at nearby Plaster Creek. Even schoolwork was banned. "You won't get a blessing on it," my father would declare. Increasingly, those restrictions seemed arbitrary to me.

When I was about sixteen, I enrolled, as was expected of me, in what was called a "pre-confession" class at church. This was the first of three steps that made up the rite of passage into adulthood in the Christian Reformed Church. Here is how I anticipated the process would go: in the class we would learn the Great Doctrines; I would wrestle with Big Questions about God and faith and the universe; the class would eventually lead me in the way I was to go, and at last I would comprehend the mysteries. Then I would meet, as required, with the church consistory, the group of elders who were eager to hear about my young faith and my relationship with God. Finally, I would stand before the entire congregation to profess my faith.

A few months later, I waited in a hallway with other teenagers to meet with the church elders. We had completed the class, where my attempts to grapple with my questions — What does God want of me? What is God? What is eternity? — had been waved aside. Crestfallen, I learned the purpose of the class: to memorize the answers listed in the Heidelberg Catechism. Now each of us, alone, entered the dark-wood-paneled consistory room. When my turn came, I took a seat in a large armchair at the polished wood table. The leaders of the church — all men — sat in their own upholstered armchairs. All of this spoke to me: something important happens here.

I still hoped the alchemy of faith would work some miracle. But there was no miracle. Someone asked me, "What is your only comfort in life and death?" and I parroted the answer to the first question of the Heidelberg Catechism. The words felt like sand in my mouth. Other questions and their expected answers followed, none of which I remember. Perhaps there was a bit of small talk, though the Dutch elders were not much skilled at patter with a teenage girl. One of the men nodded off in his chair.

And instead of the joy I anticipated would link me to the body of believers, I felt bereft, cut off, abandoned. My faith in the church, if not in God, withered at that moment. Disillusioned, I left my questions, still awaiting answers, in that consistory room. Weeks later, I did stand before the congregation, but I felt like an empty vessel.

I had had my fill of being Dutch and of being a Calvinist. A year or so later, I announced to my sister that I would never marry a Dutchman, not even someone who could be mistaken for Dutch. The man I married, I said, would be either Jewish, Japanese, or black. And I think now that the missionary dream of my early years was as much a yearning to see what else the world had to offer as it was a zeal to spread the gospel. But when the missionary dream evaporated, I did not lose the desire for adventure. If I would not be Margaret Dykstra, neither would I be my Aunt Margaret. No Kent Cleaners for me. No typewriter in the closet. I graduated from Calvin College and, despite my declaration to my sister, did indeed marry a Dutchman. But I chose one who shared my desire to seek life's answers outside the church and outside Grand Rapids. For a year we traveled the country in a Chevy van, calling it a spiritual journey. Soon afterwards, we divorced. Tossed into a new life, I lived in six different states as a journalist, a job in which daily events can be as breathtakingly unpredictable as Mux's life at Kent Cleaners was safely routine. I married again. He is Polish-Irish, raised a Catholic. When I met him, he had never been to Michigan. He struggled to pronounce Dutch names, and he had barely heard of John Calvin.

Mux has been dead for more than a dozen years now. She and Em had moved out of the family home and into a suburban condominium, then into an apartment at the Holland Home, and finally into separate rooms in the nursing wing there. She began having seizures; she got dizzy and fell. Pneumonia often knocked and sometimes visited. Her back curled in on her body and her chest seemed to disappear. She died, at eighty-one, in late January of a cold Michigan winter.

When I think of her now, I reflect on our different choices. In staying close to home, Margaret gave up adventure, financial independence, and a life of her own. What she gained was an absolute certainty that she belonged — in the church, in her home, in her family — and that she was where God intended her to be. She never expected to be anywhere else. When I was young, she and Em used to take me to Woodlawn Cemetery on Kalamazoo Avenue, where they tended the graves of their parents. They had planted flowers, and they kept a watering can in the crook of a nearby tree. My aunts told me to remember where that can was so that someday, when the years had passed, I could take up the burden of remembering the dead.

But when Mux died, I was too far away to go to her funeral. I live two thousand miles from my own mother's grave. Though I planted tulips there after she died twelve years ago, the flowers have long since disappeared. I do not share the utter sense of belonging in one place that sustained Mux throughout her life. My life has taught me to belong in many places and to seek more widely for those answers I couldn't find in the consistory room so many years ago. But sometimes now, when I hear the old hymns, I weep.

One of my favorite memories of Mux is a story she told me in the 1970s. She and Em were in their sixties and still in the family home. Watson Court had long ago been renamed Olympia Street, and the neighborhood had changed. My two aunts were among the last Dutch residents in their block. The world had come to them — had, in fact, surrounded them.

Late one hot summer night, Mux was awakened in her small single bed upstairs by noise from next door. The neighbors were drinking again. The houses, built by immigrants who valued community over privacy, were separated by, at most, ten yards. In her bare feet, Mux padded into the bathroom. From the window, she could see into the bedroom of the house to the east. Telling me the story, she giggled at the naughtiness of the show she had seen. She had not turned away. She stayed at that window, hidden from view in the dark bathroom. Enthralled, she listened and watched as the drunken couple next door hit and slapped each other. They leaned out the window and vomited. And then they made love.

Watching those naked bodies tangling the sheets made her think of purity and beauty, she said, of Adam and Eve in the Garden of Eden. She did not consider the violence or the vomit. It was as though she had witnessed the world before Original Sin.

Michigan and Fuller

Hank Meijer

Hank Meijer, co-chairman of Meijer Inc., joined the family business at the age of eleven as a trash handler at the Michigan and Fuller store. After graduating from Creston High School, he attended the University of Michigan, where he received a Hopwood Award for his essays. Upon graduation in 1973, he served as a reporter for a southeast Michigan suburban newspaper group; he became editor and later publisher of *The Crier,* a weekly newspaper in Plymouth, Michigan, before rejoining Meijer Inc. in 1979.

In 1984, Meijer published *Thrifty Years,* a biography of Hendrik Meijer, the company's founder and his grandfather. His articles on Michigan Senator Arthur Vandenberg have been published in the *Michigan Historical Review,* and he has written the entry on Vandenberg for Simon & Schuster's *Encyclopedia of the United States Congress.* Meijer is a trustee of the Gerald R. Ford Museum Foundation, and he is a fellow of the Hauenstein Center for Presidential Studies at Grand Valley State University.

I was eleven — too young to work, according to the Michigan Department of Labor. But this was not a choice. My dad had started young and so would I. My mother picked me up after school and drove me to the supermarket on Fuller Avenue at Michigan Street — maybe four miles away. We drove up Diamond, past Blessed Sacrament School and the cemetery, to Knapp Street and then to Fuller, passing the water tower on one side and the site of Auburn Hills, the planned integrated subdivision, on the other. There was Hines and Sons Appliances and a barn as the remnant of a farm, the big TB sanatorium, then an overpass above the new freeway before we dropped down toward Michigan and saw the store, where the grinning Thrifty Boy waved above the entrance.

All day the stockers saved up cardboard and refuse for my Friday evening shift. When I started, early in the fall, the days were longer, and the sun would still be up as I edged my way along the lip of a back dock crowded with heaping carts. At the far end stood the incinerator. I yanked a rope that opened the jaws of the furnace, locked it open, and began to pitch in boxes and trash. Sometimes embers were quickly rekindled. Sometimes I needed to touch match to paper.

When the labor department notified the company that it was violating child labor laws, they said we would be required to get a family business exemption. (I only learned about that part twenty years later.) This was in 1963, the fall the President was shot in Dallas — news that began as wild rumor on the bombardment court during recess at Aberdeen School. The world was still black and white — properly funereal. The incinerator was a glimpse of something more vivid. Flames leaping, sparks shooting out, a heat that seared my cheeks even as the Friday nights grew cold.

The sun set a little earlier every week. Beyond the hardware store and the cleaners, three or four blocks away, shone the lights above Houseman Field. As I chucked in boxes, the crowd of high school kids roared — clutches of mysterious teens, excited cheerleaders, all that spotlit glory on the bright green gridiron. As I pitched a broken jar against the back of the furnace, its crackle and hiss merged with distant whistles and shouts.

In the back room the floors were always sticky. After I had burned all the trash, I became the bottle boy. Friday night customers brought cartons and cases and shopping carts full of bottles to the register at the back of the store: all the beers — Falstaff, Stroh's, Blatz, and Black Label — and an exotic array of sodas, "pop" in this part of the world, a corner on the northeast side of Grand Rapids.

I tried to find a home for every bottle. Tired cases were propped against a long wall. There were cardboard slots for Tab and Nehi and

Nugrape, Dr. Pepper, Royal Crown, even Diet Rite. Offshoots of Coke and Pepsi were side by side with the Seven-Up and Mountain Dew and Fresca and Fanta — the last, I learned much later, a World War II improvisation by a beleaguered German bottler who was denied his shipments of Coke syrup. Then the buzzer would sound, and out at the register someone was waiting with a rumpled bag nearly soaked through at the bottom. The sugary sodas would have left a sticky mess, but the beer was the worst, the smell of it yeasty and fetid, in paper left too long wet by some back door.

This supermarket was my exact contemporary, opened the week I was born. I could be melodramatic and call it a large and rather demanding sibling, but my father never neglected me, or my younger brothers, in his passion to nurture the business. My mother had been laying out the week's grocery ad for the *Grand Rapids Press* at a card table in the living room when she felt the first labor pains. Tears streamed down her cheeks as she put aside her pencil, called to my father, and packed for the hospital. (I was born cesarean — two grand openings the same week.)

Above the backroom was the office of our family business, up until the fire in the late 1950s, when my father and grandfather and their colleagues moved to the big basement underneath the store. Downstairs was the snack bar where we went for breaks. There had also once been a redemption center for the trading stamps awarded to Meijer shoppers. When Goodwill Stamps were discontinued in favor of lower prices, the basement became a place to sell kitchen gadgets and beauty care and other non-food articles — the "home center." There were even toys there. It was where we did much of our Christmas shopping. When the store burned, the redemption center turned home center became a swamp of damaged goods. I found one of my first 45 rpm records there. Who sang "Tammy"? It didn't really matter. There was a high school girl across the street by that name who liked to sunbathe.

I wonder now at this place. It was always the Northeast Side. Not the Northeast Quadrant, not the Northeast Quarter. Not like the West Side either, with its Polish and Dutch neighborhoods, or the South side, Dutch or African-American. Only a quarter of the city, really, just a slightly more polyglot neighborhood, a mundane slice of pot pie. At that time, after Sputnik and before the moon landing, a perfect TV dinner of a place.

This corner of Michigan Street and Fuller Avenue, a few blocks east of downtown Grand Rapids, was the commercial heart of my childhood. It was hub enough of a neighborhood to have its own festivities. Parades marched up Michigan from the National Guard armory down the block. I was first introduced to Congressman Gerald Ford when he was walking alongside a convertible with his name on it. Maybe it was Memorial Day when he greeted my mother, brother, and me. I must have been five or six. All I remember are kids on the curb, pastel convertibles, flags, maybe candy. My dad was in Washington, by coincidence, and Mr. Ford quipped to my mother that Betty was there, too, while he was here with Fred's wife.

What was one-hour martinizing? That happened across the street, but what it was I never knew. Laundry loomed large in my mother's life. Dry cleaners were a service for city people; my parents were still pretty fresh from Greenville, up in Montcalm County. Our store shared parking with Rylee's Hardware, home of the BB gun I would always covet and never own. (Dad was an all-but-declared pacifist.) Across Michigan Street from the store, the Afendoulis family built, next to their cleaners and tuxedo rental, the Glass Hut. Fast food was a novel idea. Hamburgers and fries became staples for the high school kids who convened there after the football game. By the time I could drive, and was still working at the store, neither our basement café nor the Hut could match the appeal of the new Burger King and its strawberry shakes across the tracks on Fuller.

Across from the Burger King, the Corduroy Rubber Company must have made something for cars — fan belts, I imagined. We bought our color television from Decker and Sons across Fuller Avenue. On Michigan Street to the east, across from the armory, was the Dog 'n' Suds, where we dined often — the root beer mugs suggestive of something more grown up. Special occasions would find us further up Fuller at Bill Knapp's. To the west on Michigan, toward downtown, stores and bars yielded after a block or two to narrow, wood-framed houses. One was a faded gray bungalow whose weathered sign promised adventure and mystery: "Live Chameleons." It survived until I reached middle age, but I never got inside — or owned a chameleon.

One week in October came a coup in Vietnam, and the killing of President Diem. There was something provisional then, on the cusp of adolescence, that made me feel as if I were living week to week. The years stretched so far ahead. A couple of weeks later our President was shot. I was puzzled by my reaction. I would not know the word "dispassionate" until years later, but that was how I felt. This was a momentous thing to ponder, to report on, but I felt more excited than moved. Walking home from school with my friend Dan, whose father was an arch and sardonic Republican, I was surprised at his tears. I worried a little that I felt no such sadness, just a sudden shift in a world of ebbs and flows.

No one was impressed by my part-time job. Very part-time, really — four hours on Friday nights. Still, it was my work, even if I felt vaguely childish bustling around with a grown-up stock clerk's white apron doubled over in the middle so I wouldn't trip. The cheers from Houseman Field seemed so much like the revelry of a big kids' party to which I might never be invited.

When football gave way to winter, the back dock was my own arctic and equator. I edged through snow to reach the incinerator, but there, when the flame was rekindled, waited all the warmth of a raging bonfire. The violence of fire was the only violence in my life. My father was a liberal, peaceable fellow who would get exercised about any mistreatment of a customer or coworker. He had inherited socialist tendencies from my grandmother and her radical kin, leavened by my grandfather's good humor, immigrant gratitude for American democracy, and insistent common sense.

Though Puritan and thoroughly Protestant in their outlook, my parents had little truck with the prevailing faiths. I had essentially failed remedial choir at Second Congregational Church. After one dissonant performance of "Bring a Torch, Jeanette, Isabella," one of their chief motivations for churchgoing faded quickly.

My father's and grandfather's office hours downstairs rarely overlapped with my time in the backroom. Besides, they were on the road a lot in those days and busy with the first of the one-stop shopping stores across town. When my mom dropped me off at the store, she gave me money for a date-filled cookie from the bakery. I cherish the memory of

Three generations of the Meijer family stand proudly in front of their Eastern Avenue store, which opened in the early 1950s.
GRPL, Robinson Studio Photo Collection

that cookie, my own homely madeleine. The date filling was domed up in the middle of a scalloped circle of soft dough.

My grandfather, for whom I was named, had turned eighty, but he still came to work most days. He'd kept his barber's license, too, though he hardly needed that to cut my hair and my brothers' every third or fourth Sunday on a stool in his kitchen. He was "Mr. Meijer" to the people I worked with, the high school and college kids, mostly guys in the backroom, usually from Christian High or Central High or Calvin College. The cashiers were mostly female. They found amusement when I helped out at a register up front but could not, as a minor, ring up alcoholic beverages. They were older women — in high school or college or beyond — in white smocks and skirts. I would push an order down the belt, then stop the flow and ask whoever was on the next lane to reach over and punch the key for me for a six pack of Stroh's or a bottle of Gallo.

The guys I remember working with were mostly Dutch, Calvin kids with names like Dekker, Ippel, Penning — earnest and insouciant, knowledgeable in ways I envied. Their boss in the grocery department was the voluble Walt Andrakowicz. Walt reported to Ted Rhoda, the store manager. And each of us, in our white shirts, wore the little plastic name badges with our handwritten first names inserted below the smiling silhouette of Thrifty Boy.

As winter yielded to spring and the days grew longer, the loneliness of the back dock eased into a sort of backroom sociability. I had come to know many of the delivery people. The drivers for the soda bottlers and the beer distributors, the bread man. I was entrusted to count loaves at the receiving door, tray by tray, as the driver waited to wheel the bread racks onto the floor.

But warmer weather also somehow made the working life more isolating. I had turned twelve; junior high was in my future. Kids were playing Little League. The drama of the fire lost a little of its magic when the air was no longer so cold. Come summer, schedules would change. We had bought a cottage on a little lake north of Grand Rapids. My dad would commute; I would not.

But school was not out on that morning in late May when my dad came into the bathroom my brothers and I shared. His eyes were red, and he had that quavering around the mouth that he gets when he's about to cry. I think he must have been up most of the night, because my grandma had called sometime while we were sleeping and asked him to come quickly. My grandparents lived down the block, on the chestnut-shaded corner of Knapp and Meadowfield. My grandmother had gone to bed and found my grandfather. She thought at first he was asleep, but he was dead. His second heart attack was his last.

At school the next day, kids were let out of class. It was a brilliant morning in late May, awash in sun, a day we looked forward to all spring. The playground was marked off for various events, races and jumping — it was the annual field day. Teachers and other kids had heard about my grandfather. It wasn't a secret for long. This was a new experience — the condolences and thanks — my first experience of a death in the family. When people said they were sorry, they were serious and thoughtful about it.

My grandfather was my hero, but I didn't cry, really, although I felt like I should have. At work it was the same way, only these were people who knew Mr. Meijer, exchanged greetings with him at the checkouts or over coffee, snapped to a sort of attention when he strode down the aisles where they were stacking cereal or laundry detergent. My shifts with the incinerator and hours in the bottle return were nearly over. I was done burning things for the year. My brothers and I had a funeral to attend.

I never got to burn things again. When I worked at the store over the next few years, I was driving my mother's yellow Plymouth Fury and bagging groceries. My world widened. The Burger King added a drive-up window. My dad and his colleagues moved to a new suburban office out by our warehouse. By then I was going to Creston High football games at Houseman Field and thumbing a ride on Friday nights to the Burger Chef on Plainfield. And when I punched in on Saturday mornings, the apron finally fit.

First and Second Childhoods in Grand Rapids

Charles Honey

Charles Honey has been writing for newspapers since 1978. Before coming to *The Grand Rapids Press,* he worked at the *Murray Ledger and Times* in Murray, Kentucky, was editor of *The Enterprise* in Williamston, Michigan, and sports editor of *The Towne Courier* in East Lansing. Honey graduated with a bachelor's degree in English from Murray State University in 1984, and also did undergraduate work in creative writing at Michigan State University.

Honey has been writing for *The Grand Rapids Press* since 1985, and after stints as feature writer for the "Flair" section and covering education and Wyoming city government for the newspaper, became the religion editor in 1994. During his time as religion editor, *The Grand Rapids Press* has won the Religion Newswriters Association award for best religion section in both 2000 and 2002 among U.S. and Canadian mid-sized newspapers; it placed third for large newspapers in 2005.

Honey has won personal awards for column writing from the Michigan Press Association, the Associated Press, and the Kentucky Press Association, as well as a School Bell award from the Michigan Education Association. He has won a Public Service Award from the Michigan Association of Local Public Health for a five-part series on infant mortality in 1991. He has particular interests in spirituality and personal growth, the work of the church and individuals for social welfare, interfaith understanding, the arts, community history, and minority concerns. He wrote the following remembrance specifically for this book.

I don't know if both things happened on the same night or were separated by years. But I have put them together in my mind as the most vivid memory of my Grand Rapids childhood. It was a winter night. The power was out. Candles lighted up our house. For a little boy with a lively imagination, this was magic. I looked out the picture window on Philadelphia Avenue Southeast. Everything was white and still — like an old black-and-white movie. It was as if the world had stopped and there was nothing to do but pull a sled, take a walk, or look out the window. My father read to us by candlelight. He read aloud in the hushed darkness, while the flame threw a soft light on his rugged features. It seems to me that he was reading the Bible, though it might well have been a Western adventure story. In any event, that night stays with me, and it sums up my feeling about growing up in Grand Rapids. It was secure, it was picturesque, and it was good.

No doubt I have augmented this memory over the years as life has grown ever more complex, challenging, and not nearly as secure. But however much of it comes from my embellishments, I remember Grand Rapids as a good place to begin growing, and that memory itself has served me well. I grew up for five golden years in this city. From 1956 through 1960 my father, Keith, was the city planning director. We had come from Toledo to a city of stalwart faith and restless development. We landed smack in the middle of a postwar America that was stretching its arms at the dawn of its most prosperous era.

Dad put on a white shirt and tie for work. My mother, Betty, packed his lunch and ours. I walked two blocks to Ottawa Hills Elementary School. My older sister and brother, Maureen and Mike, walked to the same building, which at the time housed everyone from my kindergarten classmates to Ottawa Hills High School seniors. On my way to school I passed the home of a blind boy. It was said that he had gone to sleep with a fever and had awakened sightless. I had a great fear of fevers for years after hearing that.

Dad worked hard at old City Hall, toiling through urban renewal, the planning of U.S. 131, and the politically charged clashes of big-wheel developers and civic power brokers. Mom fully entered into the life of a supportive wife and involved mother. When Dad came to town in 1955 for a job interview, *The Grand Rapids Press* ran a feature on my mom explor-

Ottawa Hills Elementary School, part of what was then Ottawa Hills High School (now Iroquois Middle School), a focal point of Charles Honey's formative years
GRPL, Library Postcard Collection

ing the city's shopping treasures. And a four-column photo showed her lovingly adjusting Dad's tie on the steps of City Hall.

Most of Mom's energies went into her children. That included serving on the Ottawa Hills PTA, where she came up against a turf-conscious principal over a guest speaker on education reform in the wake of Russia's wake-up call known as Sputnik. Mom firmly pressed for the speaker, who attracted a large crowd. She also helped out in "character school" at Fountain Street Church, where my parents listened respectfully to the Rev. Duncan Littlefair's fiery sermons. It was there I was taught that all people had dignity, and I digested the simple curiosity of the song "Tell Me Why." These lessons would serve me well later in life, when I became religion editor of *The Grand Rapids Press.*

At Ottawa Hills Elementary, I learned other valuable things. One thing I learned was what happens when you touch the icy monkey bars with your tongue. Yes, I really did this at recess one day, and yes, the horror stories are true. More pleasantly, I learned to love the feel of the cool plastic mats at nap time in Dorothy Cryder's kindergarten. Hers was a kind and gentle introduction to formal education. Her classroom had a goldfish pond in the floor, which was later covered over when the room was converted to a library.

In kindergarten through second grade, I also learned to hone my penmanship with careful loops on my P's and exacting hooks on my J's. I loved the delicate water-colored paintings in our Dick and Jane readers. And I lovingly drew my own versions of our 1957 Ford Fairlane, with its sleek tail fins — along with dinosaurs, Popeye, and elaborate military clashes.

The Ottawa Hills neighborhood was well suited to the social life of a young boy, as was our colonial home just south of Hall Street. Saturday mornings were given over to Sky King, Bugs Bunny, and Woody Woodpecker on our RCA black-and-white TV. I owned an ample collection of records, brightly colored vinyl 45s with titles such as "Little Orly and the Bubble Gum." I could also mooch Ricky Nelson records off my brother, who, at five years older than I, was unquestionably cool. Mike's bedroom was a forbidden chamber of shrunken heads, *Mad* magazines, and a see-through plastic man. Sadly, I could not tag along when he cruised around in David Thwaites's convertible or holed up in a tree fort over on Sylvan Avenue with his buddy Russell Jaqua.

My sister, Maureen, was in another world, a world of poodle skirts and algebra equations I could not hope to approach. She made fast friends with Patsy Livingston and Janice Truax, and she attended high school with future Detroit Tiger Mickey Stanley. She danced in the gym to the safe-as-milk tunes of Pat Boone and Brenda Lee, wearing a dance card on her wrist and dutifully executing the fox trot she had learned in dance class.

At Christmas, Mom played piano while we sang carols, and she fixed holiday dinners of pheasant that Dad had bagged. As for the presents, they shine in my mind's eye like emeralds: Colorforms, a "Wagon Train" coloring book, Dr. Seuss snap-together figures, and Lincoln Logs. Mom also kept our house cultured, with paintings she rented from the Grand Rapids Public Library (she adored the weird, abstract figures of Joan Miro). With the second-highest median income in Grand Rapids, the Ottawa Hills neighborhood was a couple steps up from her working-class upbringing. But it was the cultural wealth of an arts-rich city that Mom truly treasured. Dad found his more rustic outlets shooting skeet at the

Kent County Conservation League or on family getaways to Rice's Resort on Round Lake, near Traverse City. Exploring nature or reading a good Civil War book were his refuges from the political pressures of City Hall.

Me, I took refuge in the playground of our neighborhood. Our backyard was bounded by a stone wall, a battlement I climbed many times to get into the adjoining neighbor's yard on Allerton Avenue. Next to the wall was the wire basket in which I burned the household papers, fancying myself an evil giant burning down a city. Down the block lived Jimmy Freeman, a freckled, sandy-haired boy who never stopped smiling. The other way lived Gordy Alward. I killed them many times in "cowboys and Indians." I myself was slain frequently, dropping with delicious drama into the cool, moist grass and relishing the tragedy of the fallen hero.

Dad often walked us to the new city branch library at the corner of Hall and Giddings, where Maureen wolfed down books like gumdrops. Saturday afternoons we might hike with him to the Eastown Theater for a matinee of Tarzan or John Wayne. There was a Jewish deli nearby where Mom picked up kreplachs after church. But no sweeter pleasure could be had than a good game of Ping-Pong with Dad, Maureen, or Mike in the basement, or flinging a Frisbee back and forth in the driveway. Friday nights were a kind of home ritual, as we gathered around the hearth of the TV watching *Gunsmoke, Rawhide,* or some other Western drama that stirred a young boy's exotic dreams.

All in all, it was a safe and secure neighborhood from which we seldom strayed. It offered adventure aplenty within a few square blocks. I recall no sense of menace anywhere except under my bed, which I checked every night to ensure there was nothing evil lurking there. Still, I almost managed to get myself seriously injured one afternoon. I did The Most Forbidden Thing: I crossed Philadelphia Avenue. I did so at the exact moment a car was barreling down the hill. The blood-curdling screech of brakes brought my mother running, panicked, from the house into the yard. It was a transgression neither my conscience nor my pride would soon forget.

There was safety in the fact that my parents knew almost everyone on our tree-lined block. Next door were Ralph and Virginia Truax. Ralph was a feature writer for *The Grand Rapids Press,* and Virginia was a diligent gardener who chatted with Mom over the low driveway wall. Their son Ron made a joyful racket drumming in the basement, laying down a backbeat for my future romance with rock 'n' roll. There is a photograph that crystallizes for me my childhood in Grand Rapids. It is the first day of kindergarten. I am standing in the driveway in a checked cowboy shirt with stiff, rolled-up jeans. My right hand is held up in an awkward, Scout-like wave good-bye. My smile is wide and confident. In the late 1950s, anything seemed possible.

We all waved goodbye to Grand Rapids in the fall of 1960. Dad had resigned as city planner to go back to Michigan State University for a master's degree. This cut his salary in half and increased his professional happiness tenfold. We moved to Williamston, a dusty farm town ten miles out of East Lansing, a place where we had often stopped for lunch on the long cross-state drive down Grand River Avenue to visit our grandparents in Detroit. But first we took a trip to Disneyland, cruising cross-country on a Vistadome train. On the brink of the riskiest move they had ever made, my parents wanted their children to know the thrill of racing down the Matterhorn Mountain ride and experiencing Fisherman's Wharf in San Francisco.

As we pulled out of the driveway on our last day in Grand Rapids, neighbor Lottie Gibson dropped a kitten in my lap. Mom wasn't thrilled with this unexpected addition to our family, but I was. The kitty was a cuddly reminder of the home I was leaving. I named her Tigerina.

When we drove into rural Williamston, I had the sinking sense that we had just slipped a rung down the social ladder. But it was, in fact, a wonderful place to live. Mike and I played basketball in the barn of our one-acre property that was dappled with apple and cherry trees. I hit rocks with my baseball bat in the gravel road out front. Williamston was a little world jumping with frogs, buzzing with cicadas, and pounding with the giddy drumbeats of Friday night football games.

I covered those games as a cub reporter for *The Williamston Enterprise.* Years later I became editor of that weekly tabloid, which was full of school board news and 4-H award winners. My wife, Wendy, taught at the same high school I had attended, and we began married life in an upstairs apartment with seven-foot ceilings. As I cranked out small-town news, I sometimes chatted with a fellow reporter named Chris Meehan. He was a former postman from Detroit who thought big and wrote well.

We agreed that, once we had worked up our journalistic chops, it might be good to write for *The Grand Rapids Press,* a quality newspaper big enough to stretch our legs but small enough to make an impact.

I'm not sure what attracted me back to Grand Rapids. Maybe it was a lingering sense of nostalgia. Maybe it was paging through the family photo album at those pictures of Dad tossing a Frisbee to us. But when Wendy and I drove over to visit, we liked the look of its gentle hills and pretty downtown. Whatever the pull, in March 1985, after a three-year layover in Murray, Kentucky, I tenaciously worked my way into a job at the *Press.* There I joined Chris Meehan, who had been hired a few years earlier, and Pat Shellenbarger, a Williamston friend and former *Detroit News* reporter who was hired the same month as I was.

Once I returned to my boyhood home, however, I discovered an entirely different world from Ottawa Hills. They called it the West Side. My parents had seldom ventured across the Grand River, save for Dad's stormy urban renewal meetings. He knew the West Side as a rough-and-tumble territory where city commissioners such as Bernard "Bunny" Barto and Mayor Stan Davis wielded clout, and tough working-class folks banded together against threats real or perceived. It was another world entirely from the more middle-class and comfortable power base of the Southeast Side.

But when I drove down west Fulton Street looking for housing, I felt a sense of familiarity. With its neighborhood grocery stores and cozy bungalows nestled around John Ball Park, it felt much like the small town of Williamston. We started in a rented house off the park. We were close enough to Sacred Heart of Jesus Catholic Church for our daughter, Emily, to walk to kindergarten there. Though she was being raised in the United Methodist Church, Emily came home on Ash Wednesday proudly bearing a smudge on her forehead.

A year later we ventured up the breathtaking incline of Bridge Street Hill and found the perfect home. Ball Park Boulevard Northwest issued southward from Mount Mercy, an old convent and Catholic girls' school on a bluff overlooking the city. Mighty maples arched protectively over the divided street. The sidewalks were plenty wide for bicycles and roller skates. The front porches had people on them. The house we were looking at was a jewel: stained glass, oak woodwork, high ceilings, pillared front porch. We walked through it and, then and there, our house search ended.

So began my second childhood in Grand Rapids. This one was made up of my children and the joy of fathering them in a quiet neighborhood filled with little kids and long-lived retirees. Emily played with two neighborhood girls named Sarah, drew on the sidewalk, and learned eagerly at Shawmut Hills Elementary. Like my sister, Maureen, she loved nothing more than spending a Saturday afternoon at the public library. Later, at Blandford School, she explored the wonders of the woods while raising chickens and making maple syrup with her sixth-grade class.

Our son, Max, came along in 1987 to make his own special brand of boyhood trouble. He was part of a population explosion of deceptively charming boys that swept through the neighborhood in that era: Caleb, Kam, Casey, Ryan, Noel, et al. Years later, the boy boom manifested itself in endless games of street hockey and, still later, ear-splitting punk-rock jams emanating from our basement. Every kid within two miles knew where Max Honey lived, and many afternoons you could find most of them sprawled on our front porch.

My kids grew up according to the slow rhythm of the West Side. It was the glide of a bike ride down to Sullivan Field, where you could watch a baseball game and sip lemonade on a hot summer afternoon. It was the saunter of twilight walks through the neighborhood. It was the breakneck rush of a sled down Union High hill, a double-dipper run that was steep enough to thrill a kid and bruise his dad's tailbone.

The neighborhood environs were different, but I believe the experiences were similar for my children and me. We all had friends, churches, sidewalks, and good sledding hills. We had modest but lovely two-story homes with leafy yards for adventuring. We had adults watching over and watching out for us. And, I hope, Max and Emily grew up — as I did — with a sense of belonging. We had a sense of being cared for by a close-knit neighborhood that didn't let its children wander far, but filled them with great expectations for the world beyond.

Baseball Nut, Altar Boy, Urchin . . .

TOM RADEMACHER

A native of Grand Rapids, Tom Rademacher was born in 1954 and lived most of his formative years on the city's West Side. A graduate of Grand Rapids Junior College and Grand Valley State University, he earned a degree in psychology and a teaching certificate, but eschewed a job in the classroom in favor of a career in writing and reporting. He joined *The Grand Rapids Press* in 1978 and covered a variety of beats before signing on as a columnist in 1986.

Rademacher's specialty is taking a microscope to "the guy next door" and finding something extraordinary in the ordinary. Before working for *The Grand Rapids Press,* he worked part-time as a swim instructor, coach, playground supervisor, silkscreener, factory rat, and taxicab driver. He currently lives in Rockford, Michigan, with his schoolteacher wife, Hollie, and their three teenage sons, Tom, Patrick, and Andrew. Rademacher wrote the following reminiscence for this book.

Had I designed a business card for myself as an eleven-year-old kid growing up in Grand Rapids, it probably would have read: "Baseball nut. Altar boy. Urchin. Happy." And every one of those cards would have been smeared with whatever else I had tucked in my pockets that day: Chum Gum, milkweed pod, Mercury dimes, transistor radio, cricket guts.

My life experiences as a native of Grand Rapids have been alternately fantastic and plain, affected by both rigid rules of conduct and winds of fate, shaped by everything from golf courses to teachers. But I wouldn't be worth two cents — or been asked to pen this memoir, I'm certain — were it not for my parents. Both helped me understand the beauty and power of words.

I was barely a teenager when my mother, Patricia, teamed up with one of my classmate's moms and decided that it would be in everyone's best interest to meet after school and discuss the likes of Emerson, Poe, Hawthorne, and Twain. It was part of a program known as "Great Books," and I still have the dusty volumes. It doesn't take much to travel back in time to see my mother's faintly freckled face, framed by her curly black hair, softly grounded in blue eyes, imploring me for a response to some question like, "What do you think Thoreau was really trying to say here?"

"Is Thoreau the guy with the, um, pond?" I'd wonder. And she'd turn to Mrs. Magin and say, "Maybe your daughter Mary can help here."

My father, Thomas, was just as adept at language, especially the written variety. On those occasions when he wrote a letter to someone, it was like an essay by E. B. White that had been edited by the School Sisters of Notre Dame. He could execute beautiful prose and still practice word economy. Not bad for a guy who spent his immediate post-high-school days driving truck and working in factories. He earned a college degree, but not until he was seventy, just months before his death.

My mother, on the other hand, graduated from Grand Rapids Catholic Central High School and then earned a degree in English — along with a teaching certificate — from Michigan State University. She taught just a few years at Godwin Heights High School, then fell in love, married, and switched careers to raise us six kids. She never went back to a classroom full-time, but that's not to say she ever quit teaching. Together, my parents exerted subtle influences on my life and the lives of my brothers and sisters, allowing us to roam, grow, succeed, fail, and learn. They encouraged us in everything from piano to sports to art lessons. So whenever I'm asked to name someone I admire, I don't have to look much further than my lineage. That includes a trio of brothers — Dan, Joe, and Matt — as well as sisters Mary and Molly, all of whom have gifts and talents from which I will continue to draw inspiration.

Even with caring parents, however, coming of age in the 1950s and '60s meant I spent a lot of time independent of them. During summer, especially, it wasn't unusual to leave the house around 8:00 in the morning and not check in again until dark. What baseball or riding bikes didn't provide in the way of sustenance, some neighbor lady would — peanut butter sandwiches at the Davison house, for instance. Or snacks at the O'Briens' or Bechtolds' or the Siegels' homes, or any number of other friends, cousins, and neighbors. Decades before Hillary Clinton popularized the term, we were already being "raised by a village." In my case, it was Grand Rapids' West Side.

To this day, some folks dismiss that quadrant of town as a blue-collar melting pot with more nerve than sophistication. Thanks for the compliment, I tell them. Our own family grew up on Ball Park Boulevard Northwest, a sanctuary emanating from the top of Bridge Street Hill that boasted a soft cathedral of trees unmatched by any in the city. As I write this, my mother lives there still — she has since 1956 — taking comfort in a rickety front porch from which my siblings and I waited our turn to play games of catch with my father on the parkway.

I spent all my formative years on and around that boulevard, playing out a life I can revisit any time I want, via the Super 8 movies my father recorded. Our sliding hill was barely three feet high, on a lot that measured just 50-by-100 feet and included a tidy foursquare home built in the 1920s. It was heaven on earth.

As a kid, I could walk from my house south through a lush stand of woods to John Ball Park, taking in "Rocket Hill" along the way, where we'd slide in wintertime. Since that time, however, that windswept knoll has been gutted to make way for the Gerald R. Ford Freeway, specifically the spot where motorists exit off of and onto Lake Michigan Drive.

Just as central to our identities then were the Catholic parishes and companion elementary schools from which we were hatched. In the beginning, the Polish were served by St. Isidore, St. Adalbert, and Sacred Heart, while the Germans congregated at St. Mary's, and the Lithuanians at Saints Peter and Paul. We settled in with the Irish at St. James, and I spent many a mass reading inscriptions on the stained-glass windows, gifts from first-generation families that hailed from the Emerald Isle itself.

Taking in mass every day of the week but Saturday was a blessed opportunity, but tedious for a kid. That's one reason I became an altar boy.

Young Tom Rademacher spent many a mass at St. James Church during his early years as an altar boy.
GRPL, Morris Photo Collection

Why merely attend when you could participate? I loved the crisp feel of the cassock and surplice, the mysterious union of water and wine. There was such ceremony in the lighting of candles and incense, the ringing of a gang of bells at the consecration. And when you served at a funeral, chances were you could ride to the cemetery in that fine black hearse. After a wedding, the "rich" couples would tip you a buck or two for your time.

Being an altar boy meant that they trusted you to run an errand on school time. "Take this to Father Magoon at the rectory," Sister Rose Elaine might instruct. Or, even better, you'd be asked to clean up a holy mess of hymnals the choir had left askew in the church balcony, a dark and mesmerizing place that housed the groaning organ and its bellowing gold pipes. My larger religious experience wasn't limited to that of an altar boy. Being a part of the church's Holy Name Society meant that I attended a glorious breakfast now and then — with my choice of tomato or orange juice. And it was made even better on a Sunday when Grand Rapids native and Detroit Tigers great Mickey Stanley held us spellbound as the guest speaker. I still have an autographed ball from the day my father took us.

My extended family included two great-uncles who served as Redemptorist priests across the Grand River at St. Alphonsus parish. Two of their three sisters never married or left the family homestead on Plainfield Avenue Northeast, where they sold religious articles from a room on the main floor. While my great-aunts sipped manhattans straight up, my brothers and sisters and cousins and I would explore everything from missals to relics to holy water fonts. My favorite item was a tiny orb through which you peered into a peephole to read the entire Lord's Prayer.

Being immersed in the Catholic faith had such a deep impact on me as a kid that I signed on for two consecutive summers at a camp near Detroit designed for youngsters who felt drawn to the priesthood. During the same period, I was mimicking clerics by "saying mass" in my own basement. I knew the entire liturgy in Latin, made vestments from old sheets, and fashioned Eucharistic hosts from flattened white bread, using a shot glass like a cookie cutter to render bite-sized wafers.

The pull the church had on me, however, was probably second to that exerted by the great outdoors. Since there were just three television stations available (and those aired in black and white), our playtime revolved around baseball, swimming, making forts, and otherwise devising our own fun. It was nothing to rubber-band a swimsuit and towel to our handlebars and ride our Sting-Rays several miles to Richmond Park for an afternoon of swimming and diving. The water was always cold, but the surrounding concrete hot, and I can still feel the incredible warmth that radiated upward when you were lying face down on that pocked poolside surface. When we had a few coins in our pockets, my cousin Mick and I would ride our bikes to Lincoln Lawns or Gracewil golf course, our raggedy bags with an incomplete set of clubs slung across those same handlebars.

If my father was in the mood, we'd rent a little boat out at Wabasis or Fresca Lake and fish for bass until well after dark. Uncle Bob Bechtold sometimes accompanied us, and he showed me how to roll my first smoke with Bugler tobacco. I was barely a teenager.

On special Saturdays, friends and I would hop a city bus for fifteen cents at Sibley and Bristol, and it would escort us into the grandeur that was downtown Grand Rapids. This was before the advent of malls, of course, and so it was the only place to shop outside of big stores like Arlans on Plainfield or "The Stadium," better known these days as the DeltaPlex. Downtown was a world of intrigue around Christmastime, with Herpolsheimer's and Wurzburg's resplendent with their ornate window displays. Inside, the same stores would entice you with polished glass counters framing fine scarves, perfumes, and leather goods.

As kids with just a buck or two, though, we were more likely to mug inside the curtained camera booth at Woolworth's, buy a few trinkets at Kresge's, and then spend any leftovers on palm buzzers and disappearing ink and magic tricks at the novelty shop across from Veteran's Memorial Park. If our parents were part of the shopping scene, it usually involved getting new sneakers — "rejects" from the Kinney shoe store at the river. Two bucks a pair.

It's against that sort of backdrop — which sometimes seems so near — that I recoil at the notion of spending $300 for a kid who "needs" an iPod. It's not that we didn't love music; we were simply content to spin LPs and 45s in someone's shag-carpeted rec room.

Money was rarely just doled out to kids of my era and ilk. To earn some, you shoveled snow or cut lawns or did chores. My first paycheck stemmed from my employment, during the seventh grade, doing odd jobs at Bechtold Bros. Furniture Co., which my grandfather had founded on lower Sibley Street Northwest. I was hired by the two uncles who had taken over the business, Bob and Dick Bechtold, to lug hardwood frames up a ramp to the second floor, reglaze failing windows, cut and glue foam rubber, and even spit a few tacks. I loved the sight and sound of the cupped plank floors, the exotic scents of varnishes and lacquers, and the occasional glimpse of a Vargas girl on a workbench calendar. I started at something like 40 cents an hour, and I made enough working after school there to keep myself in plenty of candy, sodas, and baseball cards, mostly purchased at Schichtel's party store, which we got to via a tunnel under Bridge Street across from St. James.

During that same era, I spent my evenings doing homework, or practicing basketball or football under the tutelage of Mr. Jerry Stapleton and Mr. Gordon Froman, who coached most of the boys' sports at St. James the years I attended — from 1960 through 1968. School itself was an arduous affair, with plenty to learn and too little time for shenanigans. You remembered the ones who made you learn: Mrs. Otterbacher, Mr. Nethercott, Sister Adelinda, and Mr. Murphy. The school playground was hardly that; it was merely a parking lot where you invented your own fun. When snow was plentiful, we played King of the Mountain from what the plows would pile up, then re-entered our classrooms smelling of wet wool. Lunch was whatever you brought in your bag, though once a month or so, Mrs. Weller and the other moms would host a hotdog sale. You could gorge yourself for less than a buck; glazed doughnuts were a nickel.

We lived for summers then. Aside from swimming at the Richmond and Lincoln pools, there was Little League. I always felt very important putting on my uniform — among the finest clothes I owned. And just as much fun as playing in games for sponsors such as American Laundry and Matthew's Drug Store and McInerney Spring & Wire was circulating the Southwest Little League newsletter at the start of each season. It meant dressing in uniform and hawking the little handouts at barbershops, bars, and businesses up and down Bridge and Fulton and Leonard streets. Afterwards, we'd thrill to ten-cent Dilly Bars at the Dairy Queen.

Summertime also meant a proper vacation, and for sixteen consecutive years we reveled in my maternal grandparents' cottage on Memory Lane in Grand Haven, where we stayed the same two weeks every year in August. It was the only time off my father ever got in exchange for selling industrial chemicals for more than two decades at the same firm. He could have spent the time in a chaise lounge. Instead, he rose early and rousted us on cool, sweet mornings to go perch fishing on the fabled Grand Haven pier with cane poles across our laps.

As tots, we could always count on his shoulders for the best view of the annual Coast Guard parade. Miniature golf was usually part of the plan, at least two times during our stay. But the highlight of every day was going down to the lake with a jug of homemade lemonade and simply swimming in what I still consider the most beautiful body of water in the world. At dinnertime, we'd feast on grilled burgers with corn-on-the-cob, play whiffleball or shuffleboard, then settle into sandy sheets and drift off to the sound of the foghorn. Those were perfect postcards.

Summers were also the best time to court trouble. Before I was fourteen, I'd had my first cigarette, swilled beer, and committed a half-dozen misdemeanors. And my plans for the priesthood were put on permanent hold once my imagination gleaned more of what swished beneath the plaid uniforms that hugged the girls in my eighth-grade class. My first real brush with a member of the opposite sex came during a dance to celebrate our graduation from St. James, at Rick Jackson's house on Carpenter Avenue Northwest. It was there, in his basement, that Stephanie Wood mercifully — and slowly — danced with me to the refrain of "Just Call Me Angel of the Morning." I never played Mass after that.

My first kiss wouldn't present itself until two years later, between my sophomore and junior years at West Catholic High School, where I didn't play much baseball, but parlayed my fondness for swimming into the only sport at which I would ever excel, thanks to Coach Jim Schaak, and later, David Clark. My love of the pool would later mushroom into jobs as swim instructor, lifeguard, and coach. And it was swimming that largely took me away. When, at age eighteen, my Grand Rapids Junior College team boarded a bus bound for Florida during Christmas break, it was only the second time I'd stepped across the Michigan state line in my life.

As a teenager growing up in Grand Rapids, I spent way too much time just hanging out, even with the jobs I had at various pools and in factories such as Sackner Products and Steelcase, Inc. In one of Monroe Center's many incarnations, it served during the 1960s as the mainstay of "the circuit," a haphazard route through downtown where you went with high hopes of meeting girls; unfortunately, at least in my case, I shot more gas money than Cupid did his arrows. More of the same happened at drive-in movies, where you usually ignored what was showing and tried to ignite your own screenplay. Or worse, got into a fight.

After two years at Grand Rapids Junior College, I spent a year at Alma College, then took a year off before finishing up at Grand Valley State, where I earned a degree in special education and a teaching certificate. But my parents' influence and love of English won out: the summer after graduating from Grand Valley State, I did a 180-degree turn and applied to work at *The Grand Rapids Press.* Michael Lloyd had just ascended to editor and took a huge chance on me when I pounded on his door. He hired me as a largely untested writer after I begged to do anything, even if it meant driving trucks or sweeping floors.

With mixed emotions, I moved away from the West Side shortly after marrying my wife, Hollie. We live with our three teenaged boys — Tom, Patrick, and Andrew — in Rockford now, and its core city is in some ways more like the Grand Rapids I grew up in than the one that exists now. Our home is more than a century old, the street lined with ancient hardwoods. We walk to the library, the hardware store, the meat market. It could use a tunnel, though.

When I tramp the streets of my youth now, I can still see my mother — outside helping us with a wayward snow boot or cheering from behind the backstop at Rumsey Field. My father is driving us in a Ford Country Squire station wagon to get burgers and fries at Sehler's, his left arm propped out the open window to create his only tan line. As for downtown Grand Rapids, I can hardly walk it without seeing a matronly woman in a white uniform and hairnet handing me a lemon phosphate from behind a linoleum counter at one of the luncheonettes I frequented. City Hall has a massive bell tower. And the ever-changing skyline that nowadays dotes on those who are rabid for a hot condo deal and a trendy bistro will always be the place, for me anyway, where the McKay Tower and its fourteen floors stood sentry as the tallest joint in town.

When I walk by the newly improved facade of the Amway Grand Plaza Hotel, I don't see so much gleaming glass and copper as I do a little kid being led by his late father into the Knife & Fork restaurant. It anchored what, to me, is still the Pantlind Hotel, where the kid gets to order almost anything he wants. His father alternately chats with him and reads his Sunday paper, giving the boy a chance to rubberneck his way around the little eatery, and then fix on the scene outside, where he watches the street people mingle with cabbies and window-washers and deliverymen. He has no idea that, years from now, he'll have the opportunity to work for the same newspaper his father holds in his hands. And that he'll actually help chronicle the very changes to his beloved city that he can't now even begin to imagine.

For now, though, it's enough that the hotcakes are here.

Even Though I Was Not "Raised Indian"

Levi Rickert

Levi Rickert is a tribal member of the Prairie Band Potawatomi Nation, and is the former executive director of the North American Indian Center of Grand Rapids. He has served as president of the City of Grand Rapids Historical Commission and as vice-chair of the City of Grand Rapids Community Relations Commission, as well as on many boards and commissions in Grand Rapids and at the state level to further the quality of life for American Indians.

Rickert is a senior loan officer at Broadmoor Financial Services, Inc., and owner of the White Pigeon Group, a Grand Rapids–based consulting group that is currently involved in a project with Dwelling Place of Grand Rapids and Kendall College of Art and Design to establish the Great Lakes American Indian Institute of Art, which will make it possible for American Indian students to get a college degree in American Indian art.

Rickert has written book reviews and guest editorials for *The Grand Rapids Press,* and has also written for the now-defunct *The Paper;* his article entitled "American Indian Grandparents Raising Their Grandchildren" appeared in *The American Indian Review* (Spring 2000). He is a speaker/presenter on American Indian affairs throughout Michigan, and in 2005 was the featured guest on WGVU's *Newsmakers with Fred Martino* to discuss contemporary American Indian views of Christopher Columbus. Rickert wrote the following essay specifically for this book.

In traditional American Indian lives, it was thought that a boy became a man when he killed a bear for the first time in his life. Other American Indian traditionalists held that a twelve-year-old boy should go on a vision quest, where he would go into the wild and fast, with a limited amount of water, surviving there for days until he discovered where he would ultimately fit into the tribe.

My coming of age as a Potawatomi in Grand Rapids took a different journey. Perhaps it had to do with growing up in the urban setting of Grand Rapids, away from a reservation. Perhaps it had to do with the era in which I grew up in America. My true sense is that it was the combination of these things that brought me through my journey of discovery to clarify my identity as an American Indian. This clarity has allowed me to function relatively well in two cultures — the "American" culture and the "Indian" community.

As I reflect on it, my coming of age as an American Indian in Grand Rapids has to take into consideration how generations of my family survived various federal policies toward American Indians.

I

There was something paradoxical about my upbringing. Even though I am Potawatomi, I was not "raised Indian." Or, to put it another way, even though I was not raised Indian, my DNA composition is Potawatomi and I am still an Indian. "Raised Indian" is a term that is often used by American Indians when discussing their upbringings. What it really denotes is that parents, grandparents, or guardians followed the traditional ways of our American Indian forefathers: the native language was spoken in the home, and the ceremonial ways were practiced. Actually, the term is somewhat nebulous, because practices begun one hundred years ago by our great-grandfathers were not practiced by their fathers. So when we discuss traditional ways, it is important to put things in their proper perspective, which should include time and place.

While people can never be certain what the thought process was in their own family concerning their upbringing, assumptions can be made. As for mine, I believe that my family thought that more success would come if we attempted to assimilate within the broader society. This idea actually became prevalent among many American Indian families decades before I was born. The idea followed the American Indian policy maintained by the U.S. government for several decades that supported the notion "Kill the Indian and save the man." The idea was that the Indian needed to be "civilized."

The "Kill the Indian and save the man" policy was a deliberate effort to destroy the fabric of American Indian traditions and culture. It forbade Indians from wearing attire they were accustomed to wearing; it meant that men's hair had to be cut short to mimic non-Indian hairstyles. Of course, the policy in practice followed a government policy that allowed for American Indians to be killed or put onto reservations as the country moved westward. One key component of the "Kill the Indian and save the man" policy, a practice begun in the 1800s in various parts of the country, allowed for American Indian children to be taken from their homes to live in Indian boarding schools — sometimes for years at a time, without the love and affectionate support of their families' presence.

From a sociological perspective, this policy caused a vast erosion of American Indian family life. The pangs of sorrow in the hearts of parents who had their children removed simply because they were American Indians must have been unbearable. I have heard Michigan Indian elders tell stories of how they resent the fact that they did not get the proper physical affection from their parents; it was because their parents, the ones who had been raised in boarding schools, had been robbed of the proper development of their interpersonal relationship skills by that government action.

My own grandmother was taken from her home in the Prairie Band Potawatomi Nation's reservation at Mayetta, Kansas, to live in an Indian boarding school in Genoa, Nebraska. The full impact of her boarding-school experience will never be known to me, because she never spoke to me about it. She did confide to my sisters, Nancy and Debbie, that the tattooed number on her forearm was put there by the officials of the boarding school.

By the time I was born, in the mid-1950s, some American Indians had settled in cities and suburbs. They did what they could to survive in a society they had been assimilated into. Obviously, there was no going back to the times of our forefathers. But when I look back on it, my upbringing allowed me to see American Indians functioning in modern society. Even though I was not "raised Indian," I was constantly around American Indians.

II

When I was a little boy, Potawatomi people were still called Indians, not Native Americans. It was not until the late 1960s that the term "Native American" — a term that originated with the U.S. government — became popular. Arguably, both terms are misnomers. Generally, I enjoy the duality of the term American Indian because it allows for a rightful placement within two cultures. As American Indians, we use our *tribal* affiliations to denote our identities. Back in elementary school, on the first day of school each year, my new teacher would ask me what my tribal affiliation was. When I responded "Potawatomi," my fellow classmates would yell, "Pot-a-what?!"

Historically, the Potawatomi tribe has been part of the Three Fires Confederacy, also known as the People of the Three Fires; the confederacy includes two other American Indian tribes, the Ojibwe and Ottawa. Within the People of the Three Fires, the Potawatomi have been known as the "keepers of the fire," because we are the tribe that keeps the fire going during council meetings. Perhaps due to the small size of the tribe, the Potawatomi were not then — nor even today — well known outside of the Great Lakes region. Yet historical maps show that the Potawatomi tribe at one time occupied land in the Great Lakes region that today includes populous Detroit, Chicago, and Milwaukee.

My family is the White Pigeon family. We trace our ancestry back to an eighteenth-century Potawatomi *ogema,* or leader, named Wahbememe. The English translation of his name is White Pigeon, and the oldest incorporated village (1837) in Michigan is named for him. When I was young, my grandfather would go to the village of White Pigeon at the end of each year to gather calendars from local merchants, such as the gas station and the pharmacy, with the name White Pigeon on them. He proudly passed them out to members of the family, as they bore our family name.

I was named after my grandfather, Levi White Pigeon, Sr. Though the name Levi is a Hebrew name from the Bible (one of Jacob's sons), American Indian tribal rolls in Michigan from the early 1900s contain a number of males with the first name Levi, demonstrating the influence of Christianity on American Indians during a portion of the late 1800s. Even the American Indian who performed a silly dance every time the Atlanta Braves hit a homerun in the late-1960s, known as Chief Noc-a-Homa, was Levi Walker. (Walker grew up in Cross Village, Michigan, before he moved to the South.)

My grandfather grew up in old Indian Salem in Allegan County, some thirty miles southwest of Grand Rapids. He grew up on forty acres that were allotted to my great-grandfather, James White Pigeon, a Methodist minister, in the early 1900s. All but ten acres were lost due to back property taxes owed during the Great Depression.

During a portion of the last century, many Americans moved from rural communities to cities for educational and employment opportunities, and American Indians followed the same pattern. My grandparents became one of these families when they left Allegan County and moved to Grand Rapids in the late 1920s. Many of my fondest childhood memories are of the time I spent at my grandparents' home prior to entering elementary school. It gave me an opportunity to see an almost constant stream of relatives and friends who would come to visit. As is legendary in American Indian homes, there was always a hot pot of coffee on the stove to share.

Two frequent visitors in my grandparents' home were my grandfather's sister and husband, Lena and Jim Strong. They would come to visit on their way to and from the Isabella Indian Reservation in Mt. Pleasant, Michigan. Or they would stop by on their way out West, the trunk of their car filled with all sizes of Indian black-ash baskets that they made to sell. As I sat in my grandparents' kitchen listening, their conversations were filled with soft and caring words. They were gentle people who were very thoughtful and deliberate with each word they spoke. Sure of his identity as an Indian, Jim Strong always wore Indian beaded ties instead of the regular ties that I was used to seeing on "urban Indians."

III

When I was born, the American Indian population of Grand Rapids was less than one percent of the general population, fewer than two thousand "urban Indians." While I was in school, my family was the only American Indian family in the entire school system, except for a couple of years when some cousins from the Medawis family attended the same school we did. Back then, we were taught strictly from an Anglo-Saxon perspective. Of course, we learned how "Columbus sailed the ocean blue in 1492." Even though I was not raised Indian, my Potawatomi intellect rejected many of the stories that my teachers taught me.

At home, my mother taught her children the power of reading and learning. When I was in elementary school, she took me and my siblings to the city library on Saturdays. My lifelong love of biographies began then. I remember reading most of the biographies in the library that were written for my age group by the time I was in the sixth grade. I read about George Washington, Nathan Hale, Benjamin Franklin, Thomas Jefferson, and others from that era. These figures in American history became heroes to me.

Those perceptions changed dramatically one day during eighth-grade American history. The assignment was to read the Declaration of Independence in our red, white, and blue history book. As I read Thomas Jefferson's words in the Declaration of Independence, I recognized the context of how American Indians were viewed historically. The same man who wrote the words "we hold these truths to be self-evident, that all men are created equal" continued, in the fourth paragraph from the end, with these words: ". . . the merciless Indian Savages whose known rule of warfare. . . ." At that exact moment an enlightenment came to me that changed how I have viewed written history ever since. I was sitting in the last seat of my section, and as I put my history book down and leaned back in my seat, I accidentally hit my head against the concrete-block wall behind me. Those words of Jefferson that depicted Indians so unfavorably angered me, because the "Indian savages" he wrote about were not the American Indians I knew.

A year later, the circle of the Indians I knew expanded drastically, and none of them were "savages" either. I have my sister Jessica to thank for expanding my circle. She was home for the summer from her studies at the University of Michigan, where she had been hired to conduct a survey of the American Indian community in Grand Rapids. Her surveys were part of a statewide endeavor, undertaken by Deloitte Touche for the Michigan Commission on Indian Affairs, to study the socio-economic conditions of Michigan Indians. Jessica made a deal with me: she would buy me either lunch or dinner if I would accompany her while she conducted those interviews.

Of the many interviews Jessica conducted that summer, one sticks out in my mind: it speaks of how one American Indian woman living in Grand Rapids dealt with her Indian-ness back then. Early one Saturday evening, as we were making our way home, we stopped by this woman's house to do an interview. When the woman, who clearly looked American Indian, came to the door, she was visibly upset that her name was even on the list.

"How did you get my name?" she exclaimed. "I'm not Indian! You need to leave right now. My husband just went to the grocery store and will be back in a few minutes. You can't be here when he comes home." Jessica told her that her name had been provided by the company that was having her conduct the survey.

"No one is supposed to know that I am Indian. Just leave! I cannot be part of your survey. I just don't want any trouble. You know how it is when people find out that you are Indian. Hurry, please leave." The woman was obviously scared.

Fortunately, not all urban Indians that Jessica interviewed that summer denied their heritage out of fear of being known as an Indian. Many of them did seem to want to downplay their Indian heritage, or did not want to be part of another Indian survey. This is a common thought among American Indians: "Indians have been surveyed to death!" It was obvious to me that most of them simply wanted what others in society wanted for their families, that is, to have the opportunity to work, to be healthy, and to live decent lives.

IV

As I was growing up, our country was in an era of rediscovering its identity. The civil rights movement, race riots, and the assassinations of Martin Luther King, Jr., and two Kennedys had the nation in a state of turmoil. Fortunately, I had a strong mother who guided me through this time in American history.

Mother was — and still is — a woman of great determination. She has never been afraid to voice her opinions or concerns to anyone. She would rally for her children in the school principal's office if she thought some teacher was picking on one of her children because he or she was American Indian. I appreciate that she always kept up on current events. She talked to me and my siblings constantly about what made the news. This provoked us to think for ourselves rather than simply rely on opinions of others.

My mother showed us her strong character during the week following the assassination of Martin Luther King, who was assassinated the Thursday before spring break in 1968. Since there was no school the following Monday, my brothers and I went up north with a widow friend of our family. She had a cottage and recruited us to help her "open it up" for the upcoming summer. We stayed overnight in order to get all the work done. On the day of Dr. King's funeral, I sneaked into the cottage to watch it on television.

In the early evening of the next day, we drove back to Grand Rapids. As we entered the city, our friend's car radio was tuned to a call-in talk show on WLAV. The evening's topic dealt with race relations in Grand Rapids and other parts of the country. As is usually the case when race relations are discussed, the conversation that night dealt with black and white relations. But as we listened to this talk show, a woman called in to tell the audience that the conversation should also include American Indians.

"That's our mother," blurted one of my brothers. And indeed it was. We continued to listen as my mother told how American Indians were the first people here and that we were always forgotten whenever people talked about how bad other ethnic groups had it in this country.

Two days later, my mother took us downtown to see Senator Robert Kennedy at Campau Square, which I consider one of the great events of my childhood. We stood about two hundred feet from him, and to this day I still hear his words echoing in my ears. Here was Robert Kennedy, running for the presidential nomination of the Democratic party, speaking to the citizens of West Michigan and asking for their support. Here was Robert Kennedy, brother of the slain President, speaking of healing an America torn by the recent King assassination. He spoke of Americans living together in harmony at a time when our nation was ravaged by the division of racial unrest and an unpopular war in Vietnam. He spoke of a promise and hope for a better America. He spoke to the hearts of those in downtown Grand Rapids. I stood among the crowd and welcomed the speech about working together as Americans. (Kennedy was destined to be killed less than two months later in California.)

To demonstrate how balanced my mother was in raising us politically, later that year she also took us to see Richard Nixon campaigning for the presidency at the Civic Auditorium. We must have arrived early, because I can recall getting first-row seating at the auditorium. I don't remember a word he said, but I do remember him walking around the platform showing the V-sign with a large smile on his face.

My mother also taught me the valuable lesson of how one person's voice can make a difference. One wintry Saturday morning when I was fifteen, Mother and I attended an Indian meeting at the old Westside Complex near downtown Grand Rapids. There were perhaps eight American Indians present, including my mother and me, to discuss American Indian affairs with Michigan State Senator Milton Zaagman. He apparently was reaching out to the American Indian constituency that particular morning. My mother raised her hand and told the senator that it was just ridiculous that the Michigan Commission on Indian Affairs consisted of more people who were not Indian than of those who were. She asked him how people who were not Indian could even know what Indian concerns were. The state senator listened and told her that he would look into the matter.

One day after school, a few months later, my mother showed me a small article in *The Grand Rapids Press* that, as I recall, consisted of only two small paragraphs: it reported that Senator Zaagman had created

Levi Rickert's great-grandfather and great-grandmother, Levi and Martha Whitepigeon, gather at the grave of the Potawatomi leader White Pigeon. The little boy is Rickert's grandfather, also named Levi Whitepigeon, along with his sisters Iva (left) and Lena.
Photo courtesy of Levi Rickert

legislation calling for the Michigan Commission on Indian Affairs to be made up of primarily American Indians.

My upbringing was complicated and paradoxical: from my mother I learned to be aggressive; from my grandparents I learned humility.

V

Our elders tell us that all life is circular. In retracing my family's right to retain our heritage, I discovered that my family evolved with the various federal policies toward Indians — as did other American Indians. My assessment is that my grandparents' generation safely protected their Indian-ness; yet they did not purposely pass on the old ways to my mother's generation. Fortunately for me, there has been a resurgence of American Indian culture in my generation. Even though I was not raised Indian in Grand Rapids, I eventually found my identity as an American Indian. And it came through the connection to my grandparents.

I am constantly drawn back to memories of my Potawatomi grandparents. Sometimes the connection to my past comes in the simplest of ways. When I was a little boy, my grandmother kept her hair accessories on her dresser in a small Indian basket made of sweet grass. Dark thread wove strands of green sweet grass to form the basket; its lid was a floral design made of quills. I would go into their bedroom and lift the lid of that basket, because I loved the scent of the sweet grass.

Each year at powwows, I purchase a single braided strand of sweet grass. The scent of the sweet grass transports me back to my grandparents' bedroom and provides me the connection to my family's history, security, love, and pride.

A Farewell to Arms

John Hockenberry

John Hockenberry is a three-time Peabody Award–winning radio journalist and four-time Emmy Award–winning television journalist who joined NBC as a correspondent in 1996 after fifteen years with National Public Radio and ABC News. He spent more than a decade with NPR as a general assignment reporter, Middle East correspondent, and the host of several programs, including *Heat,* a daily two-hour public affairs program that he helped create, coproduced, and hosted — for which he won his second Peabody. Hockenberry's reporting for *Dateline NBC* earned him three Emmys, an Edward R. Murrow award, and a Casey Medal. His most prominent *Dateline NBC* reports included an hour-long documentary on the often-fatal outcomes of the medically uninsured, a report on a young schizophrenic trying to live on his own, and his extensive reporting in the aftermath of the 9/11 attack.

While at NPR, Hockenberry was the first anchor of *Talk of the Nation,* a daily two-hour live call-in show broadcast from Washington, D.C., beginning with its premiere in November 1991. He was the anchor and co-writer for the multiple-award-winning NPR series *The DNA Files,* as well as a regular contributor to the award-winning radio program *The Infinite Mind.* During the Persian Gulf War, Hockenberry filed reports from Israel, Tunisia, Morocco, Jordan, Turkey, Iran, and Iraq. He was one of the first Western broadcast journalists to report from Kurdish refugee camps in northern Iraq and southern Turkey. He also spent two years (1988-1990) as a correspondent based in Jerusalem during the most intensive conflict of the Palestinian uprising. He received the Columbia Dupont Award for Foreign News Coverage for his reporting on the Gulf War, and an Emmy for his television work.

John Hockenberry

Hockenberry was born in Dayton and grew up in upstate New York and Grand Rapids. The following "coming of age" story, set in Mary Free Bed Hospital in Grand Rapids, is excerpted from his book *Moving Violations: War Zones, Wheelchairs and Declarations of Independence* (New York: Hyperion, 1996), which he performed as "Spokeman" in his one-man, off-Broadway show in 1996. He has also written for *The New York Times, The New Yorker, The Washington Post, The Columbia Journalism Review,* and *Details.* He began writing his own blog, entitled "The Blogenberry," in May 2006 and is a contributing editor to *Wired* and *Metropolis* magazines. Hockenberry lives in New York with his wife, the producer/journalist Alison Craiglow Hockenberry, and their two sets of twins.

People always ask whose fault it was. It seems such an odd question, and yet for me the answer is just a shrug. I was hitchhiking from Chicago to Massachusetts with my college roommate. We got into a car in Pennsylvania on a sunny February day. I fell asleep in the backseat. The driver and her college roommate fell asleep in the front seat.

When I awoke our car had snapped the thread holding it to earth. We hurtled over a flimsy guardrail and down an embankment. The steel of the roof crumpled on first impact, and the car's subsequent rolls and bounces rammed the frame of the passenger compartment into my back again and again. Four times, I counted, and then it came to rest. I sat pinned in that car for a long time, feeling the life bleed out of me in a warm puddle that made my hands slippery, that covered my face with the dripping, sticky confirmation that I was very seriously injured.

I made a solitary attempt to leave the car, placing my hands on my knees in an effort to push off and straighten up. My hands felt my knees, but the sensation was not returned. The knees were warm and clearly mine, yet I could no longer feel them. It is that exact moment and that precise memory that divides my life into the time when my legs carried me and the time I have spent carrying those same legs. As these words are written, the moment falls at the exact midpoint of my life, nineteen years on either side. Upon touching those knees and feeling the sensation only in my hands, I knew. My spinal cord had been severed. Whatever else was wrong with me, I would not walk again. The most powerful sensation I have ever felt is of no sensation at all.

Breath was short and painful. The sunlight glinted off the fresh blood on my hands, chest, and lap. The forces that had torn me nearly in half had done their work quickly and had moved on. They had crushed the Chevy and killed the driver. Blue sky and yellow afternoon sun were still visible through the crack of the crumpled car roof. There was plenty of daylight left. It was still a beautiful day. . . .

There was a foggy ride in an ambulance. I remember screaming about punching someone named Meigsfield. The only Meigs Field I knew was the airport in downtown Chicago. It was dark when we arrived at the hospital in Clearfield, Pennsylvania. I had a fractured skull, a broken shoulder and collarbone. My eyesight was dim and cloudy. The shock of the guitar to my face, along with the impact on the seat, had blackened my cheeks, nose, eyes, and forehead. My eyeballs had bled under the surface, replacing the whites and my blue irises with a bright red. My scalp was sliced open, and several ribs were broken.

It appeared that the nerve damage was severe, but no one could say if it was permanent. I recall one doctor with cold hands pulling a sharp object from his pocket and poking it into my chest. I could feel one nipple and only half of the other. Below — nothing. The doctors sewed me up and hoped for improvement. The only regional hospital with a spinal cord rehabilitation facility was hours away in Williamsport, Pennsylvania, where a decompression laminectomy was performed. Doctors observed three crushed vertebrae. There was a three-inch lesion on the dura, the circulatory lining of the spinal cord. It was not severed, but as dead as an earthworm pinched in the middle of a rolling bicycle tire. . . .

I woke up in intensive care in Williamsport. There were tubes everywhere. Around me machines were beeping and humming. I was in severe pain. I tried to reconstruct what had happened. I knew that I was pretty badly injured, but I felt unmistakably that I would live. I asked the nurse if I was in serious or fair condition. She said, "Critical." I immediately looked over at the screen with my heartbeat on it. I decided I would keep an eye on this just in case. I tried to figure out what time it was. In the whispering darkness and chill of the ICU there was no sense of time. . . .

John Hockenberry

My life began in one body and will end in another. At the halfway point between my birth and the present moment lies an intermediate ending and beginning. My life is bisected between its end points. It contains two beginnings, and when death finally comes it will have a pair of ends. In geometry, one and only one line is determined by two points. Between any two points on that line lies infinity. The beginnings and ends of days, moments, thoughts, dreams. First inspection suggests that I am living in the second of two lives. Perhaps on closer inspection there are many more.

I have a permanent irreversible spinal-cord injury at the chest level. In medical terminology it is an incomplete dural lesion at the T4-6 level, which refers to the fourth, fifth, and sixth thoracic vertebrae. If you break your back at the chest level, the sensation stops at about the same place. For me, just below the nipples there is a three-quarter-inch band of an odd receding sensation, and then complete numbness. There are two places on my back where sensation divides into constituent spectra. Temperature without pressure in one spot. Pressure without temperature in another. There is a place just under my right scapula where nerves are rerouted. The point is numb to the touch, but a finger pressed down there produces a sensation about eight inches away. On the other side of my spine I feel a finger pressing down where no such finger exists. Slipped wires, sensory illusions, and the map of the body is confused.

There is nothing visible about my border of feeling and numbness. It is all the same skin and the same bones, but somewhere between the eighth and ninth rib you pass Checkpoint Charlie. It is a border that snakes around my torso, higher in front, lower in the back, following the contours of the ribs and nerve endings that flare from the sternum like gentle wings. In the summer the border is easier to notice. Only my upper body sweats. Below the spinal cord break the nerves have been yanked from the thermostat. Heat stays bottled up inside like an old office building, stuffy, no air-conditioning, plenty of closed windows.

I spent much of 1976 in two hospitals. The first was in Pennsylvania near where the accident took place. The second was in Grand Rapids, Michigan, where my parents lived. The Michigan hospital was housed in an old brick building and was originally about as wheelchair-accessible as the Tower of London. It had noisy, hesitant elevators and lots of steps that had been sledgehammered into ramps to make way for wheelchairs. It is no longer in the same building today, but it has the same name: Mary Free Bed Rehabilitation Hospital.

A rehabilitation hospital is like a prep school where they serve really awful food and talk about toilet training more than history or algebra. Rehab is also like boot camp. Mary Free Bed had some quasi-religious connotation aside from sounding like someone I would have liked to date in high school. Almost immediately, any strangeness in the name was lost in the strangeness of the cast of characters rolling around the halls, myself among them.

There was smiling Nurse O'Leary with the red tube, the rubber glove, and the K-Y jelly. On my first day at Mary Free Bed, she whipped the sheet back and jammed a long rubber tube inside me. I knew there was only one place she could have put it. But I couldn't feel a thing. There it was. When I wasn't worried about the ugly red acne on my face, this bit of my body had been the focus of most of the last eight teenage years. Now my forlorn little appendage looked like something that had escaped from the circus. The Amazing Horse-swallowing Penis. She kept pushing the tube inside. No sensation. This was a five-alarm fire intruder alert, and I could feel nothing. She kept pushing. She knew what she was doing. I knew what she was doing. I expected the tube to emerge from my mouth or ear. I couldn't decide which was more disturbing, the fact that I couldn't feel any of this, or the smile that never left this nurse's face.

"How do you know when it's inside enough?" No response. Suddenly a yellow fluid began pouring from the tube into the steel bowl.

"How am I doing that?" I wasn't pushing out. I couldn't push out even if I had wanted to.

The nurse took her eyes off the business for an instant and said, "Poke a hole in a bag of urine and it drains, honey. I don't need you to do anything."

Finding a personal concept of normal in a place where nurses patrolled your urethra was the main task in the hospital. What you imagined being able to do was one thing; what you could actually accomplish was something else again. You could imagine the tragedy of never being able to do things, only to discover that there was a way to do them after all. The concept of what is normal became quite foggy and obscure once you figured out the normal response to such an overwhelming physical change. Normal was hard to see through. There were lots of things to bump into, lots of ways to improvise.

Normal for the people in the rehabilitation hospital along with me was something else altogether. We were all fucked-up in some way. We hated the food, and we were all trying to beat the system. Days were spent finding ways to sleep in, slip out, obtain contraband, obtain privacy, simply gain a few moments of freedom. It was us versus them. We had the most fun. The staff held all of the cards. We did all of the work. They were paid minimum wage. We kept things lively. They always won.

My fellow inmates would identify themselves with the only details they could remember about their accidents. One younger man whose body was scarred and looked as though it had been scraped with a paring knife was "motorcycle collided with a station wagon." Often, he would add, "Went through two windshields." A strong burly mechanic with big, hairy arms named Larry was "put the Dodge Power Wagon into the trees." Thin, chain-smoking Harry was "end over end down the ravine." Walter was "diving." Hilda was "crazy person ran into me with a green pickup truck and ruined my life . . . we never found out who it was." There were more than a few "I was drunk. Then I woke up in the hospital."

The nurses had more succinct if far less dramatic clinical medical names for all of us. I was a para. There were quads and hemis (hemiplegic), or CP's (cerebral palsy), BS's (brain stem strokes), or CVA's. Ron was a TBI, which meant traumatic brain injury. Ron could not tell you what happened to him. It was on his chart that he had bled profusely from the ears at the scene of his accident and had gone into a coma. Ron's misshapen skull was a welcome explanation for why he constantly stared at the ceiling, drooled, and had periodic uncontrollable seizures. Ron never spoke and never argued. Ron laughed a lot. He was the floor psychologist's favorite, which seemed to say more about the psychologist that it did about Ron.

Roger had been injured very high in the neck in a car accident. He was a "high quad." Only his head moved. He was sixteen years old. Roger had a crew cut and a round head that recalled one of those freckled and overly jolly faces in magazine ads from the fifties and early sixties. Roger operated his chair by using a joystick with his mouth. His hands sat, pink and motionless, palms down on a tray in front of him. His neck bore the pink scar of the tracheal tube inserted in neck fracture patients whose respiration fails as a matter of course. The tube is placed in the base of the neck by paramedics and is only removed many days later when they can breathe on their own.

Roger and I would devise ways of disrupting the schedule. He would roll into my bedroom while I was still asleep and wake me up, saying, "You can't be asleep." Roger's schedule was determined by attendants who woke him, dressed him, washed him, fed him, and plugged in his batteries. He was on their schedule. I could dress myself, barely. So I could sleep in.

Roger would crash his heavy electric chair into my bedside rail. On his tray table was a Styrofoam cup with a long straw. His mouth could go from joystick to straw in an instant. He would give his joystick a sudden, perfectly precise movement and ram his chair into my bed just enough to disturb me but not to be heard by any of the white coats in the hall. When I would peek out from the covers he would be smiling, his mouth peacefully drinking from the straw. I would drag my reluctant body upright and blink at him. He was always perfectly groomed and dressed in the morning, like a doll from a horror movie.

"Is it fun to get up this early?" I knew the answer to that question. Roger was the highest quad on the floor: C-1, the first vertebra in the neck. The nurses who worked the hall would do him first since he involved the most labor. He was the big item on the daily to-do list. If the nurses did Roger first, they could expect to take their break at ten sharp. It was the peculiar tyranny of being someone else's task.

In his former life Roger had been a regular teenager. He stayed up late and hugged the pillow until well past noon. Now he only indulged vicariously in the slovenly yawns of sleeping late by witnessing my unkempt hair and tardiness. "I'm going to steal your breakfast," he said. I blinked at his face and watched him stare at my untouched tray of cornflakes, milk, and cranberry juice. I knew my breakfast wasn't going anywhere.

"John, would it still count as stealing if you fed me your breakfast?" Roger wasn't hungry, he was starved for volition. He told me that he used to steal cars for fun. Now he couldn't make a pencil roll off his tray table.

Roger would get his life back on the night shift. The nurses on nights would put him down last, sometimes waiting until after the eleven o'clock shift change so they could watch Johnny Carson while they stripped and washed him. I would hear his comments out in the hall. He described his body as a collection of mischievous boys, himself the pack leader. His legs would be spastic, his body difficult to move; he would make an embarrassing noise. Each difficulty Roger would claim as his own intended sabotage of the nurses. He orchestrated the campaign of resistance from his moving, animated head. It was good fun, but Roger had nothing to do with it. His body did what it wanted. Roger simply claimed the credit. The nurses played along.

Any choice denied the nurses, we would try to claim for ourselves. We wondered if Roger could sleep in if we unhooked the battery to his electric wheelchair. One night after the "Tonight Show" I went in and at Roger's suggestion removed a condenser, which shut the chair down without betraying its malfunction right away.

The next morning Roger was there in my room at the same ungodly hour ramming my bed and talking about stealing my breakfast. "They got the custodian to fix the chair," he said. "He has a drawer full of condensers. I had to tell him you stole the first one. I couldn't just say I did it." Roger grinned at me and wiggled his head with a "no jury would convict" expression on his face. It was just the look you could imagine seeing from Roger in the middle of an empty bank vault surrounded by crime lab police looking for the stolen cash.

"If I have to pay the day shift to all call in sick, I swear, Roger, one of these days you are going to sleep in so I can." "You're a paraplegic, John," Roger would say. "You can do anything you want . . . what's the problem?" For Roger, paraplegia was about as serious a disability as an untied shoe. To complain about it was whining, and Roger would have none of it.

Roger and I usually went to PT (physical therapy) at the same time in the morning. There he would sit and do shoulder lifts and head moves with sandbags weighing him down for resistance. Roger also used the blow bottle to exercise his lung capacity. The more muscles you had, the harder you worked in PT. I had to lift weights and do sit-ups and transfers and push-ups. Roger would provide the commentary, noting with glee any struggle, strain, or sweat on my part, and especially any stains on my shorts. The obsession for all of us in PT was to not have an accident on the floor mats. The therapists didn't care. The entire room could be hosed down in case of an attack of dysentery. The transformation from physically strong, self-assured adults to pathetic, marginally toilet-trained wretches meant that the slightest exertion would put us back to personal hygiene's square one. It was to live in fear of grunting.

As time went on we managed to find the humor in all of this. Or someone would find it for us. Usually it was Roger. Whenever anyone would slip behind the count, or fade and stop before the allotted time or number of push-ups, Roger would note it immediately and call out. Roger sat comfortably doing his shoulder lifts while the rest of us sweated like pigs. He watched covetously as we went through our pitiful motions like a chorus line from some telethon. Roger was the choreographer. Mostly we just ignored Roger or threatened to move the straw on his evening milk shake away from his mouth as revenge. But Roger had one good motivator. If he saw any of us frustrated and angry he would call out, "Hey, look over there, it's one of Jerry's kids." To be identified with the young poster people in wheelchairs dressing the set on the Jerry Lewis muscular dystrophy telethon each year was the lowest of the low.

Roger's custom-crafted insult fused two powerful and contradictory themes in American life: sympathy and self-reliance. In rehab we were taught never to allow people to push our chairs. We were taught to do things ourselves and never ask for help. We were proud crips who were going to play basketball and win races and triumph over our disabilities. Outside rehab, self-reliance was a high-risk proposition. To people raised on telethons, it looked suspiciously like a chip on the shoulder. Somewhere between bitterness and anger and Jerry's kids, we would all have to live. After listening to Roger, we all knew which pole we wanted to stay closest to. . . .

Long before anyone worried about the health-care system in America, we could see its bizarre priorities and patterns of care at the Mary Free Bed hospital. If we had another identity besides our injury it was the label of our insurance policy. So much was determined by the patterns of insurance coverage. The most confident fully covered folks were the ones injured in car accidents. With the pool of all licensed drivers in America paying for it, insurance companies could afford to be generous. Car accident injuries could expect almost complete medical coverage, with wheelchairs provided for the rest of patients' lives in many cases.

People injured in public places such as playgrounds or swimming pools, where liability was a question, came next. They usually benefited from the payout of some insurance policy on the facility where they were injured. They also generally could count on some kind of legal settlement if they sued the facility. The next group were those injured at work, who came under workers' compensation. Coverage here was less than for auto accidents, but fairly complete nonetheless. Medical bills were paid, but the purchase of wheelchairs was more problematic.

In considerably worse shape were those people with degenerative conditions that came on suddenly. These people often exhausted their insurance in the first weeks of acute care and had little or nothing left for rehab. Such people could count on charity to buy less than state-of-the-art wheelchairs and accessories. They were the recipients of a kind of medical rationing. One chair would have to last a long time. It could not be used or abused too much. If it broke down, the Easter Seals donors did not have the resources simply to replace it.

This set of medical priorities meant that a drunk driver who lost control of a vehicle, someone whose injury was nearly self-inflicted, received a full ride from the health-care system. But someone whose disability was the result of disease and had occurred through no fault of his own was left out in the cold.

The absolutely worst off were the people with the rare degenerative diseases that no one had ever heard of. They had no insurance, no treatment, and the most expensive care. A six-year-old covered with oozing bandages roamed our halls in a little electric cart. His name was Roger, so we called him Little Roger. He had a disease I never heard called by any name other than "his skin is falling off." The adhesive that was supposed to bind his layers of skin together was defective, and the slightest touch to his skin caused it to fall off. Little Roger's disease had no treatment, its rarity meant that it was not considered by insurance companies, and it had little chance of finding its own telethon. Roger would never be able to live outside the hospital because no one could afford to pay for his support.

Insurance also determined what life would be like outside the hospital. In particular, it determined whether you would get a car paid for or modified to the special needs of a disability. Everyone hoped for a car. The biggest prize was to score a van. In the van world, the quadriplegics ruled. Paraplegics would be able to get out of their chairs and sit behind the wheel of a regular car with hand controls, but quadriplegics would need to roll aboard their vehicles.

They required electric doors and chain-operated lifts and other advanced technology. And there was plenty of technology applied to the problem of getting a car to move when most of a driver's body couldn't. Driving was an option for even the highest quads. Vehicles could be outfitted with electronic devices that connected the steering brakes and throttle to motion sensors worn on the head. Some of the most advanced vans could be driven solely by moving the head or eyes. Some had no regular steering wheel at all.

Of the cast of white-coated physical therapists, shrinks, nurses, and professional nurturers (social workers), the most popular staff person in the hospital was Doug, the driver's training instructor. While most everyone else was either measuring out urine or running around monitoring who was in denial and who was in remorse, Doug at least had a real job. He had none of the rehab speak or the black humor of the nurses. Doug said things like, "If you push this, it's your brake. Pull this, it's your gas. When the chain on the wheelchair lift gets stuck, put a little grease on it like this." Here were problems we could all solidly put our minds to solving.

As much as anything else, rehab was committed to getting broken bodies back behind the wheel of a car. Everyone wanted to get back on the road. Technology was the cure-all. We loved to watch the machines work. But it was the same old twentieth-century con: the gadgets will save you. Technology will make you free. This was ironic, principally because cars were responsible for putting most of the people in this place to begin with.

Bob was the van expert in our group. He was a C-4 quadriplegic, and would explain his injury by saying that he had been hunting trees. His car had left the road, and he was discovered by paramedics, drunk and near death. He had found a tree. But, as he used to say, the tree had bagged him. He knew he had been drunk. He could remember nothing else.

Bob could use his arms and had some use of his hands. He was a funny man who wore thick Coke bottle glasses and had red hair. At night in the ward where four of us slept, he would talk about the van he was going to get. His van was going to be the place where he would get away from it all. Being in a wheelchair, he said, was his big break. He could barely see as it was. His thick glasses suggested a profound vision impairment even when Bob wasn't hitting the beer. He used to say, "John, I'm so fucked-up now, the license people will never notice my bad eyes. If I can make a right turn with these arms, they'll hand me the license right then and there. I could be drunk and blind." He was right.

Back in the seventies, Dodge made the longest, biggest van. Bob wanted it; he assured us that Dodge vans were the best. Bob had all of the brochures. We looked at the brochures and came to the same conclusion. We all wanted the big, long Dodge. Bob's was to have a water bed in the back. His stereo and fishing equipment would be in the van, ready to go at all times. "You can't bait a hook, Bob," we would say. "You can't turn over in bed by yourself."

"I'll get myself a woman who can slide a crawler on to a fishhook, and herself down on my big pink hook. She can turn me over if she wants. She can do everything; I'll just lie there with a smile on my face."

When he talked like this, I would blush like the teenager I was. I had never had such close contact with adults. Even at the steel factory where I had worked as a welder the previous summer, we had all gone home after work. Here we slept, ate, and wet the bed together. Adults made everything real. Their tragedies were real, like their mortgage payments; the sense of change was far more real for them than for me. I was just a kid; my life was still ahead of me. They had spent their lives doing things they would no longer be able to do. But for as long as we were in rehab, we shared the same questions and predicaments.

Adults had wives, husbands, and families. They told the most disturbing off-color jokes; they had been teenagers long ago and had done it all. We pried into the details of each other's lives like nosy mothers. Having the output of your intestines and kidneys known by everyone around you generates a certain familiarity impossible to achieve in normal, everyday interactions.

The charts next to our beds indicated how many cc's of urine we had produced in the past twenty-four hours. A large amount of output immediately created the suspicion that you had been drinking somewhere away from the nurses. When the output on any one chart rose, you were immediately suspected of holding out on the others. Larry, in the bed next to me, watched my chart. With a straight face, some nights I would return to my room and try to fill two jugs without my roommates noticing. They always did.

"Where's the beer, John?" Bob would say. "John had a party and didn't invite us." Bob would point the straw he always kept near him for drinking right at me.

When someone went home on a family or friend visit, upon their return everyone gathered around to see the kidney's verdict on the outing. If the output was high, everyone remarked that it must have been a good time. Low output meant you had been forced to attend church or something. Five hundred cc's was a good result. A thousand was a tribute to the floor. Anything over 1,400 was outstanding and would dominate the conversation during physical therapy the next day.

"Larry had a fourteen hundred-cc party last night," Bob would say. "I think we may have to call Larry's insurance company and tell them to get Larry a tanker truck instead of just a van. I figure he might just explode one night at the bars and injure an innocent person."

Bob had a certain charm. He fell in love with his physical therapist, who eventually moved in with him. She seemed like someone who could bait Bob's hooks. Harry's and Larry's marriages crumbled in the hospital, and the ward where we slept was often closed while Harry and his wife had emotional discussions that ended with Harry red-faced and his wife tearful, running out the door with a child in tow. Larry said he was going to ditch his wife before she ditched him. He lost that race. She filed for divorce one afternoon while we were in physical therapy and Roger was calling somebody a Jerry's kid and somebody else had had an accident on the exercise mat. Larry didn't talk much after that. Mostly he worked to master his crutches and leg braces. He checked himself out of the hospital the next week.

Roger and I were single teenagers with no romances to lose or gain. We watched the trials of Larry and Harry and Bob with sympathy and befuddlement. We cared more about finding a way to shut down physical therapy so we could sleep in at least one morning before we were discharged. With two wheelchairs, no legs, no sharp objects, and only a pair of arms between us, we had our work cut out for us. "I've got my shoulders," Roger said. "Great, Roger, you can be in charge of dialing the phone or wrestling intruders to the ground."

The elevator operator needed a key to stop and start the car to load people on board with their chairs and walkers and stretchers. Roger came up with the idea of removing the control panel and ripping out a wire. Roger rolled down to the far end of the hall with me, and motioned with his head for me to look in the pocket on the back of his chair. "I got Doug to give me a Phillips head screwdriver from the driver's education room." Roger's voice was soaked with larceny and vandalism. He could make thoughts seem like crimes. In Roger's case, they were all he had. "The trouble with ripping out a wire, Roger, is that we will have to spend the night in the elevator after it breaks." We needed some slow-acting sabotage short of a bomb.

We found some white carpenter's glue and some epoxy in one of the therapy rooms. If we could pour enough glue inside the keyhole on the elevator panel, by morning it would be stuck solid. The plan was clever enough, but it lacked a certain dramatic flourish. If we were going to commit small-time terrorism, then we teenaged boys needed a way to claim responsibility for the terrorist attack.

Before getting on the elevator to return to the upper floors where the wards were, we stopped by the main office, which was open. I told Roger to hold the door and watch for nurses in the hall. One office contained the building-wide public-address system with a big, old-fashioned taxi dispatcher microphone. I called to Roger.

"Go and call the elevator, and hold it with your chair."

"What are you doing?"

"I'm mixing the glue, and when I'm finished I'm going to make an announcement on the public-address system."

Roger left his post in the hallway and came into the office. Using the force of his electric chair, he noisily bludgeoned the doors open.

Mary Free Bed Rehabilitation Hospital
GRPL, Mary Free Bed Hospital Collection

"Let me make the announcement. Let me talk on the microphone," he said flatly.

"It was my idea, Roger." I wanted to make a final statement of protest before we left Mary Free Bed for good. Taking over the public-address system had the quality of history about it, echoing the Attica prison uprising, or prefiguring the Romanian revolution.

"I'll read whatever announcement you write. Just let me read it. If they hear my voice, it will really freak them out." Roger certainly had a point. Putting me on the PA was just a straightforward prank. The thought of the voice from Roger's bobbing head and motionless body commanding the nurses and doctors who decided when he got up and when he got down was a truly inspired protest. I quickly jotted down some notes. Roger jammed himself through the door and planted himself in front of the microphone table, knocking down a couple of chairs in the process.

He was still a few feet away. I placed the paper on his lap table. "Can you read it?" I asked. "Yes, put the microphone up to my mouth." I squeezed the Talk button, held the mike out, and said, "Go!" I could hear the clicking over the hall speakers. We were on the air.

"This is Roger Duncan speaking. Unfortunately, physical therapy will be canceled tomorrow so that we may present a movie for your enjoyment."

He whispered at me, "Is it on?"

"Yes, yes. Continue."

"This is Roger Duncan again. The title of the movie will be *A Farewell to Arms.* The story of a family of amputees during World War One."

We grabbed the glue and raced down the hall to the elevator. Roger held it open while I dumped two kinds of glue, epoxy and white, down inside the keyhole. As I worked, Roger said, "I always wondered what that book was about." I wiped the keyhole clean so that dripping glue could not be detected, then said to Roger, "Get in." We rode back to the second floor.

Physical therapy was canceled on my last day at the hospital. Nurse O'Leary found the two kinds of glue in the bag on Roger's chair. There in the morning, banging against my bed asking about my breakfast, was Roger; he had not slept in. He had his sandbag weights on his shoulders. They had brought physical therapy upstairs. But Roger was smiling. "I'm a hero this morning, John. Even drooling Ron was laughing when I went to bed. Of course, the nurses want to kill you."

"Thank you for letting me know, Roger," I called out from under the covers.

"You haven't packed yet," he said.

"I was sleeping, Roger."

When I sat up I could see that Roger wasn't smiling. It was the last time I would ever see him or any of the other characters in this rehab class of 1976: Roger, Harry, Larry, Ron, Hilda, Bob, and Little Roger.

"What's going to happen to me?" Roger asked quietly, and I could see that he was afraid. I was fully awake now. But I had no answer. There was a nine-and-a-half-inch difference in where his spine was broken and where mine had been injured permanently. The difference in our lives could not be measured. I felt the distance between us. I would miss Roger. “The nurses said my voice sounded good on the loudspeaker. Maybe I could get a job in radio? Do you think I could do that, John?”

I nodded. “There’s an idea, Roger.”

Harry and Larry both got divorced and returned to the hospital with serious complications of their original injuries. Bob got his van and married his physical therapist. They had a child. Years later, Bob’s body was found in his van. He had asphyxiated in a closed garage with the motor running. Some people suggested that he had been unable to reach the ignition key and get out of the vehicle. He had very poor eyesight, they said, and as it was dark in the garage he might have been a little drunk and couldn’t get the seat belt off. Only with a quadriplegic crip would people assume that you could turn your own garage into Dachau by simply fumbling with your car keys.

There was no proof that Bob had killed himself, but many of us understood. Bob was a quadriplegic, but he needed no Kevorkian. The tree he had been hunting had finally found him and finished the job. Bob did get away from it all in his big, long Dodge van. I have no doubt that he was thinking about fishing at the end.

I left the hospital three months after arriving there from the intensive care unit in Pennsylvania. It was the training for the outside world. I came in weak, scared, and sick. I departed in a coral-red wheelchair that reflected my intention of aggressively taking on the world, wheelchairs be damned. I got a blue General Motors van with a lift that got fourteen miles to the gallon back when gasoline was just beginning to cost more than a dollar a gallon. It had seemed like a good idea at the time, but a coral-red vinyl chair and a blue gas guzzler were not going to work in my new real world. My second wheelchair was black, as was every chair I have since owned. I eventually got rid of the blue van. I got tired of the crowds who gathered to watch the electric lift work and tell me they had seen the same van on “Ironside,” the TV show. I learned how to toss my chair into the backseat of a normal passenger car.

We imagine one life and live another. We trace our lives on a map of places we will never visit and landmarks we wish we had missed. Each journey alters the map. Our signatures are written in possibilities; the ink dries as the indelible mark of change. Roger went off to live in a nursing home. I went back to Chicago to college, where I dropped out, moved out west, and eventually ended up riding a donkey in Kurdistan.

Life's end points come in pairs; all else defies counting. Down long corridors, possibilities beckon and vanish at the horizon. It is with the pain and resentment preceding wisdom that we gradually discover the doors that have closed behind us and how the straight path ahead is not ours, though we may claim it as our own dream. Life removes possibilities one by one from the pillows beneath our sleeping heads. The dreams are not stolen; they just go quietly by themselves, passing like time, replaced by real events beyond imagining. I lost touch with Roger. It was me who, years later, ended up with the job in radio.

Before That Was There

Laura Kasischke

Laura Kasischke grew up on the east side of Grand Rapids. Her mother was a speech therapist in the public schools, and her father was a mail carrier. Her grandparents immigrated to Grand Rapids from Southampton, England, in the 1920s. Kasischke graduated from East Grand Rapids High School in 1980, and then attended the University of Michigan, where she received her B.A. in writing and literature (1984) and her M.F.A. in creative writing (1987).

Kasischke's books include six collections of poetry, the most recent being *Gardening in the Dark* (Ausable Press, 2005), and five novels, most recently *Be Mine* (Harcourt, 2007). Her first novel, *Suspicious River,* was made into a feature film, and her third novel, *The Life Before Her Eyes,* is currently in production (the movie title will be *In Bloom*), with Uma Thurman in the starring role. Kasischke's work has been translated into many languages and published internationally. She has been the recipient of numerous writing awards, including fellowships from the National Endowment for the Arts and several Pushcart prizes.

Kasischke credits her high school creative writing teacher, Willis Brenner, for encouraging her writing career, and for guiding her in directions that helped it flourish. She also credits her mother, who died in 1985, and her father, who now lives in St. Joseph, Michigan. Currently an assistant professor at the University of Michigan, Kasischke is married and lives with her husband and eleven-year-old son in Chelsea, Michigan. She wrote the following narrative specifically for this book.

Laura Kasischke

Why should it be a matter of wonder that the dead should come back? The wonder is that they do not. Ah! That is the wonder. How one can go away who loves you, and never return, nor speak, nor send any message — that is the miracle. . . . All my life it has been a marvel to me how they could be kept away.

Margaret Oliphant

I

There wasn't much room for the ghosts. Wherever one thing had once been, there was something else now. "That's where your grandmother and grandfather lived when they first came to Grand Rapids," my aunt said, pointing to an automotive repair shop. "That's where your mother was born," pointing to the new addition to a nursing home. "It's been gone longer than you've been alive."

My grandparents built their own house in the country. I would stand next to my grandmother at the kitchen window, look into her back yard and across it, into a neighborhood of bright new houses that stretched for miles until it ended at the mall.

"Cows," she'd say. "When we first moved in, all you could see were cows. Miles and miles of green grass and cows."

Our own house stood where another house had burned to the ground. The elementary school behind our house had been built, they said, on what had once been the town dump — and, in truth, that was easy to imagine, because of the inexplicable sledding hill, the one that rose out of nothing.

But it was harder to imagine, looking at the sepia photograph of my grandmother and grandfather in their wedding clothes, standing on the steps of St. Mark's Episcopal Church, that they were, now, the couple with an oxygen machine in their house, the clothesline strung between the garage and the side door, the matching canes leaning up against the couch. Later, when they became the blank-eyed patients at Springbrook Manor, it was hard to remember them with a house (which smelled, always, of sweetly burned jam), an oxygen machine, a clothesline, canes. After a while they couldn't walk at all, and then they could not breathe, and then they became the absence of grandparents — with markers bearing their names over the places where they supposedly rested, under the ground. But before those markers had been laid, there had been only two squares of emerald grass, or patches of mud or snow, I suppose. Cows perhaps? Or a house in which someone's mother had been born? And I suppose a time will come when something I can't imagine any better than the miles of cows or the town dump rolls over even those stones. Of course. Who am I kidding, to believe anything else?

But the occasional ghost comes back to Grand Rapids. Perhaps.

We moved into the new house on Lakeside Drive in summer. For twenty dollars, a man my father knew from work helped put the furniture from the old house into the trailer, then drove it across town to the new house. He was a young man, I think — or at least in my memory he is younger than my father, who would have been only in his mid-thirties. He had to strip off his shirt when the temperature rose over ninety degrees. I remember he asked my mother if he could have a glass of water, but she couldn't find the glasses. The box labeled KITCHEN had nothing in it but bowls and butter knives. So Bob went to the spigot outside the house, turned it on, and plunged his head under it, came up gasping, said he wasn't feeling well, and sat down in our new front yard.

My father pulled into the driveway in the car he'd borrowed from my grandparents. He called out, "You okay, Bob?"

Bob sank back into the grass, and my mother and I stood on the front steps holding hands and looking from Bob to my father. "Hey, Bob," my father said, getting out of the car. "Bob!" He leaned over Bob.

My mother told me to go into the house. My father went to our new next-door neighbors' house and pounded on their front door. I could hear him calling for help, and then calling to my mother that no one had answered. We had, of course, no phone in our new house yet. My father ran across the street — I could see him from the window, there were no curtains either — and pounded on the door of another house. He went inside it. My mother was in the front yard with Bob, but I could only see her shadow draped across the lawn, the occasional shadow-flapping of her arms.

It seemed to me that hours passed in our new house, without furniture, without carpet or towels or television or toys, before the sirens screamed into our driveway, and my mother came back in and stood in the doorway of what would be my new bedroom, and said, "This is bad."

No one ever told me that Bob had died. I was only five and wouldn't have been taken to a funeral. Bob wasn't a close friend. In fact, I think I'd only seen him once before, at a Post Office picnic where my father and I had won a hot plate together for winning the father-daughter three-legged race. (To be fair, my father had carried me on his hip through the race.) I don't know if Bob had children. I knew nothing then, and know almost nothing now, about Bob.

And his dying like that on our front lawn the day we moved into the new house might have been the kind of thing my parents might have preferred not to tell me about — although they didn't generally shield me from such things. Usually I got all the gory details of surgeries and diagnoses, divorces and bankruptcies, whether I wanted them or not. I was one of those Midwestern children who learned to read my grandmother's *National Enquirers* long before anyone bothered to tell me that there weren't, necessarily, UFO's, and that Bigfoot probably never did mate with the homecoming queen of a suburban San Diego high school, despite the convincing article and the photograph of their strangely attractive child.

We didn't really have any relationship with Bob. Why would they have told me what happened to Bob? He was just a guy my father knew from work, a guy with a weak heart he didn't know he had, who needed twenty dollars, had a day off, and so had offered to help us move.

And then he lay back on the grass of our new front lawn and died.

So, imagine my surprise when, one night — summer again, at least a decade later — Bob came back. I was sitting on the love seat in the living room of this house — no longer the new house, now simply the house I'd grown up in, the old house — watching television with my mother, who had her fuzzy slippers propped up on the arm of the couch. My father, a mailman, was already in bed. It could only have been nine o'clock or nine-thirty, but he had to get up every morning at four, and was always deeply asleep before the sun set in the summer. My mother was wearing a robe. Our cat, Pumpkin — an obese tom with a grudge against all the other cats in the neighborhood and my father — was stretched out the full length of him, purring loudly.

Outside, the evening sky was purple. The smell of mowed lawns drifted in through the screen door. Down the street, Lori Graves's little dog was yapping. Crickets were trilling. The smell of my mother's rose garden — a dense intoxicating floral perfume mixed with the tang of pesticides — drifted in through the other side of the house. We were watching *One Day at a Time,* when suddenly there were headlights in the picture window, lighting up the living room, impossibly close to the house. My mother stood up, dumping the enormous weight of Pumpkin on the floor with a thud, and went to the door.

From where I stood behind her, I could see that a beat-up red Volkswagen had been driven across our front yard and had come to a stop in the space between the sidewalk and our driveway. We watched as a man fumbled his way out from behind the wheel, leaving the door open behind him, the dome light illuminating the interior of the car. I remember that there were actual fuzzy dice hanging from the rearview mirror — and this was before fuzzy dice became a statement *about* fuzzy dice, before they were retro, back when they just *were.*

The man looked about thirty. He was wearing Levis, tennis shoes, and a pale-blue T-shirt, untucked. He stumbled up the walk to our house, watching his feet carefully as he did so — clearly, or so I thought, drunk, blotto, blitzed. And then he looked up at my mother, standing at the screen door, and said, in a voice I can still hear — passionate and sad and resigned — "Baby, I'm back."

My mother slammed the door, locked and chained it, and then she screamed. By the time my father rose from his deep dreams (he always claimed he dreamed, every night, that he was delivering mail, until he retired, when he began to dream, every night, that he was golfing), the Volkswagen had managed to drive over the curb and back down Lakeside Drive in the direction it had come from, never to be seen again, and leaving nothing behind but tire tracks in our front yard.

I know, because I watched from the picture window.

"What the hell is going on?" my father asked.

My mother clasped her robe around her more closely, with the drama and timing of the theater major she had been and the local-theater celebrity she still was, and said, "It was Bob."

The Kasischke family home on Lakeside Drive that became the "haunted house" of Laura Kasischke's memoir
GRPL, Betty Gibout Real Estate Card Collection

My father's reaction was the same as mine: "Who the hell is Bob?" Or who *was* Bob?

She reminded us about Bob, and we both just stared at her. No, it wasn't Bob. It was a drunk guy looking for the house where his ex-wife used to live. Our house looked exactly like every other house on the block — a small, stark, aluminum-sided box — so how was he supposed to know? And perhaps my mother, backlit in the fuzzy blue television light, looked like his ex-wife, standing in the doorway of his ex-house.

Baby, I'm back.

And when she slammed the door and screamed, he realized his mistake and sobered up enough to make his getaway. But there was no convincing my mother, who finally had a chance to tell us that she'd known all along that Bob had left something — his soul? — in our house. That she'd heard his voice, once before, in the basement, under the stairs, right behind the furnace. That she'd felt his presence there in the front yard, under the tree, for years.

My father grumbled, went outside in his shorts and looked at the tire tracks, then went back to bed. I told my mother *my* theory: Drunk guy/ex-wife/wrong house. But she would have none of it. She'd seen him: it was Bob.

That night I lay in bed for a while imagining the story I'd tell my best friend on the phone the next morning. We had lots of laughs about our crazy mothers. Hers worked at Planned Parenthood and was forever handing out condoms to strangers as if they were peppermints or car-wash tokens. (We were, I suppose, both proud and horrified to have such mothers, and relieved to have each other to tell about them.) *Wait'll Kris hears this one.* But I also remember that I couldn't get to sleep that night, not for a long time. The window was open. The air smelled like earth. I remembered him now. Now it was coming back to me from across the decade, during which I'd never thought of him at all: Bob.

I hadn't known that he'd died, had I?

I remembered his head under the spigot. Before that, he'd come into the kitchen. What he'd wanted was a glass of water. I remembered that. I remembered my mother hunting for the glasses, and never finding them. Still, that drunk guy wasn't a ghost. I lay awake a long time that night, rehearsing my funny story, but also listening to the summer breeze in the branches of the trees.

It seemed to be whispering: *I'm back, I'm back, I'm back.*

II

My mother died when I was twenty, of cancer, in the gray light of a hospital room on a brilliant April morning. I will tell you here, she did not pass away gently. And the nurses on the oncology unit of Blodgett Hospital were not nice to me, or to her. They grew impatient, I think, that she wouldn't die. When they'd brought her in, she was supposed to go within hours, and it took days. One young nurse became exasperated while clearing my mother's lungs, and said, inches from the stark terror of my mother's suffocating face, "Goddamn you!" And still, in good Midwestern fashion, my aunts sent me up to the hospital wing with a big box of chocolates and a thank-you card for the nurses the week after my mother died.

For days after her death, every time the phone rang, I was sure it was her. This was nothing rational — or psychotic. I knew she was dead. But some part of me expected that she would still be able to phone home, to check in. When I listened to the radio at night, in my bed, I had the eerie sense that if I could just find the right frequency, I would hear her voice. She couldn't be that gone, could she? She'd only been ill for a few months before she died. Her gardening shoes were still on the porch. Her clothes in the closet still smelled of her perfume. My father and I still had a few dinners she'd made for us in the freezer. She'd frozen the leftovers. A special gumbo she was good at. A bit of beef stew. And it seemed every night at six o'clock, while my father and I pondered how to eat without her, that she was right there, in the kitchen, urging us to sit down at the table.

Dinner will be ready in a minute. Don't forget to wash your hands. (We never ate those frozen meals. How could we? As far as I know, my father threw them out when I went back to college.)

And a couple of strange things happened. A few days after her death, a photograph of me — my high school senior picture — which had been in a frame on a table near our back door, disappeared. The frame was left. The photograph had been slipped out, was gone. My mother loved that picture of me, though I'd often — to annoy her — turn it upside down in its frame and lay it flat on the table. I said (and still say) that this picture — the photographer had made me look up at the ceiling, then poured an orange light down all over my face before he snapped it — made me look like a doped-up, sunburned would-be angel.

But where had the photograph gone?

And then there was the day a man my mother knew from a civic theater production of *Harvey,* in which she'd had a role a year before the cancer, saw me at the grocery store, wandering stupefied through the aisles. It was a week, to the day, after her death. "Hey, Laura! How are you? What a coincidence, I just saw your mom."

What?

"Yeah, she was making a right turn onto 28th Street. We waved."

I explained that it could not have been my mother, and why, and right there in the baked-goods aisle we cried. He was, as well as being shocked, mortified at his blunder.

It hadn't been her, of course; we both agreed about that. He'd seen someone who resembled my mother, turning right onto 28th Street — a street, coincidentally, onto which my mother had turned right nearly every day of her life, to visit my grandmother, who lived on East Paris Road, just off of it. It was the busiest street at the time in Grand Rapids, and my mother had been terrified to drive on it. I can still see her knuckles, white on the steering wheel. "I'm going to get killed on this street some day," she said more than once. "I had a dream about it."

But my mother was always having prophetic dreams. And my mother saw ghosts. I never listened to any of it. Still, a decade after she died, after a divorce and during an admittedly difficult and emotional time in my life, I found myself walking down a street when, I could have sworn, I saw my mother walking directly toward me.

That's her, I thought. Her face, her gait. She was even wearing her camel's hair coat. It was raining, and she was carrying a black umbrella, but I swear I would have known her anywhere. I even recognized her shoes. I was so sure it was her — but not, in the end, *that* sure. . . .

I didn't say anything. I let the woman I'd mistaken for my mother pass by, just brushing her shoulder with mine. But, as I passed her, I whispered, "Don't worry, Mom, I wasn't crying. That was rain on my face."

III

In my family, on the maternal side, every woman I could name (some of the stories were passed down from female relatives who'd lived and died long before I was born) had claimed at one time or another in my youthful presence to have seen a ghost. My great-grandmother told a story of having seen her eldest son standing at the foot of her bed the night he was killed in France during World War I. He was covered, head to toe, in mud and blood.

My grandmother said she once saw a cousin of hers, a little boy who'd died of pneumonia, in the house she herself had grown up in. She'd been turning the corner from the parlor to the stairwell when she caught a glimpse of him ("Completely solid, just as if he were alive") running off toward the kitchen.

One great-aunt was visited by my grandfather (her brother) the night after his funeral. Another met a woman in her bathroom one night, a woman she'd never seen before, but who knew my aunt's name, and who screamed when she saw her.

And my mother — my mother saw ghosts everywhere. Yet I, her daughter, never believed in them. Never. Not even after I saw, one night in 1967, an old woman with long black hair standing in the doorway of my childhood bedroom. The old woman looked at me, and I looked at her, and then she turned toward me and began to run. Fast. Faster than anyone could run across such a short space between my bed and the hallway. And then she leapt into the air — a kind of soaring that, had she been subject to the laws of gravity, would have brought her down hard on my torso. I screamed. But she just soared straight over me and disappeared.

My screams woke my grandmother, who was sleeping in our living room on the pull-out couch. She came quickly, but was too groggy to really attend to me. She suffered from anxiety, and whatever it was that the doctors had prescribed for her had the effect of making her into a kind of gentle zombie after six o'clock at night. I was five years old. I must have told her what I'd seen: the long black hair. Did I mention that she was wearing a white nightgown? That she was thin and old, and that she did not look angry when she saw me, only mildly surprised?

My grandmother stared at me with a look I'd already begun to recognize on the faces of the women around me. A kind of horror that was more like a memory of horror than the thing itself. And even then, at five or six years old, I disliked it. I doubted it. I'm sure I said to her, "It was just a bad dream, Grandma. I'm going back to sleep now." I suppose, if she'd been the one who'd said, "Go back to sleep, you were just dreaming," I might have cried and insisted that, no, it had been a real woman. A hag. She'd come after me. She might come back. But because the melodrama of it was all there already in my grandmother's drugged expression, I was able to dismiss it myself, even at that age understanding how much trouble might be drummed up if I were to say much more about it.

Well, the trouble was drummed up anyway. My grandmother had been spending the night with me because my mother was in the hospital having her gallbladder removed. There had been "complications," about which I'd been told more than it's probably wise to tell a five-year-old — something about an infected incision oozing yellow pus, and my mother convinced that she would die in the night, and wanting my father at the hospital with her. (She would recover quickly, however. At least that time. And she was home in time to have a rousing fight with my grandmother over whether or not it was an insult to her that my grandmother had washed all the clean dishes in the house while she was in the hospital.)

In the morning, after my bad dream, my grandmother called my mother in the hospital and told her that I'd seen a ghost. When she got home, my mother (looking pale and flushed at the same time) took me by the shoulders, looked me in the eyes, and asked me to describe, precisely, the hag I'd seen.

"It was just a bad dream, Mommy," I said.

But after being badgered long enough, I gave her the details. Not much was said afterward, but at Thanksgiving I overheard my mother talking to her aunts; they all agreed that, yes, it sounded as if, unfortunately, the house we were living in was haunted; but they also said that, despite what was always said, it wasn't always true that children who were visited by "the Hag" died within the year.

Well, I was happy about this last part at least.

Our home, I was sure, even at that impressionable age, couldn't possibly be haunted. The house, it seemed clear to me, was the least likely house on the planet to be haunted. Aluminum-sided. Two bedrooms. Tossed up hastily in the fifties. Exactly like every other house on the block. No long hallways. Just one short, shag-carpeted passageway between the bedrooms and the bathroom. No nooks or crannies. For a ghost, what would it have to offer? Now, looking back, I think, *Of course. It would have to be the least likely house that would be the one to be haunted.* Those Victorian things with the chandeliers, that was too cliché. Ours would be the kind of house a self-respecting ghost could haunt without feeling like a *ghost.*

But I didn't believe in ghosts — especially because the aunts all insisted that I'd seen one.

IV

When I was a child, I thought it was actually illegal to mow your lawn on a Sunday. I still feel strange in a store on a Sunday — a little frantic, as if they might lock the door behind me and trap me in my sacrilegious act of shopping on the day of rest. I usually call ahead to make sure the store is open. Target, even. CVS. Of course it's open. But in Grand Rapids in the 1960s and early '70s, it was inconceivable to me that a day would come when, if you ran out of milk or gas on a Sunday, you wouldn't simply be out of luck.

I hated Sundays. I dreaded Sundays. I so loathed Sundays that it seems to me possible that it was the very force of my desire that altered that terrain, as if I were Carrie — hating Sundays with such passion that I could move lawn mowers out of their garages and push them around on the grass, break the locks on the convenience stores, throw open the gates to the zoo, the doors to the skating rinks, the libraries, the arcades, activate the electrical eyes on the doors to the supermarkets so that they slid open freely when a shopper passed by. Now, of course, on Sundays in Grand Rapids you can have a pizza delivered. But then, whatever you had in the house was what you were going to eat, and if you played too loudly in the back yard, you could be sure your parents were going to hear about it from the neighbors, and you'd be sent back in to watch one of the exhausted four channels of Sunday programming — *Mutual of Omaha's Wild Kingdom,* two identical religious programs, and professional bowling.

It made going to church appealing.

It was there, one Sunday, when I was seven or eight years old, that I heard one of the first ghost stories told by an adult outside of my own family. Our Sunday school teacher's name was Mrs. Schmidt. She was young and pretty, and, as I look back, I suspect she chose to teach Sunday school as a way to get out of the house on Sundays herself, and also so she had a good excuse for leaving her three children under the age of five in the church nursery for an hour. We were no picnic, but she didn't have to change our diapers.

We met in the basement of the church, which was dank and unfurnished except for some folding chairs, and which always smelled of sauerkraut and potato salad, no matter how long it had been since the last church banquet. Usually, we got pictures of Mary and Jesus, or rainbows and arks, or lambs lying down beside lions, and spent an hour or so coloring those while our parents drank coffee and talked to each other above us in the nicely carpeted church lobby.

Occasionally, Mrs. Schmidt gave us some dire warning about not lying, or she read the Ten Commandments out loud, but usually she just took one of the dittoed pictures and spent the hour like we did — coloring. This routine went on for what seemed like lifetimes. We were a multi-age group, so we took little interest in one another. If I ever had a conversation with any of my Sunday school classmates, I don't remember it. I didn't go to school with any of them, and as far as I could tell, except for a couple of siblings, they didn't know each other, or care to get to know each other either. We were simply occupying the same gray space on those same gray Sundays, a sharp-cornered square of time cut out of the week. It was just something to be gotten through, a little better than its alternatives. Boredom blanketed us in heavy, itchy wool, stifling communication, and we were too used to it to complain.

Then, one Sunday morning, we came into the basement to find Mrs. Schmidt weeping in a folding chair. We simply took our seats as we'd always done and watched her, awaiting instructions. And then she looked up from her damp hands and told us that one of us had died.

I remember looking around. Panicked. Which one? But since I'd never, once, looked so closely at the group of children assembled around me, I couldn't guess which one it was. All of us, in the ashen light of February in a windowless basement in uncomfortable clothes, wearing expressions of grim determination, were candidates, it seemed. Then I remembered: he'd been gone for weeks, hadn't he? Months? That boy with the braces. The one whose name she had quit calling for roll. Jeremy. I'd simply forgotten about him. If I had noted his absence at all, I suppose I assumed he'd refused to come to Sunday school any longer (this was not uncommon among the pre-adolescents), or that his family had moved. But he had died!

We were given dittos and crayons anyway, as soon as Mrs. Schmidt quit crying, and we were dutifully coloring in the outlines of Jesus hanging on the cross (it was almost Lent) before she spoke again. She said, in a strange new voice that was deep and serious and full of portent, "I want you to know that Jeremy visited me the night after he died. He said that he was at peace. And that he'll miss all of us very much."

So, not only had one of us died, but one of us had died and already returned from the dead with his well-wishes and reassurances! There was some shifting. No one was looking at her any longer. We continued to color.

The next Sunday, I took my seat at the table as usual, and saw, written in crayon on the edge of it: *Jeremy was here.* It was dated two days after the day of his death.

Smart aleck.

V

I come back to Grand Rapids looking for them. Visit graves. Drive past old houses. I would walk up to the door and say, "I'm back." But no one would know I'd been gone except for the ones who wouldn't, themselves, be there.

The cherry tree my father planted for my mother must have snapped in a snowstorm. It's no longer in the front yard. There's nothing there. Not even a circle of dirt where that tree used to be. Now, just grass. Or snow. Or something in between.

Before, in any case, before I lived in the house I grew up in, there was another house.

Another girl? Another ghost?

After all these years away, she might as well have been me. I am as gone as she is: that child I was with the Hoola Hoop or the Day-Glo orange jump rope in the front yard — the mother doing laundry in the basement, the father nailing something to a wall in the garage.

You can sit and stare for a long time, trying to remember it, imagine it, conjure it up with goodwill, or sarcasm, or doubt, or prayer, trying to believe that what was there was ever really there.

In fact, I now know, you can spend half of an April morning idling outside it in your car, looking through the condensed breath on your windshield, trying to believe that, before this, *that* ever was — looking for it, waiting for it — and see little more than a vague outline that refuses to be filled in. A shadow that passes too fast for you to see its shape.

You get that quick glimpse, and you think, for a second, that it's still there. (But it isn't.) That it's come back. (But it hasn't.)

Eventually, you drive away.

Bissell's Haunt

KAYE LONGBERG

Kaye Longberg attended East Grand Rapids High School, and she graduated from Calvin College in 1989. In 2001, she earned an M.F.A. in creative writing at Western Michigan University, where she is currently a doctoral candidate. She has taught creative writing, literature, and composition at Grand Rapids Community College, Aquinas College, and Western Michigan University.

Longberg's work has been published in *Alaska Quarterly Review, So to Speak, The Macguffin, The South Carolina Review,* and other journals. She has been nominated twice for the Pushcart Prize and once for the Best New American Voices. She lives in East Grand Rapids. She contributed the following story for this anthology, and it appears in print here for the first time.

The carpet sweeper was designed in the late 1800s by a man who was allergic to dust: Melville Bissell, who is now at one with dust, came from Grand Rapids, Michigan, my hometown. His estate was a grand old mansion on four acres of coveted land that bordered a private lake in the wealthiest part of town. I lived a block away, but what a difference that block made — in socio-economic terms. I walked past the place every day on my way to school and back home without even noticing it, so sheltered was it by the looming old trees and a cedar hedge. A sign on the gatepost at the cobbled drive gave a warning: KEEP OUT.

This was in the mid-1970s, a period when an oil embargo and inflation made my parents bristle with stories of the Depression and of how poor they'd been as kids. So when the mansion on Plymouth went on the market in disrepair, a steal if you were rich, we were surprised to hear who bought it. The buyers lived on our street, in a house not much better than ours. Their youngest son, Chris, had become my closest friend.

Their name was Law and the father was a lawyer. He wasn't home much, and when he was, the house became an office. I never saw him wrestle or tickle his kids like my father did. For tickling, Chris came to our house, where he seemed to be the favorite, since we didn't have a boy. My father must have thought sometimes of Craig, the brother I never knew, whose pictures stopped at five. Sometimes I wondered whether Chris had come over to play with me or with my father.

Chris had mean older brothers. My sister wasn't as bad as his brothers, but even so, he and I were always escaping together, pretending we were running away from home. We climbed trees and stayed in them for hours, hidden by the leaves, lost in a private world while spying on the real one. Our favorite was the old apple tree by the driveway at my parents' house on Briarwood. The strongest branches were horizontal; we could eat plenty of apples, and we had a good view of Rudy's house across the street. Rudy was a blustery old suspender-wearing Hungarian with fifties-style glasses and a drinker's nose. He would rant and swear and threaten to get his shotgun if we stepped on his grass, which looked like a carpet, or if our bikes rode over the hose stretched across his sidewalk to sprinkle the marigolds in the parkway. After dark we swung out of the tree, and I would gather the soft bad apples on the ground and pitch them down the driveway. The apples bounced under the dim street light, jumped the curb and the marigolds, and disappeared into Rudy's grass. For a while Chris just watched, sounding ashamed of himself for laughing. When he finally joined in, he boasted about his aim. The next day Rudy would rake the apples into a pile at his curb. How easy it would have been for him to knock on our door, shove a rake at me, and say, "I know where the apples came from." But he never did.

Our parents thought Chris and I would marry. Maybe Chris thought so too, but my feelings were muddled. In a brand-new diary I wrote *I love Chris Law,* locked it, and threw it away. There was so much about him I envied. He was prettier than me, for a start. Actually beautiful, yet solidly male. He had money and culture, and he was also brilliant: he eventually skipped grades and graduated ahead of me. Sometimes he followed a bad impulse, misguided by his brothers' influence or by mine; but he was basically kind. I couldn't compete. I could have tried to match him in kindness, but his kindness made me meaner, wanting to corrupt it, and here I felt my failing the most. I didn't deserve him and, curiously, didn't want to.

It bothered me that his parents were friendly with mine in just a neighborly way. They weren't real friends. We tried to nudge them into it. "We're different," they said, or, "Even our dogs clash." Dogs roamed free then. Chris had a bear-like golden retriever named Yeats. Ours was a scruffy mutt my mother had saved from being stoned by the kids she taught in alternative ed. We named him Rags. I took a scissors to his matted fur so his coat would be sleek, but he wouldn't let me near his head, so he ended up with a lion's mane. I cut his tail to match. When Yeats came looking for Chris, he ignored our barking lion long enough to squirt every bush and tree trunk. Before leaving he'd attack, proudly pinning Rags on his back for a humiliating sniffing over.

On a bare, thawing day when spring was a new smell in the air, Chris came over with the news that his parents had bought the Bissell house. I didn't know the house he meant. I was afraid of losing him to a different part of town, a different school. I didn't think a different *world.* He said the house was on the corner of Wealthy and Plymouth.

"There's no house on that corner," I said.

"Yes, there is," he laughed, "that big gray house. You can see it through the trees. You know the one. It's huge, you couldn't miss it."

"That? That's a *house?*"

His laugh was embarrassed.

"What're you gonna do with it?"

"We're gonna live there." He blushed.

I began to tingle as if in some sort of danger. I remembered the time we'd been playing with my father's tin-snips, and Chris had held them open and dared me to put my finger in. It was something his brothers might have tried on him. We were five and curious about ourselves, about skin and bones, trust and friendship. I held out my finger. He cut down to the bone but couldn't cut through it. He ran from my scream.

Recalling the pain, the swollen look of my nail-less finger, dark as a black tulip, I felt wary of the Bissell house. It wasn't just the KEEP OUT sign. There was a feeling about the place. It seemed lost to the present, as if only a horse and buggy belonged on the cobbled drive. I'd never seen a car go in or out. Instead of a garage, there was a carriage house. I couldn't believe I'd be a friend to someone living there.

Summer was on its way, then junior high. I thought my summer would be lonely, and in junior high I'd get just a nod from Chris as we passed in the halls.

"Will we still be friends?" I asked.

To him this was funny. He said, "Why wouldn't we?"

They moved in before school let out, when the grass was lush and the trees were budding. I wanted proof that they were in, and that some old ghost of a butler wouldn't put me off the property. I asked Chris to meet me at the entrance to the drive, where there had once been a gate. The lone gatepost had a companion, a crumbly stone stump I'd never noticed before. I'd always imagined it intact. I'd imagined a gate, too. Now I walked right through. The KEEP OUT sign was gone. Behind Chris, the drive cut a snaky path up to the house. Somewhere beyond the house was Fisk Lake. I looked down at my feet. "The cobblestones are cracked," I said.

"They have to be fixed," he said. "Everything has to be fixed."

It wasn't the first time I'd heard this, but I hadn't believed him then. I thought he'd been saying it out of modesty. We went halfway up the drive, enclosed in a shaggy paradise so inviting it made me laugh. My sense of exclusion disappeared. New-leafing hedges were screening us in. My gaze skipped along them, looking for their ends. We walked among trees too tall for climbing and others just right.

"Some of them were imported," he said. "We have a map of the grounds that shows where all the different species are. They need some pruning, I guess."

"Pruning? Who says? Pruning means hacking, you know."

"My dad says they need it. But he has to wait till they're done flowering."

"Let's hide his pruners."

"He's got a lot of other stuff to do. Maybe he won't get to it."

Fisk Lake, on which the Bissell mansion is located, is a private environmental preserve in an urban setting.
GRPL, Library Postcard Collection

The trees were left to thrive, even though a lot of them were the "dirty" kind. When summer came, their lawn was littered with bean pods, stringy catalpa and plump locust, with willow whips and horse chestnut burs, bleeding mulberries and cottony catkins from poplars that sounded like static when the wind blew, their leaves glinting in the sun like coins and a summer snow wafting down from the catkins still aloft. A small orchard stood against Wealthy Street, lined with the tall cedar hedge I had walked by every day, unaware of the aging grandeur beyond it.

Grandeur is a ballroom so sure of itself it's blind to the view of the lake. It faced the driveway, and the opposite view showed a short stretch of yard walled in by junipers. Inside, it had become the biggest, shabbiest storage room I'd ever seen. Its high ceiling was dingy, curdled, and mildew-speckled. A rusty pull-chain hung from the trap door, which had layers of filthy handprints fanning out along its dark seams. There were holes where the chandeliers had been. The walls had cracks; the windows were cloudy. The air felt as cold as spring, and a dead fireplace at each end gave it a smell of soot. We wore our jackets in there. It became the place to skateboard.

Every week or so we made a new obstacle course with the easiest things to move: the boxes of old clothes and Christmas ornaments, the monkey lamp, the swordfish with the broken sword, the dining room chair Yeats had gnawed as a puppy. He lumbered beside our skateboards, nipping at our legs. In giant mirrors on opposite walls, between the windows and around both fireplaces, we saw ourselves roll by, reflected forever. When we tired we fell on the boxes, all so crumpled they were as soft as beanbags. Yeats panted at our feet, his tail sweeping the floor and gathering cobwebs and dead bugs. Shadows shaped like junipers crept in through the blurry windows.

Breathless, Chris said, "What would we do without this room?"

"Whatever we used to do," I said, as if we wouldn't be disappointed.

"My dad wants to tear it down."

"Don't let him," I said.

"My mom wants to make it a greenhouse."

"We can't skateboard in a greenhouse. What's wrong with fixing it?" I'd raised my voice, and it echoed. I looked at Chris and we laughed, me at my echo and he at my question.

"It would cost too much," he said. "It needs a whole new roof. The chimneys are plugged, and one winter, when no one was here, the pipes froze. It's cheaper to tear it down. I like the greenhouse idea, though. I know we don't need a ballroom."

"You need a greenhouse? A ballroom is a million times better. Think of it all fixed up. You could have parties like they used to." I wanted to help. I was willing to sweep and scrub and paint. On warm summer nights it would hum with talk, full of the kind of people my parents didn't know, people in glamorous clothes who drank martinis. And there would be dancing. I had taken a dance class. I could wear mascara and lip-gloss. My chest was growing painful bumps, hard as apples. I pictured myself in a gown. But Chris didn't care about society parties.

Then one day his mother popped in with a surprised look, as if it were news to her that we had been skateboarding in there. Maybe it was. His parents weren't very observant. "You kids can't play in here," she said, "you'll ruin the wood floor."

The rest of the house seemed to snatch our voices away. Worn carpet and dark waxed wood muffled everything we said. We whispered. Chris led and Yeats trailed behind me. In every room, we'd sit in the first chair or couch for a minute before moving on, as if expecting a ghost to poof out of the last century and ask us why we were there, and we'd need an excuse, something like, "Oh, we're with the furniture."

The Laws' furniture looked misplaced. It could have been doubled and the house would have still felt bare. Yeats followed us as far as the library, but he wouldn't go in there. He'd turn and go the long way around to meet us on the other side. We peeked around corners and checked the closets, the creaky little elevator, and the stale dark niches behind secret panels in the walls. We expected a jolt. Chris's brothers, Dave and Jim, would lie in wait, becoming the ghosts that lurked in every silent cavity of the house.

His brothers were envious of our whispering. If they caught us at it they'd haul Chris upstairs and throw him down the laundry chute, or cram him in the dumbwaiter on the third floor and drop him to the first. Sometimes they were getting revenge because Chris had booby-trapped their rooms. Their mother couldn't stop them. His brothers were strong, and if she tried to grab them, they'd shove her off. She'd pull at their shirts, which ripped as they fought. "Stop it, you'll kill him!" she'd yell. They'd yell right back in her face with crazy grins, while Chris echoed, "Mom!" from the falling dumbwaiter.

When his brothers were gone, we played hide and seek. I didn't hide in rooms Yeats avoided. I figured something unearthly was in there, something with vibes a dog could sense. Whether I was crouched in hiding or looking for Chris, the promise of a good scare made my skin crawl. The best hiding places also hid mousetraps, either baited or clamping stiff mice.

Sometimes we leapt out of hiding at Chris's mother, mistaking her for the seeker. One time I knew it was her, but I wanted the laugh. The whir of her sewing machine had stopped. Through a crack I saw her coming, a tape measure over her shoulders, a tomato pincushion like a growth on her wrist. Even barefoot, her steps thudded. I hopped out with a merry "Boo!" and she jumped, gasping as if actually confronted by a ghost.

She struck back by putting us to work. She had us cutting circles out of the filmy white netting used for veils, putting candy-coated almonds into the circles and tying them up with ribbon. We sat on the floor of the sewing room finding quiet ways to make each other laugh as we worked. She asked us not to talk because she needed to concentrate: she was making a wedding gown. We'd eaten so many of the candied almonds that we'd become sick of the sight of them. We put them in our ears to show we'd had our fill. We stuck them with pins and stood them on their feet. We cut them in half with zigzag scissors and stifled our laughter as the halves shot in opposite directions and met the wall or floor with a tiny knock.

The bride was a relative or a friend, and the reception was held on their lawn. My parents hadn't been invited, but I went on my own as Chris's guest. I wore a flowered skirt and a satin-trimmed top I thought were too casual, but they were the nicest things I had. My mother wouldn't buy new. "You don't have to be fancy," she'd said. "You're not one of them."

It was a clear blue day, fresh with the smell of cut grass and trees in full bloom. A confetti of loose petals wafted in the breeze, and drifting along with the petals was the music, played by a string quartet dressed in tails and a black silk gown. People wanted the sun. They plucked folding chairs covered in crisp white paper out of the shade. They ate cold shrimp and mushroom caps stuffed with cheese and garlic. They brought plastic flutes to a fizzing champagne fountain that Chris and I stood grinning beside. Some of the guests wanted to give us a glass, but it was more fun sneaking it. When their backs were turned we'd think up a ploy.

"I wonder how this fountain works," Chris would say, rubbing his chin as if puzzled. He'd study the pedestal as if figuring out the mechanics, then tilt his head and open his mouth under a spout. He came out chuckling and wiping his face. I sensed people watching me, measuring me up. They thought I was his girlfriend, and he hadn't told them differently. I felt flattered, and happy and silly — even aside from the champagne. We stole sips whenever we could. We eyed the guests and checked the bubbles in the fountain's three tiers. We sampled from the middle tier and kept a greedy watch of the swell at the top. Soon we were fanning ourselves with small plastic plates and swaying like the trees.

"Another bee," I'd say, waving a plate. They'd land on the rim of a tier, creep toward a spout and fall into the next pool if we didn't wave them off. Behind our waving plates we'd dip under a spout and get our faces splashed as the champagne poured into our mouths. I turned my face to the breeze, to the rain of spent buds and blushing petals that fell in the fountain and spun in its pools. I started hiccupping.

We tried not to laugh. "Hold your breath," Chris said, "you're giving us away."

I couldn't hold my breath. I felt woozy. "Nobody cares," I said. The music had stopped, and the party had begun moving down to the lake, where guests were swimming in their underwear. The champagne was going flat, but we both filled a plastic flute and veered for the orchard. Chris held bundles of candy-coated almonds pouched in his shirt.

The lawn dipped and the grass went tall where the orchard began. Instead of rows there was a scatter of trees all bulging with flowers. We took off our shoes and swished in. Crickets sprang from our feet to swing on grass that still chirped.

"Who was supposed to mow?" I asked.

"It's hard to mow in here. It's bumpy, and going around all the trees is a pain."

He dropped a shoe. It disappeared with a whish. I hiccupped even as I laughed. He swept the grass with his foot, wobbling and laughing. "Now I spilled my champagne," he drawled. He dropped the other shoe and it also disappeared. I looked back at our weaving trail. I could glimpse the fountain through branches rippling with pale blossoms.

"I'm glad you didn't mow," I said. "I like it this way."

"My dad was pissed." We started laughing and kept each other going until we were teary and red. Chris glowed like he was sunburned, and it made his eyes even bluer.

We tapped our glasses together. "To summer," I said.

"To the bride and groom," he said. We entwined glasses and emptied them. He said, "Now we're supposed to kiss."

We'd been kissing since the time he almost cut my finger off. He'd kissed me the next day in apology. I always felt strange about the kisses, as if I were kissing my lost brother. I'd been wondering when I'd feel the magic. What more could it take than a champagne daze in a flowery, bee-buzzing grove? I closed my eyes to let it hit. Chris was supposed to drop his shirtful of almonds, grope and ravish me. But it was like always, a plain kiss, flat as a mirror. Unbelievably, he wanted another.

I felt too giddy to be disappointed. I laughed — and not to mock. I was happy the magic was still ahead of us, and if it wasn't, I felt too good to care. "I don't want to play bride and groom," I said. "Let's climb a tree." The ground seemed to be pitching.

"We'll fall. Let's get more champagne."

"Falling won't hurt. It's not that high. The fountain's gotta be dead."

"Whoever falls has to take off her skirt."

"I'm not falling. You'll lose your pants." I gathered my skirt between my legs and tucked the hem into the waistband in front, then started up the tree. Chris climbed jerkily onto the lowest branch, still pouching his shirt. I went into the perfume of the blossoms, looking for the right fork to rest in. The tree swirled faster the higher I went. On a swingy high branch I sat rocking, waggling my feet as if they were in water. "You're not climbing," I said.

He sat on the fattest branch, leaning against the trunk, munching almonds. He said, "Here, catch," and tried to pelt me with the nuts.

I lay on the branch, spanning it, my arms and legs dangling, my head cradled in a crook. My eyes wanted to blur everything. I'd steady them on a trembly blossom a bee was in, but they'd glide past the blossom to the chinks in the canopy, to the scraps of blue sky I wanted to catch and hold. I felt so exquisitely happy, so numb with pleasure that I kept smiling even when a bumblebee came buzzing around my face, wanting me to swipe at it and fall. It hovered so close I could feel the breath of its wings. I blew at it. My skin felt taut with dried champagne. The buzzing got angry. The bee made furious little swoops at my face. I held the branch and shut my eyes. My cheek felt the creeping tickle of its feet. I turned to wood.

"The party must be over," Chris said. "Here comes Yeats."

I let my hands dangle; my eyes fluttered open. The bee rose with a hum and flew to a blossom. I sat up and rubbed my cheek.

"Don't go home," Chris said. "I've gotta help clean up, but you could stay. Sleep over. Some of the guests from out of town are staying. I don't see why you couldn't."

Our parents were growing leery of our sleepovers. Back when we were five and our friendship began, our parents had assumed we were young enough to be trusted. As we grew, and his parents or mine would express their doubts, we kept reminding them that they trusted us, and that they should trust us more, not less, as we matured. But now they were starting to ask us embarrassing questions. We'd blush and play innocent, which we were — somewhat. Though we were interested in sex, though we privately questioned why it was wrong for us but right for adults, though we knew from dirty magazines how it was supposed to work and had sort of tried, we always gave up disappointed. Our touching was as feeble as our kissing. We were too bashful, our bodies too young. We'd part and fall asleep feeling strangely distant, ashamed for trying and for failing.

"You really want me to?" I said.

"Of course I do."

I looked for the bee where I heard its drone. Three bees were on that bough. Bees were on every bough, hovering choosily above the flowers before setting down and digging in. I pictured apple weights where flowers were, the happy white canopy gone. Overnight the flowers would fall. Dull leaves would grow, and we wouldn't climb again until the apples were apples.

We broke the rule about staying out of the third floor, which led to the attic, which led to the roof, where we dared each other to scale from one attic window to another. It was especially risky because some of the roof's clay tiles were loose. Once, while we were arguing over who would go first, my father unexpectedly came walking up the drive. He'd come on the pretext of calling me home to supper. Crouched like gargoyles, we watched him approach. Chris took a loose tile and flung it down, intending to miss; but the tile looked dead-on to hit my father. Chris yelled a frantic "Hey!" which made my father jump clear and left me wondering why I had stayed silent.

I remember my father's fury and Chris chanting "Sorry sorry . . . sorry" as he scrambled for the closest window, desperate to reach his parents before my father did. When he was angry, my father seemed huge and very powerful. And he *was* powerful: he could ground me, or end my friendship with Chris. But before Chris had thrown the tile, while my father was walking up the cobbled drive — taking everything in, the house itself and the matching carriage house, the beautiful grounds sweeping down to the lake, where the upper half of the boathouse was visible and probably part of the groundskeeper's house — I saw from the roof how my father was small. I saw the wistful look on his face, his awareness of his limits, of the things he couldn't have or give.

I was told I couldn't go back to the Bissell house, though Chris was forgiven. He came to our house on Briarwood, sheepishly at first. He tried flattering my parents. "It's cozy here. . . . I like your small house better than mine." It was the truth, but my mother quibbled.

"This is not a *small* house. That place of yours must be constant work."

He agreed. One day he said, "My dad broke three ribs falling out of a tree. He was trying to saw off the branches that got twisted in the storm."

"Lawyers should stay out of trees," my father crowed.

Chris took it well, but he blushed and said, "It was just a dumb maple. If it had been the black walnut, we could've sold it for thousands."

My father gazed out the window, silent.

It was more than a fluke that Chris's father would climb into a wrecked maple and do his own sawing. He also rode the bus to work. Taxes had been hiked that summer, and by October, OPEC had imposed the oil embargo. Gas had nearly tripled in price, if it could be found at all. There was a bus stop on Wealthy near the estate's entrance, and when I walked past it on my way to school, I often saw Mr. Law waiting there with his briefcase. He was a striking man, especially among the janitors and orderlies going home from the night shift at Blodgett Hospital across the street, still wearing paper on their shoes and heads.

All summer, since my father didn't want me in their house, Chris and I met in the orchard, our sanctuary, nestled behind the carriage house and sheltered by the hedge on Wealthy, where the bus stopped. We knew every tree, its ease of climbing and store of fruit, its frailties and strengths. His brothers didn't bother us, because they had found other pursuits. Jim speared bullfrogs, and Dave, the eldest and most volatile, had become a poet-painter-pianist. His poems and paintings were angry, even the sexy ones. His music thundered, reaching us in the orchard. He played Beethoven, seated at one of two baby grands that stood side by side in the long living room. He played in his father's tails and tie, shirtless, with boxer shorts and bunchy socks, his hair as wolfish as the composer's and his eyes as ravenous.

The Appassionata burned into my memory before I knew its name. It silenced us in the orchard. I loved every leap and flicker of it, especially the heat in the third movement. I had watched Dave play it once. I had stood rooted by the piano, terrified, clenching my teeth at the power of it, but too thrilled to walk away. Even listening in the orchard my breath went short, as if the music were a plume I could snuff out if I breathed too hard. Chris knew missed notes the second they happened. I knew them only after, because Dave would go back a few bars and repeat them, brutally, endlessly, like an old record stuck on a scratch.

Chris teased me then. "You're sighing," he said, chomping on an apple.

"I can't stand it. Why doesn't he get on with it?"

"He's trying to perfect it. It's like looking for the perfect apple. No worm holes."

"Bull. He's sick and he's torturing us."

"It's because he's pissed. We might have to sell this place." Chris was probably glad, but for my sake he didn't show it. "We'll know for sure by spring."

The music paused, leaving us with cricket chirp and birdsong.

"There, he's going back to the very beginning," Chris said. The music began in a new mood.

"Let's always be friends," I said. "Let's make a pact. Even if we both move away and we don't see each other for years, we'll be all old, and we'll meet somewhere."

"Like how old?" He tossed the core and wiped his hands on his shirt.

"You know, about fifty."

"Too old."

"Thirty?"

"Yeah," he said, "but where'll we meet? School?"

"School sucks. I wouldn't wanna go back there. What about the bus stop on Wealthy? Right here on your corner?" From the tree we could watch the traffic light flash its three colors over the intersection, but the bus stop was hidden by the hedge.

"We need a special day so we don't forget. Like my birthday," he said.

"In December? I don't think so. I don't wanna stand around freezing. Let's make it my birthday: June's the best month of the year."

"Be there at noon," he said. "Swear? It's not a real pact unless there's blood."

"What do you mean?" I said, conscious of my virginity. "What kind of blood?"

"Blood. In the movies they use a sharp knife and then put their cuts together. If I go get a knife, will you do it?" He was already starting down the tree.

"Oh, just that. We don't need a knife. Let's pick a scab. What've you got?"

We were both in shorts. He sat on the branch and held out his legs. His legs made me hate my own. His were sculpted; mine were bony. He had twice the tan I had, and for some reason he wasn't dotted with mosquito bites. He had thick dark scabs on his knees and hands, probably from his descents down the laundry chute.

"Your choice," he said. "What about you?"

"This." I showed him my ankle. "It's a mosquito bite I scratched too hard."

We brought out the blood, and he held my ankle on his knee.

We stayed in the orchard until suppertime, when Chris's father came home from work. He'd want to play the piano, and since Dave wouldn't be shouldered out, *The Appassionata* became a roiling cacophony of argument between them. On pianos meant for accompaniment they poundingly disputed which was the better piano, who the better pianist, and more importantly, who the greater composer — Beethoven or Bach.

Chris could listen with a calm smile. "They're both wrong," he said. "The greatest was Mozart." He held out his handsome legs to look at the bright new scab on his knee. How I adored him then, and how frightened I was of change.

He walked me home. We didn't talk. The musical racket stayed with me. I heard it in the quiet of my home, seated at supper with the same old thing on the plate: fried potatoes and beans. I didn't eat, didn't speak, even when my sly sister said, "You smell like apples," a bid for news of the

Bissell house. Envious as she was, she'd gloat if the house had to be sold and Chris had to move away.

As winter came, Chris visited more often. Our thermostat never went above 68, as Nixon had asked, but Chris would say how warm we were. Finally, near Christmas, I was allowed go to his house again, and I found it deathly cold. Most of it was closed off. Sheets draped the furniture. Floors that once shone were hazed with dust, as if in the chill a frost had settled. Beside the sheet music on one of the baby grands was a pair of fingerless wool gloves. The library was livable, warmed by a fire, and so were the two kitchens, their ovens open for heat. In the library we played billiards — not *pool* — and in the kitchens I repeatedly lost to him in chess.

As spring approached, the Bissell house went on the market quietly, without a sign out front. The family worked at pruning, repairing, and cleaning. The living room grew as one of the pianos and some furniture was sold. The mousetraps disappeared. They took down Dave's paintings, many of which were bloody, featuring orgies and fire-lit cannibals. But without them the walls seemed cold.

They accepted the first offer that came. And later, when the buyer tried to renege, they held him to the purchase agreement with a legal threat. One acre of land was divided from the estate to be the last buildable lot on the lake, and this was to become the site of the Laws' future, more affordable home — what they called the "little house." Construction began. Bulldozers ripped a path through the hedge on Wealthy and tore up our orchard, felling a world of trees. The trees were still bare and looked their weakest, gnarled and vulnerable. Chris and I watched from the roof of the carriage house, where we sat leaning against the cupola.

Chris was guardedly enthusiastic about the new house. He tried to appease, pointing out the positive, painting a warm cozy picture of the future blot on our sanctuary. The house would have a double fireplace, he said, vaulted ceilings and bedrooms with balconies facing the lake; it would have a sauna, a sunken whirlpool under a skylight; there would be no mice. He had his parents' promise that a few of the trees would be spared. But I knew it would never be the same. The few spared trees — in plain view of the new house — became reminders of a lovely lost refuge, and we never climbed them. He must have sensed that would happen. Watching and listening as steel struck against trunks, our trees shook and fell, he muttered, "We'll still have the lake."

The shore of their acre was swampy, and the rustic yet modern "little" house, with its stolen side view of the sprawling Bissell lakefront, looked like the encroachment it was, especially when seen from the lake. We walked up huge old weeping willows that leaned over the lake as if they were made just for us to jump from onto inner tubes floating below. The Bissell kids had probably walked those trees, their arms out for balance, the same as ours. Sometimes I sat on a humped root and watched Chris walk up alone. I worried he'd slip if he knew I was watching, but he was too practiced to slip. I wondered if it meant he could forget me more easily than I could him. I couldn't walk up unless he was ahead of me. Knowing he was watching ruined my concentration, my balance.

In summer the trees were flecked with mating dragonflies. They wept yellow leaves in the fall, when we tried to net turtles but never had any luck. Yeats swam after our canoe and we'd pull him in and he'd jump after the turtle when he saw us raise a net. In winter we skated in the swamp, where the trees made us an obstacle course on harmless shallow ice. We held hands and looped around the wet trunks until we were dizzy.

I felt watched by the little house with its slant view, a new and intrusive presence, so quiet. Dave had gone to study physics at the University of Michigan, taking *The Appassionata* with him. When there was music, it was Mr. Law's funereal Bach, played at an easy volume. The other brother, Jim, had dropped out of high school and was rarely home except at night. Chris and I were nearing the end of junior high, but he was already choosing a college. He'd grown taller than his mother, and she'd begun hugging, kissing, and caressing him as I'd rarely seen before. I watched with jealousy and fear, dreading perhaps more than she did the day he'd leave.

She might have caught my expression once while she was kissing him or wiping her lipstick off his face. "You're all grown up," she said, bending him to her height by rubbing his shoulders. "You two shouldn't be sleeping over any more."

It seemed a wise decision. If we were friends instead of sweethearts or lovers, I thought I'd have less to cry about when he went off to college and I didn't.

I started avoiding him — to get used to the idea of distance. Except in school, we didn't see each other until spring, when I went to his house, where the smell of the lake drew us to the shore. The Bissell lawn was spreading a blanket of pale blue veronica. The swamp, newly seeded, was pushing up wispy grass that was hopelessly soggy and full of toads the size of my fingernail. Every step crushed one or two of them. Chris's brother Jim liked to pinch them until their guts popped out their mouths. But Chris and I weren't much better. It began while we were mucking around at the shore. I caught a toad and cupped it in my hands.

"Don't pinch it," Chris said.

"Why would I want to?" Its weak little struggle tickled like wet kisses. It tried to squeeze out wherever light squeezed in. I started wondering about its sense of direction, its instinct for life. I shook it and tossed it into the lake. "Let's see if it knows where shore is."

Chris wagged his head, chuckling.

It floated for a few seconds and then swam for shore, a tiny ripple on the surface that suddenly disappeared in a gulp from below. It was so sudden and irrevocable, I couldn't help laughing.

"Like you didn't know it'd get eaten," he said. "It's a given." He caught another and tossed it in to prove it.

I threw another one in, too. "Let's see whose toad can make it back first."

Soon there was a feeding frenzy, in the middle of which one of my toads actually made it back. I slopped after it in the mud. I was going to wave it in the air — the winner.

"Leave it," Chris said. "You're no fair, it made it back. It deserves to live now."

It didn't struggle in my hand. It sat on my palm, as still as a stone except for its pulsing throat. Suddenly it hopped. It plinked into the lake, into the expanding rings the fish were making. "They all deserve to live," I said, "but they won't."

That summer we hardly saw each other. Chris went to summer school and then skipped the ninth grade. He kept his freshman friends but tried to fit in with sophomores, too. In his junior year he took college courses and was too busy studying to bother with friends. He finished his senior year in one semester, graduated without the usual ceremony, and took a scholarship to Yale.

He gave me a call just minutes before he left. I could have missed the call. I went over, but didn't go inside. He'd packed all his things in the back of his car, an old white station wagon that had been his grandfather's. Yeats sat in the front seat, a patient look on his white face. Chris joked about taking him, then laughed nervously and gave me a hug that felt strange with his parents watching. He was parked under our apple tree, the one we'd made the pact in. We didn't mention the pact. It had already become, and for years would remain, a promise held in silence, open to the whims of time.

The Good Immigrant Student

BICH MINH NGUYEN

Bich Minh Nguyen was born in Vietnam in 1974 and immigrated to Grand Rapids with her father, sister, uncles, and grandmother after the fall of Saigon in 1975. A self-proclaimed "insufferably good immigrant student" in Grand Rapids at Spectrum School for the Gifted and Talented, City School, and Forest Hills Northern High School, she established herself as a writer in her high school years — and in college at the University of Michigan, where she received an M.F.A. degree.

Nguyen has won major awards for both her poetry and essays. She is the coeditor of *The Contemporary American Short Story: A Longman Anthology* (2003) and *I & Eye: Contemporary Creative Nonfiction* (2004). Her work has appeared in *Watermark: Vietnamese American Poetry and Prose* (1998), *Scribner's Best of the Fiction Workshops* (1999), and *Dream Me Home Safely: Writers on Growing up in America* (2003), as well as in *Gourmet* magazine and the *Chicago Tribune.* Her latest book, *Stealing Buddha's Dinner: A Memoir,* was published in early 2007. Currently she teaches at Purdue University in West Lafayette, Indiana. This memoir of her coming-of-age experiences in Grand Rapids schools first appeared in *Tales Out of School: Writers on Their Student Years* (2000).

My stepmother, Rosa, who began dating my father when I was three years old, says that my sister and I used to watch *Police Woman* and rapturously repeat everything Angie Dickinson said. But when the show was over Anh and I would resume our Vietnamese, whispering together, giggling in accents. Rosa worried about this. She had the idea that she could teach us English and we could teach her Vietnamese. She would make us lunch or give us baths, speaking slowly and asking us how to say *water,* or *rice,* or *house.*

After she and my father married, Rosa swept us out of our falling-down house and into middle-class suburban Grand Rapids, Michigan. Our neighborhood surrounded Ken-O-Sha Elementary School and Plaster Creek, and was only a short drive away from the original Meijer Thrifty Acres. In the early 1980s, this neighborhood of mismatching street names — Poinsettia, Van Auken, Senora, Ravanna — was home to families of Dutch heritage, and everyone was Christian Reformed, and conservative Republican. Except us. Even if my father hadn't left his rusted-through silver Mustang, the first car he ever owned, to languish in the driveway for months we would have stuck out simply because we weren't white. There was my Latina stepmother and her daughter, Cristina; my father, sister, uncles, grandmother, and I, refugees from Saigon; and my half-brother born a year after we moved to the house on Ravanna Street.

Although my family lived two blocks from Ken-O-Sha, my stepmother enrolled me and Anh at Sherwood Elementary, a bus ride away, because Sherwood had a bilingual education program. Rosa, who had a master's in education and taught ESL and community ed in the public school system, was a big supporter of bilingual education. School mornings, Anh and I would be at the bus stop at the corner of our street too early, hustled out of the house by our grandmother who constantly feared we would miss our chance. I went off to first grade, Anh to second. At ten o'clock, we crept out of our classes, drawing glances and whispers from the other students, and convened with a group of Vietnamese kids from other grades to learn English. The teachers were Mr. Ho, who wore a lot of short-sleeved button-down shirts in neutral hues, and Miss Huong, who favored a maroon blouse with puffy shoulders and slight ruffles at the high neck and wrists, paired with a tweed skirt that hung heavily to her ankles. They passed out photocopied booklets of Vietnamese phrases and their English translations, with themes such as "In the Grocery Store." They asked us to repeat slowly after them and took turns coming around to each of us, bending close to hear our pronunciations.

Vietnamese refugee children and a new Grand Rapids friend on the statue of John Ball in John Ball Park

GRPL, Vietnamese History Collection, Carol Russo photo

Anh and I exchanged a lot of worried glances, for we had a secret: we already knew English. It was the Vietnamese part that gave us trouble. When Mr. Ho and Miss Huong gave instructions, or passed out homework assignments, they did so in Vietnamese. Anh and I received praise for our English, but were reprimanded for failing to complete our assignments and failing to pay attention. After a couple of weeks of this, Anh announced to Rosa that we didn't need bilingual education. Nonsense, she said. Our father just shrugged his shoulders. After that, Anh began skipping bilingual classes, urging me to do the same, and then we never went back. What was amazing was that no one, not Mrs. Eunice, my first grade teacher, or Mrs. Hankins, Anh's teacher, or even Mr. Ho or Miss

Huong said anything directly to us about it. Or if they did, I have forgotten it entirely. Then one day my parents got a call from Miss Huong. When Rosa came to talk to me and Anh about it we were watching television the way kids do, sitting alarmingly close to the screen. Rosa confronted us with "Do you girls know English?" Then she suddenly said, "Do you know Vietnamese?" I can't remember what we replied to either question.

For many years, a towering old billboard over the expressway downtown proudly declared Grand Rapids "An All-American City." For me, that all-American designation meant all-white. I couldn't believe (and still don't) that they meant to include the growing Mexican-American population, or the sudden influx of Vietnamese refugees in 1975. I often thought it a rather mean-spirited prank of some administrator at the INS, deciding with a flourish of a signature to send a thousand refugees to Grand Rapids, a city that boasted having more churches per square mile than any other city in the United States. Did that administrator know what Grand Rapids was like? That in school, everywhere I turned, and often when I closed my eyes, I saw blond blond blond? The point of bilingual education was assimilation. To my stepmother, it was preservation: she didn't want English to take over wholly, pushing the Vietnamese out of our heads. She was too ambitious. Anh and I were Americanized as soon as we turned on the television. Today, bilingual education is supposed to have become both a method of assimilation and a method of preservation, an effort to prove that kids can have it both ways. They can supposedly keep English for school and their friends and keep another language for home and family.

In Grand Rapids, Michigan, in the 1980s, I found that an impossible task.

I transferred to Ken-O-Sha Elementary in time for third grade, after Rosa finally admitted that taking a bus all the way to Sherwood was pointless. I was glad to transfer, eager to be part of a class that wasn't, in my mind, tainted with the knowledge of my bilingual stigma. Third grade was led by Mrs. Andersen, an imperious, middle-aged woman of many plaid skirts held safe by giant gold safety pins. She had a habit of turning her wedding ring around and around her finger while she stood at the chalkboard. Mrs. Andersen had an intricate system of rewards for good grades and good behavior, denoted by colored star stickers on a piece of poster board that loomed over us all. One glance and you could see who was behind, who was striding ahead.

I was an insufferably good student, with perfect Palmer cursive and the highest possible scores in every subject. I had learned this trick at Sherwood. That the quieter you are, the shyer and sweeter and better-at-school you are, the more the teacher will let you alone. Mrs. Andersen should have let me alone. For, in addition to my excellent marks, I was nearly silent, deadly shy, and wholly obedient. My greatest fear was being called on, or in any way standing out more than I already did in the class that was, except for me and one black student, dough-white. I got good grades because I feared the authority of the teacher; I felt that getting in good with Mrs. Andersen would protect me, that she would protect me from the frightful rest of the world. But Mrs. Andersen was not agreeable to this notion. If it was my turn to read aloud during reading circle, she'd interrupt me to snap, "You're reading too fast" or demand, "What does that word mean?" Things she did not do to the other students. Anh, when I told her about this, suggested that perhaps Mrs. Andersen liked me and wanted to help me get smarter. But neither of us believed it. You know when a teacher likes you and when she doesn't.

Secretly, I admired and envied the rebellious kids, like Robbie Wilson, who came to school looking bleary-eyed and pinched, like a hungover adult; Robbie and his ilk snapped back at teachers, were routinely sent to the principal's office, were even spanked a few times with the principal's infamous red paddle. Those kids made noise, possessed something I thought was confidence, self-knowledge, allowing them to marvelously question everything ordered of them. They had the ability to challenge the given world.

Toward the middle of third grade, Mrs. Andersen introduced a stuffed lion to the pool of rewards: the best student of the week would earn the privilege of having the lion sit on his or her desk for the entire week. My quantity of gold stars was neck and neck with that of my two competitors, Holly and Jennifer, both sweet-eyed blonde girls with pastel-colored monogrammed sweaters and neatly tied Dock-Sides. My father did not have a lot of money and my stepmother had terrible taste. Thus I attended school in such ensembles as dark red parachute pants and a nubby pink sweater stitched with a picture of a unicorn rearing up. This only propelled me to try harder to be good, to make up for everything I felt was against me: my odd family, my race, my very face. And I craved that stuffed lion. Week after week, the lion perched on Holly's desk or Jennifer's desk. Meanwhile, the class spelling bee approached. I didn't know I was such a good speller until I won it, earning a scalloped-edged certificate and a candy bar. That afternoon I started toward home, then remembered I'd forgotten my rain boots in my locker. I doubled back to school and overheard Mrs. Andersen in the classroom talking to another teacher. "Can you believe it?" Mrs. Andersen was saying. "A foreigner winning our spelling bee!"

I waited for the stuffed lion the rest of that year, with a kind of patience I have no patience for today. To no avail. In June, on the last day of school, Mrs. Andersen gave the stuffed lion to Holly to keep forever.

The first time I had to read aloud something I had written — perhaps it was in fourth grade — I felt such terror, such a need not to have any attention upon me, that I convinced myself that I had become invisible, that the teacher could never call on me because she couldn't see me.

More than once, I was given the assignment of writing a report about my family history. I loathed this task, for I was dreadfully aware that my history could not be faked; it already showed on my face. When my turn came to read out loud, the teacher had to ask me several times to speak more loudly. Some kids, a few of them older, in different classes, took to pressing back the corners of their eyes with the heels of their palms while they chanted, "Ching-chong, ching-chong!" during recess. (This continued until Anh, who was far tougher than me, threatened to beat them up.)

I have no way of telling what tortured me more: the actual snickers and remarks and watchfulness of my classmates, or my own imagination, conjuring disdain. My own sense of shame. At times I felt sickened by my obedience, my accumulation of gold stickers, my every effort to be invisible.

Yet Robbie Wilson must have felt the same kind of claustrophobia, trapped in his own reputation, in his inability to be otherwise. I learned in school that changing oneself is not easy, that the world makes up its mind quickly.

I've heard that Robbie dropped out of high school, got a girl pregnant, found himself in and out of first juvenile detention, then jail.

What comes out of difference? What constitutes difference? Such questions, academic and unanswered, popped up in every other course description in college. But the idea of difference is easy to come by, especially in school; it is shame, the permutations and inversions of difference and self-loathing, that we should be worrying about.

Some kids want to rebel; other kids want to disappear. I wanted to disappear. I was not brave enough to shrug my shoulders and flaunt my difference; because I could not disappear in the crowd, I wished to disappear entirely. Anyone might have mistaken this for passivity.

Once, at the end of my career at Sherwood Elementary, I disappeared on the bus home. Mine was usually the third stop, but that day the bus driver thought I wasn't there, and she sailed right by the corner of Ravanna and Senora. I said nothing. The bus wove its way downtown, and for the first time I got to see where other children lived, some of them in clean orderly neighborhoods, some near houses with sagging porches and boarded-up windows. All the while, the kid sitting across the aisle from me played the same cheerful song over and over on his portable boom box. *Pass the doochee from the left hand side, pass the doochee from the left hand side.* He and his brother turned out to be the last kids off the bus. Then the bus driver saw me through the rearview mirror. She walked back to where I was sitting and said, "How come you didn't get off at your stop?" I shook my head, don't know. She sighed and drove me home.

I was often doing that, shaking my head and staring up wordlessly. I realize that while I remember so much of what other people said when I was a child, I remember little of what I said. Probably because I didn't say much at all.

I recently came across in the stacks of the University of Michigan library *A Manual for Indochinese Refugee Education 1976-1977.* Some of it is silly, but much of it is a painstaking, fairly thoughtful effort to let school administrators and teachers know how to go about sensitively handling the influx of Vietnamese children in the public schools. Here is one of the most wonderful items of advice: "The Vietnamese child, even the older child, is also reported to be afraid of the dark, and more often than not, believes in ghosts. A teacher may have to be a little more solicitous of the child on gloomy, wintery days." Perhaps if Mrs. Andersen had read this, she would not have upbraided me so often for tracking mud into the classroom on rainy days. In third grade I was horrified by my muddy shoes. I hung back, trying to duck behind this or that dark-haired boy.

In spite of this, in spite of bilingual education, and shyness, and all that wordless shaking of my head, I was sent off every Monday to the Spectrum School for the Gifted and Talented. I still have no idea who selected me, who singled me out. Spectrum was (and still is) a public school program that invited students from every public elementary school to meet once a week and take specialized classes on topics such as the Middle Ages, Ellis Island, and fairy tales. Each student chose two classes, a major and minor, and for the rest of the semester worked toward final projects in both. I loved going to Spectrum. Not only did the range of students from other schools prove to be diverse, I found myself feeling more comfortable, mainly because Spectrum encouraged individual work. And the teachers seemed happy to be there. The best teacher at Spectrum was Mrs. King, whom every student adored. I still remember the soft gray sweaters she wore, her big wavy hair, her art-class handwriting, the way she'd often tell us to close our eyes when she read us a particular story or passage.

I believe that I figured out how to stop disappearing, how to talk and answer, even speak up, after several years in Spectrum. I was still deeply self-conscious, but I became able, sometimes, to maneuver around it.

Spectrum may have spoiled me a little, because it made me think about college and freedom, and thus made all the years in between disappointing.

In seventh grade I joined Anh and Cristina at the City School, a seventh through twelfth grade public school in the Grand Rapids system that served as an early charter school; admission was by interview, and each grade had about fifty students. The City School had the advantage of being downtown, perched over old cobblestone roads, and close to the main public library. Art and music history were required. There were no sports teams. And volunteering was mandatory. But kids didn't tend to stay at City School; as they got older they transferred to one of the big high schools nearby, perhaps wishing to play sports, perhaps wishing to get away from City's rather brutal academic system. Each half semester, after grades were doled out, giant dot-matrix printouts of everyone's GPAs were posted in the hallways.

I didn't stay at City, either. When my family moved to a different suburb, my stepmother promptly transferred me to Forest Hills Northern High School. Most of the students there came from upper-middle-class families. The rich kids were the same as they were anywhere in America: they wore a lot of Esprit and Guess, drove nice cars, and ran student council, prom, and sports. These kids strutted down the hallways; the boys sat in a row on the long windowsill near a group of lockers, whistling or calling out to girls who walked by. Girls gathered in bathrooms with their Clinique lipsticks.

High school was the least interesting part of my education, but I did accomplish something: I learned to forget myself a little. I learned the sweetness of apathy. And through apathy, how to forget my skin and body for a minute or two, almost not caring what would happen if I walked into a room late and heads swiveled toward me. I learned the pleasure that reveals itself in the loss, no matter how slight, of self-consciousness. These things occurred because I remained the good immigrant student, without raising my hand often or showing off what I knew. Doing work was rote, and I went along to get along. I've never gotten over the terror of being called on in class, or the dread in knowing that I'm expected to contribute to class discussion. But there is a slippage between being good and being unnoticed, and in that sliver of freedom I learned what it could feel like to walk in the world in plain, unselfconscious view.

I would like to make a broad, accurate statement about immigrant children in schools. I would like to speak for them (us). I hesitate; I cannot. My own sister, for instance, was never as shy as I was. Anh disliked school from the start, choosing rebellion rather than silence. It was a good arrangement: I wrote papers for her and she paid me in money or candy; she gave me rides to school if I promised not to tell anyone about her cigarettes. Still, I think of an Indian friend of mine who told of an elementary school experience in which a blond schoolchild told the teacher, "I can't sit by her. My mom said I can't sit by anyone who's brown." And another friend, whose family immigrated around the same time mine did, whose second grade teacher used her as a vocabulary example: "Children, this is what a *foreigner* is." And sometimes I fall into thinking that kids today have the advantage of so much more wisdom, that they are so much more socially and politically aware than anyone was when I was in school. But I am wrong, of course. I know not every kid is fortunate enough to have a teacher like Mrs. King, or a program like Spectrum, or even the benefit of a manual written by a group of concerned educators; I know that some kids want to disappear and disappear until they actually do. Sometimes I think I see them, in the blurry background of a magazine photo, or in a gaggle of kids following a teacher's aide across the street. The kids with heads bent down, holding themselves in such a way that they seem to be self-conscious even of how they breathe. Small, shy, quiet kids, such good, good kids, *immigrant, foreigner,* their eyes watchful and waiting for whatever judgment will occur. I reassure myself that they will grow up fine, they will be okay. Maybe I cross the same street, then another, glancing back once in a while to see where they are going.

Permissions

The editors and publisher gratefully acknowledge permission to include material from the following sources:

"Sketches for an Autobiography," excerpted from *The Essays of A. J. Muste,* edited and with an introduction by Nat Hentoff, preface by Jo Ann O. Robinson (2nd ed. 2001), published by the A. J. Muste Memorial Institute, Murray Rosenblith, Executive Director. Used by permission of A. J. Muste Memorial Institute.

"The Cut of My Jib," from *Toys of a Lifetime* by Arnold Gingrich. Copyright © 1966 by Arnold Gingrich. Used by permission of Alfred A. Knopf, a division of Random House, Inc.

"Belly Fulla Straw," from *Belly Fulla Straw* by David Cornel DeJong. Copyright © 1934. Published by Alfred A. Knopf, a division of Random House, Inc.

"Boyhood — and Beyond," from *A Time to Heal* by Gerald R. Ford. Copyright © 1979. Reprinted by permission of William Morris Agency, LLC, on behalf of the author.

"The Times of My Life," from *The Times of My Life* by Betty Ford (with Chris Chase). Copyright © 1978. Reprinted by permission of William Morris Agency, LLC, on behalf of the author.

"Yesterdays in Grand Rapids," from "Yesterdays in Grand Rapids" by John Thompson. Copyright © 1969 by *Harper's Magazine.* All rights reserved. Excerpted from the May issue by special permission.

Permissions

“Technicolor Paddy,” from *A Man's Life.* Copyright © 1982 Roger Wilkins. Reprinted by Ox Bow Press. Used by permission. All rights reserved.

“Rocky and Me,” from *Roommates: My Grandfather's Story* by Max Apple. Copyright © 1994 by Yom Tov Sheyni, Inc. Used by permission of Warner Books, Inc.

“Half a Chance to Prove Myself,” from *Take Me to the River* by Al Green and Davin Seay. Copyright © 2000. Reprinted selections by permission of Harper-Collins Publishers.

“The Good Immigrant Student,” by Bich Minh Nguyen. Copyright © 2004 from a collection entitled *The Presence of Others.* Published by Bedford/St. Martin's. Used by permission of the author.

“A Farewell to Arms,” from *Moving Violations* by John Hockenberry. Copyright © 1995 John Hockenberry. Reprinted by permission of Hyperion. All rights reserved.

Contributors

Max Apple has written two nonfiction books about growing up in Grand Rapids, *I Love Gootie,* about his grandmother, and *Roommates,* about his grandfather, Rocky (made into a 1995 movie). He has also published two collections of stories, two novels (*Zip* and *Profiteers*), and two screenplays that have been made into movies, *Smokey Bites the Dust* and *The Air Up There.* Five of his books have been *New York Times* Notable Books, and his stories have appeared in *Best American Stories* and *Best Spiritual Writing.*

Albert Baxter, a nineteenth-century journalist with the *Detroit Tribune* and the *Grand Rapids Eagle,* was the first historian of Grand Rapids, Michigan. His monumental work *A History of Grand Rapids* was first published in 1891.

Charles E. Belknap made his father's blacksmith shop into the Belknap Wagon Company and became a prominent Grand Rapids citizen as firefighter, Civil War veteran, alderman, and mayor of the city. He served two terms in the U.S. Congress, was Boy Scout Commissioner, and published his memoir *The Yesterdays of Grand Rapids* in 1922.

William Brashler, a journalist whose work has appeared in *Newsweek, Sports Illustrated, Esquire,* and *New York* magazines, and a longtime contributor to the *Chicago Tribune* and the *Chicago Sun-Times,* is the author of fourteen books, including *The Bingo Long All-Stars and Traveling Motor Kings, The Chosen Prey,* and *Traders.* He has collaborated with Reinder Van Til (under the pen name Crabbe Evers) on five murder mysteries, including *Murder in Wrigley Field* and *Fear in Fenway.*

David Cornel DeJong published poetry and short fiction in *Atlantic Monthly, The New Yorker,* and *Saturday Review* while still in college. He published five children's books, three volumes of poetry, and thirteen novels, including *The Desperate Children* and *Belly Fulla Straw.* He taught creative writing at Brown University, as well as North Carolina and Rhode Island.

Betty Bloomer Ford was a student of dance (under Martha Graham) and a teacher of dance in Grand Rapids before she married Gerald Ford in October 1948. She became one of the most candid and best-loved First Ladies in the history of presidential politics. After leaving the White House, she established the Betty Ford Center for the treatment of chemical dependency. Her 1978 autobiography is entitled *The Times of My Life.*

Gerald R. Ford represented Grand Rapids (Michigan's 5th District) for twenty-four years (1949-1973) before becoming the 40th Vice President and the 38th President of the United States. His autobiography is entitled *A Time to Heal.*

Edward V. Gillis was born in Lithuanian Town, Grand Rapids (1920), and was a lifelong resident. He was president of the Michigan Archaeological Society and the editor of its newsletter. He was also a scholar of Native American culture and cofounder of the Grand Valley American Indian Lodge, as well as the editor of the Lodge's newsletter.

Arnold Gingrich was the founding editor of *Esquire* magazine, as well as of *Apparel Arts* (now *Gentleman's Quarterly*), and the moderator of *Esquire*'s famous literary symposia in the late 1950s. He was also a novelist (*Cast Down the Laurel*, set in Grand Rapids) and autobiographer (*Toys of a Lifetime*).

Al Green recorded eight albums between 1969 and 1976 that sold 20 million copies worldwide. In 1976, the Reverend Al Green felt called to the ministry at the Full Gospel Church in Memphis, and in the next decade he released nine best-selling gospel albums. He has won eight Grammy awards, as well as a Grammy Lifetime Achievement Award (2002); he has been inducted into the Rock and Roll Hall of Fame (1995) and the Gospel Music Hall of Fame (2004). His autobiography is entitled *Take Me to the River.*

Jim Harrison is the author of nine novels, including *True North, Dalva,* and *Sundog,* eight collections of poetry, three works of nonfiction, and five volumes of novellas, including *Legends of the Fall* and *The Woman Lit by Fireflies.* His most recent novel, *Returning to Earth,* was published early in 2007. He has been called "a national treasure" (*The Washington Times*) and "a writer with immortality in him" (*London Times*).

John Hockenberry is a three-time Peabody Award–winning radio journalist and four-time Emmy Award–winning TV journalist. He was the first anchor of NPR's *Talk of the Nation* show, and his later reporting for *Dateline NBC* earned him three Emmys, an Edward R. Morrow award, and a Casey Medal. He was one of the first Western journalists to report from Kurdish refugee camps in northern Iraq. He has written for *The New York Times, The New Yorker,* and *The Washington Post.*

Charles Honey has been writing for *The Grand Rapids Press* since 1985. After stints as feature writer for the "Flair" section and covering education for the newspaper, he became the religion editor in 1994. The *Press* has won several awards for its religion section from the Religion Newswriters Association during his tenure there.

Laura Kasischke is the author of five novels, most recently *Be Mine* (2007), and six collections of poetry, most recently *Gardening in the Dark* (2005). Her first novel, *Suspicious River,* was made into a feature film; her third novel, *The Life Before Her Eyes,* is currently in film production. She has won numerous awards, including a National Endowment for the Arts fellowship and several Pushcart prizes.

Kaye Longberg earned an M.F.A. in creative writing at Western Michigan University, where she is currently a doctoral candidate. Her stories have been published in *Alaska Quarterly Review, So to Speak, The Macguffin,* and *The South Carolina Review.* She has been nominated for Pushcart and Best New American Voices prizes.

Hank Meijer is co-chairman of Meijer, Inc. in Grand Rapids. He has been a reporter, editor, and publisher at various Michigan newspapers, and his articles on Arthur Vandenberg have been published in *Michigan Historical Review* and the *Encyclopedia of the United States Congress.* In 1984 he published

Thrifty Years, a biography of Hendrik Meijer, the company founder and his grandfather.

A. J. Muste, the foremost U.S. pacifist in the first half of the twentieth century, was a mentor to Bayard Rustin, Martin Luther King, Jr., and David Dellinger, and played a prominent role in the founding of the American Civil Liberties Union, the Congress on Racial Equality, and the War Resisters League. He was the founding editor of *Liberation* magazine and the author of *Nonviolence in an Aggressive World.*

Bich Minh Nguyen earned an M.F.A. at the University of Michigan and has won major awards for both her poetry and essays. Her work has appeared in several anthologies, as well as in *Gourmet* magazine and the *Chicago Tribune.* Her acclaimed first book, *Stealing Buddha's Dinner: A Memoir*, was published in early 2007.

John Otterbacher has been a professor at Aquinas College and was a member of both the Michigan House of Representatives and Senate for eight years during the 1970s. He has had a private practice in clinical psychology in Grand Rapids, and he has spent six years sailing the world's oceans with his family. His first book, *Sailing Grace*, is being published in the spring of 2007.

Glen Peterson has had a clinical psychology practice in Grand Rapids for many years, as well as a consulting firm working with law enforcement agencies to evaluate the psychological fitness of police officers. He has lectured frequently on opera, and he created the radio program "All About Opera" for a west Michigan classical music frequency.

Tom Rademacher joined *The Grand Rapids Press* in 1978 and covered a variety of beats before becoming a columnist there in 1986. His approach is taking a microscope to "the guy next door," finding the extraordinary in the ordinary.

Levi Rickert is a tribal member of the Prairie Band Potawatomi Nation and the former executive director of the North American Indian Center in Grand Rapids. A senior loan officer at Broadmoor Financial Services, Inc., and owner of the White Pigeon Group, he has served as president of the Grand Rapids Historical Commission and vice-chair of the Grand Rapids Community Relations Commission.

Paul Schrader has been one of America's most respected screenwriters and filmmakers for three decades. His creative collaboration with Martin Scorsese has produced *Taxi Driver, Raging Bull, The Last Temptation of Christ*, and *Bringing Out the Dead*. He has been the writer-director of *Hardcore, Blue Collar, Mishima, Light Sleeper*, and *Affliction*, among others. His most recent film, *The Walker*, a conceptual progression of *American Gigolo* (1979), will be released in 2007.

John Thompson was a poet, novelist, essayist, and the book review editor of *Harper's* magazine during the editorship of Willie Morris. His essay "Yesterdays in Grand Rapids" inaugurated the "Going Home in America" series in *Harper's*. He was also the author of *The Founding of English Metre* and *The Talking Girl and Other Poems*.

Robert VanderMolen is a poet and a member of the Grand Rapids Historical Commission. He has published ten collections of poetry, including, most recently, *Peaches* and *Breath*. His frequently published poems have appeared in *London Review of Books, Poetry, Parnassus, Driftwood, Epoch, St. Ann's Review*, and other poetry journals.

Reinder Van Til has written two books of nonfiction, *Lost Daughters* (1997) and a history of the Michigan Veterans Facility. He has also collaborated with William Brashler (under the pseudonym Crabbe Evers) on five murder mysteries, including *Tigers Burning* and *Bleeding Dodger Blue*. He is an editor with Eerdmans Publishing Company.

Sheri Venema has been a reporter for the *Norwich* (CT) *Bulletin* and the *Baltimore News American*, a reporter and bureau chief at the *Hartford Courant*, and an associate editor of the *Arkansas Democrat-Gazette*'s business section. She has run her own writing consulting business and is now a professor at the University of Montana's School of Journalism. She has won a fellowship from the American Society of Newspaper Editors.

Roger Wilkins, a leading civil rights advocate and activist for the last half-century, was Assistant Attorney General of the United States in the Johnson administration, after which he became a Pulitzer Prize–winning columnist for the *Washington Post* and served on the editorial board of *The New York Times*. His autobiographical memoir is *A Man's Life* (1982).